Good Faith in Insurance and *Takaful* Contracts in Malaysia

Haemala Thanasegaran

Good Faith in Insurance and *Takaful* Contracts in Malaysia

A Comparative Perspective

Springer

Haemala Thanasegaran
Monash University
Melbourne, VIC
Australia

and

Monash University
Subang Jaya, Selangor
Malaysia

ISBN 978-981-10-0381-3 ISBN 978-981-10-0383-7 (eBook)
DOI 10.1007/978-981-10-0383-7

Library of Congress Control Number: 2015960218

Printed on acid-free paper

This Springer imprint is published by SpringerNature
The registered company is Springer Science+Business Media Singapore Pte Ltd.

Foreword

The duty of utmost good faith is perhaps the single most important distinguishing characteristic of insurance contracts. In civil law jurisdictions, contractual good faith is a pervasive concept. In common law jurisdictions, by contrast, utmost good faith is confined to insurance law and extends to both pre-contractual and post-contractual dealings between the insurers and their policyholders. The law has undergone dramatic changes in recent times. In Australia, the *Insurance Contracts Act 1984* distinguishes between pre-contractual presentation of information and post-contractual conduct, rendering the latter an implied contractual term with both contractual and regulatory sanctions if the duty is broken. In the UK, exactly 250 years after the duty was laid down in the seminal case of *Carter v Boehm*, the *Insurance Act 2015*—which comes into force in 2016—has recast the duty of utmost good faith, reclassifying the pre-contractual duty as one of fair presentation and laying down a more general principle for post-contractual dealings.

Dr. Haemala Thanasegaran's text, which is now in front of you, is the first major published work to demonstrate systematically how the principles of utmost good faith apply to *takaful*. Islamic insurance has a number of unique features not reflected in common law rules, and utmost good faith has been adapted from the common law so that it complies with principles of *takaful*. The focus in the text is on Malaysia and, in particular, on changes introduced in 2013, but scholars of both common law insurance rules and *takaful* will find this book an excellent and rewarding study of utmost good faith under both sets of rules. A particularly important feature of the book is its currency, taking in the most recent developments in all jurisdictions discussed. It will become a key point of reference for practitioners, academics and indeed, market professionals who wish to understand how the principles interact and how they differ, and indeed how they apply in practice.

Dr. Thanasegaran is to be congratulated on her excellent and timely scholarship.

Sidmouth, England

Rob Merkin QC

Preface

The past 10 years or so have witnessed tremendous activity in the insurance industry in the UK and Malaysia, in terms of regulatory and infrastructural improvements. This has been a long-time coming, for an industry that has been regulated primarily by Lord Mansfield's 18th century common law pronouncement of utmost good faith as codified in the *Marine Insurance Act 1906* (UK).

The *Marine Insurance Act 1906* (UK)'s application to both insurance and *takaful* contracts in Malaysia has been by virtue of Malaysia's British colonial roots as reinforced by the *Civil Law Act 1956* (Malaysia). Although *takaful* or Islamic insurance is a relatively new entrant compared to its conventional insurance counterpart, it has shown great potential for growth in Malaysia within the dual mainstream mercantile law system of the country subject of course to *Sharia* requirements. This has been due to the Muslim majority population in the country, as well as its strategic positioning by the government as a regional and global Islamic financial hub.

Nevertheless, the insurance and *takaful* industry in Malaysia has been regulated by the *Insurance Act 1996* (Malaysia) and the *Takaful Act 1984* (Malaysia) that have both not explicitly nor adequately addressed the duty of utmost good faith, despite its acknowledged acceptance by case law as forming the cornerstone of such contracts which are *uberrima fidei* in nature.

The Malaysian government has however taken steps over the years to enhance the industry in terms of its infrastructure and education. In 2003, it launched a 10-year Consumer Education Programme to educate consumers of their rights and responsibilities arising under insurance and *takaful* contracts. This was followed by the amalgamation of the Insurance and Banking Mediation Bureaus into the highly effective Financial Mediation Bureau in 2005 which handles the majority of insurance and *takaful* complaints to date. The Law Harmonisation Committee was in turn established in 2010 to facilitate a more conducive legal system to achieve certainty and enforceability of Malaysian Islamic finance laws. This was followed in 2011 by the Central Bank's *Sharia Governance Framework* for Islamic Financial

Institutions in order to enhance the role of the key organs responsible for executing *Sharia* compliance.

Major regulatory reform of the Malaysian insurance and *takaful* industry in the form of the *Financial Services Act 2013* (Malaysia) and the *Islamic Financial Services Act 2013* (Malaysia) however came about following the substantial reforms undertaken in the UK. Both these statutes came into effect on 30 June 2013 following a much awaited repeal of their predecessors, the *Insurance Act 1996* (Malaysia) and the *Takaful Act 1984* (Malaysia).

It is important to note that prior to the Malaysian reforms taking place, the Law Commission of England and Wales and the Scottish Law Commission had, in 2006, commenced a major review of insurance law in the UK. This has since culminated in the enactment of the *Consumer Insurance (Disclosure and Representations) Act 2012* (UK) which came into effect on 6 April 2013, introducing substantial reform with respect to consumer insurance contracts. This in fact formed the basis of the Malaysian reforms undertaken in 2013.

The Law Commissions have since gone on to enact the *Insurance Act 2015* (UK) which is meant primarily but not exclusively for non-consumer insurance contracts. The *Act* received the royal assent on 12 February 2015 and will take effect in August 2016, following an 18-month lead-in period. This was inspired by the urgent need for reform of insurance contract law in the UK which has had numerous calls for reform dating back more than 50 years, as well as the progressive Australian insurance law reform package, the *Insurance Contracts Act 1984 (Cth)*, that has proven to be highly effective.

It is against this backdrop of development in the UK and Australia that this book proposes to evaluate the Malaysian reforms pertaining to utmost good faith in insurance and *takaful* contracts undertaken in 2013, with the aim of achieving reform that serves to strike a fair and workable balance between the competing interests of insurers/*takaful* operators and insureds/*takaful* participants.

Apart from offering a comparative analysis of the law in this area which is hoped would prove useful to its readers, this book serves to highlight the importance of undertaking law reform in a holistic sense. This in turn involves a sociocultural evaluation of Malaysian society as well as the economic efficiency of the reforms proposed, in order to further substantiate the need for and viability of such reform, as insurance and *takaful* contracts are underpinned by social and economic considerations. This is done in the firm belief that a balanced legal framework is crucial to achieving comprehensive and sustained improvement in the law of utmost good faith, like any other law of a commercial nature for that matter.

It remains to be seen what further reforms would be undertaken by the Malaysian government in this respect. It is hoped that some of what is contained herein proves useful in this regard.

I wish to take this opportunity to thank my publishers: Springer and the staff responsible for this project; my mentor and colleagues at Monash University Australia and Malaysia for their support; and Professor Robert Merkin for his gracious and insightful foreword to this book.

Finally, my sincere thanks go to my family—my husband Dinesh, daughters Marisha and Anoushka, son Dravid and my parents, for their love and encouragement.

The research undertaken for this book has been applied to a number of law review articles, and this book draws upon those works as indicated in the text. The law and legal issues analysed herein is as at 30 June 2015.

August 2015 Haemala Thanasegaran

Contents

Table of Cases

Chapter 1
Introduction

Abstract The central aim of this book is to set out and analyse the duty of utmost good faith in non-marine insurance and *takaful* (Islamic insurance) contracts in Malaysia, against the backdrop of the development in the United Kingdom and Australia. This is done to evaluate the extent to which Malaysian insurance and *takaful* law and practice addresses insurer and insured rights in a balanced manner. In this context, comparable *takaful* regulations from Muslim-majority jurisdictions will also be briefly examined. The book then goes on to evaluate the holistic adequacy of the reforms undertaken in Malaysia to date, from a socio-cultural and economic perspective.

1.1 Introduction

The law provides a wide range of 'technical' defences potentially available to an insurer wishing to avoid liability under his policy. By 'technical' is meant a legally valid, though morally dubious, point, outstanding examples of which are the rights of an insurer to avoid a policy for innocent, immaterial non-disclosures or breach of warranty and to avoid a claim for innocent, immaterial breach of condition… [and] it seems highly questionable that insurers should be permitted effectively to remain judges in their own cause.[1]

This observation was made by John Birds in 1977 on the state of the law governing utmost good faith in insurance contracts[2] in the United Kingdom which has existed for over 100 years.

---

[1]Birds (1977, p. 677).

[2]Reference to 'insurance' contracts throughout this book covers only non-marine insurance and *takaful* contracts, which include life insurance, general insurance and family and general *takaful*. Marine insurance contracts are beyond the scope of this book because an examination of them would unduly widen its scope and as a result, lose its intended aim and effect. Furthermore, international traders and conglomerates acquiring marine insurance policies are usually on a comparable footing with insurers, as they possess adequate legal representation to protect their interests. This is unlike most average purchasers of non-marine insurance policies.

H. Thanasegaran, *Good Faith in Insurance and Takaful Contracts in Malaysia*,
DOI 10.1007/978-981-10-0383-7_1

One of the central aims of this book is to set out and analyse the duty of utmost good faith in non-marine insurance and *takaful* (Islamic insurance) contracts in Malaysia, against the backdrop of the development in the United Kingdom and Australia, in evaluating the extent to which this observation might still be applicable or relevant today. The other, is to evaluate the holistic adequacy of the reforms undertaken in Malaysia to date, from a socio-cultural and economic perspective.

Consider an insured who acquires an intangible product like insurance which cannot be enjoyed or appreciated immediately. 'By its nature, an insurance contract is about future uncertain events. Precision with regard to all possible contingencies is all but impossible…[and] there remains a certain inevitability about disputes of this kind'.[3] And yet,

> the purchase of insurance, whether by *layman* or by *professional*, represents a "purchase" of greatest importance. The failure of this "purchase" will in most cases involve far more serious results for the "purchaser" than is likely to be true in the event of any other defective goods or commodity the insured acquires (author's emphasis added).[4]

Hence, it is commonplace for an insured who takes up an insurance policy to assume that by making premium payments regularly, any genuine claim made would be met without excuses or delays. The thought of facing obstacles when making a claim, is especially distressing to an insured, as it is usually preceded by a loss. The legalese in which insurance policies are normally worded, adds to the insured's feeling of helplessness, as it often results in them not understanding or appreciating the precise content of the policy. This in turn, results in adverse consequences for the insured when it transpires that the risk or loss in question is not covered by the policy or that the quantum is substantially less than expected.

On the other hand, it is natural for insurers to assess the validity or genuineness of a claim in a rigorous manner, as it may have a direct bearing on the insurers' viability of remaining as a going concern. This has therefore, resulted in the insurer-insured relationship being inherently fraught with tension.[5] Ironically however, there has long been 'a remarkable lack of control over the terms of insurance contracts,'[6] until recent years.

This is indeed surprising, for unlike ordinary contracts, insurance contracts are *uberrima fidei* in nature, which essentially requires both the insurer and insured to act in utmost good faith towards each other in a positive sense, rather than merely refrain from engaging in fraud, misrepresentation or undue influence, for instance. As a result, the duty of utmost good faith has long been recognized at common law,

---

[3]Brown (1994, p. 195).

[4]Hasson (1969, p. 634).

[5]This section draws on research appearing in: Thanasegaran (2011, p. 191).

[6]Hasson (1984, p. 517). This has not been the case however, with other types of contracts such as employment, sale of goods, supply of services and consumer credit contracts.

as constituting the cornerstone of insurance contracts[7] and the same can also be said of insurance and *takaful* contracts in Malaysia.[8]

It is against this backdrop that this book proposes to evaluate whether and, if so, the extent to which the duty of utmost good faith is effectively regulated and observed by insurers/*takaful* operators and insureds/*takaful* participants in Malaysia. This book examines the problems and shortcomings in the Malaysian legal framework until the recent amendments introduced in 2013, evaluates the adequacy of these amendments and proposes holistic reform that serves to strike a fair and workable balance between the competing interests of the parties involved. This is done in the firm belief that only a balanced legal framework would go the distance in bringing about comprehensive and sustained improvement to the current position.

In doing this, a comparison is made with other common law jurisdictions with progressive insurance regulations like Australia and in recent times, the United Kingdom, so as to provide a broader perspective to the issues faced with respect to utmost good faith in insurance and *takaful* contracts in Malaysia. This is done with the aim of improving law reform in the area, not just for Malaysia but also other common law countries in the region.

1.2 Background

For more than a century, the United Kingdom and Malaysia[9] have been shackled by the outdated and draconian provisions of the *Marine Insurance Act 1906* (UK). This is because the *Marine Insurance Act 1906* (UK) which is a codification of English common law, has long formed the basis of not just marine but also non-marine insurance regulation in the United Kingdom. Steyn J's dicta in *Banque Keyser Ullmann SA v Skandia (UK) Insurance Co Ltd*[10] is a clear reflection of this sentiment, where his Honour said that '[t]he Act was a codification of the common law, and it is inconceivable that the common law regarded marine insurers as bound by a duty of utmost good faith but not other insurers'.

The same can be said for Malaysia as well, being a former British colony, with its legal framework based on English common law in many respects, except where it is inconsistent with specific Malaysian legislation governing the subject matter. The application of English insurance and mercantile law to Malaysia is facilitated

[7]See: *Carter v Boehm* (1766) 3 Burr 1905 (Lord Mansfield).

[8]See: *Leong Kum Whay v QBE Insurance (M) Sdn Bhd* [2006] 1 CLJ 1 (insurance), *Seah Cheoh Wah v Malayan Banking Bhd & Anor* [2009] 7 CLJ 485 (*takaful*).

[9]This applies to other common law jurisdictions like Singapore as well.

[10][1987] 1 Lloyd's Rep 69, 93; Also see: *Britton v Royal Insurance Company* (1866) 4 F & F 905, 909 where Willes J voiced a similar sentiment in a case involving a fraudulent claim made under a fire insurance policy.

by s5 of the *Civil Law Act 1956* (Malaysia) which shall be set out in the next chapter.

The insurance industry in Malaysia comprises both conventional insurance and *takaful*, which is the Islamic system of mutual insurance that is built on principles of *Sharia* or Islamic law. The former was governed by the *Insurance Act 1996 (Malaysia)* and the latter by the *Takaful Act 1984* (Malaysia).[11] Both statues have however, been repealed and replaced by the *Financial Services Act 2013* (Malaysia) and *Islamic Financial Services Act 2013* (Malaysia) respectively, which came into effect on 30th June 2013.[12]

It should be noted that *takaful* is viewed as part of the mainstream mercantile law of Malaysia.[13] As a result, it is subject to the same civil court structure, instead of being part of *Sharia* or Islamic law per se like in jurisdictions such as Sudan and Saudi Arabia. The *takaful* scheme in Malaysia came about upon the enactment of the *Takaful Act 1984* (Malaysia) and since it is treated as part of the mainstream mercantile law of the country, legislative gaps within the governing regulation have in the past been filled by the common law (much like that of conventional insurance), rather than *Sharia*.[14] This is because like many common law jurisdictions, the source of the basic tenets of conventional insurance and *takaful* as practiced in Malaysia is the common law.[15]

The regulation of the Malaysian insurance and *takaful* industry (which forms part of the larger banking and finance sector) is handled by the Central Bank of Malaysia,[16] with respect to prudential regulation, market supervision and control and consumer protection. Insurance and *takaful* dispute resolution has in turn been handled primarily by the Financial Mediation Bureau ("FMB") since 2005, which has proven to be a viable alternative to litigation.[17]

Apart from this, insureds and *takaful* participants may direct their complaints and enquiries directly to the Customer Services Bureau of the Central Bank ('Customer Services Bureau') set up in 1998. The Customer Services Bureau is a less formal avenue that has the task of analysing complaints received and liaising with industry and relevant trade associations to resolve the same. It also serves to

---

[11]Both statutes have been supplemented by the Central Bank of Malaysia's Guidelines issued as and when necessary, the most important of which being the *Guidelines on Claims Settlement Practices* ('*Claims Settlement Guidelines*') issued in 1995 and revised in 2003.

[12]Section 271 of the *Financial Services Act 2013* (Malaysia) and s282 of the *Islamic Financial Services Act 2013* (Malaysia) are the relevant provisions repealing the same.

[13]This is by virtue of Articles 73, 74, 75, 121 (1), 121(1A) and the Ninth Schedule of the *Federal Constitution of Malaysia*. See: Mohamed (2005, p. cv).

[14]Ibid.

[15]The concept of *takaful* will be developed further and a brief comparison with other major *takaful* offering nations will be made in Chap. 5 of this book.

[16]The Central Bank of Malaysia is also known as *Bank Negara Malaysia*.

[17]The FMB (which replaces the Insurance Mediation Bureau set up in 1991) was established in 2005 in line with the Central Bank of Malaysia's *Financial Sector Master Plan 2001*, to integrate the redress mechanisms for the whole banking and finance sector.

identify and channel insurance and *takaful* practices that may require regulatory action by the Central Bank. In 2003, the Malaysian government launched a 10-year Consumer Education Programme to educate consumers of their rights and responsibilities arising under insurance and *takaful* contracts, and in 2013, passed the *Financial Services Act* and *Islamic Financial Services Act* to amend the law regulating insurance and *takaful* as a whole, in line with legislative developments in the United Kingdom and Australia in the area.

It is important to note that the Law Commission of England and Wales and the Scottish Law Commission ("the Law Commissions") commenced a major review of insurance law in the United Kingdom in 2006. This has since culminated in the enactment of the *Consumer Insurance (Disclosure and Representations) Act 2012* (UK) for consumer insurance which came into effect on 6th April 2013 and the *Insurance Act 2015* (UK) which is meant primarily but not exclusively for non-consumer insurance contracts. The *Insurance Act 2015* (UK) received the royal assent on 12 February 2015 and will take effect in August 2016, following an 18-month lead-in period. This was inspired by the urgent need for reform of insurance contract law in the United Kingdom, as well as the progressive insurance law reform package adopted by Australia since 1984 via the *Insurance Contracts Act 1984 (Cth)* (Australia) as amended in 2013, that has proven to be highly effective.[18]

1.3 Objective and Scope

The objective of this book is two-fold. First, it aims to examine whether the duty of utmost good faith in insurance and *takaful* contracts is effectively regulated and observed by insurers/*takaful* operators and insureds/*takaful* participants, in Malaysia. Secondly, if not, how can the legal framework regulating utmost good faith be improved so as to achieve a fair and workable balance between the competing interests of these parties?

This objective is in turn important for two reasons. First, because of the social and economic importance of insurance and *takaful* to the nation for as at 31 December 2012, the Central Bank of Malaysia estimated the life insurance and family *takaful* penetration rate in Malaysia to be at 54 %.[19] This coupled with the inherent tension that exists between insurer-insured (and *takaful* operator-participant) expectations, reflects the need for balanced regulation. Since the insurance (and *takaful*) industry is widely viewed as a key part of the financial services industry of any nation, in that it provides an important social service to

---

[18]See: Coonan (2003).

[19]See: Central Bank of Malaysia (2013). The Central Bank's penetration rate is based on the ratio of the number of policies and certificates in force, to the total Malaysian population. The Malaysian government's aim is to increase this to 75 % as soon as possible.

individual consumers as well as underpins most forms of economic activity,[20] it is essential that a fair and workable balance is struck between the interests of insurers/*takaful* operators and insureds/*takaful* participants in order for the industry to truly achieve sustained growth and development in a meaningful manner.

The second more important reason is to evaluate the adequacy or effectiveness of the recent reforms introduced in 2013, in addressing the shortcomings which have plagued the Malaysian legal framework regulating utmost good faith in insurance and *takaful* contracts since the enactment of the *Insurance Act 1996* and *Takaful Act 1984*. In reality, the 'normal' expectations of insureds have thus far been more of a legal misconception. This is apparent from the fact that a large proportion of insurance and *takaful* complaints by insureds and *takaful* participants in Malaysia have related to allegations by insurers and *takaful* operators of breach of utmost good faith by insureds/*takaful* participants in one form or another.

Proof of this problem is evident in the Financial Mediation Bureau's *Annual Reports*,[21] which have over the years consistently shown that a large proportion of public complaints or cases in insurance and *takaful* stem from alleged breaches of this fundamental duty of good faith.

For example, from 2000 to 2014 an average of more than 1000 new insurance and *takaful* cases per year have been referred to the Financial Mediation Bureau. Of these, an average of 92 % of the cases involved avoidance of the policy or claim by insurers and *takaful* operators based on allegations of breach of utmost good faith in one form or another by insureds/*takaful* participants.[22] These statistics are a valuable indicator of the current state of affairs, as most cases on insurance and *takaful* in Malaysia are filed with the Financial Mediation Bureau and Customer Services Bureau (with respect to enquiries and less serious complaints), and few are taken to the courts.[23]

In response to this, however, the enactment of the *Financial Services Act 2013* (Malaysia) and *Islamic Financial Services Act 2013* (Malaysia) forms the first substantive reform of the law on utmost good faith in insurance and *takaful*

---

[20]This section draws on research appearing in: Thanasegaran (2013, p. 104).

[21]The same is also evident in its predecessor, the Insurance Mediation Bureau's *Mediator's Annual Reports and Case Reviews*.

[22]See: Table of Cases Referred to the Financial Mediation Bureau from 2000 to 2014 in the Appendix. It should be noted that the Financial Mediation Bureau's Annual Reports from 2012 to 2014 do not provide a breakdown of the type of complaints referred to them, unlike that which was available until 2011. Part of the Table of Cases in the Appendix, specifically, data from 2000 to 2009 draws on research appearing in: Thanasegaran, above n 5, 199.

[23]This may be supported by the fact that the number of cases on insurance and *takaful* decided by the civil courts in Malaysia from 1 January 2000–31 December 2014, amount to less than 100. A comparison between the number of insurance and *takaful* complaints 'referred' to the Financial Mediation Bureau is made with the number of insurance cases 'decided' by the Malaysian civil courts from 2000 to 2014, because it has not been possible to obtain the number of cases on insurance and *takaful* which have been filed in the Malaysian courts for that period, as no such record is available.

contracts, thereby warranting a thorough analysis of its effectiveness in terms of according clearer and fairer rights and responsibilities to the parties concerned.

In evaluating this, the full length of the insurance and *takaful* contract is considered because the duty of utmost good faith is of a continuing nature, although its juristic basis may differ at different stages. It spans from the pre-contractual stage which concerns non-disclosure and misrepresentation of material facts through to the post-contractual claims settlement stage.[24] The book is therefore, structured in a manner which reflects this continuing nature of the duty.

This book is primarily doctrinal in nature, involving a comparative analysis of the Malaysian position pertaining to the law and practice governing insurance and *takaful* contracts, with that of the United Kingdom and Australia, with the view of proposing reform most suited to Malaysia.

The concluding chapters of the book provide a socio-cultural evaluation of Malaysian society and the economic efficiency of the reforms proposed, in order to further substantiate the need for and viability of such reform. The law and legal issues analysed herein is as at 30th June 2015.

1.4 Structure

This book comprises seven chapters, with this first chapter forming the introduction.

Chapter 2 sets out the duty of utmost good faith by examining its meaning, juridical basis and scope or extent of its continuing nature within insurance contracts. In doing so, the origins of the duty, namely, s17 of the *Marine Insurance Act 1906* (UK) will be set out together with its applicability to non-marine insurance contracts mainly in the United Kingdom and Malaysia with extensive comparison being made to the Australian position. In this respect, the effect of recent reforms in the United Kingdom and Malaysia on the scope and application of the duty of utmost good faith in insurance contracts will be analysed.

Chapter 3 examines the existing legal framework regulating insurance contracts and practice in Malaysia pertaining to the pre-contractual duty of disclosure and misrepresentation. A comparative analysis will be made with the United Kingdom and Australia, with suggestions for possible improvement to the recent reforms being made. The pre-contractual duty of disclosure is a unique component of the duty of utmost good faith in insurance contracts which although historically has had a legitimate juridical basis owing to the information imbalance between insurer and insured, has the potential to affect insureds adversely. Even innocent non-disclosure of a material fact which has no bearing on any ensuing loss, may result in the insurer avoiding the contract and refusing payment.

---

[24] Hasson, above n 4, 634. Justification for the continuing nature of the duty shall be provided in Chap. 2.

Pre-contractual misrepresentation on the other hand, is a false statement of fact addressed to the insurer to induce it to enter into the insurance contract and in fact does. Insurers have frequently relied on both non-disclosure and misrepresentation interchangeably to avoid insurance contracts, thereby, often blurring the distinction and increasing the potential for avoiding insurance contracts. In this context, the role of intermediaries in effecting insurance policies and the widespread use of 'basis of contract' clauses in insurance proposal forms which have the effect of incorporating the insured's answers into the insurance policy and converting them into warranties of fact, will also be examined.

Chapter 4 examines the post-contractual aspect of utmost good faith involving claims settlement practices by insurers. In this respect, the use of wide exclusion clauses and strict construction of policy terms by insurers as a means to defeat insureds' otherwise legitimate claims, along with other undesirable claims settlement practices such as undue delay in the processing of claims and reduced settlement of claims as a matter of course, will be examined. On the flipside, fraudulent claims made by insureds will also be addressed.

Chapter 5 will set out the concept of *takaful* which has its juridical foundations in *Sharia* or Islamic law. It will then examine the applicability of the duty of utmost good faith to *takaful* contracts and address the shortcomings in the *Takaful Act 1984* (Malaysia) with respect to this duty at both the pre and post-contractual stage of *takaful* contracts. The adequacy of the recent reforms introduced by the *Islamic Financial Services Act 2013* (Malaysia) will in this regard be evaluated, along with a brief comparison with *takaful* regulations in other major *takaful* offering nations in the region, namely, Pakistan, Bahrain, Egypt, Indonesia, Brunei, Iran, the United Arab Emirates (UAE), Saudi Arabia and Sudan with the view of proposing reform most suited to Malaysia. This additional comparison is made because Malaysia does not adopt the British and Australian method of having conventional insurance regulation apply to both the insurance and *takaful* industries, preferring separate regulations instead.

Chapter 6 will demonstrate that in addition to the doctrinal justification for reform of the law and practice regulating insurance and *takaful* contracts in Malaysia provided in Chaps. 2–5, such law reform is also important from a socio-economic perspective since law reform is part of the broader social sciences namely sociology, economics and political science. As such, an examination of the socio-cultural influence on law reform along with the economic efficiency of the suggested reforms is useful in proposing any suitable law reform package. This chapter will set out the literature on legal culture and analyse the effect of Malaysian legal culture on the proposed reforms.

Chapter 7 concludes this book by comprehensively outlining the proposals for further reform of the law and practice regulating insurance and *takaful* contracts in Malaysia, suggested throughout the book and evaluates the economic efficiency of the same, in assessing its viability in striking a workable balance between insurer/*takaful* operator and insured/*takaful* participant rights and responsibilities.

References

Birds John (1977) The Statement of insurance practice: a measure of regulation of the insurance contract'. Mod Law Rev 40:677

Brown C (1994) Unfinished business: misrepresentation and non-disclosure in insurance proposals. N Z Univ Law Rev 16:195

Central Bank of Malaysia (2013) Concept paper on life insurance and family Takaful framework, 7 Nov 2013

Coonan H (Minister for Revenue and the Assistant Treasurer, Australia), 'Insurance Contracts Act Reform Package' (Press Release, 10 Sept 2003)

Hasson RA (1969) The Doctrine of uberrima fides in insurance law—a critical evaluation. Mod Law Rev 32:615

Hasson RA (1984) The special nature of insurance contracts: a comparison of the American and english law of insurance. Modern Law Review 47:505

Mohamed S (2005) The legislative jurisdiction of the federal parliament in matters involving islamic law. Malayan Law J 3:cv

Thanasegaran H (2011) Settlement of claims by Malaysian insurance and *Takaful* companies: a genuine prospect or merely suspect? Int Company & Commercial Law Rev 22(6):191

Thanasegaran H (2013) Making an entrance—can Australia contribute to *Takaful* (islamic insurance) law reform? Insurance Law J 24:104

Chapter 2
Duty of Utmost Good Faith

Abstract The duty of utmost good faith forms the cornerstone of insurance law codified in s17 of the *Marine Insurance Act 1906* of the United Kingdom. It is a wide and all-encompassing duty that has arisen as a result of insurance contracts being *uberrimae fidei* in nature. This chapter examines the origin, meaning and juridical basis of the duty of utmost good faith; its applicability to non-marine insurance contracts in the United Kingdom, Malaysia and Australia; its scope or continuing nature with respect to the insurer's and insured's obligations; and the recent legislative reforms in the area in the jurisdictions examined.

2.1 Introduction

The duty of utmost good faith, which is the cornerstone of insurance law, has long been codified in s17 of the *Marine Insurance Act 1906* of the United Kingdom. The section provides that:

> A contract of marine insurance is a contract based upon the utmost good faith, and, if the utmost good faith be not observed by either party, the contract may be avoided by the other party.

This wide and all-encompassing duty has arisen as a result of insurance contracts being *uberrimae fidei* in nature. This chapter proposes to examine the origin, meaning and juridical basis of the duty of utmost good faith; its applicability to non-marine insurance contracts in the United Kingdom, Malaysia and Australia; its scope or continuing nature with respect to the insurer's and insured's obligations; and the recent amendments in the area in the jurisdictions examined.

It should be noted at this juncture, that there has been substantial reform in the area with respect to the United Kingdom following the enactment of the *Consumer Insurance (Disclosure and Representations) Act 2012* to regulate consumer

H. Thanasegaran, *Good Faith in Insurance and Takaful Contracts in Malaysia*,
DOI 10.1007/978-981-10-0383-7_2

insurance contracts and the *Insurance Act 2015* to primarily regulate non-consumer insurance contracts.[1] Malaysia has also followed suit with the introduction of its *Financial Services Act 2013* and *Islamic Financial Services Act 2013*, regulating insurance and *takaful* contracts respectively, with Australia having led the way, as far back as 1984 via its *Insurance Contracts Act 1984* (Cth). Nevertheless, this chapter traces the historical development of this important duty in order to effectively evaluate the adequacy of the recent amendments.

The duty of utmost good faith is essentially a broad duty existing in *uberrimae fidei* contracts, of which insurance contracts are a type. It requires both parties to the contract to disclose all material facts and act honestly towards each other without any underhanded behaviour. It is a positive duty imposed on the parties that goes beyond the obligation present in ordinary contracts, which merely requires parties to refrain from engaging in conduct that is fraudulent, misrepresentative or causes undue influence. Over and above this however, there has been some support for the view that it might also be wide enough to include conduct depicting fair play and co-operation as highlighted by Steyn J in *Banque Keyser Ullmann SA v Skandia (UK) Insurance Co Ltd.*[2]

2.2 The Meaning of and Juridical Basis for the Duty

The question that arises when addressing the meaning that should be assigned to the concept of utmost good faith is whether it should receive a broad or narrow interpretation. As mentioned earlier, the duty of utmost good faith can generally be described as a positive requirement on both the insurer and insured to act honestly towards each other without deception, with 'utmost' merely serving to emphasize the duty.

As far as the English courts have been concerned, a rather conservative stance seems to have been taken. This is apparent from Slade LJ's concern voiced at the Court of Appeal in *Le Banque Financiere v Westgate Insurance Co Ltd*[3] in response to an indication by Steyn J in *Banque Keyser Ullmann SA v Skandia (UK) Insurance Co Ltd*[4] that utmost good faith may be wide enough to include broad based notions such as fair dealing and co-operation:

> …in the case of commercial contracts, broad concepts of honesty and fair dealing, however laudable, are a somewhat uncertain guide when determining the existence or otherwise of an obligation which may arise even in the absence of any dishonest or unfair intent … More importantly, in our judgment, it would be too broad a proposition to state that any fact is

---

[1]The *Insurance Act 2015* (UK) is however, not exclusively applicable to non-consumer insurance contracts, in that it also contains provisions dealing with consumer insurance.

[2][1987] 1 Lloyd's Rep 69.

[3][1988] 2 Lloyd's Ll Rep 513.

[4][1987] 1 Lloyd's Rep 69.

> material if it is [in the language of the *Marine Insurance Act 1906*] calculated to influence the decision of the insured to conclude the contract of insurance. To give one example, it might well be that in a particular case proposed insurers would be aware of another reputable underwriter who would be prepared to underwrite the same risk at a substantially lower premium. In our judgment the mere existence of the relationship of insurers and insured would not place upon them the duty to inform the insured of this fact. …[The duty on the insurer, however] must at least extend to disclosing all facts known to him which are material either to the nature of the risk sought to be covered or the recoverability of a claim under the policy which a prudent insured would take into account in deciding whether to place the risk for which he seeks cover with that insurer.[5] (Author's clarification added)

The Australian[6] and American courts on the other hand, have adopted a more liberal and progressive description of what amounts to utmost good faith, by ascribing to it the essential elements of fairness, reasonable conduct and propriety or honesty, although it is not necessary to show dishonesty for there to be a lack of utmost good faith. In fact, in as far back as 1933, it was held in the leading American case of *Kirk La Shelle Co v Paul Armstrong Co*[7] that:

> In every contract there is an implied covenant that neither party shall do anything which will have the effect of destroying or injuring the right of the other party to receive the fruits of the contract, which means that in every contract there exists an implied covenant of good faith and fair dealing.[8]

Academics[9] in the area have generally had a consensus that utmost good faith in insurance contracts requires more than mere mechanical performance according to the letter of the contract. The question however, remains as to how much more.

Some help can be found in the foreword to Steven Burton's article where he argues that:

> …the duty to perform in good faith applies when one party exercises discretion in performance and thereby controls the other party's anticipated benefit. The discretion exercising party performs in good faith when it exercises discretion for any purpose within the reasonable contemplation of the parties, and in bad faith when discretion is used to recapture foregone opportunities.[10]

His analysis takes the concept of good faith far beyond that of a mere absence of bad faith but not so far as to secure the other party's expectations under the contract. His theory may well be relevant to insurance contracts because one party, namely the insurer, usually controls both the content (being contracts of adhesion) and administration of the insurance contract which includes the disposition of the

---

[5] *Le Banque Financiere v Westgate Insurance Co. Ltd.* [1988] 2 Lloyd's L1 Rep 513, 544.

[6] See: Sutton (1999, pp. 157–158); *CGU Insurance Ltd v AMP Financial Planning Pty Ltd* (2007) 235 CLR 1.

[7] 263 NY 79, 188 NE 163 (1933).

[8] Ibid. 167; Also, unlike other common law jurisdictions, the American *Uniform Commercial Code* defines 'good faith' as 'honesty in fact in the conduct or transaction concerned'.

[9] See: Finn (1989a, 1989b, p. 87), Tarr (1989).

[10] Burton (1980, p. 369).

benefits thereunder to the insured. In focusing on the conduct of the party having the principal discretion as to the time and manner of performance of the contract, he argues that the proper 'expectation interest' of one party to a contract is that the other will not take advantage of any discretion granted to it by the type of agreement, in order to avoid the sacrifice of economic opportunity necessitated by performance.

In this regard, it has been said that:

> ...the rhetoric of 'utmost good faith' must never substitute for a careful consideration of what is good law in the particular and modern context...[and] the future development of the doctrine of utmost good faith must take place against an evaluation of the extent to which it continues to be appropriate for parties to insurance contracts.[11]

The juristic basis for the pre-contractual duty of utmost good faith has long been entrenched in s17 of the *Marine Insurance Act 1906* (UK). This is because s17 provides that insurance contracts are 'based upon' the utmost good faith which presupposes that it relates to the formation of the contract, and is supported by its positioning at the beginning of ss17–20 of the *Marine Insurance Act 1906* (UK) under the heading 'Disclosure and Representation', that relate to the formative process.[12] This coupled with the information imbalance that exists in favour of the insured justifies its imposition.[13] The remedy for its breach therefore, is that of avoidance of the contract ab initio under s17, which is a severe remedy that has retrospective effect and no right to damages.[14]

The justification for the post-contractual duty of utmost good faith on the other hand, is in response to the problem that unlike most other general contracts which have some device for policing unfair terms, there has been a 'remarkable lack of control in insurance contracts' in favour of insurers. Therefore, in addition to the *contra proferentum* rule, something along the lines of a post-contractual duty of utmost good faith was needed.[15]

The juristic basis for this post-contractual duty however, is less settled. First, since the words of s17 are wide enough to cover 'a continuing mutual duty of disclosure that runs throughout the duration of the contract of insurance,'[16] and unlike ss18–20 which are restricted to the pre-contractual stage, it would appear that

---

[11]Bennett (1999, p. 221).

[12]Bennet, above n 11, 219. Sections 18–20 of the *Marine Insurance Act 1906* (UK) have however, been repealed in recent times by s21 (2) of the *Insurance Act 2015* (UK).

[13]See: *Carter v Boehm* (1766) 3 Burr 1905 (Lord Mansfield); *Pan Atlantic Insurance Co Ltd v Pine Top Insurance Co* [1994] 3 All ER 581.

[14]This section draws on research appearing in: Thanasegaran (2011, p. 193). It is worth noting that this much criticized remedy of avoidance ab initio has been deleted from s17 by s14 of the *Insurance Act 2015* (UK).

[15]Hasson (1984, pp. 517–518); See: *The Mercandian Continent* [2001] EWCA Civ 1275 [11] (Longmore LJ).

[16]Naidoo and Oughton (2005, p. 347).

avoidance of the contract would be the drastic remedy for breach. Support for this reasoning can be found in Hirst J's judgment in *Black King Shipping v Massie (The Litsion Pride)*[17] where a post-contractual duty of good faith was clearly said to exist between both insurers and insureds.

On the other hand, the view in favour of detaching the post-contractual duty from s17 altogether as its juristic basis and fragmenting it into post-contractual terms and claims handling; and fraudulent claims has much to be said for it.[18] The former has been convincingly argued to be based on an implied term of the insurance contract but applicable in a more flexible manner than at the pre-contractual stage.[19] This would in turn give rise to the more equitable remedy of prospective avoidance of the relevant claim and/or damages.[20] As for the juristic basis for fraudulent claims in turn, it is founded on the public policy argument that no one should benefit from their wrong doing.[21]

Amongst the reasons for this view is that since the *Marine Insurance Act 1906* (UK) was a codifying statute, it would have been intended to retain the common law position prior to 1906, where such a wide post-contractual duty giving rise to avoidance as a remedy was in fact rejected at the time by Blackburn J in *Cory v Patton*.[22] Furthermore, as there is no longer an information imbalance between the parties post-contract, express contractual provisions can more than adequately regulate the rights and obligations of the parties concerned without the need for an overarching duty based on s17.[23] It would appear that this reasoning is more in line with the recent reforms that have taken place in insurance.

2.3 Continuing Nature of the Duty of Utmost Good Faith

The notion of good faith in insurance contracts as embodied in s17 of the *Marine Insurance Act 1906* (UK) was introduced in the landmark case of *Carter v Boehm*[24] where Lord Mansfield stated that:

[17][1985] 1 Lloyd's Rep 437.

[18]See: Naidoo and Oughton, above n 16, 367–371; *Agapitos v Agnew (The Aegeon)* [2002] 2 Lloyd's Rep 42, [45] (Mance LJ).

[19]See: Australian Law Reform Commission (2001); Derrington (2002); *The Star Sea* [2001] 1 Lloyd's Rep 389 (Lord Hobhouse).

[20]See: Naidoo and Oughton, above n 16, 371.

[21]See: *The Star Sea* [2001] 1 Lloyd's Rep 389 (Lord Hobhouse), *The Mercandian Continent* [2001] EWCA Civ 1275 (Longmore LJ), *Agapitos v Agnew (The Aegeon)* [2002] 2 Lloyd's Rep 42 (Mance LJ). This section draws on research appearing in: Thanasegaran, above n 14, 193.

[22](1872) LR 7 QB 304, 309.

[23]Soyer (2003, p. 42).

[24](1766) 3 Burr 1905.

> Insurance is a contract upon speculation. The special facts, upon which the contingent chance is to be computed, lie most commonly in the knowledge of the insured only: the under-writer trusts to his representation, and proceeds upon confidence that he does not keep back any circumstance in his knowledge, to mislead the under-writer into a belief that the circumstance does not exist, and to induce him to estimate the risqué, as if it did not exist.
>
> The keeping back such circumstance is a fraud, and therefore the policy is void. Although the suppression should happen through mistake, without any fraudulent intention; yet still the under-writer is deceived, and the policy is void; because the risqué run is really different from the risqué understood and intended to be run, at the time of the agreement ... Good faith forbids either party by concealing what he privately knows, to draw the other into a bargain, from his ignorance of that fact, and his believing the contrary.[25]

Although the doctrine of utmost good faith is primarily associated with the pre-contractual stage of insurance contracts, aspects of it are also applicable post-contract, right up to the settlement of claims.[26] The scope of the duty and the remedies available for breach however, may vary with the stage, as observed by Leggatt LJ when expressing the view of the Court of Appeal in *Manifest Shipping & Co Ltd v Uni-Polaris Insurance Co Ltd*:

> It was common ground between assured and underwriters that the duty of utmost good faith continues to subsist after the making of the contract. There is less common ground as to the content of the duty or as to the remedy for breach of the duty. Whatever its origin, there is force in the argument that the scope of the duty of utmost good faith will alter according to whether underwriters have to make a decision under the policy or the assured decides to make a claim, and may also be affected according to the stage of the relationship at which the scope of the duty becomes material.[27]

Since the pre-contractual duty is of a reciprocal nature (owing to the words of s17), it follows that the post-contractual duty should also reflect the same. This post-contractual duty can arise in relation to whether the insurer's decision to avoid the policy had been made in breach of good faith[28] or whether the insurer's conduct involving claims handling amounts to a breach.[29] 'Overall the application of the insurer's duty to avoid and the claims handling process represent an emerging principle of good faith in the way in which insurers handle claims.'[30] However, the remedies available in the event of breach should be prospective termination of the contract and/or damages based on the implied term theory, as explained above.

At this point it is necessary to take into account the debate on the scope of the continuing duty of good faith that was started by Hirst J's wide pronouncement that

---

[25]Ibid. 1909, 1910.

[26]Bennet, above n 11, 197.

[27][1997] 1 Lloyd's Rep 360, 370.

[28]See: *Pan Atlantic Insurance Co Ltd v Pine Top Insurance Co Ltd* [1994] 3 All ER 581, 623 (Lord Lloyd); *Drake Insurance plc v Provident Insurance plc* [2004] 1 Lloyd's Rep 268.

[29]See: Naidoo and Oughton, above n 16, 359.

[30]See: Naidoo (2005).

it arose 'whenever there is a contractual duty for the insured to give the underwriter information'.[31] This was followed by the House of Lords overruling *The Litsion Pride*[32] in *The Star Sea*[33] and a subsequent evaluation of the House of Lords' reasoning, undertaken by the Court of Appeal in *K/S Merc-Skandia xxxxii v Certain Lloyd's Underwriters*.[34] The Court of Appeal's[35] position on the matter, led by Longmore LJ, was that there is an inextricable link between the continuing duty of good faith and the terms of the insurance policy. This is because the insured's post contractual duty is mainly governed by the insurance contract itself, although the *Marine Insurance Act 1906* (UK) does in effect recognize the existence of such a continuing duty.

Based on this, the post-contractual duty of utmost good faith continues to exist but is limited in its application. It arises in the form of a pre-contractual obligation when renewals and variations of a policy are sought; and in claims settlement and management by the insurer, but does not apply to fraudulent claims.[36]

Further support for this limitation pertaining to fraudulent claims is apparent in cases like *Agapitos v Agnew (The Aegeon)*,[37] *Bonner v Cox Dedicated Corporate Member Ltd*[38] and *HLB Kidsons (A Firm) v Lloyd's Underwriters,*[39] which reinforce the juristic basis for fraudulent claims to be instead the public policy reasoning of not benefitting from your own fraud.[40] Once viewed in this manner, it becomes clear that there is a continuing duty of utmost good faith in insurance contracts but with different juristic basis accorded to it at the pre and post-contractual stages, giving rise to appropriate remedies in the event of breach. This, instead of the disproportionate all or nothing remedy of avoidance of the contract *ab initio* generally associated with s17 of the *Marine Insurance Act 1906* (UK).[41]

---

[31]*Black King Shipping Corp v Massie (The Litsion Pride)* [1985] 1 Lloyd's Rep 437. This was followed by Evans J in *The Captain Panagos DP* [1986] 2 Lloyd's Rep 470.

[32]Ibid.

[33][2001] Lloyd's Rep IR 247.

[34]*(The Mercandian Continent)* [2001] 2 Lloyd's Rep 563.

[35]Ibid.

[36]A useful account of this debate can be found in Merkin (2010, pp. 291–302).

[37][2002] Lloyd's Rep I R 573 (Mance LJ).

[38][2006] Lloyd's Rep I R 385 (Waller LJ).

[39][2008] EWCA Civ 1206 (Toulson LJ).

[40]Soyer, above n 23, 59 however argues that there is still a possibility that the treatment of fraudulent claims may be based on the implied term theory proposed by Hoffmann LJ in *Orakpo v Barclays Insurance Services* [1995] LRLR 443 (that has not been discredited) which might come in handy where an insurer incurs expenditure in investigating fraudulent claims.

[41]This distinction is of less importance in the United Kingdom in recent times, following the amendment to s17 brought about by s14 of the *Insurance Act 2015* (UK).

2.4 Application of the Duty of Utmost Good Faith

It has long been accepted in the United Kingdom that the *Marine Insurance Act 1906* (UK) which is essentially a codification of the common law, applied equally to marine and non-marine insurance contracts.[42] This pre-empted the need for a separate piece of legislation to govern non-marine insurance contracts in the United Kingdom. This approach has in fact been retained in recent times, with the *Consumer Insurance (Disclosure and Representations) Act 2012* (UK) applying to all types of consumer insurance contracts and the *Insurance Act 2015* (UK) applying primarily (but not exclusively) to non-consumer insurance contracts.

As far as Malaysia is concerned, the application of English common law with respect to insurance and mercantile matters is facilitated by s5 of the *Civil Law Act 1956* (Malaysia), as endorsed in decisions such as *Leong Brothers Industries Sdn Bhd v Jerneh Insurance Corporation Sdn Bhd.*[43] Section 5 (1) of the *Civil Law Act 1956* (Malaysia)[44] imports into the states of West Malaysia (other than Malacca and Penang), insurance and mercantile law administered in England in the like case as at 7 April 1956. As for the states of Penang, Malacca, Sabah and Sarawak however, s5 (2) provides for the application of insurance and mercantile law administered in England in the like case at the corresponding period.

The meaning of 'corresponding period' in s5 (2) has been interpreted to include English law up to the cut-off date of the advent of the *Federal Constitution of Malaysia* on 31 August 1957 following Malaysia's independence from Britain. This is because Article 44 of the *Federal Constitution of Malaysia* vests the legislative authority of the Federation in the Malaysian Parliament. Hence, any post-Constitution application of English law in Malaysia is at best only of persuasive value, provided there is no Malaysian law on point.[45]

The application of the *Marine Insurance Act 1906* (UK) and common law to marine insurance cases in Malaysia is well established, as there is no corresponding

---

[42]*Banque Keyser Ullmann SA v Skandia (UK) Insurance Co Ltd* [1987] 1 Lloyd's Rep 69, 93 (Steyn J); See also: *Britton v Royal Insurance Company* (1866) 4 F & F 905, 909 where Willes J voiced a similar sentiment in a case involving a fraudulent claim made under a fire insurance policy.

[43][1991] 1 MLJ 102.

[44]Section 5 (1) provides:

In all matters pertaining to the law of marine insurance, average, life and fire insurance and mercantile law generally, to be decided in the States of West Malaysia other than Malacca and Penang, the law to be administered shall be the same as would be administered in England in the like case at the date of the coming into force of this Act (7 April 1956).

This section draws on research appearing in: Thanasegaran, above n 14, 192.

[45]See: Abu Bakar (2013, p. 19).

Malaysian statute addressing the same. As for non-marine insurance cases however, it has been the accepted practice for the *Marine Insurance Act 1906* (UK) and common law to apply in Malaysia, unless they are inconsistent with domestic insurance or *takaful* regulation, in which case the latter would prevail.[46] In this context, conventional insurance in Malaysia has been governed by the *Insurance Act 1996*[47] up until its repeal by the *Financial Services Act 2013* on 30th June 2013. Similarly, *takaful* in Malaysia is now governed by the *Islamic Financial Services Act 2013* which repealed the *Takaful Act 1984* on 30th June 2013.

A clear example of the continued application of the *Marine Insurance Act 1906* (UK) and common law in non-marine insurance and *takaful* contracts in Malaysia is the fact that the general principle of utmost good faith laid down in s17 of the *Marine Insurance Act 1906* (UK) has long been accepted as the foundation of insurance law in Malaysia. This has been the case although there was no corresponding provision to that effect in the *Insurance Act 1996* (Malaysia) or its predecessor, the *Insurance Act 1963* (Malaysia) or even the *Takaful Act 1984* (Malaysia) for that matter. The fact that Malaysian cases have repeatedly given effect to the principle of utmost good faith in both marine and non-marine insurance and *takaful* contracts indicates that the omission appears to be an oversight rather than deliberate.[48]

2.5 Reciprocal Duties

The words of s17 of the *Marine Insurance Act 1906* (UK) reflect the reciprocal application of the duty of utmost good faith to both insurers and insureds. However, this was only explicitly acknowledged as such by the English courts in the 1980s in *Banque Keyser Ullmann SA v Skandia (UK) Insurance Co Ltd.*[49] Steyn J in the case, in holding that insurers like insureds, were under a duty to exercise utmost good faith in disclosing facts that were material to the insurance contract, said:

> I am of the opinion that it is established beyond doubt that the *uberrima fides* principle, as it is sometimes called, imposes reciprocal duties on the insured and insurer. … In other

[46]See: Mahmood (1992, p. 43).

[47]The *Insurance Act 1996* in turn repealed and succeeded the first insurance regulation in Malaysia, namely the *Insurance Act 1963*.

[48]See: *Kurnia Insurance (M) Bhd v Nik Mohd Faizul bin Nik Mustafa & Anor* [2013] 9 MLJ 675; *Leong Kum Whay v QBE Insurance (M) Sdn Bhd* [2006] 1 CLJ 1; *Cheong Heng Loong Goldsmiths (KL) Sdn Bhd v Capital Insurance Bhd* [2004] 1 MLJ 353; *Aetna Universal Insurance Sdn Bhd v Fanny Foo May Wan* [2001] 1 MLJ 227; *Seah Cheoh Wah v Malayan Banking Bhd & Anor* [2009] 7 CLJ 485 (*takaful*).

[49][1987] 1 Lloyd's Rep 69.

words, reciprocal duties rest on both parties to an insurance contract not only to abstain from bad faith but to observe in a positive sense the utmost good faith by disclosing all material circumstances.[50]

Steyn J's view was subsequently endorsed on appeal by the Court of Appeal in *Banque Financiere v Westgate Insurance Co Ltd.*[51] It is interesting to note that Steyn J in the case, went on to award the plaintiffs damages for the insurer's failure to disclose the fraud. This was based on the alternative ground of breach of duty of care in the tort of negligence, as the remedy of avoidance of the contract provided for in s17 would have been totally inadequate for the plaintiff in the circumstances.

However, his Honour's decision on the point of recoverability of damages by the insured for the insurer's breach of its duty of disclosure was reversed on appeal. Although the Court of Appeal found Steyn J's reasoning to warrant some merit, they nevertheless, unequivocally held that the insured was entitled to only rescission of the contract and a refund of premiums paid without any right to damages, as the contract becomes void ab initio.[52]

Slade LJ[53] at the Court of Appeal cited several reasons for this. First, that the court has the power to grant rescission of the contract in cases of duress and undue influence as well as for bad faith, none of which carries any right to damages. Secondly, the words of the *Marine Insurance Act 1906* (UK) provide no indication that Parliament contemplated the remedy of damages; and lastly, it would also have to be reciprocal and therefore, result in causing greater hardship to the insured if the roles were reversed, since there is no need to prove fault.

This view was subsequently upheld by the House of Lords,[54] albeit from the point of view of causation rather than a breach of good faith, without a final view on the matter being expressed. Nevertheless, the House of Lord's decision has been followed in later cases through the operation of judicial precedent.[55]

Despite this, however, there has been a great deal of academic criticism levelled against the legal justification given by the Court of Appeal and the House of Lords in *Banque Financiere v Westgate Insurance Co Ltd,*[56] preferring instead Steyn J's

[50]Ibid. 92–93. Further support for the proposition that the duty of good faith and the duty of disclosure are reciprocal in nature can be found in Lord Jauncey's restatement in *Banque Financiere v Skandia (UK) Insurance Co Ltd* [1990] 2 Lloyd's Rep 377of Lord Mansfield's dicta in *Carter v Boehm* (1766) Burr 1905, 1909.

[51][1988] 2 Lloyd's Rep 513.

[52]This section draws on research appearing in: Thanasegaran (2004, pp. 155–157).

[53]*Banque Financiere v Westgate Insurance Co Ltd* [1988] 2 Lloyd's Rep 513, 546, 550–551.

[54][1990] 2 All ER 947. Although the House of Lords did not specifically consider the issue of remedies, Lord Templeman agreed with the Court of Appeal that damages were not available for a breach of the duty of utmost good faith.

[55]See: *Aldrich v Norwich Union Life Insurance Co Ltd* [2000] Lloyd's Rep IR 1 where Evans LJ reluctantly decided that there was no duty on the insurer to disclose facts that could induce a proposer to enter into an insurance contract.

[56][1988] 2 Lloyd's Rep 513 (Court of Appeal); [1990] 2 All ER 947 (House of Lords).

view on the point.[57] The criticisms highlight how the *Marine Insurance Act 1906* (UK) which is a codification of the common law position as enunciated by Lord Mansfield in *Carter v Boehm*[58] could purportedly give rise to an equitable relief for failure to exercise good faith. On the point of Parliament's intention being limited to that which is reflected in ss17 and 18 of the *Marine Insurance Act 1906* (UK) alone, it is difficult to reconcile with the House of Lord's decision in *Pan Atlantic Insurance Co Ltd v Pine Top Insurance Co*[59] where the element of 'the particular insurer having to be induced' was implied into the prudent insurers' test in s18 (2), although such a requirement is not apparent in the words of the section itself.

Finally, the suggestion that reciprocity of damages as a remedy would cause hardship to the insured is untenable, as it also applies to a breach of contract situation without any element of fault or blame having to be present. On the other hand, the reciprocity of damages as a remedy would do more justice to the insured in balancing the scales, than retaining the avoidance of contract as the sole remedy for the insurer's breach of good faith, would. This is because the latter does not adequately redress the loss suffered by the insured or exposure to risk. Meanwhile, a claim for damages by the insurer in the event of the insured's breach of utmost good faith should not significantly affect the insured's position, as the insurer's loss would in most cases be only that of opportunity cost.[60]

In fact, damages or a proportionate reduction of the policy monies paid out would be preferred over the long standing 'all or nothing' remedy of avoidance of the insurance contract by insurers for breach of the duty of utmost good faith by insureds.

Be that as it may, however, the position in the United Kingdom and Malaysia up until the recent amendments in 2012–2015 was that a breach of the duty of utmost good faith by the insurer would only avail the insured of a refund of premiums paid upon avoidance of the contract ab initio. Likewise, any breach of the said duty by the insured would entitle the insurer to do the same, thereby discharging the insurer of its payment obligations under the insurance contract.[61]

There were however, encouraging signs leading up to the major reform in this area that a distinction may be drawn between fraudulent conduct of the insured justifying avoidance of the claim by the insurer and lesser breaches of the duty; as well as the possible availability of damages for a breach of the post-contractual duty of utmost good faith by an insurer.

---

[57]Birds (2013, pp. 157–158), Kelly (1989).

[58](1766) 3 Burr 1905.

[59][1994] 3 All ER 581.

[60]This section draws on research appearing in: Thanasegaran, above n 52, 157.

[61]Unless of course an award of damages is given based on a different ratio, as was the case in *Bank of Nova Scotia v Hellenic Mutual War Risks Association (Bermuda) Ltd. (The Good Luck)* [1991] 2 Lloyd's Rep 191 where the insurer was held to be in breach of an express undertaking in the insurance policy to inform the insured of any information within the insurer's knowledge which was material to the risk insured.

Longmore LJ in *K/S Merc-Scandia XXXXII v Lloyd's Underwriters (The Mercandian Continent)*,[62] which is widely regarded as a seminal case on the common law duty of utmost good faith in insurance contracts in the United Kingdom, succinctly set out the remedies available:

> The insurer can treat the insured as being in repudiation of what will normally be an innominate term of the contract if there is a serious breach or there is a breach with serious consequences for the insurer. Avoidance ab initio is an even more extreme form of contractual termination than an acceptance of repudiatory conduct and, for the extreme remedy of avoidance to be available, there must, in my view, be at least the same quality of conduct as a repudiation of the contract. It is only in this way that the requirement of inducement for pre-contract conduct resulting in avoidance can be made to tally with the post-contract conduct said to entitle the insurer to avoid the contract. It would not be just to the insured to enable the insurer to by-pass the rights and duties, imposed on the parties by the contract in order to enable him to claim the disproportionate remedy of avoidance, with the result that he can avoid liability for all other claims under the policy as well as the instant claim, without requiring that the conduct relied on be as serious as conduct which would be viewed as repudiatory. In this way the operation of Section 17 post-contract has the appropriate symmetry to the operation of the section pre-contract.[63]

Some commentators have also gone on to suggest that the duty of utmost good faith on the part of the insurer may operate to limit the insurer's ability to exercise its 'right' to avoid an insurance contract for breach of utmost good faith or non-disclosure by the insured.[64] Unanimous support for this view can be found in the Court of Appeal's judgment in *Drake Insurance plc v Provident Insurance plc*,[65] with Rix LJ saying (obiter) that:

> The doctrine of good faith should be capable of limiting the insurer's right to avoid in circumstances where that remedy…would operate unfairly…It may be necessary to give wider effect to the doctrine of good faith and recognize that its impact may demand that ultimately regard must be had to a concept of *proportionality implicit in fair dealing*. (Author's emphasis added)

The rationale for the limitation on good faith was likely as a result of concern that the law on non-disclosure in the United Kingdom operated unfairly at the time. In this context, it was recognized that any sensible law reform should make specific changes to aspects of non-disclosure like materiality and inducement, instead of adding 'an overarching and uncertain duty of good faith' to it.[66] Similarly, where

---

[62] [2001] 2 Lloyd's Rep 563.

[63] Ibid. 575. The subsequent cases of *Agapitos v Agnew (The Aegeon)* [2002] Lloyd's Rep I R 573 and *Axa General Insurance Ltd v Gottlieb* [2005] Lloyd's Rep I R 369 (Mance LJ) went on to endorse the view that the appropriate remedy for fraudulent claims by insureds was a matter derived from the terms of the insurance contract and the public policy reasoning that an insured should not be entitled to benefit from his or her own wrongdoing.

[64] Eggers (2003, pp. 262–271), Clarke (2003, p. 558).

[65] [2004] QB 601, [87]–[89].

[66] Campbell (2005, p. 438).

the insurer fails to act in good faith towards the insured in the handling of a claim or any other post-contractual breach, it was clear that the insured's ability to only avail himself of avoidance of the policy and a refund of the premiums paid, was unfair and of little value.[67]

The law on utmost good faith in insurance and *takaful* contracts in Malaysia has operated in a similar manner, by virtue of s17 of the *Marine Insurance Act 1906* (UK) being applicable via s5 of the *Civil Law Act 1956* (Malaysia), where avoidance (and not damages) has been the only remedy available for breach of the duty.[68]

Before setting out the recent revamp of the law on utmost good faith and its ensuing remedies in the United Kingdom and Malaysia, it is worth noting that the Australian legislature had back in 1984 addressed this issue in a bold and progressive manner by incorporating the duty of utmost good faith as an implied term of contract in s13 of its *Insurance Contracts Act 1984* (Cth) whilst omitting the remedy of avoidance. In its place, more proportionate and innovative remedies were introduced, in ss14, 28 and 29 read together with ss31 and 33.[69] Section 13 provides that:

> A contract of insurance is a contract based on the utmost good faith and there is implied in such a contract a provision requiring each party to it to act towards the other party, in respect of any matter arising under or in relation to it, with the utmost good faith.

Section 14 (1) goes on to provide that:

> If reliance by a party to a contract of insurance on a provision of the contract would be to fail to act with the utmost good faith, the party may not rely on the provision.

Central to this package of remedies in ensuring that the duty of utmost good faith is complied with, is that s13 makes the mutual obligation of utmost good faith an *implied term* of the insurance contract. This has paved the way for damages as a remedy for its breach to be assessed according to the contractual loss of profits principle rather than in tort.

It is worthwhile noting that the comprehensive provisions of the *Insurance Contracts Act 1984* (Cth) have been recently improved by the *Insurance Contracts Amendment Act 2013* (Cth). A new s13 (2)–(4) has been inserted to provide for a breach of utmost good faith to be a breach of the Act entitling the Australian Securities and Investments Commission (ASIC) to take action against the insurer; and also extends the good faith obligation to a third party beneficiary under the contract, from the time the contract is entered into. Section 14A inserted by the

---

[67] *Cox v Bankside Members' Agency Limited* [1995] 2 Lloyd's Rep 437.

[68] *Leong Kum Whay v QBE Insurance (M) Sdn Bhd* [2006] 1 CLJ 1; *Seah Cheoh Wah v Malayan Banking Bhd & Anor* [2009] 7 CLJ 485 (*takaful*).

[69] These provisions apply to the remedies for breach of the pre-contractual duty of utmost good faith which shall be examined in Chap. 3. Sections 54 and 56 that address the remedies for post-contractual breach of the same will in turn be examined in Chap. 4.

amendment goes on to provide that the ASIC may exercise its powers under the *Corporations Act 2001* (Cth) against the insurer for failure to comply with the duty of utmost good faith in the handling or settlement of a claim.

Recent reforms in the United Kingdom have in turn, seen s2 (5) of the *Consumer Insurance (Disclosure and Representations) Act 2012* (UK) limiting the application of the duty of utmost good faith in s17 of the *Marine Insurance Act 1906* (UK) and subjecting it to the provisions of the former, which as the name suggests, deals with consumer insurance contracts. This has since been superseded and repealed by s14 (4) of the *Insurance Act 2015* (UK) which abolishes the remedy of avoidance of contract for a breach of utmost good faith in all types of insurance contracts. The result is that only the first part of s17 of the *Marine Insurance Act 1906* (UK) which provides that 'a contract of marine insurance is a contract based upon the utmost good faith,' is retained and deletes the rest, via ss14 (1) and 14 (3).

It should be noted that although the *Insurance Act 2015* (UK) primarily deals with non-consumer insurance contracts, some provisions especially those contained in Parts 5 and 6 of the Act, apply to consumer insurance contracts as well. This therefore, paves the way for more proportionate remedies like damages to be available to aggrieved parties. There are no specific provisions made for remedies with respect to a breach of utmost good faith as such in both the English statutes however, as the emphasis is on the insured's duty of fair presentation and the consequences of failure thereof. This aspect shall be set out in Chap. 3, that deals with pre-contractual non-disclosure and misrepresentation.

As for Malaysia, Paragraph 5 (9) of *Schedule 9* to the *Financial Services Act 2013* provides that both 'consumers' and insurers shall exercise the duty of utmost good faith in their dealings with each other, including the making and paying of a claim, after a contract has been entered into, varied or renewed. This explicit pronouncement of a general duty of utmost good faith that covers claims handling and renewals as well has been a long time coming. However, the provision should have been made applicable to **all** insurance contracts instead of just consumer contracts and should have also addressed the remedy available in the event of its breach by either party. This has resulted in some uncertainties in the law. For example, does the duty of utmost good faith which explicitly includes the insurers' conduct in claims handling apply to non-consumer insurance contracts as well? Also, in the event of a breach of the duty of utmost good faith by either party, would there be an opportunity for the common law remedy of avoidance to apply or has it been abolished?[70]

Having set out the reciprocal nature of the parties' duty of utmost good faith owed to each other, an examination will now be made of the scope of both the insured and insurer's respective obligations pertaining thereto.

---

[70]This section draws on research appearing in: Thanasegaran and Shaiban (2014, p. 338).

2.6 Scope of Insurer's Duty of Utmost Good Faith

Much of the emphasis has been with respect to what is expected of the insured in observing the duty of utmost good faith in insurance contracts. As a result, the ambit of the continuing duty of utmost good faith with respect to the insurer is less clear. Nevertheless, it has been shown that such a duty exists from the pre-contractual stage based on s17 of the *Marine Insurance Act 1906* (UK); right up to claims settlement, based instead on the implied term and public policy reasoning.[71] The various aspects of the insurer's duty of utmost good faith can be categorized as follows.

2.6.1 Clear Warning in Proposal Forms

The Malaysian legislature had by virtue of s149 (4) of the now repealed *Insurance Act 1996* (Malaysia) provided for the insurer to give a clear warning in proposal forms to prospective insureds, regarding the consequences that can ensue under the insurance contract as a result of pre-contractual non-disclosure. Section 149 (4) provided:

> A proposal form and, where no proposal form is used, a request for particulars by the licensed insurer shall prominently display a warning that if a proposer does not fully and faithfully give the facts as he knows them or ought to know them, the *policy may be invalidated.*[72] (Author's emphasis added)

The requirement for a statutory warning to be provided is an example of compliance with the duty of utmost good faith on the part of the insurer, and is a positive measure. However, the *Insurance Act 1996* (Malaysia) did not go on to explicitly provide for a remedy in the event of a breach of or non-compliance with s149 (4) by insurers. To compound matters, it retained the common law remedy of avoidance of the contract for pre-contractual non-disclosure and misrepresentation.

The new Paragraphs 5 (7) and 4 (4) of *Schedule 9* to the *Financial Services Act 2013* (Malaysia) have replaced s149 (4) by improving it to an extent. In referring to consumer and non-consumer insurance contracts respectively, they make no mention of avoidance as a remedy and require insurers *before* a contract is *entered into, varied or renewed*, to *clearly inform* the proposer or consumer/non-consumer *in*

---

[71]Bennet, above n 11, 197.

[72]A similar provision existed previously under s16 (4) of the *Insurance Act 1963* (Malaysia) that was repealed upon the enactment of the *Insurance Act 1996* (Malaysia). By comparison, it should be noted that although the United Kingdom did not have a statutory equivalent before the recent amendments, Clause 4.3.2 (3) of the *Insurance Conduct of Business 2005* ('*ICOB*') (which is in substance similar to Clause 1 (c) of the previous *Statement of General Insurance Practice 1986* ('*SOGIP*') but since 14 January 2005 had been regulated by the Financial Services Authority instead of self-regulation as was the case since 1977, contained a similar provision.

writing of their pre-contractual duty of disclosure and of its continuing nature until the contract is entered into, varied or renewed. Although it is largely based on Australia's s22 (1) of the *Insurance Contracts Act 1984* (Cth), it still does not provide for a remedy against insurers for failing to provide such a statutory warning in the first place.[73]

This is unlike the position in Australia for instance, where s22 (3) of the *Insurance Contracts Act 1984* (Cth) clearly provides that non-compliance with s22 (1)[74] would result in the insurer not being entitled to exercise a right in respect of the proposer's failure to comply with the duty of disclosure, unless the failure was fraudulent.

Apart from this, the persistent problem due to the state of the law in Malaysia is the all or nothing remedy of avoidance of the insurance contract that has remained in the event of non-disclosure by the insured. However, there appears to be some improvement with reference to avoidance being omitted in the recent provisions giving rise to the statutory warning.

Another criticism that could still be levelled against the statutory warning is that although it is useful in reminding prospective insureds regarding the duty of disclosure, it may not be very effective otherwise. This is because it would only be truly effective if proposers of insurance (be it consumers or non-consumers) are able to 'understand and appreciate its significance'.[75] This sentiment is also prevalent in Singapore which has a similar provision, in that 'compliance with this section does not go anyway in explaining the substance of the warning, which is the common problem faced by befuddled insureds'.[76]

Furthermore, the widespread misconception that proposers only need to answer the questions posed, honestly and correctly, is compounded by the fact that insurance proposal forms are designed to contain numerous questions interspersed with sufficient space for proposers to insert their answers, without any additional space being provided for further material information to be provided that is not covered in the questions posed.[77]

On the contrary, this is far from what is expected, as reflected in the words of Whiteley JC of the Malaysian Supreme Court in *Teh Say Cheng v North British and Mercantile Insurance Co Ltd.*[78]

---

[73]This section draws on research appearing in: Thanasegaran and Shaiban, above n 70, 341.

[74]Section 22 (1) of the *Insurance Contracts Act 1984* (Cth) provides that:

The insurer shall, before the contract of insurance is entered into, clearly inform the insured in writing of the general nature and effect of the duty of disclosure.

[75]This was a criticism that was levelled by Mahmood, above n 46, 49, with respect to the previous s16 (4) of the *Insurance Act 1963* (Malaysia) and is applicable to the *Insurance Act 1996* (Malaysia) as well.

[76]Lee (1997, p. 224).

[77]This section draws on research appearing in: Thanasegaran, above n 52, 149–150.

[78](1921) 2 FMSLR 248, 253.

> In order then, that the plaintiff may derive any benefit from this line of argument, it is necessary for him to establish the proposition that his duty of disclosure is limited to the subject matter of the question. There is an abundance of authority to contradict such a contention.

In order for the statutory warning to be more effective, however, it should *expressly* require the proposer to be under a positive duty to truthfully and accurately answer the questions posed in the proposal form *as well as* provide any other information which he or she knows *or* a reasonable person in the circumstances could be expected to know to be relevant to the insurer's decision on whether to accept the risk and the rates and terms to be applied. An expanded warning of this nature would effectively draw the standard of the pre-contractual duty of disclosure previously contained in s150 (1) of the *Insurance Act 1996* (Malaysia) to the proposers' attention. Anything short of this would only serve to exacerbate this widespread misconception on the part of proposers highlighted above.[79]

This rings true for Paragraph 4(1) of *Schedule 9* to the *Financial Services Act 2013* (Malaysia) as well, with respect to non-consumer insurance contracts which still requires voluntary disclosure by the proposer. This criticism however, does not apply to consumer insurance contracts in Malaysia and **all** insurance contracts in the United Kingdom, as they have adopted an inquiry based disclosure instead.

Although admittedly, in order for any statutory warning to be truly effective it would have to be appreciated as such by the proposers, a broader warning coupled with the provision of some conspicuous space in the proposal form below it for the proposer to volunteer information, would better serve its intended purpose. In addition, insureds should be provided with a copy of the proposal form filed with the insurer that contains a prominent warning requiring the proposer to keep a record of all information supplied to the insurer for the purpose of *entering into and renewing* the insurance contract. This would serve to further impress upon the insured regarding the existence and importance of the pre-contractual duty of disclosure at the inception of the contract as well as at renewals and variations,[80] thereby reinforcing the improvements introduced in the recent reforms which make explicit reference to the insurer's duty as also applying at renewals and variations.[81]

Having said this, the new and expanded statutory warnings in Paragraphs 5 (7) and 4 (4) of *Schedule 9* to the *Financial Services Act 2013* (Malaysia) are a welcome change, in that they would prevent a situation like that of *Leong Kum Whay v QBE Insurance (M) Sdn Bhd*[82] from recurring. The case was decided based

[79]This section draws on research appearing in: Thanasegaran, above n 52, 150.

[80]Ibid. See: *CE Heath Underwriting & Insurance (Australia) Pty Ltd v Edwards Dunlop & Co Ltd* [1993] 176 CLR 535; *Lumley General Insurance Ltd v Delphin* (1990) 6 ANZ Ins Cas ¶60-986.

[81]See: Merkin, above n 36, 36–37: This takes cognizance of Merkin's criticisms leveled against the previous position, of insureds not being made aware of the duty at renewals and the remedy of avoidance for this being inadequate.

[82][2006] 1 CLJ 1.

on the old *Insurance Act 1963* (Malaysia) (repealed)[83] which was similar to s149 (4) of the recently repealed *Insurance Act 1996* (Malaysia), as the policies concerned were taken out in 1991 and 1992.

The appellant insured in the case sought a reversal of the High Court of Malaya's decision refusing to set aside an arbitrator's award relating to claims made by the appellant against various insurance companies on personal accident policies he had taken out with each of them. The appellant had made a claim on the policies following an accident on 26 June 1992. The insurers in the case were however, permitted to avoid the insured's personal accident insurance contracts and refuse payment on the basis of non-disclosure of a material fact, which was the acquisition of two life insurance policies by the insured prior to the renewal of the personal accident policies, despite the fact that no statutory warning was given to the insured at renewal.[84]

The recent Malaysian reforms take cognisance of their Australian counterpart in s22 (1) of the *Insurance Contracts Act 1984* (Cth) which requires insurers to 'clearly inform' the insured in writing of the general nature and effect of the duty of disclosure, before the 'contract of insurance' is entered into, and take it a step further to encompass the renewal stage as well.[85] In fact, in Australia, the recurrent issue has been whether (save for fraudulent non-disclosure) the written warning or information given by the insurer in fact amounted to 'clearly informing' the insured,[86] for otherwise, the insurer would not be able to rely on non-disclosure by the insured.[87]

This arose in *Suncorp General Insurance Ltd v Cheihk*,[88] where the New South Wales Court of Appeal had to consider whether the insured had been 'clearly informed' of the duty of disclosure by the insurer in the case. The insurer had sent three documents to the insured in renewing the policy. The duty of disclosure only appeared on the back of a Certificate of Insurance without any reference being made to it either on the front of the said document or anywhere in the other two

[83]The said Act also contained a similar obligation on the insurer's part to provide a statutory warning in proposal forms (making no mention of renewals) in s16 (4):

No insurer shall use in Malaysia a form of proposal which does not have prominently displayed therein a warning that if a proposer does not fully and faithfully give the facts as he knows them or ought to know them, he may receive nothing from the policy.

[84]This section draws on research appearing in: Thanasegaran (2007, pp. clii–cliii).

[85]The Australian courts have nevertheless, applied it to renewals as well, as a matter of course. See: *Lumley General Insurance Ltd v Delphin* (1990) 6 ANZ Ins Cas ¶60-986; *Alexander Stenhouse Ltd v Austcan Investments Pty Ltd* (1993) 7 ANZ Ins Cas ¶61-166. Also see: Section 11 (10) of the *Insurance Contracts Act 1984* (Cth) which was retrospectively introduced in 1986 to cover the insurer's duty at renewals as well.

[86]See: *GIO General Ltd v Wallace* (2001) 11 ANZ Ins Cas ¶61-506; *Suncorp General Insurance Ltd v Cheihk* (1999) 10 ANZ Ins Cas ¶61-442.

[87]Section 22 (3) of the *Insurance Contracts Act 1984* (Cth).

[88](1999) 10 ANZ Ins Cas ¶61-442; This section draws on research appearing in: Thanasegaran, above n 84, cliv.

documents. The insurer was in the circumstances held not to have 'clearly informed' the insured, as the requirement of clarity not only applied to the contents of the documents but also the way in which the contents were brought to the insured's attention. Giles JA went on to say:

> It will always be a question of fact and degree, but the purpose of s22 is to ensure that the insured is informed of the *significance and important matters of his duty of disclosure* and the *consequences of failure to comply* with the duty of disclosure, so that his insurance cover will not be imperilled by ignorance of those matters. The insured is to be *informed clearly*. Both the purpose of s22 and its terms call for insistence *on a proper standard of information giving*.[89] (Author's emphasis added)

2.6.2 Unduly Strict Construction of Policies and Exclusions

Another aspect of the insurer's duty of good faith and disclosure would be with respect to the enforceability and meaning of the insurance contract itself. This was pointed out by Lord Lloyd at the House of Lords in *Pan Atlantic Insurance Co. Ltd. v Pine Top Insurance Co Ltd*[90] where his Lordship said that'...there may be circumstances in which an insurer, by asserting a right to avoid for non-disclosure, would himself be guilty of want of utmost good faith'.[91]

Such a duty would likely cover situations where insurers seek to construe policy terms in an unduly strict manner or rely on technical exclusions to defeat or reduce otherwise valid claims put forward by insureds. It is indeed ironic that such practices still occur today, when the English courts almost a century ago recognised that good faith warranted insurance policies to be drawn up in clear and unambiguous terms, according to the proposal forms 'so as not to deceive and entrap the unwary'.[92] This aspect shall be developed further in Chap. 4 of this book under the post-contractual duty of good faith.

2.6.3 Good Faith in Claims Settlement

As for good faith in claims settlement, the courts seem to have given precedence to clear words contained in insurance policies even though they may fly in the face of good faith. This is apparent from cases such as *Lambert v Cooperative Insurance Society Ltd*[93] and *Chiew Swee Chai v British American Insurance Co Sdn Bhd*[94]

[89]Ibid. 75–024.

[90][1994] 2 All ER 581.

[91]Ibid. 623.

[92]*Re Bradley and Essex and Suffolk Accident Indemnity Society* (1912) 1 KB 415, 433 (Farwell J).

[93][1975] 2 Lloyd's Rep 485.

[94][1987] 1 MLJ 53.

which has led to the frequent contesting of claims by insurers, and resulting in a rejection of claims and reduction of policy monies paid out. As a result, it has given rise to a growing trend amongst insureds to make exaggerated claims as a counter measure, in order to facilitate 'price haggling' between insurers and insureds, which has become commonplace.

On the issue of fraudulent claims, insureds typically put forward an inflated claim with the intention to defraud the insurer. Such a claim can be defeated by the insurer on the basis of the insured's failure to act in good faith.[95] It is however, a question of fact to be inferred from surrounding circumstances, as to whether a particular claim is tainted with fraud.

Section 17 of the *Contracts Act 1950* (Malaysia) may be of assistance in this regard, as it contains a general definition for 'fraud'. Section 17 provides that:

> "Fraud" includes any of the following acts committed by a party to a contract, or with his connivance, or by his agent, with intent to deceive another party thereto or his agent, or to induce him to enter into the contract: (a) the suggestion, as to a fact, of that which is not true by one who does not believe it to be true; (b) the active concealment of a fact by one having knowledge or belief of the fact; (c) a promise made without any intention of performing it; (d) any other act fitted to deceive; and (e) any such act or omission as the law specially declares to be fraudulent.

The Explanation (or proviso) to s17 goes on to provide that:

> Mere silence as to facts likely to affect the willingness of a person to enter into a contract is not fraud, unless the circumstances of the case are such that, regard being had to them, it is the duty of the person keeping silent to speak, or unless his silence is, in itself, equivalent to speech.

This reinforces the fact that in *uberrimae fidei* contracts such as insurance, a failure to disclose material facts with intent to deceive would amount to fraud, the consequence of which (along with misrepresentation or coercion) makes the contract voidable at the option of the innocent party, by virtue of s19 (1) of the *Contracts Act 1950* (Malaysia).[96]

Alternatively, s19 (2) provides that 'a party to a contract, whose consent was caused by fraud or misrepresentation, may, if he thinks fit, insist that the contract shall be performed, and that he shall be put in the position in which he would have been if the representation had been true'.

In this regard, the Court of Appeal in *Galloway v Guardian Royal Exchange (UK) Ltd*[97] held that the insurer was entitled to avoid the entire policy due to the insured's fraudulent claim put forward for an exaggerated sum. Fraud on the part of the insured was clear in this case, as he sought to claim an additional loss of £2000

---

[95] *Tuong Aik (Sarawak) Sdn Bhd v Arab-Malaysian Eagle Assurance Bhd* [1996] 1 AMR 871; *Britton v Royal Insurance Company* (1866) 4 F & F 905.

[96] Unless of course the party whose consent was vitiated had the means of discovering the truth with ordinary diligence or was in fact not induced by the fraud (or misrepresentation) to consent to the contract: proviso to s19 (2).

[97] [1999] Lloyd's Rep IR 209.

by submitting a forged receipt relating to the purchase of a computer. The court's position on the matter was succinctly set out by Millett LJ as follows:

> The result of a breach of this duty leaves the insured without cover. In the present case the insured took advantage of the happening of an insured event to make a dishonest claim for the loss of goods worth £2,000 which to his knowledge had not occurred...The making of dishonest insurance claims has become all too common. There seems to be a widespread belief that insurance companies are fair game, and that defrauding them is not morally reprehensible. The rule which we are asked to enforce today may appear to some to be harsh, but it is in my opinion a necessary and salutary rule which deserves to be better known by the public. I for my part would be most unwilling to dilute it in any way.[98]

Where the insured puts forward an inflated claim without any express act of fraud or forgery on the other hand, the position becomes less clear. The inflated claim in this case, would give rise to a *prima facie* presumption that the insured is not acting in good faith. This is however, merely a presumption and therefore, not conclusive. The insured would still be entitled to succeed in making the claim, if the presumption could be rebutted, in which case, the insurer would have failed to prove fraud.[99]

In *Norton v Royal Fire and Life Assurance Co*,[100] the insured who had presented an exaggerated claim was held not to have intended to defraud the insurers, as he had worked out the claim based on his recollection and had subsequently reduced it. If however, the claim is grossly exaggerated as to the amount and/or the quantity of goods lost, an inference of fraud would be more likely to be drawn and harder to rebut.[101]

The true question in an exaggerated claim presented by an insured, however, is whether the insured intended to deceive the insurer by it.[102] This is a recurrent problem in the insurance industry today, where inflating the claim to some degree is seen to be the norm as a means to commence bargaining. The inflated claim is merely seen as a bargaining figure, without any real intention to defraud the insurer. This practice appears to have emerged as a means to counter the insurers' general reluctance to award claims put forward without strict scrutiny and frequent contesting and reduction wherever possible.

This has in fact been acknowledged by MacKinnon J in *Ewer v National Employers' Mutual General Insurance Association Ltd.*[103] Here, an insured who had put forward an exaggerated claim for items lost in a fire based on the cost price of the said items even though they were at the time no longer new, was held to have

---

[98]Ibid. 21.

[99]*Globe Trawlers Pte Ltd. v National Employers' Mutual General Insurance Association Ltd* [1989] 1 MLJ 463; This section draws on research appearing in: Thanasegaran, above n 52, 153.

[100](1885) 1 TLR 460.

[101]*Chapman v Pole P O* (1870) 22 L T 306.

[102]The requisite mental element is therefore, whether a representation was made either 'knowingly without belief in its truth or recklessly without caring whether it is true or false': *Derry v Peek* (1889) 14 App Cas 337 (HL).

[103][1937] 2 All ER 193, 203.

done so not to defraud the insurers but merely as a bargaining figure. A similar view acknowledging the commercial phenomenon of 'price haggling' is apparent in Vincent Ng J's judgment in *Wong Cheong Kong Sdn Bhd v Prudential Assurance Sdn Bhd*[104] where his Honour said:

> Even so, concerning exaggerated claims, the practice in business to exaggerate demands in order to accommodate the commercial phenomenon of "price haggling", ought not to be ignored by the court in its deliberation, as it is quite prevalent and hence not necessarily an *ipso facto* fatal element in an insurance claim.[105]

Despite the fact that an exaggerated claim may give rise to a presumption of fraud by the insured (which may in turn be rebutted), the burden of proving the allegation that the insured intended to defraud the insurer rests with the insurer. The standard of proving fraud in such an instance in the United Kingdom and Australia is on the balance of probabilities for civil cases, with strong evidence of intention to defraud having to be adduced in practice but not so high as to be proof beyond a reasonable doubt.[106] With respect to Malaysia however, the Federal Court decisions of *Yong Tim v Hoo Kok Chong*[107] and *Asean Securities Paper Mills Sdn Bhd v CGU Insurance Bhd*[108] have settled the standard of proof to be that of beyond reasonable doubt.[109]

On the issue of good faith in claims settlement, Paragraph 5 (9) of *Schedule 9* to the *Financial Services Act 2013* (Malaysia) is an improvement with respect to *consumer* insurance contracts as it requires the duty of utmost good faith to be exercised by a consumer and insurer in their dealings with each other 'including the making and paying of a claim.' The uncertainty remaining, however, is with respect to the status of non-consumer insurance contracts and the remedy available in the event of breach.

As for the United Kingdom on the other hand, it is interesting to note that the draft *Insurance Contracts Bill 2014* that was tabled in Parliament, contained a s14 (1) which *implied* a term into *every* contract of insurance that if the insured makes a claim under the contract, the insurer must pay any sums due in respect of the claim within a reasonable time. The implications of the proposed duty being an implied term of contract, was that damages would have been an available remedy in the event of breach. This proposal would have been in line with s13 of the *Insurance*

104[1998] 3 MLJ 724.

105Ibid. 737–738.

106*Danepoint Limited v Allied Underwriting Insurance Limited* [2005] EWHC 2318; *Von Braun v Australian Associated Motor Insurers Ltd.* (1999) 10 ANZ Ins Cas 61-419.

107[2005] 3 CLJ 229.

108[2007] 2 MLJ 301.

109There was however, some doubt raised by Gopal Sri Ram JCA at the Court of Appeal in *CGU Insurance Bhd v Asean Security Paper Mills Sdn Bhd* [2006] 3 MLJ 1, 33 as to the standard of proof for fraud in civil cases in Malaysia being on a balance of probabilities, but was rejected by the Federal Court on appeal. This section draws on research appearing in: Thanasegaran, above n 14, 195.

Contracts Act 1984 (Cth) of Australia. However, when the *Insurance Act 2015* (UK) was eventually passed on 12 February 2015, this provision was dropped owing to a lack of consensual support by all the market players, which made it unsuitable to be passed though the Law Commission's uncontroversial bill procedure. This aspect of good faith in claims settlement and the recent reforms shall be examined further in Chap. 4 under the post-contractual duty of good faith.

2.6.4 Tort of Bad Faith

It is worth noting however, that in the United States the aspect of good faith on the insurer's part has been taken much further where it is viewed as a tortuous obligation. This tort of bad faith is essentially described as follows:

> In every contract (not just insurance policies) there is implied by law a covenant of good faith and fair dealing which provides that neither party will do anything which will injure the right of the other to receive the benefits of the agreement. The violation of this duty is a tort, which may give rise to liability over and above that for breach of contract. In a proper case, general damages (such as those for mental distress) and punitive damages may be recovered.[110]

The American position is motivated by the need to prevent insurers from acting unreasonably in claims settlement, although not necessarily limited to this.

The Australian Law Reform Commission[111] had in 1982, considered the possibility of introducing the same into Australian law but decided against it in favour of contractual damages instead. This decision was made based on the sentiment that it would not substantially add to the contractual remedies already available to the insured and compounded by the fact that Australian courts are not generally in the habit of awarding punitive damages.

Although the tort of bad faith does not apply to contracts of insurance governed by the Australian *Insurance Contracts Act 1984* (Cth), the possibility that such a tortuous obligation may exist with respect to insurance contracts not governed by the Act has been left open by the judgments of Badgery-Parker J in *Gibson v Parkes District Hospital*[112] and McDonald J in *Gimson v Victorian Workcover Authority*,[113] although this has remained an increasingly academic issue with the passing of time.

A duty of good faith founded on tort is in fact not a common feature in the United Kingdom, Malaysia and Australia, as the awarding of punitive damages by the judiciary is uncommon in these jurisdictions. Australia by virtue of ss13–14 of

---

[110]Parkes and Heil (1973, p. 63).

[111]Report No 20, *Insurance Contracts* (1982) [328].

[112](1991) 26 NSWLR 9.

[113][1995] 1 VR 209; This section draws on research appearing in: Thanasegaran, above n 52, 157–158.

the *Insurance Contracts Act 1984* (Cth) has clearly adopted a *contractual* duty of utmost good faith and although the Malaysian provisions for utmost good faith under the *Financial Services Act 2013* (Malaysia) and *Islamic Financial Services Act 2013* (Malaysia) and that of the United Kingdom under the *Insurance Act 2015* (UK) have not explicitly provided so, there is nothing to indicate a wider reaching tortuous duty being envisaged. Nevertheless, some clarification on this would prove useful.

2.7 Scope of Insured's Duty of Utmost Good Faith

The scope of the duty of utmost good faith with respect to the insured on the other hand, has been the focal point of and therefore, fairly clearly addressed by the legislatures of the United Kingdom, Malaysia and Australia. It also spans from the pre-contractual stage of negotiations between the parties right up to the submission and settlement of claims there under.

2.7.1 Pre-contractual Duty of Disclosure

The common law pre-contractual duty of disclosure imposes a positive duty on the insured to make disclosure of all material information as well as any material change in the risk to be insured[114] right up to the moment the insurance contract is concluded. Failure to do so would entitle the insurer to avoid the contract ab initio. This right to avoid the contract is available to the insurer before or after a loss occurs and the insurance contract remains in force until and unless the insurer exercises the option to avoid.

The justification for this duty is broadly based on insurance contracts being *uberrimae fidei* in nature and more specifically on the information imbalance existing at that stage of the transaction. This information imbalance is in favour of the insured who possesses knowledge of his own circumstances, vis-à-vis the insurer who does not but nevertheless, needs to assess the viability of the risk to be undertaken. It has however, been argued that claims of this information imbalance placing the insured in a position of strength over the insurer may be more of a perception than reality. This is because the insured is often unaware as to which parts of the information the insurer wishes to have and is as a result in a weaker position.[115]

[114]*Allis-Chalmers Co v Fidelity & Deposit Co of Maryland* (1916) 114 LT 433; *Looker v Law Union and Rock Insurance Co Ltd* [1928] 1 KB 554.

[115]Hasson (1969, p. 633).

In fact, the pre-contractual duty of disclosure has been viewed at common law as arising as a matter of law in all *uberrimae fidei* contracts (of which insurance is a type),[116] as opposed to being an implied term of contract like in Australia, for instance.[117]

This 'all or nothing' common law remedy of avoidance or affirmation of the contract however, has the potential for injustice in situations where the insurer avoids a policy on grounds of non-disclosure of information that has only a marginal effect on the premium. To compound matters, the remedy of proportionate recovery for the insured that commensurate with the premium actually paid based on the non-disclosure, which has been adopted by other European jurisdictions and Australia,[118] was also not available in the United Kingdom and Malaysia until recently.

Section 18 (1) of the *Marine Insurance Act 1906* (UK), which laid down this pre-contractual duty of disclosure, provided that:

> Subject to the provisions of this section, the assured must disclose to the insurer, before the contract is concluded, every material circumstance that is known to the assured, and the assured is deemed to know every circumstance which, in the ordinary course of business, ought to be known by him. If the assured fails to make such disclosure, the insurer may avoid the contract.

The burden of proving non-disclosure of a material fact by the insured, in accordance with general legal principle, rests with the insurer,[119] which may be further justified by the fact that the issuance of the insurance policy would have raised the presumption that everything was in order.[120]

In this regard, a circumstance was described in s18 (2) as being material if it

> ...would influence the judgment of a prudent insurer in fixing the premium or determining whether he will take the risk.

And whether an undisclosed circumstance is in fact material is essentially a question of fact, according to s18 (4).

The pre-contractual duty of disclosure comes to an end upon the conclusion of the insurance contract and although the duty of utmost good faith continues thereafter,[121] the insured is no longer under a duty to disclose any changes in the

---

[116]This is apparent from *March Cabaret Club & Casino Ltd v London Assurance Ltd* [1975] 1 Lloyd's Rep 169, 175 (May J).

[117]See: Section 13 of the *Insurance Contracts Act 1984* (Cth) (Australia).

[118]This is available by virtue of the Australian remedy of common law damages for non-disclosure in general insurance contracts (s28 of the *Insurance Contracts Act 1984* (Cth)) and proportionate recovery in life insurance contracts (s29 of the *Insurance Contracts Act 1984* (Cth)).

[119]*Joel v Law Union and Crown Insurance Company* [1908] 2 KB 863; *Lee Bee Soon v Malaysia National Insurance Sdn Bhd* [1980] 2 MLJ 252.

[120]*Elkin v Janson* (1845) 13 M & W 655.

[121]*Manifest Shipping & Co Ltd v Uni-Polaris Insurance Co Ltd* [1997] 1 Lloyd's Rep 360.

risk insured which may occur during the subsistence of the contract.[122] The House of Lords in *Niger Co Ltd v Guardian Assurance Co Ltd*[123] in fact rejected an attempt made by the insurer to extend the insured's duty of disclosure concerning the risk insured beyond the conclusion of the insurance contract. In deciding so, Lord Sumner was mindful of the potential threat to the insured if insurers were allowed to extend the pre-contractual duty of disclosure, when his Lordship said:

> There remains the question of non-disclosure. The object of disclosure being to inform the underwriter's mind on matters immediately under his consideration, with reference to the taking or refusing of a risk then offered to him, I think it would be going beyond the principle to say that each and every change in an insurance contract creates an occasion on which a general disclosure becomes obligatory, merely because the altered contract is not the unaltered contract, and therefore the alteration is a transaction as the result of which a new contract of insurance comes into existence. This would turn what is an indispensable shield for the underwriter into an engine of oppression against the assured.[124]

The position has been largely the same with respect to Malaysia until the recent reforms introduced in both countries, as can be seen from the decision of Yusoff J in *Lee Bee Soonv Malaysia National Insurance Sdn Bhd*,[125] a case involving marine insurance. Here, s21 of the *Marine Insurance Act 1906* (UK)[126] was applied with respect to when a contract of marine insurance was deemed to be concluded, connoting the end of the insured's duty of disclosure pertaining to the risk insured.

It may be worthwhile to note that the duty of disclosure continues to apply to the period between when an insured applies for a policy and the time the policy is issued, should the insured come into possession of material information. As Hasson points out, this obligation should be clearly stipulated in the proposal form or application, as lay applicants for insurance often think that the contract is concluded when the application is submitted and hence inadvertently open themselves up to a breach of the duty.[127]

This duty of disclosure arises again whenever the insurance policy is renewed, whereby the insured is required to disclose to the insurer all material changes that

---

[122]It should be noted that certain insurance contracts like fire insurance, in practice impose a duty on the insured to disclose facts which occur during the subsistence of the contract that materially increase the risk insured. This is done usually by inserting a promissory warranty in the contract, providing that the insurer is discharged from liability in the event of failure by the insured to make such disclosure.

[123](1922) 13 Ll L Rep 75.

[124]Ibid. 82.

[125][1980] 2 MLJ 252.

[126]Section 21 provides that:

A contract of marine insurance is deemed to be concluded when the proposal of the assured is accepted by the insurer, whether the policy be then issued or not; and for the purpose of showing when the proposal was accepted, reference may be made to the slip or covering note or other customary memorandum of the contract, although it be unstamped.

[127]Hasson, above n 115, 635–636.

have taken place since the last renewal. Such was the case in *Lambert v Co-operative Insurance Society Ltd*[128] where the English Court of Appeal held that the insurer was entitled to avoid the 'all risks' insurance policy taken out by the insured on jewellery belonging to herself and her husband. This was on the basis that she had failed to disclose at the time of renewal of the policy that her husband had been convicted of two offences involving dishonesty and was sentenced to fifteen months' imprisonment.[129]

This is also the position in Malaysia where in the Supreme Court decision of *Syarikat Pembinaan Lida Sdn Bhd v Talasco Insurance Sdn Bhd,*[130] the appellant was not entitled to claim under the fire insurance policy, for failure to inform the insurers that part of the risk insured had been damaged by fire the day before the policy was renewed. A similar decision was reached by the Court of Appeal in *Leong Kum Whay v QBE Insurance (M) Sdn Bhd*[131] where the insured was not entitled to claim under a personal accident insurance policy for failing to inform the insurer of two life insurance policies taken out prior to renewal of the policy in question.

This surfacing of the duty of disclosure whenever an insurance policy is renewed however, does not apply to life insurance policies as they are intended to provide insurance coverage for the entire duration of the insured's life. Most life insurance policies therefore, expressly provide for such an automatic right to renewal and even when they do not, such a term may be implied into the contract, so as not to defeat the essential objective of life policies.[132]

Besides renewals, the duty of disclosure also arises in the case of variations and reinstatements of insurance policies when the same tantamount to entering into a new contract, although most likely limited to the variation itself.[133]

Although it is trite law that the duty of utmost good faith and the duty of disclosure are reciprocal in nature, ss18 (1) and (2) of the *Marine Insurance Act 1906* (UK) and s150 (1) of the *Insurance Act 1996* (Malaysia) nevertheless made specific mention of only the insured's pre-contractual duty of disclosure. This is because the insured is in possession of information or facts peculiar to him or herself that is not known to the insurer.[134] It is this information or facts that would

[128][1975] 2 Lloyd's Rep 485.

[129]Ibid. 487. See also: *Sharp and Roarer Investments Ltd v Sphere Drake Insurance Plc (The Moonacre)* [1992] 2 Lloyd's Rep 501.

[130][1993] 2 MLJ 121.

[131][2006] 1 CLJ 1.

[132]Poh (2005, p. 377).

[133]See: Section 11 (9) of the *Insurance Contracts Act 1984* (Cth) (Australia) which provides some guidance by including renewals, variations and extensions of insurance contracts as giving rise to 'entering into an insurance contract' which would in turn give rise to the duty of disclosure.

[134]This does not however, mean that there is no such duty on the insurer at the pre-contractual stage, although presumably governed by the general duty of utmost good faith as opposed to s18. See: *Banque Financiere v Skandia (UK) Insurance Co Ltd* [1990] 2 Lloyd's Rep 377, 389 (Lord Jauncey).

be likely to influence the prudent insurer in deciding on the amount of premium to fix or whether to accept the risk and provide coverage at all. Hence, it would appear to be fair to place such an obligation on the insured.[135]

It should be noted however, that both s18 of the *Marine Insurance Act 1906* (UK) and s150 (1) of the *Insurance Act 1996* (Malaysia) have been repealed by s21 (2) of the *Insurance Act 2015* (UK) and s283 of the *Financial Services Act 2013* (Malaysia) respectively, and shall be addressed in Chap. 3 of this book.

On the flipside, however, an insurance company with its vast experience and industry knowledge would most likely know exactly what sort of information it would require, pertaining to the risk to be underwritten. Furthermore, most insurance companies today are multinational corporations with huge resources, dealing in turn, with insureds who are often taking out their first insurance policy. Therefore, any previous justification for a strict application of the pre-contractual duty of disclosure may be placed in doubt, as the insured who is often inexperienced in the matter, would be totally unfamiliar with what sort of facts the insurance company would like to be informed of, in order to assess the viability of the risk to be underwritten.

As a result, insureds may often act in good faith and yet fall short of the duty of disclosure required by law, either due to failure to realise that certain facts are material in law or not realising that the duty encompassed more than having to truthfully answer the questions posed on a proposal form.[136] As Hasson pointed out in his critique of the duty of good faith[137] this imbalance between the insurer and insured in favour of the insurer, was largely due to the assignment of a wider interpretation of a 1766 decision[138] by later English courts, whereas American courts have read the case as stating a much narrower duty.

Despite this, however, the strict position of the common law remained unwavering up until the recent reforms in the United Kingdom in 2012–2015 and Malaysia in 2013. Scrutton LJ in *Rozanes v Bowen*[139] had in fact dismissed any notion of the pre-contractual duty of disclosure on the part of the insured as being limited to questions put forward by the insurer.

This rigid attitude of the courts is also apparent in the Malaysian case of *Teh Say Cheng v North British and Mercantile Insurance Co Ltd*,[140] where Whiteley JC categorically rejected the insured's argument (under a fire policy) that he was justified in assuming that the insurer only required no more information than that which was asked by the questions in the proposal form.

---

[135]See: Romer LJ's comment on the rationale for the rule in *Seaton v Heath* [1899] 1 QB 782, 793.

[136]It should be noted that numerous calls for reform of this position were made by the Law Reform Committee back (1957), the Law Commission (1980) and the Insurance Ombudsman in the United Kingdom.

[137]Hasson, above n 115, 632–633.

[138]Lord Mansfield's dicta in *Carter v Boehm* (1766) 3 Burr 1905, 1909, 1910.

[139](1928) 32 Ll L Rep 98, 102.

[140](1921) FMSLR 248, 255.

In *March Cabaret Club & Casino Ltd v London Assurance Ltd*[141] May J clearly stated the position with respect to questions posed to the insured in proposal forms as '...whereas there is a presumption that matters dealt with in a proposal form are material, there is no corresponding presumption that matters not so dealt with are not material'.[142]

The justification for this has always been that the insured's duty to disclose material information to the insurer existed independently and irrespective of any proposal form.[143] It would appear that since insurers in Malaysia were not up until the enactment of the *Financial Services Act 2013* (Malaysia), obliged to issue proposal forms to begin with, they should not as a result be prejudiced by it should the questions posed be incomplete. Therefore, the proposal form although a common feature in the Malaysian insurance industry, was seen as a mere guide as to the type of information that may be material to the insurer and by no means an avenue to relieve the insured of the duty to disclose, in the event that it was not comprehensive.[144] Such is no longer the case however, by virtue of Paragraphs 4 (4) and 5 (7) of *Schedule 9* to the *Financial Services Act 2013* (Malaysia).

Based on this reasoning, it was held in *Arterial Caravans Ltd v Yorkshire Insurance Co Ltd*[145] that the insurer's acceptance of a proposal form in which the insured had omitted to answer certain questions, did not give rise to an inference of waiver or estoppel against the insurer as to the insured's duty of disclosure with respect to the information omitted. In this respect, the insured's conduct of giving a blank answer may also amount to a misrepresentation of fact, where the blank answer is taken as a negative reply and it turns out to be untrue.[146] That which seems more logical and consistent an approach however, is that whatever the inference, the overriding consideration should be whether the incomplete proposal form ought to have put the insurer on guard.[147]

In fact, the English Court of Appeal in *Roberts v Plaisted*[148] did accept that the way in which a question was framed in a proposal form could in certain circumstances have the effect of limiting the insured's pre-contractual duty of disclosure. In this case, the plaintiff obtained insurance coverage for a motel that had a function room, a lounge bar and a discotheque. The proposal form inquired as to whether the premises were occupied as a hotel or an inn, whether it had any other purposes and if there was a casino in any part of the building. The insured correctly answered the latter two questions in the negative.

---

[141][1975] 1 Lloyd's Rep 169.

[142]Ibid. 176; This was reiterated in *United Oriental Assurance Sdn Bhd v WM Mazzarol (The Melanie)* [1984] 1 MLJ 260, 262 (Salleh Abbas CJ).

[143]*Asia Insurance Co Ltd v Tat Hong Plant Leasing Pte Ltd* [1992] 1 CLJ 330.

[144]*Schoolman v Hall* [1951] 1 Lloyd's Rep 139.

[145][1973] 1 Lloyd's Rep 169.

[146]*Roberts v Avon Insurance* [1956] 2 Lloyd's Rep 240.

[147]Legh-Jones et al. (2003, p. 447).

[148][1989] 2 Lloyd's Rep 341.

During the currency of the policy, the motel was destroyed by fire and the insurers refused to indemnify the insured for the loss on the grounds that the insured had failed to disclose that the motel had a discotheque. The Court of Appeal held that the way in which the questions in the proposal form were framed, in particular that pertaining to the existence of a casino, had the effect of waiving the insured's duty to disclose the presence of a discotheque on the premises, even though such a fact may have otherwise been material. Furthermore, it was reasonable for an insurer to assume that a motel that provided public entertainment would also have a discotheque.

The courts were therefore only willing to accept questions posed in proposal forms as giving rise to the defence of waiver or estoppel in the insured's favour, in clear and limited situations as above. There has however, been a substantial change in this area in Australia and Malaysia in favour of the insured, by virtue of s21 (3) of the *Insurance Contracts Act 1984* (Cth) (Australia) and Paragraphs 4 (3) and 5 (6) of *Schedule 9* to the *Financial Services Act 2013* (Malaysia) (based on s150 (3) of the now repealed *Insurance Act 1996* (Malaysia)) respectively, that will be addressed in Chap. 3.

Another alternative may be where questions asked in a proposal form are ambiguous in which case the courts have been inclined to provide a fair and reasonable construction in construing them *contra proferentum*, which is against the party seeking to rely on them.[149] It should be noted however, that where the insured is seeking to rely on the ambiguity of the questions posed in the proposal form as a means to defeat an allegation of non-disclosure or misrepresentation, the courts in construing the ambiguity have been mindful of any inconsistency in the answers to other questions in the proposal form which leaned towards an indication that the insured was in fact not misled by the ambiguity.[150]

The *contra proferentum* rule, albeit a fair and useful tool of construction protecting insureds against their understandable ignorance of technical insurance provisions, can however, only be deployed in cases of ambiguity and does not quite address the imbalance in information and understanding existing at the pre-contractual stage, like it does with respect to resolving post-contractual disputes.[151]

A detailed analysis of the application of the pre-contractual duty of disclosure in the United Kingdom, Malaysia and Australia, along with its exceptions and concepts such as 'materiality' and the 'prudent insurer test' reflected in the now repealed s18 (2) of the *Marine Insurance Act 1906* (UK), as well as the recent amendments in the United Kingdom and Malaysia that incorporate an enquiry based disclosure for consumer insurance contracts and voluntary disclosure for non-consumer contracts, will be made in Chap. 3 of this book.

---

[149] *Sweeney v Kennedy* (1948) 82 Ll L Rep 294.

[150] *Asia Hotel Sdn Bhd v Malayan Insurance (M) Sdn Bhd* [1992] 2 MLJ 615.

[151] Tarr (2001).

2.7.2 Misrepresentation

Another aspect of the insured's pre-contractual duty of utmost good faith towards the insurer is the duty to refrain from making material misrepresentation. Misrepresentation in the general law of contract is a vitiating factor, resulting in the contract being voidable at the option of the innocent party.[152] It is divided into three categories, namely, fraudulent, negligent and innocent misrepresentation. Fraudulent misrepresentation is where one knowingly makes a false statement without belief in its truth or recklessly as to whether it is true or false.[153] Negligent and innocent misrepresentation on the other hand which lack the intent to deceive on the part of the maker of the statement, are defined by s18 of the *Contracts Act 1950* (Malaysia).[154]

Misrepresentation as a vitiating factor in the general law of contract addressed in ss17–19 of the *Contracts Act 1950* (Malaysia) necessarily envisages pre-contractual misrepresentation. This is because unlike *uberrimae fidei* contracts like insurance, there is no continuing post-contractual duty of good faith in general contracts.

As far as the law of insurance is concerned, the corresponding provision to the pre-contractual duty of disclosure with respect to the duty to abstain from material misrepresentation at the pre-contractual stage was contained in s20 of the *Marine Insurance Act 1906* (UK) which provided as follows:

> Every material representation made by the assured or his agent to the insurer during the negotiations for the contract, and before the contract is concluded, must be true. If it be untrue the insurer may avoid the contract.

Like s18 (2), a representation would be material if it influenced the judgment of a prudent insurer in fixing the premium or determining whether to take the risk and offer coverage,[155] with the materiality of a particular representation essentially being a question of fact.[156] Such a representation may either be as to a matter of fact or expectation or belief,[157] with a representation of fact being true if it is

---

[152] See: Section 19 (1) of the *Contracts Act 1950* (Malaysia).

[153] *Derry v Peek* (1889) 14 App Cas 337; Section 17 of the *Contracts Act 1950* (Malaysia) covers this in its definition of fraud.

[154] Section 18 of the *Contracts Act 1950* (Malaysia) provides that:

Misrepresentation includes: (a) the positive assertion, in a manner not warranted by the information of the person making it, of that which is not true, though he believes it to be true; (b) any breach of duty which, without an intent to deceive, gives an advantage to the person committing it, or anyone claiming under him, by misleading another to his prejudice, or to the prejudice of anyone claiming under him; and (c) causing, however innocently, a party to an agreement to make a mistake as to the substance of the thing which is the subject of the agreement.

[155] Section 20 (2) of the *Marine Insurance Act 1906* (UK).

[156] Section 20 (7).

[157] Section 20 (3).

substantially correct[158] and a representation of belief or expectation being true if it is made in good faith.[159]

Section 20 (6) completed the provision on pre-contractual representations by providing that a representation may be withdrawn or corrected before the contract is concluded, without affecting the validity of the ensuing contract. Section 20 has however, been repealed by s21 (2) of the *Insurance Act 2015* (UK) and replaced by a duty of *fair presentation* on the insured's part, which shall be examined in Chap. 3.

It should be noted at this juncture, that there was no corresponding provision to s20 of the *Marine Insurance Act 1906* (UK) on pre-contractual misrepresentation in the now repealed *Insurance Act 1996* (Malaysia), resulting in the position with respect thereto being governed by s20. This was the case up until the enactment of the *Financial Services Act 2013* (Malaysia). Paragraphs 4 and 5 of *Schedule 9* to the *Financial Services Act 2013* (Malaysia) now provide for a voluntary disclosure mechanism similar to Australia, with respect to non-consumer insurance contracts; and an inquiry based disclosure mechanism similar to that of the United Kingdom and eligible contracts in Australia, with respect to consumer insurance contracts, respectively. The details of these and the corresponding remedies available in the event of breach shall be addressed in Chap. 3.

As far as post-contractual misrepresentation is concerned, it is presumably on the same footing as that of the general duty of utmost good faith, which is based on the implied term of contract reasoning.

It is worth noting that misrepresentation in the insurance context has always played second fiddle to the duty of disclosure, largely due to the wide scope of the latter. The fact that insurers in bringing an action for avoidance of contract in the past, have often pleaded both non-disclosure and misrepresentation as their defence, has added to the blurring of the two principles. The rationale for this seems to have been that the insured's duty to correctly answer questions posed in a proposal form, in essence forms part of the insured's duty of good faith and disclosure. There have however, been instances in cases like *Economides v Commercial Assurance Co Plc*[160] where the insured's conduct in underinsuring the contents of his house as a result of not realizing the actual value of the items subsequently brought in by his parents from Cyprus, was held to be an innocent misrepresentation as opposed to material non-disclosure warranting avoidance.

It should be noted that there is a distinction between innocent misrepresentation of belief or expectation which would not entitle the insurer to avoid the contract and innocent non-disclosure on the other hand, which would, as the latter is a situation

---

[158]Section 20 (4). It goes on to stipulate that a representation of fact would be substantially correct if the difference between what is represented and what is actually correct would not be considered material by a prudent insurer. This goes to show that a representation must be considered in its entirety and in the context in which it was made. See: *Morrison v Muspratt* (1827) 4 Bing 60, 63 (Burrough J).

[159]Section 20 (5).

[160][1997] 3 WLR 1066.

where the insured knows the truth but does not appreciate the fact that it is material and should therefore, be disclosed.

By virtue of s20 (1) of the *Marine Insurance Act 1906* (UK), the insurer was entitled to the remedy of avoidance of contract for material misrepresentation at the pre-contractual stage, irrespective of whether such misrepresentation by the insured was negligent or fraudulent. Although s20 (1) failed to make a distinction on the remedy available for different types of misrepresentation, the insurer was under common law entitled to the additional remedy of damages in the tort of deceit and could retain any premium paid, in the face of fraudulent misrepresentation by the insured.

Where the misrepresentation was innocent however, the insurer was entitled to avoid the contract only if it was with respect to a statement of fact and not expectation or belief. This was because s20 (5) provided that a representation of belief or expectation was true if it was made in good faith, as was the case in *Economides v Commercial Assurance Co Plc.*[161]

Most cases involving avoidance of insurance contracts by insurers for material misrepresentation however, tend to involve incorrect answers given by insureds to questions posed in proposal forms. This is apparent from cases like *Goh Chooi Leong v Public Life Assurance Co Ltd,*[162] *National Insurance Co Ltd v S Joseph*[163] and *Taylor v Eagle Star Insurance Co Ltd.*[164] Although this need not necessarily be the case always, as can be seen in *St Paul Fire & Marine Insurance Co (UK) Ltd v McConnell Dowell Constructors Ltd.*[165] Here the insurers were entitled to avoid the Contractors All Risks policy in response to the appellant contractors' submission on their own accord of drawings and plans for the projected buildings as having piled foundations when in actual fact, spread foundations were subsequently used, resulting in subsidence damage to the buildings.

Albeit different provisions of the *Marine Insurance Act 1906* (UK) dealt with the issue of pre-contractual non-disclosure and misrepresentation, the consequence of a breach of both was the same, namely avoidance of the contract by the insurer.

It would appear that damages as a remedy in addition to avoidance of the contract would be available where there was fraud or negligent misrepresentation involved.[166] This being in line with s76 of the *Contracts Act 1950* (Malaysia) read together with s19 of the same Act, whereby, should a contract be avoided on the basis that it was obtained by coercion, fraud or misrepresentation, the party rightfully avoiding the contract would be entitled to compensation for any damage sustained thereby.

---

[161]Ibid.

[162][1964] MLJ 5.

[163][1973] 2 MLJ 195.

[164](1940) 67 Ll L Rep 136.

[165][1995] 2 Lloyd's Rep 116.

[166]*Toomey v Eagle Star Insurance Co. Ltd. (No 2)* [1995] 2 Lloyd's Rep 88.

It is interesting to note however, that prior to the recent amendments in the United Kingdom and Malaysia which shall be examined in Chap. 3, English judges like Steyn J and Rix J in *Highlands Insurance Co. v Continental Insurance Co.*[167] and *HIH Casualty and General v Chase Manhattan Bank,*[168] as well as the Insurance Ombudsman in the United Kingdom[169] had indicated the possible application of s2 (2) of the *Misrepresentation Act 1967* (UK) as a restriction on the insurer's right to avoid contracts for misrepresentation. Especially so, in consumer or non-commercial insurance contracts, thereby, permitting damages instead to be awarded in lieu thereof.

2.7.3 Fraudulent Claims

The final aspect of the insured's duty of utmost good faith is at the claims settlement stage, where the insured is required to put forward a genuine claim to the insurer within the contractual time limit prescribed. In this regard, the submission of a fraudulent claim would by virtue of public policy be a breach of utmost good faith, entitling the insurer to avoid the claim and forfeit the premiums paid.[170] An allegation of fraud by the insured would however, have to be pleaded and proven by the insurer.[171] In this context, the submission of exaggerated claims by insureds would not in itself necessarily amount to fraud. The courts would be mindful of the possibility of such exaggeration as merely being a means to facilitate the now common phenomenon of 'price-haggling' between the parties.[172]

2.8 Remedies for Breach of the Duty of Utmost Good Faith

Since it is well established that the duty of utmost good faith is reciprocal in nature, it is therefore necessary to evaluate the suitability of the remedies available to both insurers and insureds alike, in the event of breach by the other.

---

[167] [1987] 1 Lloyd's Rep 109.

[168] [2001] Lloyd's Rep IR 702.

[169] Financial Ombudsman Service (1991, pp. 7–8).

[170] See: *The Star Sea* [2001] 1 Lloyd's Rep 389 (Lord Hobhouse), *The Mercandian Continent* [2001] EWCA Civ 1275 (Longmore LJ), *Agapitos v Agnew (The Aegeon)* [2002] 2 Lloyd's Rep 42 (Mance LJ).

[171] *Hornal v Neuberger Products Ltd* [1957] 1 QB 347.

[172] *Ewer v National Employers' Mutual General Insurance Association Ltd.* [1937] 2 All ER 193; *Wong Cheong Kong Sdn Bhd v Prudential Assurance Sdn Bhd* [1998] 3 MLJ 724; This aspect has been addressed earlier in this chapter under the insurer's duty of good faith in claims settlement.

As far as breach of the duty of utmost good faith by the insurer is concerned, the United Kingdom and Malaysia were up until the recent amendments in the *Insurance Act 2015* (UK) and *Financial Services Act 2013* (Malaysia) still bound by the shackles of s17 of the *Marine Insurance Act 1906* (UK) and its solitary remedy of avoidance of the insurance contract by the insured with a refund of premium paid, without any right to damages.[173]

The effect of these recent amendments in the United Kingdom and Malaysia, as well as the position in Australia, as to the remedies available in the event of breach, shall be broadly divided into the pre-contractual and post-contractual stages and examined in Chaps. 3 and 4.

2.9 Conclusion

In view of the wide scope of the insurers' and insureds' duties of utmost good faith highlighted above, which span from the pre-contractual stage of negotiating an insurance contract right up to claims settlement, the following Chaps. 3 and 4 will be dedicated to a detailed analysis of the reforms undertaken thus far and still required, at the pre and post-contractual stages. This will then be followed by an evaluation of the position pertaining to *takaful* in Chap. 5.

References

Abu Bakar B (2013) The commercial law of Malaysia revisited—Section 5 (2) of the Civil Law Act 1956; Constitutionality, the EU and Islamisation. Int Islam Univ Malaysia Law J 21(1)
Australian Law Reform Commission (1982) Report No 20, Insurance Contracts
Australian Law Reform Commission (2001) Report No 91, Review of the Marine Insurance Act 1909
Bennett H (1999) Mapping the doctrine of utmost good faith in insurance contract law. Lloyd's Marit Commer Law Quart 165
Birds J (2013) Birds' Modern Insurance Law, vol 9. Sweet & Maxwell, London
Burton S (1980) Breach of contract and the common law duty to perform in good faith. Harv Law Rev 94:369
Campbell N (2005) Insurance law. N Z Law Rev 3:431
Clarke M (2003) Refusing rescission: contracts of utmost bad faith. Camb Law J 556
Derrington (2002) Marine insurance law in Australia: the Australian law reform commission proposals. Lloyd's Marit Commer Law Quart 214
Eggers P (2003) Remedies for the failure to observe the utmost good faith. Lloyd's Marit Commer Law Quart 249
Financial Ombudsman Service (1991) Insurance Ombudsman Annual Report 1990, London
Finn P (1989a) Good faith and fair dealing. Paper presented at the Australian Insurance Law Association Conference, Melbourne, Nov 1989

[173] *Banque Financiere v Westgate Insurance Co. Ltd.* [1988] 2 Lloyd's Rep 513.

Finn P (1989b) Commerce, the common law and morality. Melb Univ Law Rev 17:87
Hasson RA (1969) The doctrine of uberrima fides in insurance law—a critical evaluation. Mod Law Rev 32:615
Hasson RA (1984) The special nature of insurance contracts: a comparison of the American and English law of insurance. Mod Law Rev 47:505
Kelly D (1989) The insured's rights in relation to the provision of information by the insurer. Insur Law J 2:45
Law Commission (1980) Insurance law: non-disclosure and breach of warranty, Report No 104, Cmnd 8064
Law Reform Committee (1957) Conditions and exceptions in insurance policies, Report No 5, Cmnd 62
Lee KS (1997) Ubi Jus Ibi Remedium? Insurer's duty to disclose—time for another look? Singap J Leg Stud 185
Legh-Jones N, Birds J, Owen D (eds) (2003) MacGillivray on insurance law, vol 10. Sweet & Maxwell, London
Mahmood NR (1992) Insurance law in Malaysia. Butterworths, Malaysia
Merkin R (2010) Colinvaux's law of insurance, 9th edn. Sweet & Maxwell, London
Naidoo A, Oughton D (2005) The confused post-formation duty of good faith in insurance law: from refinement to fragmentation to elimination? J Bus Law 346
Parkes JE, Heil RJ (1973) Insurers beware: "bad faith" is in full bloom. Forum 9:63
Poh CC (2005) Principles of insurance law, 6th edn. Butterworths, Singapore
Soyer B (2003) Continuing duty of utmost good faith in insurance contracts: still alive? Lloyd's Marit Commer Law Quart 39
Sutton K (1999) Insurance law in Australia, 3rd edn. Law Book Co, Sydney
Tarr A (1989) Insurance law and the consumer. Bond Law Rev 1:79
Tarr J-A (2001) The insured's reasonable expectations. Insur Law J 12:9
Thanasegaran H (2004) Insurers' good faith in Malaysia: does a search for a fairer balance in non-marine insurance contracts lead to Australia?' Insur Law J 15:143
Thanasegaran H (2007) To renew or not to renew—what are the questions? An evaluation of the statutory warning in insurance contracts' Malay Law J 2:cxlvii, clii–cliii
Thanasegaran H (2011) Settlement of claims by Malaysian insurance and *takaful* companies: a genuine prospect or merely suspect? Int Co Commer Law Rev 22(6):191
Thanasegaran H, Shaiban M (2014) Harmonization of Takaful (Islamic insurance) regulation—a realistic goal or improbable ideal? Singap J Legal Stud 328

Chapter 3
Pre-contractual Duty of Disclosure and Misrepresentation

Abstract This chapter builds on the preliminary description of the pre-contractual duty of disclosure and misrepresentation and their relationship to the concept of utmost good faith offered in Chap. 2. It analyses the elements of the duties as embodied in ss18 (2) and 20 (2) of the *Marine Insurance Act 1906* (UK) and their development with respect to the United Kingdom and Malaysia, as well as the effect of selected provisions of the *Insurance Act 1996* (Malaysia) and its successor, the *Financial Services Act 2013* (Malaysia) with respect to Malaysia, before providing a comparison with the Australian *Insurance Contracts Act 1984* (Cth).

3.1 Introduction

A preliminary description of the pre-contractual duty of disclosure and misrepresentation and their relationship to the concept of utmost good faith has been offered in Chap. 2. In that chapter, the origins of the duties,[1] their application in Malaysia, the United Kingdom and Australia, and the consequences of their breach were set out. This chapter will in turn analyse the elements of the duties as embodied in ss18 (2) and 20 (2) of the *Marine Insurance Act 1906* (UK) and their development with respect to the United Kingdom and Malaysia, as well as the effect of selected provisions of the *Insurance Act 1996* (Malaysia) and its successor, the *Financial Services Act 2013* (Malaysia) with respect to Malaysia. Since the law pertaining to pre-contractual disclosure and misrepresentation in Malaysia has been heavily reliant upon the English common law, the position in the United Kingdom will first be set out before turning the analysis to Malaysia and Australia, respectively.

---

[1]The pre-contractual duties of disclosure and misrepresentation were a codification of the common law position in the United Kingdom at the time, as expounded by Lord Mansfield in *Carter v Boehm* (1766) 3 Burr 1905 and set out in ss18 and 20 of the *Marine Insurance Act 1906* (UK) until its recent repeal by s21 (2) of the *Insurance Act 2015* (UK).

H. Thanasegaran, *Good Faith in Insurance and Takaful Contracts in Malaysia*,
DOI 10.1007/978-981-10-0383-7_3

The common law based pre-contractual duty of disclosure that remained applicable to the United Kingdom and Malaysia until recent amendments[2] imposed a positive duty on the insured to make disclosure of all material information and change in the risk to be insured up until the insurance contract was concluded or renewed. Failure to do so entitled the insurer to avoid the contract ab initio. This was justified by the fact that insurance contracts were contracts of utmost good faith and the information imbalance which existed in favour of the insured at that pre-contractual stage of the transaction.

Misrepresentation in insurance contracts on the other hand, albeit connected to the duty of disclosure, has always played second fiddle to it, owing to the wide scope of the latter. This is because any information that is disclosed must be full and accurate. Therefore, any false representation of material facts or partial omission thereof would amount to a material misrepresentation and/or non-disclosure. As a result, insurers have often resorted to pleading both non-disclosure and misrepresentation as grounds for avoiding insurance contracts, which has added to the blurring of the two principles.[3]

In a general sense, the duty to refrain from making material misrepresentation would encompass the pre and post-contractual stages of insurance contracts. However, its effect at the pre-contractual stage has the potential to cause serious repercussions, and shall be addressed in this chapter. Post-contractual misrepresentation on the other hand, is primarily governed by the terms of the insurance policy itself and shall be dealt with in Chap. 4. A clear distinction between the effect of pre and post-contractual misrepresentation was made by Greer LJ in *Toller v Law Accident Insurance Society Ltd.*[4] His Lordship explained that where an insurer relies on pre-contractual material misrepresentation by the insured, it is in effect avoiding the contract ab initio, by rejecting the very existence of the contract. A claim of post-contractual misrepresentation on the other hand, is an affirmation of the existence of the insurance contract but the insurer is relying on a term of the contract to avoid making payment of the claim.[5]

---

[2]The common law position remained applicable to the United Kingdom until the *Consumer Insurance (Disclosure and Representations) Act 2012* altered it with respect to consumer insurance contracts and the *Insurance Act 2015* (UK) did so with respect to primarily but not exclusively, non-consumer insurance contracts. As for Malaysia, the application of the common law to insurance contracts was altered in 1996 and again in 2013 by virtue of the *Insurance Act 1996* (Malaysia) and *Financial Services Act 2013* (Malaysia) respectively, and the *Islamic Financial Services Act 2013* (Malaysia) did the same with respect to *takaful*, contracts in Malaysia which shall be addressed in Chap. 5 of this book.

[3]Birds (2013, pp. 114–115).

[4][1936] 2 All ER 952, 956.

[5]It should be noted that the law on pre and post-contractual misrepresentation in insurance contracts is distinct from that applying to the general law of contract. In general contract law, misrepresentation (whether innocent, negligent or fraudulent) necessarily occurs at the pre-contractual stage, as there is no continuing duty of utmost good faith. It is treated as a vitiating factor which makes the contract voidable at the option of the innocent party. See: ss17–19 of the *Contracts Act 1950* (Malaysia) as discussed in Chap. 2 of this book.

3.2 Development and Application of the Pre-contractual Duties in the United Kingdom

The legislation governing the pre-contractual duty of disclosure in insurance contracts in the United Kingdom was s18 of the *Marine Insurance Act 1906* (UK) until its recent repeal with respect to consumer insurance contracts via ss2 (5) and 11 (1) of the *Consumer Insurance (Disclosure and Representations) Act 2012* (UK) and in general (including non-consumer insurance contracts) via s21 (2) of the *Insurance Act 2015* (UK). Section 18 (1) had provided:

> Subject to the provisions of this section, the assured must disclose to the insurer, before the contract is concluded, every material circumstance that is known to the assured, and the assured is deemed to know every circumstance which, in the ordinary course of business, ought to be known by him. If the assured fails to make such disclosure, the *insurer may avoid the contract* (emphasis added).

Section 18 (2) went on to provide that:

> Every circumstance is material which would *influence* the *judgment of a prudent insurer* in fixing the premium or determining whether he will take the risk (emphasis added).

The question of materiality of any particular circumstance not disclosed was in each case, a question of fact.[6]

The corresponding provision in s20 of the *Marine Insurance Act 1906* (UK) with respect to the duty to abstain from making material misrepresentation at the pre-contractual stage, has also been repealed by s21 (2) of the *Insurance Act 2015* (UK). Section 20 (1) had provided that:

> Every material representation made by the assured or his agent to the insurer during the negotiations for the contract, and before the contract is concluded, must be true. If it be untrue the *insurer may avoid the contract* (emphasis added).

Like s18 (2), s20 (2) provided that a representation would be material if it influenced *the judgment of a prudent insurer* in fixing the premium or determining whether to take the risk and offer coverage, with the materiality of a particular representation being a question of fact.[7] According to s20 (3), such a representation may either relate to a matter of fact or expectation or belief, whereby a representation of fact would be true if it was substantially correct[8] and

---

[6]Section 18 (4) of the *Marine Insurance Act 1906* (UK).

[7]Section 20 (7) of the *Marine Insurance Act 1906* (UK).

[8]Section 20 (4); It went on to stipulate that a representation of fact would be substantially correct if the difference between what is represented and what is actually correct would not be considered material by a prudent insurer. This goes to show that a representation must be considered in its entirety and in the context in which it was made: *Morrison v Muspratt* (1827) 4 Bing 60, 63 (Burrough J).

a representation of belief or expectation would be true if it was made in good faith.[9]

Despite different provisions of the *Marine Insurance Act 1906* (UK) dealing with the issue of pre-contractual non-disclosure and misrepresentation, the consequence of a breach of either obligation was the same drastic remedy of avoidance of the contract by the insurer.

Section 2(2) of the *Misrepresentation Act 1967* (UK) however, sought to provide some reprieve for the insured and has been used by the courts and the Insurance Ombudsman in misrepresentation cases involving private individuals, in order to restrict the insurers' right to avoid insurance contracts for misrepresentation.[10] This was done by the exercise of discretion to award damages in lieu of rescission, primarily in cases where insurers tried to avoid policies for purely innocent misrepresentation unconnected to the loss insured.[11]

Another avenue for reprieve was through the application of the *contra proferentum* rule by the judiciary. Where there was ambiguity,[12] whether in the proposal form or in the policy itself, the courts would construe the ambiguity against the party responsible for drafting or seeking to rely on it, thereby, often coming to the aid of the insured.[13] Despite this however, the ensuing discussion on the prudent insurer test will illustrate the unsatisfactory state of the law that existed in the United Kingdom and its reform proposals, as well as its influence on the development of the law in Malaysia.

Before moving on to an evaluation of the elements of the pre-contractual duty of disclosure and misrepresentation that were embodied in ss18 (2) and 20 (2), it would be helpful to take a brief look at what the insured was required to disclose generally under s18 (1) and the limited exceptions to disclosure contained in s18 (3) of the *Marine Insurance Act 1906* (UK).

3.2.1 What Must the Insured Disclose

Section 18 (1) although appearing fairly straightforward upon a first reading, has given rise to three questions, namely, whether the insured knows of this pre-contractual duty of disclosure, whether the facts to be disclosed need to be

[9]Section 20 (5); See: *Economides v Commercial Assurance Co Plc* [1997] 3 WLR 1066. Section 20 (6) completed the provision on pre-contractual representations by providing that a representation may be withdrawn or corrected before the contract is concluded, without affecting the validity of the ensuing contract.

[10]See: *Highlands Insurance Co v Continental Insurance Co* [1987] 1 Lloyd's Rep 109 (Steyn J obiter) which was subsequently echoed by Rix J in *HIH Casualty and General v Chase Manhattan Bank* [2001] Lloyd's Rep IR 702. See also: Financial Ombudsman Service (1991, pp. 7–8).

[11]Merkin (2000, p. [A.4.6]).

[12]The existence of an ambiguity in any given situation however, may in itself be unclear, as could be seen in the case of *Alder v Moore* [1961] 2 QB 57.

[13]See: *English v Western* [1940] 2 KB 156; *Houghton v Trafalgar Insurance Co Ltd* [1954] 1 QB 247.

material in the insured's opinion and whether the insured is bound to disclose material facts within his or her actual, as well as constructive knowledge.[14]

On the first point, it is irrelevant whether the insured knows of this duty of disclosure, as the law imposes it. To mitigate the potential injustice to private individual insureds that may be unaware of this duty, domestic insurance laws have made it compulsory for insurers to display a warning of this requirement in proposal forms and requests for particulars.

As far as Malaysia is concerned, this was provided for in the now repealed s149 (4) of the *Insurance Act 1996* (Malaysia) and has been replaced by the improved Paragraphs 4 (4) and 5 (7) of *Schedule 9* to the *Financial Services Act 2013* (Malaysia). Both provisions are based on the Australian s22 (1) of the *Insurance Contracts Act 1984* (Cth) and have been alluded to in Chap. 2 of this book.

There was however, no corresponding provision for the United Kingdom under the *Marine Insurance Act 1906* (UK). The same has also been omitted under the recent amendments introduced via the *Consumer Insurance (Disclosure and Representations) Act 2012* (UK) and the *Insurance Act 2015* (UK), as the United Kingdom has adopted an enquiry based disclosure mechanism instead, placing on insureds a duty to take reasonable care not to make misrepresentations (in consumer insurance) and to make a fair representation of the risk (in non-consumer insurance) to the insurer.[15]

On the second point, as to whether a fact needs to be material in the insured's view before warranting disclosure, it has been settled law in the United Kingdom that it does not.[16] Materiality of a fact is judged from a prudent insurer's perspective. This is still the case under the *Insurance Act 2015* (UK) with respect to non-consumer insurance contracts,[17] whereas the standard required in consumer insurance contracts is that of a reasonable consumer.[18] The materiality of a fact warranting disclosure in Malaysia and Australia on the other hand is judged from the more favourable perspective of the reasonable insured in the circumstances,[19] as the disclosure mechanism applicable in these jurisdictions is generally that of voluntary disclosure.

---

[14]Birds, above n 3, 122–123.

[15]See: Section 2 (2) of the *Consumer Insurance (Disclosure and Representations) Act 2012* (UK) and s3 (1) of the *Insurance Act 2015* (UK), respectively.

[16]*Lambert v Co-operative Insurance Society* [1975] 2 Lloyd's Rep 485.

[17]See: Section 3 (3), 3 (4) and 7 (3) of the *Insurance Act 2015* (UK).

[18]See: Section 3 (3) of the *Consumer Insurance (Disclosure and Representations) Act 2012* (UK).

[19]See: Paragraph 6 (2) and Paragraph 4 (1) (b) of *Schedule 9* to the *Financial Services Act 2013* (Malaysia) for consumer and non-consumer insurance contracts respectively, in relation to Malaysia, which was previously regulated by the now repealed s150 (1) of the *Insurance Act 1996* (Malaysia). The position in Australia on the other hand, is governed by s21 of the *Insurance Contracts Act 1984* (Cth).

The third question in turn, concerns whether the disclosure of material facts within the insured's knowledge covers actual as well as constructive knowledge. Section 18 (1) of the *Marine Insurance Act 1906* (UK) has received a disjunctive interpretation from the English courts, which have held that the constructive knowledge of material facts can only be imposed on an insured who took out a policy in the course of business and not in a personal capacity.[20] This was presumably to ameliorate the more onerous aspects of the prudent insurer test and the remedy of avoidance that existed. It should be noted that the concept of constructive knowledge has been retained in the recent amendments with respect to non-consumer insurance, via s3 (4) of the *Insurance Act 2015* (UK), presumably in view of the enquiry based disclosure mechanism adopted.

The disjunctive interpretation taken by the English courts that is more favourable to the insured, however, has not been the position adopted by Australia[21] and Malaysia (even before the recent amendments)[22] which have enacted provisions on disclosure that clearly impose both actual as well as constructive knowledge on the insured. This is presumably because of the more favourable assessment of materiality in existence that is judged from the *reasonable insured's* perspective instead.

Having considered the three questions above, the exceptions to disclosure will now be set out in brief. This is then followed by an assessment of the extent of the information requiring disclosure, in that what sort of information pertaining to the insured's history would necessitate disclosure for instance and how far back in time the insured is required to go, in order to satisfy this obligation. This would involve the examination of concepts such as physical and moral hazards that are invariably linked to the issue of materiality.

In doing so, the guiding principle to determine the disclosure of any information in the United Kingdom has been whether such information would influence the decision of a prudent insurer in deciding whether to accept the risk or in fixing the premium for undertaking such a risk, whereas the less onerous 'reasonable insured in the circumstances' test has been adopted by Australia and Malaysia in this regard.

3.2.2 Exceptions to the Duty of Disclosure

The now repealed s18 (3) of the *Marine Insurance Act 1906* (UK) contained a limited exception to the insured's pre-contractual duty of disclosure, dealing with matters not required to be disclosed by the insured, unless expressly required to do so by the insurer. Section 18 (3) provided that:

In the absence of inquiry the following circumstances need not be disclosed, namely:

---

[20] *Economides v Commercial Assurance Co Plc* [1997] 3 WLR 1066.

[21] Section 21 (1) of the *Insurance Contracts Act 1984* (Cth) (Australia).

[22] Section 150 (1) of the *Insurance Act 1996* (Malaysia).

(a) Any circumstance which diminishes the risk;
(b) Any circumstance which is known or presumed to be known to the insurer. The insurer is presumed to know matters of common notoriety or knowledge, and matters which an insurer in the ordinary course of his business, as such, ought to know;
(c) Any circumstance as to which information is waived by the insurer;
(d) Any circumstance which it is superfluous to disclose by reason of any express or implied warranty.

This has been largely retained for non-consumer insurance contracts via s3 (5) of the *Insurance Act 2015* (UK) along with s5 which clarifies the scope of the insurer's actual, constructive and presumed knowledge; save for s18 (3) (d) which has been deleted for being of little practical value.[23]

Malaysia, which essentially followed the Australian s21 (2) of the *Insurance Contracts Act 1984* (Cth) had adopted a similar provision via the now repealed s150 (2) of the *Insurance Act 1996* (Malaysia), save for the words 'in the absence of inquiry' being omitted. This provided the insured with greater protection by indicating that the matters listed in the subsections need under no circumstances be disclosed to the insurer. Section 150 (2) of the *Insurance Act 1996* (Malaysia) has now been replaced by a similar provision in s4 (2) of the *Financial Services Act 2013* (Malaysia) with respect to non-consumer insurance contracts only, as it is no longer relevant to the enquiry based disclosure mechanism adopted for consumer insurance contracts in Malaysia.

With respect to circumstances that diminish the risk insured, it appears logical enough that they need not, in the absence of inquiry, be disclosed by the insured.[24] This is because there is no threat or risk of the insurer being disadvantaged by its non-disclosure.

As for circumstances known or ought or presumed to be known to the insurer, on the other hand, there has been more debate.[25] In *Hales v Reliance Fire & Accident Insurance Ltd*[26] for example, the insurer was presumed to know that an insured who ran a business selling groceries, provisions, newspapers, tobacco and confectionery would have fireworks on his premises during Guy Fawkes' season and was therefore not entitled to avoid the policy on grounds of non-disclosure of that fact.

[23]In fact, this provision was dropped from both the Australian *Insurance Contracts Act 1984* (Cth) and the now repealed Malaysian *Insurance Act 1996*, as well as from s4 (2) of the new *Financial Services Act 2013* (Malaysia).

[24]The Australian and Malaysian equivalent are s21 (2) (a) of the *Insurance Contracts Act 1984* (Cth) and s4 (2) (a) of the *Financial Services Act 2013* (Malaysia), respectively.

[25]The equivalent Australian and Malaysian provisions are s21 (2) (b) and (c) of the *Insurance Contracts Act 1984* (Cth) and s4 (2) (b) and (c) of the *Financial Services Act 2013* (Malaysia), respectively.

[26][1960] 2 Lloyd's Rep 391; See also: *Winter v Irish Life Assurance Plc* [1995] 2 Lloyd's Rep 274.

In the Malaysian cases of *Tan Kang Hua v Safety Insurance Co*[27] and *Pacific & Orient Insurance Co Sdn Bhd v Lim Sew Chong*,[28] the insurers were also held not to be entitled to avoid the insurance contracts on grounds of non-disclosure, as the evidence adduced in both cases indicated that the insurers were in fact aware of the facts alleged to have been concealed by the insured.[29]

Although a waiver of (material) information by the insurer also removes the insured's duty of disclosure pertaining thereto,[30] the English courts have required a clear and explicit waiver of information by the insurer. They have been slow to accept (if at all) an inference of waiver where for instance, the insurer accepts a proposal form which was incompletely answered by the insured.[31] Failure by the insurer to ask express questions to elicit information from the insured was also not generally construed as a waiver, unless perhaps the insured was placed in a genuine doubt as a result of it.[32] This position has however, been largely rectified by ss3 (5) and 5 of the *Insurance Act 2015* (UK).

The position of the insured in Australia and Malaysia has however, been more favourable. Section 21 (3) of the *Insurance Contracts Act 1984* (Cth) (Australia) and s150 (3) of the now repealed *Insurance Act 1996* (Malaysia), as well as the new ss5 (6) and 4 (3) of the *Financial Services Act 2013* (Malaysia) which apply to consumer and non-consumer insurance contracts respectively, essentially provide that the insurer is deemed to have waived compliance with the insured's duty of disclosure where the insured fails to answer or gives an incomplete or irrelevant answer to a question posed by the insurer in the proposal form.

3.2.3 The Prudent Insurer Test of Materiality

Although it is clear that in order to satisfy the pre-contractual duty of disclosure and misrepresentation, insureds need to disclose information within their knowledge which was material to the risk to be undertaken by the insurer, the 20th Century has

---

[27][1973] 1 MLJ 6.

[28][1985] 2 MLJ 60.

[29]In the former case, the Federal Court felt that the insurers were not influenced by the insured's incorrect answer in the proposal form that he had not made a claim in respect of his motor policy in the past two years, as the insurers went on to charge the insured the standard premium without any 'no claim bonus' rebate. In the latter, the court was of the view that the insurers in fact knew or at the very least, ought to have known that the motor policy was renewed on behalf of the deceased policyholder by his son, as the cover note described the insured as 'Ng Hwee Bin (Deceased)'.

[30]The equivalent Australian and Malaysian provisions are s21 (2) (d) of the *Insurance Contracts Act 1984* (Cth) and s4 (2) (d) of the *Financial Services Act 2013* (Malaysia), respectively.

[31]*Arterial Caravans Ltd v Yorkshire Insurance Co Ltd* [1973] 1 Lloyd's Rep 169; c/f *Roberts v Plaisted* [1989] 2 Lloyd's Rep 341.

[32]See: *Orakpo v Barclays Insurance Services Ltd* [1995] LRLR 443 where this was in fact not the case.

seen much debate on the question of materiality itself. The initial debate until 1975 was on whether a fact or circumstance was material if it influenced the judgment of a 'prudent insurer' or a 'reasonable insured' in warranting disclosure by the insured.

For the insured, it has always been argued that only information that a reasonable insured would consider as being material to the risk to be undertaken should be disclosed. Proponents of this view have relied heavily on Fletcher Moulton LJ's dicta in *Joel v Law Union and Crown Insurance Company.*[33] The justification for this being that imposing any test based on the insurers' need for information would be too great a burden on the insured, who would have no idea as to what an insurance company with a wealth of experience in the field would like to know.

On behalf of the insurers on the other hand, the contention has been that the insured should be under an obligation to disclose all information that would be material to a prudent insurer in deciding to undertake the risk or fix the premium. The protracted debate between the two opposing views was finally put to rest by the Court of Appeal in *Lambert v Co-operative Insurance Society Ltd*[34] where the 'prudent insurer' test was endorsed in determining the materiality of any information to be disclosed by the insured. In doing so, the Court of Appeal was influenced by the fact that stronger judicial authority existed for the said test, along with the fact that both s18 (2) (and for that matter s20 (2)) of the *Marine Insurance Act 1906* (UK) and s10 (5) of the *Road Traffic Act 1934* (UK) had also adopted the same.

As a result, the plaintiff who had taken out an 'All Risks' insurance policy to insure jewellery belonging to herself and her husband, was held not to be entitled to claim thereunder upon the loss of the jewellery. The grounds for so holding were that she had failed to disclose the fact that her husband had been fined £25 for receiving stolen cigarettes some years ago and was serving a fifteen month prison sentence for offences involving dishonesty, at the time the policy was renewed. The plaintiff's contention that she need only have disclosed information which a reasonable man would have considered material was rejected, along with her claim. This was despite their Lordships acknowledging that she had acted in good faith and her husband was in fact at the relevant time, still serving his prison sentence. MacKenna LJ in fact, went on to highlight the unsatisfactory state of the law and called upon the insurers to 'act decently' by paying the insured.[35] Lawton LJ went on to say that such injustices were for Parliament to deal with 'if they are to be got rid of at all'.[36]

It has therefore, been long settled law in the United Kingdom that the materiality of information to be disclosed by the insured in both marine and non-marine insurance contracts is to be viewed from the perspective of a prudent insurer undertaking the risk.

---

[33][1908] 2 KB 863, 884.

[34][1975] 2 Lloyd's Rep 485.

[35]Ibid. 491.

[36]Ibid. 492.

It is worth noting however, that the 'prudent insurer' test has been retained in the recent progressive reforms introduced in the United Kingdom with respect to non-consumer insurance contracts, via ss3 (4) (b) and 7 (3) of the *Insurance Act 2015* (UK). With respect to consumer insurance contracts on the other hand, it has been replaced by a 'reasonable consumer' test coupled with the insurer's awareness of 'any particular characteristics or circumstances of the actual consumer,' via ss3 (3) and 3 (4) of the *Consumer Insurance (Disclosure and Representations) Act 2012* (UK). Although the prudent insurer test has been retained for non-consumer insurance contracts, the obligation as a whole reflects a more balanced approach, as the duty of disclosure on proposers is now largely enquiry based in the United Kingdom. As a result, proposers are merely required to make a 'fair presentation' of the risk in non-consumer insurance contracts and refrain from making a misrepresentation in consumer insurance contracts. Nevertheless, it is worth taking stock of the criticisms and development of the law in this area, in order to better understand the aim and effect of the recent reforms.

3.2.4 Criticism of the Prudent Insurer Test of Materiality

It is worth considering the criticisms levelled against the 'prudent insurer' test over the years, although with hindsight, it appears purely academic in nature, in view of the major reforms undertaken in the United Kingdom in 2012 and 2015 in the area.

Robert Merkin[37] gave an excellent account of the unsatisfactory position of the law on non-disclosure and misrepresentation in insurance contracts, as a result of the Court of Appeal's decision in *Lambert v Co-operative Insurance Society Ltd.*[38] Simply put, the doctrine of disclosure as it was, together with the prudent insurer test, appeared to require insureds to possess 'clairvoyant powers to discover what a reasonable insurer would regard as material.'[39] In reality however, many insureds would not have even given a second thought to some of the matters that have in the past been held to be material to a prudent insurer, in justifying avoidance of the contract for non-disclosure.

For example, in *Horne v Poland*[40] the insured's national origin was held to be material even though he had lived in Britain for 22 years since the age of 12 and in *Locker and Woolf v Western Australian Insurance Co Ltd*[41] the previous refusals by insurers to grant a motor insurance policy were held to be material in an application for a fire insurance policy.

---

[37]Merkin (1976).

[38][1975] 2 Lloyd's Rep 485.

[39]Merkin, above n 37, 479.

[40][1922] 2 KB 364.

[41][1936] 1 KB 408.

Also, the irony of the matter was that the duty of disclosure (being a crucial part of the wider duty of utmost good faith) was often used against insureds whose conduct in the matter had in fact been acknowledged by the courts to have been in good faith. This was indeed the predicament Mrs. Lambert found herself in.[42]

This, coupled with the fact that whilst any question posed in the proposal form was deemed to be material, there was no corresponding presumption that matters not contained therein were immaterial,[43] which simply reinforced the unfortunate position of insureds whose claims were more often than not, doomed to fail. Furthermore, in annually renewable policies, the onus on the insured was to take stock of everything that had happened in the past year, by donning the eyes of a prudent insurer, to ensure that proper disclosure was made at every renewal.

Another issue was one of proof or evidence when applying the prudent insurer test, where the legal burden of proving non-disclosure or misrepresentation of material facts was on the party alleging it.[44] Unlike the 'reasonable insured' test which would have been fairly simple for the courts to apply, as it is essentially the application of a reasonable man's test that the courts have had vast experience in doing, especially in the law of tort; the prudent insurer test has had its challenges. As Merkin pointed out, 'no judge can pretend to be a prudent insurer'.[45] As such, the only way of ascertaining whether the undisclosed information was material to a prudent insurer was to allow insurance companies to tender evidence on their own behalf and the views of other insurers as evidence.

Where an undisclosed fact was so obviously material, it posed no problem to the court. It was when the materiality of a particular fact was less clear, that there was a fear of the courts relying too heavily (or even solely) on the evidence of the insurer concerned, as opposed to also calling independent witnesses to corroborate the same. This was in fact the case in *Abu Bakar v Oriental Fire and General Insurance Co Ltd.*[46]

As Nik Ramlah Mahmood observed, 'accepting the unsubstantiated evidence of an interested insurer makes a mockery of the prudent insurer test'.[47] It is fortunate therefore, that the judge in *Roselodge v Castle*[48] rejected the insurer's evidence that a man who had stolen apples at age 17 and then lived a saintly life for 50 years

---

[42]See: *Lambert v Co-operative Insurance Society Ltd* [1975] 2 Lloyd's Rep 485.

[43]See: May J in *March Cabaret Club & Casino Ltd v London Assurance Ltd* [1975] 1 Lloyd's Rep 169, 176. This was reiterated in the Malaysian case of *United Oriental Assurance Sdn Bhd v WM Mazzarol (The Melanie)* [1984] 1 MLJ 260, 262 (Salleh Abbas CJ).

[44]*Goh Chooi Leong v Public Life Assurance Co Ltd* [1964] MLJ 5.

[45]Merkin, above n 37, 480.

[46][1974] 1 MLJ 149, where the insurer's branch secretary's testimony at the Sessions Court (which was not substantiated by any independent witness) that knowledge of the presence of the four grinding mills in the insured's shop would have caused the insurer to charge a higher premium, was whole heartedly accepted right up to the Federal Court.

[47]Mahmood (1992, p. 58).

[48][1966] 2 Lloyd's Rep 112.

would be a big risk to insure against the theft of valuables. Also, as R C Evans pointed out in his article, there was a further problem of the courts being confused as to whether the expert testimony tendered on behalf of the insurer, in fact referred to the general practice within the industry or the practice of the particular insurer concerned.[49] It was therefore important that both the insurer concerned as well as independent insurers be called to give evidence on the issue of materiality.[50]

The bias of the prudent insurer test against the insured was compounded by the fact that in reality, insurance agents often dictated the questions in the proposal form to the proposer and filled in the answers, with the proposer merely signing the form thereafter. In such cases, it would be grossly unfair for non-disclosure or misrepresentation to be raised later by the insurer in order to avoid the policy. What was most disturbing is that until the recent reforms, English law supported this practice by holding an insurance agent in such circumstances to be the insured's agent, thereby preventing any adverse knowledge from being imputed onto the insurer.[51]

Merkin[52] was in fact critical of the judges' conservative attitude in addressing the said inequities that existed in the law, by merely expressing judicial regret.[53] He made a pertinent comparison with the progressive stance adopted by Sachs J in *Adams v Andrews*,[54] in ordering the Motor Insurance Bureau to pay an injured passenger and in fact asked to be informed if there was no payment made. This decision was despite the Motor Insurance Bureau's agreement in force with the Minister of Transport at the time, which did not make compensation payment obligatory. As a result, a revision of the agreement between the Motor Insurance Bureau and the Minister of Transport was made in 1969, allowing passengers to recover their losses for the first time.

Lastly, the courts' general rejection of the proposition that the 'prudent insurer' test found in marine insurance was not appropriate or necessarily applicable to non-marine insurance seemed to indicate a refusal to acknowledge commercial reality. Such a broad-brush endorsement of the application of the prudent insurer test to all areas of insurance law was apparent in the judgment of Whiteley JC of the

---

[49] Evans (1984, p. 14).

[50] Such was the case in *Teh Say Cheng v North British & Mercantile Insurance Co Ltd* (1921) 2 FMSLR 248. See also: *Godfrey v Brittanic Assurance Co Ltd* [1963] 2 Lloyd's Rep 515, 518 (Pape J).

[51] *Newsholme Bros v Road Transport and General Insurance* [1929] 2 KB 356. This has been the case in the United Kingdom, despite the Law Reform Committee (1957) having recommended that the position be changed, whereby an insurance agent negotiating a policy should be deemed to be the insurer's agent for the purposes of formation of the insurance contract, so that the agent's knowledge could be imputed to the insurer. An examination of the recent reforms in the United Kingdom and Malaysia and the position in Australia with respect to the role and effect of insurance intermediaries at the pre-contractual stage of insurance contracts will be made later in this chapter.

[52] Merkin, above n 37, 482.

[53] See: *Lambert v Co-operative Insurance Society Ltd* [1975] 2 Lloyd's Rep 485 (MacKenna and Lawton LJJ).

[54] [1964] 2 Lloyd's Rep 347.

Supreme Court in the Malaysian case of *Teh Say Cheng v North British and Mercantile Insurance Co Ltd*:

> Is there any good ground for holding that a rule which is obviously proper in marine insurance is too severe to apply in fire insurance? In my opinion there is not. The contract of fire insurance is as much a contract of *uberrimae fides* as is a contract of marine insurance. It follows that the duty to disclose material facts cannot be higher in the one form of insurance than in the other.[55]

On the contrary, there may well have been valid grounds for such a distinction being drawn between marine and non-marine insurance. This is because marine insurance contracts are generally entered into by shipping companies and other like businesses with sufficient knowledge or legal advice on insurance law. They have thus, been well equipped to be able to discharge their duty of disclosure by satisfying the prudent insurer's test of materiality.

Non-marine insurance policies on the other hand, are often taken out by laypersons having no knowledge of the existence of the duty of disclosure, let alone its standards. Therefore, the prudent insurer test has been too onerous a burden on such insureds. It is on this basis that the reasonable insured test of materiality has been felt by many to be more appropriate and equitable, whilst arriving at the same result of utmost good faith being achieved in both marine and non-marine insurance contracts.

3.2.5 The Inducement Element and Degree of Influence

The conclusion of the debate between the prudent insurer and reasonable insured tests in favour of the former in 1975 went on to witness a further debate on the intricacies of the prudent insurer test of materiality.[56] The case that sparked this off was *Container Transport International Inc v Oceanus Mutual Underwriting Association Ltd.*[57] *('CTI v Oceanus')*

The plaintiff company, which was in the business of hiring out containers for use in ocean transport, decided to insure against the risk of the containers being damaged during the hire. They were initially insured with Crum & Forster of the United States and then, by Lloyd's when Crum & Forster discontinued the insurance after realising that the plaintiffs had a high level of claims. Lloyd's later discontinued their policy for the same reasons and the plaintiff's brokers then obtained coverage from the defendants. The plaintiff's claims record with Lloyd's was presented to the defendants who in reliance upon the information granted insurance coverage to the plaintiff. The defendants then sought to avoid the policy

---

[55](1921) 2 FMSLR 248, 258.

[56]The Court of Appeal's decision in *Berger and Light Diffusers Pty Ltd v Pollock* [1973] 2 Lloyd's Rep 442 however, indicates some reference to such issues by the courts much earlier.

[57][1982] 2 Lloyd's Rep 178.

on grounds of non-disclosure and misrepresentation when the plaintiff made claims on the policy. The defendants contended that the plaintiff had failed to furnish them with a complete and accurate claims record.

The trial judge, Lloyd J, decided against the defendants based on the evidence tendered, holding that the defence of non-disclosure or misrepresentation can only be successfully pleaded if a prudent insurer *would not* have accepted the risk altogether or have charged a higher premium had it known of the facts in question and the particular insurer concerned would have also done the same.

In so holding, his Honour sought to examine the words of the now repealed s18 (2) (and s20 (2)) of the *Marine Insurance Act 1906* (UK) which defined a material circumstance as one which 'would influence the judgment of a prudent insurer in fixing the premium or determining whether he will take the risk'. In deciding what would amount to 'influencing the judgment of a prudent insurer' in that whether it is sufficient that the circumstance is one that the prudent insurer would wish to know of, as might have caused it to decline the risk or fix a higher premium or would the circumstance have in effect led to one of the two results, his Honour held in favour of the latter. In doing so, Lloyd J recognized that '...s18 is an extremely powerful weapon placed by the law in the hands of the insurer' and '...the least that should normally be expected of the underwriter is to show that a prudent insurer would have charged an increased rate'.[58]

With respect to ascertaining if the 'judgment' of the prudent insurer was influenced, his Honour went so far as to say that '[i]t can never be enough for the prudent insurer to say "[y]es, I would have liked to know this or that fact, so that I could have made up my mind what to do about it."'[59]

The Court of Appeal however, reversed the trial court's decision and rejected Lloyd J's construction of the insured's duty of disclosure under s18 (2) (and s20 (2)) of the *Marine Insurance Act 1906* (UK). The Court of Appeal held that in order for an insurer to avoid an insurance policy for non-disclosure (or misrepresentation), all that was needed to be shown was that the information not disclosed would be material to a prudent insurer, without also having to show that it had the same effect on the particular insurer concerned. Furthermore, in order for the insurer to prove that the said information would have influenced the judgment of a prudent insurer, it would only need to show that the information would merely have 'had an impact on the formation of his opinion and on his decision making process' and not necessarily affect his 'final decision'.[60]

The decision of the Court of Appeal was applied later in *Highlands Insurance Co v Continental Insurance Co*[61] which was a case involving a fire insurance

---

[58]Ibid. 187, 188.

[59]Ibid. 188.

[60]See: *CTI v Oceanus* [1984] 1 Lloyd's Rep 476, 491–492 (Kerr LJ) in delivering the judgment of the Court of Appeal. It is worth noting that Kerr LJ in his judgment had disassociated himself from his previous decision in *Berger and Light Diffusers Pty Ltd v Pollock* [1973] 2 Lloyd's Rep 442.

[61][1987] 1 Lloyd's Rep 109, 114.

policy, albeit in so doing, Steyn J expressed his misgivings about being bound by precedent to apply a marine insurance decision to a case involving non-marine insurance.

It is interesting to note however, that in the Australian case of *Barclay Holdings (Australia) Pty Ltd v British National Insurance Co Ltd*[62] also involving a fire insurance policy, Kirby P JA in delivering the judgment Court of Appeal, refused to follow the decision of the English Court of Appeal in *CTI v Oceanus*[63] and instead endorsed Samuel J's formulation offered in *Mayne Nickless Ltd v Pegler*[64] of the insured's common law obligation of disclosure.[65]

In an articulate examination of the two possible interpretations of Samuel J's test of 'reasonably affecting the mind of a prudent insurer,' Kirby P JA[66] opted for the more restrictive interpretation (over the broader one expounded by the Court of Appeal in *CTI v Oceanus*),[67] whereby the effect on the mind of the prudent insurer should be limited strictly, only to considerations which will ultimately determine whether the insurer will accept the risk and if so, at what premium and condition.

Subsequent to this, came the landmark case of *Pan Atlantic Insurance Co Ltd v Pine Top Insurance Co Ltd*[68] that presented the House of Lords with a long awaited opportunity to make an authoritative ruling on the issues raised above. The plaintiffs in the case, Pan Atlantic Insurance Company, had reinsured certain risks under their Casualty Account with the defendants. When a claim was made thereon, the defendants denied liability on grounds that the plaintiffs had failed to disclose certain additional losses sustained by them between 1980 and 1981. Whilst the documents containing the information relating to the plaintiffs' claims history were with the broker who arranged the re-insurance, they were not shown to the defendants. The decision of the trial court, that the information not disclosed was material (and therefore entitling the re-insurers to avoid the contract), was upheld by both the Court of Appeal and House of Lords.

In doing so, the Court of Appeal and House of Lords (albeit taking different routes) went on to consider the law applicable to non-disclosure and

---

[62][1987] 8 NSWLR 514.

[63][1984] 1 Lloyd's Rep 467; Ibid. 520, his Honour went so far as to comment on Kerr LJ's unfortunate disassociation in *CTI v Oceanus* [1984] 1 Lloyd's Rep 467 with his earlier judgment in *Berger and Light Diffusers Pty Ltd v Pollock* [1973] 2 Lloyd's Rep 442.

[64][1974] 1 NSWLR 228, 239.

[65]This was one of the last cases applying the common law duty of disclosure, as the position has since been governed by the *Insurance Contracts Act 1984* (Cth) that in essence views the question of materiality from the reasonable insured's perspective. Such has also been the case under the now repealed *Insurance Act 1996* with respect to Malaysia.

[66]*Barclay Holdings (Australia) Pty Ltd v British National Insurance Co Ltd* [1987] 8 NSWLR 514, 517–519.

[67][1984] 1 Lloyd's Rep 467.

[68][1994] 3 All ER 581.

misrepresentation in insurance contracts at the time, in the wake of the *CTI v Oceanus*[69] decision.

Before examining the much discussed House of Lords decision in *Pan Atlantic Insurance Co Ltd v Pine Top Insurance Co Ltd*,[70] it is worth noting the admirable attempt made by Steyn LJ (whilst delivering the judgment of the Court of Appeal) to ameliorate the harshness of the *CTI v Oceanus*[71] decision, within the confines of judicial precedent. His Lordship interpreted the *CTI v Oceanus*[72] decision as stating first, that there was no requirement for the particular insurer to have been induced by the non-disclosure and secondly, that it was not necessary for the non-disclosure to have had a decisive influence on the prudent insurer's decision to underwrite the risk or charge the premium.[73]

By interpreting the second limb of the *CTI v Oceanus*[74] decision in a negative manner, namely the rejection of the 'decisive influence' test (as opposed to the positive endorsement of the 'mere influence' test) Steyn LJ paved the way for the introduction of an alternative test. This test was more of a middle-ground of sorts that an undisclosed fact would be material if it would have 'increased the risk to the prudent underwriter' and not just be something he would have liked to have known.[75]

On appeal, by a bare majority of three to two, the House of Lords held first, that when an insurer was seeking to avoid an insurance contract on grounds of misrepresentation or non-disclosure of material facts by the insured, a requirement that the particular insurer was actually induced to enter into the contract as a result had to be implied into the contract. To this extent, the Court of Appeal's decision in *CTI v Oceanus*[76] was overruled in part as having been wrongly decided.

Secondly, once it had been shown that the particular insurer had been induced, all that was needed to be shown was that the undisclosed fact would have had an effect on the mind of a prudent insurer in weighing up the risk. This was an endorsement of the *CTI v Oceanus*'s[77] 'mere influence' approach, as opposed to the 'decisive influence' and 'increased risk' options. In doing so, Lord Goff tried to draw a link between the introduction of the 'actual inducement' requirement and the purportedly corresponding lack of necessity for the 'decisive influence' approach.[78]

---

69 [1984] 1 Lloyd's Rep 476.

70 [1994] 3 All ER 581.

71 [1984] 1 Lloyd's Rep 476.

72 Ibid.

73 *Pan Atlantic Insurance Co Ltd v Pine Top Insurance Co Ltd* [1993] 1 Lloyd's Rep 496, 503–505.

74 [1984] 1 Lloyd's Rep 476.

75 *Pan Atlantic Insurance Co Ltd v Pine Top Insurance Co Ltd* [1993] 1 Lloyd's Rep 496, 503–505.

76 [1984] 1 Lloyd's Rep 476.

77 Ibid.

78 *Pan Atlantic Insurance Co Ltd v Pine Top Insurance Co Ltd* [1994] 3 All ER 581, 588.

Lord Mustill (in delivering the judgment of the House) after spelling out the requirement for a prudent insurer as well as the particular insurer to have been induced by the non-disclosure or misrepresentation, however, went on to introduce a presumption of inducement in favour of the particular insurer, once the former was proved.[79]

It is unfortunate however, that Lord Mustill who had deemed it fit to do justice by making new law in implying the element of inducement into ss18 (2) and 20 (2), nevertheless, in the same breath introduced the concept of a presumption of such inducement once materiality was established with respect to the prudent insurer.[80]

In contrast, the strong dissenting judgment of Lord Lloyd (with whom Lord Templeman concurred) appears to be far more compelling.[81] In an impressive analysis of the same cases that Lord Mustill had also examined in his judgment,[82] and an examination of the crucial phrase in s18 (2) (and s20 (2)) of the *Marine Insurance Act 1906* (UK) word for word, his Lordship emphatically rejected the 'mere influence' test in favour of the 'decisive influence' alternative.[83] That is to say that a fact would only be material, if a prudent insurer had it known of the undisclosed fact, would have either declined the risk altogether or charged an increased premium.

Lord Lloyd in fact went on to lay down the sequence in which the tests of materiality and influence should in his view, be applied:

> Whenever an insurer seeks to avoid a contract of insurance or re-insurance on the ground of misrepresentation or non-disclosure, there will be two separate but closely related questions. (1) Did the misrepresentation or non-disclosure induce the actual insurer to enter into the contract on those terms? (2) Would the prudent insurer have entered into the contract on the same terms if he had known of the misrepresentation or non-disclosure immediately before the contract was concluded? If both questions are answered in favour of the insurer, he will be entitled to avoid the contract, but not otherwise.
>
> The evidence of the insurer himself will normally be required to satisfy the court on the first question. The evidence of an independent broker or underwriter will normally be required to satisfy the court on the second question. This produces a uniform and workable solution,

---

[79]Ibid. 617–619.

[80]Not to forget, materiality in turn only required the test of 'mere influence' to be satisfied. It should be noted that Lord Lloyd in the same case strongly disagreed with the imposition of such a presumption (at 637) and has been consistent in holding this view. See: His Lordship's decisions at the High Court in *CTI v Oceanus* [1982] 2 Lloyd's Rep 178; *Commonwealth Insurance Co of Vancouver v Group Sprinks SA* [1983] 1 Lloyd's Rep 67; and *Pan Atlantic Insurance Co Ltd v Pine Top Insurance Co Ltd* [1994] 3 All ER 581.

[81]It should be noted that the House was split on the law but was unanimous in dismissing the appeal on the facts.

[82]*Carter v Boehm* (1766) 3 Burr 1905; *Ionides v Pender* (1874) QB 531; *Stribley v Imperial Marine Insurance Co* (1876) 1 QBD 507; *Rivas v Gerussi Bros & Co* (1880) 6 QBD 222; *Tate & Sons v Hyslop* (1885) 15 QBD 368; *Mutual Life Insurance Co of New York v Ontario Metal Products Co Ltd* [1925] AC 344; *Zurich General Accident and Liability Insurance Co Ltd v Morrison* [1942] 2 KB 53; *Barclay Holdings (Australia) Pty Ltd v British National Insurance Co Ltd* (1987) 8 NSWLR 514.

[83]*Pan Atlantic Insurance Co Ltd v Pine Top Insurance Co Ltd* [1994] 3 All ER 581, 625–626.

> which has the further advantage, as I see it, of according with good commercial common sense. It follows that the *CTI* case was wrongly decided, and should be overruled.[84]

It was unfortunate however, that the above was not a pronouncement of the law applicable in the United Kingdom for a long time, for the Court of Appeal's decision in *CTI v Oceanus*[85] had only been overruled in part and stood with respect to the application of the 'mere influence' test of establishing materiality. Such was the endorsement given to the House of Lord's decision in *Pan Atlantic Insurance Co Ltd v Pine Top Insurance Co Ltd*,[86] by the Court of Appeal in *St Paul Fire & Marine Insurance Co (UK) Ltd v McConnell Dowell Constructors Ltd*,[87] where in fact, Lord Mustill's 'presumption of inducement' was followed by Evans LJ in delivering the judgment of the court.[88]

In addition, the Court of Appeal also held that it was sufficient if the undisclosed information formed 'an inducement' to the particular insurer and not necessarily 'the inducement.' Therefore, adding yet another feather in the insurers' caps with respect to discharging their burden of proof. To make matters worse, in the subsequent cases of *Aneco Reinsurance Underwriting Ltd v Johnson & Higgins*[89] and *Insurance Corporation of Channel Islands v Royal Hotel Ltd*,[90] even insurers who failed to give evidence benefited from such a presumption of inducement.

In fact, there were not many cases in which a more dynamic approach was taken on the matter. One such decision however, was by Longmore J in *Marc Rich & Co AG v Portman*[91] where his Honour held that the presumption of inducement could only operate where the particular underwriter concerned, was unable for very good reason, to tender evidence.

3.2.6 Criticism of the CTI and Pan Atlantic Decisions

There have been numerous criticisms levelled at the primary decisions which shaped the development of the prudent insurer and inducement tests affecting materiality with respect to pre-contractual disclosure and misrepresentation. It is important to take stock of this in order to appreciate the current development in the

---

[84]Ibid. 638.

[85][1984] 1 Lloyd's Rep 476.

[86][1994] 3 All ER 581.

[87][1995] 2 Lloyd's Rep 116.

[88]Ibid. 122 and 127.

[89][1998] 1 Lloyd's Rep 565.

[90][1998] 1 Lloyd's Rep IR 151.

[91][1996] 1 Lloyd's Rep 430, 442. The decision was later upheld by the Court of Appeal but without fully considering the point. It should be noted that Long more J has been consistent in subscribing to this view, as can be seen in *Sirius International Insurance Corp v Oriental Insurance Corp* [1999] Lloyd's Rep IR 343, 354 (a case involving misrepresentation).

law brought about by the *Consumer Insurance (Disclosure and Representation) Act 2012* (UK) and the *Insurance Act 2015* (UK).

In this context, the most criticised would have to be the Court of Appeal's decision in *CTI v Oceanus*,[92] which has been berated as one which is 'contrary to precedent and principle'.[93] Henry Brooke in his article[94] criticised the Court of Appeal's decision in *CTI v Oceanus*[95] in favour of the trial judge, Lloyd J's decision as one that is 'not soundly founded on authority nor on principle', 'capable of creating considerable practical difficulties' and tipping 'the balance unwarrantably in favour of insurers' in difficult cases where insurers are anxious to avoid their contractual liabilities.[96]

In doing so, he made an impressive examination of the historical development of the common law in the area, by dividing it into four parts. First, he set out the development of the rules governing non-disclosure in the years leading up to the enunciation of the 'prudent insurer' test in *Ionides v Pender.*[97] Secondly, the years leading up to the codification of the common law into the *Marine Insurance Act 1906* (UK). Then, the cases decided since 1906 both in the United Kingdom and other Commonwealth jurisdictions; and finally, a comparative look at the American position.

He argued that the Privy Council's decision in the Canadian case of *Mutual Life Insurance Co of New York v Ontario Metal Products Co Ltd*[98] and Lord Greene MR's judgment in *Zurich General Accident and Liability Insurance Co Ltd v Morrison*[99] reflected the correct proposition of English law, in favour of the 'decisive influence' test of materiality, although the Court of Appeal in *CTI v Oceanus*[100] had somewhat simplistically dismissed the same as being peculiar to the statutory position in Ontario.

In addition, Brooke pointed out[101] that the American authorities (none of which were cited by the Court of Appeal in *CTI v Oceanus*)[102] also held sway to the 'decisive influence' test of materiality, citing the judgments of Taft J in *Penn Mutual Life Insurance Co v Mechanics Savings Bank and Trust Co*[103] and Hand J in *Btesh v Royal Insurance Co Ltd of Liverpool.*[104]

---

[92][1984] 1 Lloyd's Rep 476.

[93]Clarke (1988, p. 298).

[94]Brooke (1985) (written before *Pan Atlantic Insurance Co Ltd v Pine Top Insurance Co Ltd* [1994] 3 All ER 581 came about).

[95][1984] 1 Lloyd's Rep 476.

[96]Brooke, above n 94, 438 and 452.

[97](1874) QB 531.

[98][1925] AC 344.

[99][1942] 2 KB 53.

[100][1984] 1 Lloyd's Rep 476.

[101]Brooke, above n 94, 451–452.

[102][1984] 1 Lloyd's Rep 476.

[103]72 F 413 (1896).

[104]49 F 2d 720 (1931).

A similar array of cases were also analysed by Clarke in his critique of the Court of Appeal's decision in *CTI v Oceanus*,[105] where he exposed how the decision in favour of the 'mere influence' test fell short on grounds of precedent, principle, policy and practicality.[106] Some of his salient reasons for saying so are that given the objective nature of the materiality test, it is not apparent why it would be easier and more practical to say that an undisclosed fact had 'some influence' on a prudent insurer than to say that it had a 'decisive influence'.[107] Such a test would inevitably cause total disclosure by insureds wanting to play it safe; and the *CTI v Oceanus*[108] decision ignored the basic nature of misrepresentation and non-disclosure as factors which would vitiate the insurer's consent. This would clearly not be the case if the prudent insurer would have issued the same policy on the same terms notwithstanding the non-disclosure or misrepresentation in question.

Further, in the last days of the applicability of the common law on materiality in Australia,[109] the New South Wales Court of Appeal in the case of *Barclay Holdings (Australia) Pty Ltd v British National Insurance Co Ltd*,[110] made a bold stand in rejecting and departing from the *CTI v Oceanus*[111] decision. In doing so, the court unanimously decided in favour of the 'decisive influence' test of materiality. In an interesting article analysing the case,[112] the author elucidated Glass JA's view[113] in departing from the *CTI v Oceanus*[114] decision, as being essentially one of timing. The 'mere influence or impact' approach taken by Kerr LJ in *CTI v Oceanus*[115] implies that the materiality of information is ascertained at the point when the insurer undertakes investigations of the risk to be insured, whereas in *Barclay Holdings (Australia) Pty Ltd v British National Insurance Co Ltd*,[116] the Court of Appeal felt that the assessment of materiality is only done at the point when the insurer was deciding whether or not to take the risk.

The issue of timing is of practical importance, as an insurer goes through 'the initial investigative stage' (where practically all facts isolated or otherwise, even including matters of general interest, would have been taken into account by the prudent insurer), to 'the sifting and arranging stages' (of discarding unimportant matters and arranging the seemingly important information in order of relevance),

---

105 [1984] 1 Lloyd's Rep 476.

106 Clarke, above n 93, 298.

107 Ibid. 304.

108 [1984] 1 Lloyd's Rep 476.

109 Just before the *Insurance Contracts Act 1984* (Cth) (Australia) came into effect on the 1st of January 1986.

110 (1987) 8 NSWLR 514.

111 [1984] 1 Lloyd's Rep 476.

112 Ying (1990).

113 The decision of the court in the case was unanimous.

114 [1984] 1 Lloyd's Rep 476.

115 Ibid.

116 (1987) 8 NSWLR 514.

and then onto ‘the critical decision-making stage’ (where only those material facts and all the circumstances in its full matrix would be taken into account by the said insurer).[117]

The Court of Appeal in *CTI v Oceanus*[118] however, seemed to have failed to appreciate this rather complex decision making process by holding that any information which a prudent insurer would have liked to know would be material. This would make virtually every piece of information about the insured’s past, even that forming part of the insurer’s wide initial investigations, material. Surely, there must be merit in holding otherwise, that only information important to the insurer’s critical decision making stage should be material.

Yeo Hwee Ying also criticised the Court of Appeal’s failure to appreciate this as exposing its decision’s ‘own weakness of encompassing too disastrously wide a spectrum of information and ignoring the complexities involved in the reasoning stages of the decision making process’.[119]

Much criticism has also been levelled at the House of Lord’s decision in *Pan Atlantic Insurance Co Ltd v Pine Top Insurance Co Ltd*[120] and the Court of Appeal’s decision subsequent thereto in *St Paul Fire & Marine Insurance Co (UK) Ltd v McConnell Dowell Constructors Ltd.*[121]

The House of Lord’s decision in *Pan Atlantic Insurance Co Ltd v Pine Top Insurance Co Ltd*[122] has been criticised for its dismissal of the ‘decisive influence’ test of materiality in favour of the less fair ‘mere influence’ test; the unfortunate need to introduce the ‘inducement’ element in an attempt to do justice after having rejected the golden opportunity to endorse the ‘decisive influence’ test[123]; and the suggestion of a presumption of inducement existing in favour of the insurer once the objective test of materiality was satisfied.[124]

The House of Lord’s decision in *Pan Atlantic Insurance Co Ltd v Pine Top Insurance Co Ltd*[125] therefore, did further damage to the already unsatisfactory state

---

[117]Ying, above n 112, 103.

[118][1984] 1 Lloyd’s Rep 476.

[119]Ying, above n 112, 106.

[120][1994] 3 All ER 581.

[121][1995] 2 Lloyd’s Rep 116.

[122][1994] 3 All ER 581.

[123]Birds and Hird (1996, p. 288) eloquently question the need for a ‘convoluted’ introduction of the ‘actual inducement’ element by the House of Lords, when neither the *Marine Insurance Act 1906* (UK) nor the previous authorities make any mention of it, as well as the inherent differences between non-disclosure and misrepresentation; Hird (1995a, b) goes on to state that there would not have been a need for such artificial striving had the House of Lords rejected the mere influence test to begin with.

[124]Lord Mustill alluded to such a presumption twice in his judgment in *Pan Atlantic Insurance Co Ltd v Pine Top Insurance Co Ltd* [1994] 3 All ER 581, 610, 617. This was later endorsed by the Court of Appeal in *St Paul Fire & Marine Insurance Co (UK) Ltd v McConnell Dowell Constructors Ltd* [1995] 2 Lloyd’s Rep 116.

[125][1994] 3 All ER 581.

of the law on non-disclosure and misrepresentation after *CTI v Oceanus.*[126] The reason being, as a result of the majority of the House categorically rejecting the 'decisive influence' test and endorsing the 'mere influence' test, it had removed any room for the possible application of the 'increased risk' test introduced by Steyn LJ at the Court of Appeal. Also, by introducing the purportedly insured friendly 'actual inducement' element to the equation,[127] the House had left open yet another uncertainty, in that whether the material fact not disclosed to the insurer should be 'the' inducement to enter into the particular insurance contract or only 'an' inducement to the effect.

Although the words used by the House of Lords seem to indicate the former, when the issue came up before the Court of Appeal in *St Paul Fire & Marine Insurance Co (UK) Ltd v McConnell Dowell Constructors Ltd,*[128] 'exactly the opposite was decided'. This therefore, resulted in the position being 'even more prejudiced in favour of the insurer',[129] warranting the description of 'giving the insurer a blank cheque, for with it he can claim any harmless fact not disclosed by the insured to be material and hence seek to avoid the policy'.[130] This was precisely the case in *Whitlam v Hazel*[131] where the insurer was held to be entitled to the grossly disproportionate remedy of avoidance in response to the insured having given an incomplete and hence, misleading answer in the proposal form, albeit entirely innocently.

However, there were signs of discontentment on the part of the English courts with respect to the then state of the law, where there were attempts made to stretch the law so as to accommodate insureds' interests.

One such case was *Drake Insurance plc v Provident Insurance plc*[132] where the insurer avoided a motor vehicle policy on grounds of non-disclosure of a speeding conviction by the insured, when renewing the policy. At the renewal however, the insured had also failed to disclose another fact that was in his favour, namely that a previous accident which was initially recorded as being the insured's fault had since been resolved as being the third party's instead. Had this been disclosed to the insurer it would under the insurer's regimented underwriting system, have exactly offset the speeding conviction, resulting in the insurer renewing the policy on the same terms despite the non-disclosure. It was therefore, held by a majority of the Court of Appeal that the insurer had not on a balance of probability proved that they had been induced by the non-disclosure. The court in fact, unanimously went on to

[126][1984] 1 Lloyd's Rep 476.

[127]It is however, difficult to appreciate how it may be so in light of the 'presumption of inducement' that was introduced.

[128][1995] 2 Lloyd's Rep 116.

[129]Hird (1995a, b, pp. 612–613).

[130]Ying, above n 112, 102.

[131][2004] EWCA Civ 1600.

[132][2004] QB 601.

say (albeit obiter) that an insurer's right to avoid for non-disclosure was subject to an overriding duty of good faith.[133]

3.2.7 Types of Information Requiring Disclosure

Having established that the test of materiality is one of law which in the United Kingdom has been ascertained by applying the prudent insurer's test, its application to each case however, is a question of fact. Although each case would differ on its facts, material facts have generally been classified as those relating to physical and moral hazards.

The difference between the two was explained by Whiteley JC of the Malaysian Supreme Court in *Teh Say Cheng v North British and Mercantile Insurance Co Ltd*[134] which was a case involving a fire policy as '[m]oral hazard is chiefly a man's standing and general reputation. The word 'hazard' I use as equivalent to the 'risk of fire'. The physical hazard is determined by the condition of the building and the nature of the stock'.[135]

Merkin describes physical hazards as including factors that concern the likelihood or degree of loss, with matters such as physical condition of the insured subject matter, geographical environment and use, falling within this heading.[136]

One such material factor that insurers have often required disclosure of would be the insured's claim history, provided it has a bearing on the present risk to be insured.[137] The insured's claim history would be relevant where it goes to show that the insured is a careless person, thus, constituting a bad risk, as he is more likely to make future claims or that the insured is a moral hazard, especially where previous claims were not genuine. In *Becker v Marshall*,[138] the defendant insurers were held to be entitled to avoid the insurance contract and deny liability against the insured of a burglary policy. This was on the basis that the insured had denied having sustained a loss in the past, in response to a question in the proposal form, when in fact the insured had suffered three burglaries within 10 years of the current claim, thereby constituting both a physical and moral hazard.

It is clear that when a prior claim was made on the same subject matter as the present policy applied for it should be treated as material.[139] That which is not as clear is when the previous loss or claim concerned another type of insurance. On such an issue, MacKinnon J in *Ewer v National Employers Mutual General*

[133]This view is also shared by various commentators, like Eggers (2003), Clarke (2003).

[134](1921) 2 FMSLR 248.

[135]Ibid. 260.

[136]See: Merkin, above n 11.

[137]*Lyons v JW Bentley Ltd* (1944) 77 Ll L Rep 335.

[138](1922) 12 Ll L Rep 413.

[139]*Marc Rich & Co AG v Portman* [1996] 1 Lloyd's Rep 430.

Assurance Ltd[140] rejected the insurer's contention that the proposer was under a duty to disclose his entire claim history covering all types of insurance, including those not of the same type as the policy in question.

It would therefore appear that the materiality of the insured's prior claim history is qualified by the nature of the losses previously suffered and the lapse of time between them and the present claim.[141]

Moral hazards in turn are broadly speaking, facts that throw doubt on the integrity of the proposer, thus making the proposer a bad risk to underwrite. Facts which amount to a moral hazard and therefore, require disclosure can generally be classified into those relating to the proposer's insurance history (or previous refusals) and criminal convictions.[142] The moral hazard comprising the proposer's insurance history concerns previous refusals by other insurers to undertake similar risks[143] or previous cancellations of policies by insurers.[144]

In order for the insured to be considered a bad risk to prospective insurers, the previous refusal would normally have to be of a type similar to the one currently at hand, as the refusal would have a direct bearing on the risk currently insured or being insured.[145] In support of this, it has been contended that previous refusals should only be disclosed if they reflect upon the integrity or *bona fides* of the proposer and not otherwise.[146] The New South Wales Court of Appeal's decision in *Barclay Holdings (Australia) Pty Ltd v British National Insurance Co Ltd*[147] bears out this argument, where the court rightly considered a previous refusal to renew the insured's policy for purely administrative reasons, without any suggestion of bad faith, to be immaterial.

---

[140][1937] 2 All ER 193. His Honour however, failed to go further and provide some guidelines on the extent of the duty.

[141]See: *Becker v Marshall* (1922) 12 Ll L Rep 413; Goh *Chooi Leong v Public Life Assurance Co Ltd* [1964] MLJ 5; *Toh Kim Lian & Anor v Asia Insurance Co Ltd* [1996] 1 MLJ 149.

[142]Following the coming into force of the *Race Relations Act 1976* in the United Kingdom however, issues of race, religion, nationality and origin are immaterial factors, on grounds of public policy.

[143]*Glicksman v Lancashire & General Assurance Co Ltd* [1927] AC 139. This however, is only peculiar to non-marine insurance contracts and is irrelevant to marine insurance: *Glasgow Assurance Corporation v William Symondson & Co* (1911) 16 Com Cas 109, 119 (Scrutton J).

[144]*National Insurance Co Ltd v S Joseph* [1973] 2 MLJ 195.

[145]*Glicksman v Lancashire & General Assurance Co Ltd* [1927] AC 139 where the House of Lords decided that the insured who ran a small business as a ladies' tailor and had applied for a burglary policy to insure his stock-in-trade, was duty bound to disclose to the insurer that he had been previously refused a burglary policy by another insurance company. Their Lordships held that the insured's duty to disclose this information was in addition to his duty to provide truthful answers to questions posed in the proposal form. In fact, the insurer in this case had posed a question in the proposal form that was made the 'basis of contract', asking the insured as to whether any company had declined to accept or refused to renew the insured's burglary policy, to which the insured failed to give a truthful response.

[146]Legh-Jones et al. (2003, p. 438).

[147](1987) 8 NSWLR 514.

As to claims by insurers of previous non-disclosure or misrepresentation of material facts by the insured, Lloyd J in *CTI v Oceanus*,[148] rejected such contentions as in themselves amounting to material facts by virtue of constituting a moral hazard. His Honour based his decision on the argument that a breach of the duty of utmost good faith can be committed innocently and should not therefore, automatically be regarded as affecting the insured's integrity.[149]

In addition, the lapse of a reasonable amount of time between the previous refusal and the present application should also be taken into account in determining the materiality of the refusal. In *Ewer v National Employers' Mutual General Insurance Association Ltd*[150] for instance, a refusal that took place 18 years prior to the present application for insurance was held to be no longer material for disclosure.

Apart from this, the insured's previous criminal convictions would necessitate disclosure if they had a direct bearing on the present risk to be insured[151] or concerned one of general dishonesty or cheating (if it is serious),[152] as they may well indicate that the insured is a bad risk or lacks moral integrity.

By the same token therefore, if the previous convictions do not involve general dishonesty that is serious, especially where the previous convictions have no bearing on the present policy, the courts have found against disclosure.[153]

In this regard, Merkin puts forward an interesting and thought provoking argument against criminal convictions being regarded as material facts in the first place.[154] According to him, previous convictions at best raise a presumption of further dishonesty but that fraud if suspected, should be pleaded and proved in court and not inferred from previous conduct through innovative 'anti fraud' devices like

---

[148][1982] 2 Lloyd's Rep 178.

[149]It therefore, follows that prior dishonest conduct or fraud by an insured would constitute a moral hazard and would have to be disclosed to the prospective insurer: *Insurance Corporation of Channel Islands v Royal Hotel Ltd* [1998] Lloyd's Rep IR 151.

[150][1937] 2 All ER 193.

[151]For instance, a conviction for diamond smuggling (but not for bribing a police officer 20 years ago) was held to be material to a policy on diamonds in *Roselodge v Castle* [1966] 2 Lloyd's Rep 112; and a conviction for receiving stolen furs was held to be material to a policy on furs in *Regina Fur v Bossom* [1958] 2 Lloyd's Rep 425. It is however, not easy to see how the Court of Appeal in *Lambert v Co-operative Insurance Society Ltd* [1975] 2 Lloyd's Rep 485 found Mr. Lambert's first conviction and fine of £25 for receiving 1730 stolen cigarettes, which took place more than 10 years before the policy, to be a material fact, despite the fact that the insurers had in evidence admitted that an all risks policy would have been issued even if the said conviction was disclosed.

[152]*Schoolman v Hall* [1951] 1 Lloyd's Rep 139 where the insured's previous convictions for a series of offences ranging over 10 years, were held to be material to a burglary policy.

[153]This was the case in *Roselodge v Castle* [1966] 2 Lloyd's Rep 112, 132 where McNair J held the undisclosed fact that the insured company's principal director had been convicted 20 years ago for bribing a police officer, to be immaterial as it had 'no direct relation to trading as a diamond merchant'. Likewise, in *Reynolds v Phoenix Assurance Co Ltd* [1978] 2 Lloyd's Rep 440 the insured's failure to disclose a previous conviction involving a fine for receiving some stolen goods 11 years before was held to be immaterial when taking out a fire policy.

[154]Merkin, above n 37, 481.

non-disclosure and breach of warranty. However, the mischief caused by the need to disclose previous convictions, has today, been somewhat reduced by the industry's practice of posing in proposal forms, specific questions concerning previous convictions which have occurred within a stipulated time frame.

The crucial question is therefore, whether the existence of either hazard would generally increase the chance of a claim being made by the insured under the policy, thereby influencing the insurer's decision on whether to accept the risk and if so, at what premium and conditions. This analysis on the application of the pre-contractual duty of disclosure and misrepresentation with respect to physical and moral hazards is also broadly reflective of the position in Malaysia and Australia.

3.2.8 Law Reform in the United Kingdom

The unsatisfactory state of the law on materiality in the United Kingdom was subject to a major review by the English and Scottish Law Commissions which commenced in 2006 and resulted in the reforms introduced through the *Consumer Insurance (Disclosure and Representations) Act 2012* (UK) for consumer insurance contracts and the *Insurance Act 2015* (UK) for (primarily, but not exclusively) non-consumer insurance contracts.

Section 2 (2) of the *Consumer Insurance (Disclosure and Representations) Act 2012* (UK) abolishes the common law's wide voluntary duty of disclosure, by replacing it instead with a duty 'to take reasonable care not to make a misrepresentation to the insurer'.[155] Whether the consumer has in fact taken reasonable care, is determined in 'light of all the relevant circumstances.'[156] The standard of care expected of consumers in this regard is that of a 'reasonable consumer', thereby, removing the prudent insurer element of materiality from consumer insurance contracts completely. Furthermore, the reasonable consumer standard is made subject to the balanced provisions in ss3 (4) and (5) whereby, particular characteristics or circumstances of the actual consumer that the insurer was or ought to have been aware of must be taken into account; and misrepresentations made dishonestly by consumers would always tantamount to a breach of reasonable care.

Section 4 (1) goes on to provide that an insurer only has a remedy against a consumer for a 'qualifying misrepresentation' (which can either be deliberate/

---

[155]Section 2 (4) of the *Consumer Insurance (Disclosure and Representations) Act 2012* (UK) explicitly abolishes this.

[156]Section 3 (1) of the *Consumer Insurance (Disclosure and Representations) Act 2012* (UK). The relevant circumstances to be taken into account would include the non-exhaustive list of matters set out in s3 (2), like the type of consumer insurance contract, its target market, any explanatory or publicity material produced by the insurer, the clarity, specifics and importance (as communicated to the insured) of the insurer's questions posed and the presence (if any) of an agent acting on the insured's behalf.

reckless or careless as defined in ss5 (2) and (3)) made before a contract is entered into or varied if the *insurer can show* that it 'would not have entered into the contract or agreed to the variation at all or would have done so only on different terms.' This therefore, gives statutory recognition to the 'decisive influence' test of materiality proposed by Lord Lloyd in *Pan Atlantic Insurance Co Ltd v Pine Top Insurance Co Ltd.*[157] over that of the much criticized 'mere influence test.'

Section 5 (2) defines a qualifying misrepresentation as deliberate or reckless if the consumer either knew or did not care whether the representation was untrue or misleading ***and*** knew or did not care whether it was a matter that was relevant to the insurer, with the burden of proving the same being placed on the insurer.[158] This is however, again balanced by a presumption in s5 (5) that the consumer possesses the knowledge of a reasonable consumer and that the consumer knew that a matter about which the insurer asked a clear specific question was relevant to the insurer. In the event of a deliberate or reckless misrepresentation by the consumer, Paragraph 2 of *Schedule 1* to the Act entitles the insurer to avoid the contract, refuse all claims and retain the premiums paid, except to the extent that it would be unfair to the consumer for it to retain them.

A qualifying misrepresentation that is not deliberate or reckless is in turn defined as a careless misrepresentation in s5 (3) that warrants a remedy set out in Paragraphs 5–8 of *Schedule 1* to the Act. If the insurer would not have entered into the contract on any terms but for the careless misrepresentation, the insurer may avoid the contract and refund the premiums paid; if the insurer would have entered into the contract but on different terms (not relating to the premium), the contract is treated as being entered on those terms; and if the insurer would have entered into the contract but with a higher premium charged, the insurer may proportionately reduce the amount to be paid on a claim arising there under, as calculated based on Paragraph 8.

As for non-consumer insurance contracts on the other hand, s3 (1) of the *Insurance Act 2015* (UK) requires the insured to make a 'fair presentation' of the risk to the insurer before an insurance contract is entered into, in place of the previously wide pre-contractual duty of disclosure and representation of material facts found in ss18 and 20 of the *Marine Insurance Act 1906* (UK). This was in part supported by the approach taken by judges in modern cases, as evidenced by Clarke J's dictum in *Garnat Trading & Shipping (Singapore) Pte Ltd v Baominh Insurance Corporation.*[159]

This package of provisions has been described as being both 'evolutionary' with respect to the mechanics of the insured's duty of fair presentation; and 'more radical' as to the regime of proportionate remedies introduced in place of the sole remedy of avoidance[160] and has received overwhelming support from insurers,

[157] [1994] 3 All ER 581, 625–626.

[158] Section 5 (4) of the *Consumer Insurance (Disclosure and Representations) Act 2012* (UK).

[159] [2011] 1 Lloyd's Rep. 589.

[160] Hertzell and Burgoyne (2013, p. 108).

academics and the public as being sensible in striking a right balance between insurers and insureds.[161]

What amounts to a fair presentation of the risk, both in substance and form,[162] is clearly set out in ss3 (3) and (4) of the *Insurance Act 2015* (UK). A fair presentation of the risk requires disclosure of material circumstances which the insured knows or ought to know[163] (as reasonably revealed by a reasonable search of information available to the insured[164]; as well as matters which the insured suspected and would have had knowledge of but for deliberately refraining from confirming or enquiring about them)[165] **or** failing which, disclosure which gives the insurer sufficient information to put a 'prudent insurer' on notice that *it needs* to make further enquiries to reveal those material circumstances.[166] In this regard, ss4 (3) and (8) of the Act address a practical issue with respect to corporate entities by providing that insureds who are not individuals know only what is known to one or more of the individuals 'who are part of the insured's senior management or responsible for the insured's insurance'.

Section 7 (3) goes on to provide that a circumstance or representation would be material if it would influence the judgment of a 'prudent insurer' in determining whether to take the risk and on what terms, with s7 (4) providing some useful examples of what would amount to a material circumstance.[167] Section 7 (5) clarifies that a material representation is substantially correct if a 'prudent insurer' would not consider the difference between what is represented and what is actually correct to be material.

Sections 8 (1) and (3) go on to provide that an insurer only has a remedy against the insured for a breach of the duty of fair presentation if it amounts to a 'qualifying breach' (which can either be deliberate/reckless or neither deliberate/reckless as defined in ss8 (4) and (5)). The *insurer* would have to show however, that but for the breach it 'would not have entered into the contract at all or would have done so only on different terms.' This again, gives statutory recognition to the 'decisive influence' test of materiality proposed by Lord Lloyd in *Pan Atlantic Insurance Co Ltd v Pine Top Insurance Co Ltd*[168]

Section 8 (5) defines a qualifying breach as deliberate or reckless if the insured either knew that it was in breach of the duty of fair presentation or did not care

---

[161]Ibid. 109.

[162]The insured must make disclosure in a manner that would be reasonably clear and accessible to a prudent insurer: s3 (3) (b) of the *Insurance Act 2015* (UK).

[163]Section 3 (4) (a) of the *Insurance Act 2015* (UK).

[164]Section 4 (6) of the *Insurance Act 2015* (UK).

[165]Section 6 (1) of the *Insurance Act 2015* (UK).

[166]Section 3 (4) (b) of the *Insurance Act 2015* (UK).

[167]These would include (a) special or unusual facts relating to the risk; (b) any particular concerns that led the insured to seek insurance cover for the risk; and (c) anything which those concerned with the class or field of insurance or activity in question would generally require a fair presentation of risks.

[168][1994] 3 All ER 581, 625–26.

whether or not it was in breach of that duty, with the burden of proving the same being placed on the insurer.[169] In the event of an insured's qualifying breach that is deliberate or reckless, Paragraph 2 of *Schedule 1* to the Act entitles the insurer to avoid the contract, refuse all claims and retain the premiums paid.

As for a qualifying breach that is neither deliberate nor reckless, the remedies set out in Paragraphs 4–6 of *Schedule 1* to the Act would apply. If the insurer would not have entered into the contract on any terms but for the said qualifying breach, the insurer may avoid the contract and refund the premiums paid; if the insurer would have entered into the contract but on different terms (not relating to the premium), the contract is treated as being entered on those terms; and if the insurer would have entered into the contract but with a higher premium charged, the insurer may proportionately reduce the amount to be paid on a claim arising there under, as calculated based on Paragraph 6 (2).[170]

It is worth noting however, that although the 'prudent insurer' test has been retained in the recent progressive reforms introduced in the United Kingdom with respect to non-consumer insurance contracts, the entire obligation reflects a more balanced approach, as not only does the insurer have to satisfy the decisive influence test of materiality, the duty of fair presentation on the insured is to begin with, one that is more enquiry rather than disclosure based.

Before moving on to examine the application of the pre-contractual duty of disclosure and misrepresentation in the Malaysian context, it is useful to briefly take stock of the English proposals for reform in the area which eventually led to these recent reforms, in the hope of providing an insight into the development of the law in Malaysia.

It started with the Fifth Report of the Law Reform Committee in 1957[171] which reported that the then state of the law with respect to warranties, exceptions, non-disclosure and misrepresentation in the United Kingdom was capable of leading to abuse. This was because it provided insurers with the opportunity to avoid liability in various instances, even against an honest and reasonably careful insured.[172] In order to balance the scales, the Committee proposed to introduce into the legal framework of English insurance law, the 'reasonable insured' test of materiality and misrepresentation of fact by insureds as only being actionable where the insured could not prove that the statement was true to the best of his knowledge and belief.[173]

The proposed provisions were meant to affect ss18 (1) and (2) as well as ss20 (1), (2) and (4) of the *Marine Insurance Act 1906* (UK) which concern material

[169]Section 8 (6) of the *Insurance Act 2015* (UK).

[170]It should be noted that a similar set of remedies are provided for in Paragraphs 7–11 of *Schedule 1* to the Act with respect to qualifying breaches of the duty of fair presentation in relation to variations made to non-consumer insurance contracts.

[171]Law Reform Committee (1957).

[172]Ibid. [11]–[12].

[173]Ibid. [14].

non-disclosure and representations of fact, where the test of materiality was the 'prudent insurer' test. By proposing that any allegation by the insurer of misstatement (misrepresentation) of *fact* by the insured would fail if the insured could prove that the statement was true to the best of his knowledge and belief, the Committee was attempting to achieve three objectives. The first of which was to place the benchmark for ascertaining misrepresentations of fact with the insured. Secondly, it sought to make it a subjective assessment as to whether the statement was to the best of the insured's knowledge and belief. Thirdly, it tried to overcome the widespread mischief caused by 'basis of contract' clauses used by insurers in proposal forms. The Committee's proposals for reform were however, never adopted but formed the basis of the Law Commission's proposal for reform in 1980.[174]

In 1975, the Law Commission and the Scottish Law Commission on *Exemption Clauses*[175] had in their Second Report recommended that their proposal (on which the English *Unfair Contract Terms Act 1977* was based) should be applied to all types of contracts, including insurance.[176] The provisions of the *Unfair Contract Terms Act 1977* essentially included an element of 'reasonableness' in order for any exclusion of liability to be effective.[177] Therefore, if insurance contracts were included within its ambit, it would have in effect removed the prudent insurer's perspective from the materiality equation. In its final form however, the *Unfair Contract Terms Act 1977* was enacted excluding insurance contracts from its purview owing to successful lobbying by the insurance industry to the effect. The result of this made it 'fundamentally unsatisfactory that the consumer of insurance services continue[d] to receive less favourable treatment than the consumer of goods and other services'.[178]

As a means of compromise for the exclusion of insurance contracts from the said Act, the insurance industry agreed to undertake measures of self-regulation in 1976 in the form of the *Statement of General Insurance Practice* ('*SOGIP*')[179] covering general insurance and the *Statement of Long Term Insurance Practice* ('*SOLTIP*')[180] covering life and investment insurance (together referred to as 'the Statements'). Both the Statements were subsequently amended in 1986 and continued in use until the introduction of statutory regulation in the form of the *Insurance Conduct of Business* ('*ICOB*')[181] and *Conduct of Business* ('*COB*')[182] respectively by the Financial Services Authority in January 2005.

---

174 Law Commission (1980).

175 Law Commission and Scottish Law Commission (1975).

176 Ibid. [240]–[47].

177 The exception to this being death and personal injury, for which there could be no exclusion of liability.

178 Forte (1986, p. 767).

179 Association of British Insurers, *Statement of General Insurance Practice* (1986a).

180 Association of British Insurers, *Statement of Long Term Insurance Practice* (1986b).

181 Financial Services Authority, *Insurance Conduct of Business* (2005b).

182 Financial Services Authority, *Conduct of Business* (2005a).

The Law Commission in 1980 came up with another proposal for reform[183] in addressing the contention by some representatives of the insurance industry that reform was unnecessary, owing to the voluntary observance by insurers of the Statements. The most important provision being essentially, a stipulation that insurers would not 'unreasonably' repudiate liability or reject a claim on grounds of non-disclosure or misrepresentation.

In addressing this contention, the Law Commission gave three reasons for concluding that the self-regulatory Statements failed to cure the mischief and alleviate the injustice to the insured caused by the then law on the matter. To begin with, such rules of self-regulation whilst appearing to be theoretically fair left the insurers as judges in their own cause as to whether repudiation or rejection was unreasonable in any given situation. This was unsatisfactory because the Statements merely set out the rules of insurance practice and had no force of law. Therefore, strictly speaking, insurers could always invoke their legal right to avoid policies and reject claims for non-disclosure and misrepresentation, based on the then existing law on the matter which was in itself unsatisfactory.

Secondly, the Statements were confined to policyholders effecting insurance in their 'private' capacity, thus, covering only consumers. Therefore, even if the Statements were adhered to effectively by insurers, they would still leave many businessmen whether operating in a small or large scale without any protection. Lastly, the Statements would only be enforceable by the industry (if at all) against insurers registered with the British Insurance Association and Lloyds and not others, which would clearly be an unacceptable state.[184]

In recommending the retention of the duty of disclosure but against the adoption of special rules for consumer applicants for insurance, the Law Commission suggested reform of the law much along the lines proposed by the Law Reform Committee in 1957.[185]

Special provisions were also proposed with respect to proposal forms and renewal notices, so as to provide a clear and prominent warning to proposers of the residual duty of disclosure, both at the inception of the policy and at each renewal. Also addressed, were the importance of retaining a copy of the information provided by them to the insurers in the proposal forms and renewals; as well as the possible consequence of the policy being repudiated or claim being rejected, in failing to make adequate disclosure. Failure by the insurers to comply with any of the said requirements was proposed to result in the insurer not being entitled to rely on any non-disclosure by the insured, unless the court was satisfied that such failure did not cause any prejudice to the insured with regard to his or her obligation to

---

[183]See: Law Commission (1980) [28]–[29]; *Insurance Law: Non-disclosure and Breach of Warranty* (1979) [9].

[184]This is because the *SOGIP* was drawn up by the British Insurance Association and Lloyds and *SOLTIP* was drawn up by the Life Offices' Association and the Associated Scottish Life Offices.

[185]Law Reform Committee (1957). See: Law Commission (1980) [10.9].

disclose such fact.[186] The Commission also recommended against insurers contracting out of the proposed provisions, by rendering such attempts void.

Whilst it has been acknowledged that 'the Law Commission's final recommendations were probably intended to mitigate the harshness of the law without over-antagonising the insurance industry',[187] there have been a fair number of criticisms levelled against its recommendations. The Law Commission was criticised for retaining the residual duty of disclosure, when such a duty has played an insignificant role in the United States for instance, without in any way affecting the effectiveness of its law of insurance.[188] It has also been criticised for adopting the purely objective 'reasonable insured' criterion for ascertaining the materiality of any fact not disclosed or misrepresented, as ignoring the fact that 'reasonable persons come in a wide variety of shapes and sizes' resulting in 'a rule which probably only a tiny fraction of the population know about, imposed on the entire population in the name of "reasonableness"'.[189] These issues have however, been finally laid to rest in the recent 2012–2015 reforms set out above.

Nevertheless, despite the seemingly watered down recommendations for reform proposed by the Law Commission in 1980, the United Kingdom was only subject to the self-regulating rules of the *SOGIP* and *SOLTIP* until 2005 and thereafter, the statutory regulations of the *ICOB* and *COB* issued by the Financial Services Authority.[190]

Both the Statements in their revised form applied only to policies entered into by individuals resident in the United Kingdom in their private capacity. Generally, the Statements addressed issues concerning proposal forms, policy documents, claims, renewals, 'basis of contract' clauses and dispute resolution. Although the Statements were an acknowledgment by the industry of the 'reasonable insured' test and the requirement for a causal link to be established between breach of warranty and loss occasioned, and hence, positive, it was however, technically not open for insureds to raise this against insurers in a court of law.

To some extent, this was mitigated by the welcome progressive stance taken by the Insurance Ombudsman over the years, requiring insurers to comply with the Statements, in the cases appearing before him.[191] This approach, has in practical

[186]This is in fact what was enacted by Australia via s14 of the *Insurance Contracts Act 1984* (Cth).

[187]Birds (1982, p. 452).

[188]See: Hasson (1984); Birds, above n 187, 453.

[189]Hasson, above n 188, 509.

[190]The *ICOB* and *COB* were issued by the Financial Services Authority pursuant to s138 of the *Financial Services and Markets Act 2000* (UK).

[191]See: Financial Ombudsman Service (1990–1991) [2.17] and [2.3] where the Insurance Ombudsman had in situations where an insured negligently misrepresented (or failed to disclose) a material fact, indicated that insurers would not be entitled to avoid liability entirely. They would instead be required to pay a proportionate sum based on the difference between the premium which was actually paid and that which ought to have been paid, had the insurer known the truth, despite Clause 2 (b) of *SOGIP* technically permitting avoidance of the policy in its entirety.

terms greatly mitigated the harshness of the law that was then applicable to misrepresentation and non-disclosure, for as one study pointed out, 'the British experience of self-regulation in the insurance industry suggests that the perceived advantages of self-regulation…may be more illusory than real'.[192]

Owing in part, to the drawbacks of self-regulation in the United Kingdom, the Financial Services Authority issued statutory regulation of general insurance and long term insurance contracts, in the form of the *ICOB* and *COB*, respectively in January 2005. Most of the provisions of these statutory regulations essentially mirrored those of the self-regulating *SOGIP* and *SOLTIP*.

Some examples regulating insurers in relation to customers acting in their private capacity only, were the warning or notice requirement of the duty of disclosure at the point of executing or renewing an insurance contract[193]; matters generally viewed to be material, to be the subject matter of clear questions in proposal forms[194]; not to unreasonably reject a claim or refuse to meet a claim on grounds of non-disclosure or misrepresentation in the absence of fraud[195]; the curtailment of 'basis of contract' clauses[196]; and the settlement of claims by making payment promptly.[197] However, the distinctive feature of statutory regulation vis-à-vis its self-regulatory predecessor was the availability of damages as a remedy for non-compliance[198] and the Financial Services Authority's ability to take action against any person guilty of misconduct, by imposing a penalty or publishing a statement of the said misconduct.[199]

Nevertheless, the English and Scottish Law Commission went ahead with a major exercise to reform this area of the law in 2006 which has resulted in the progressive reforms to date, as it found the 'FSA Rules or FOS practice' to be inadequate 'substitutes for law reform' as they were 'needlessly complex, confusing and inaccessible, with the potential for cases of real injustice falling into the cracks in the system'.[200]

---

[192]Hamilton (1995, p. 366), who upon analysing a sample of 10 proposal forms in relation to life insurance and five in relation to 'home and contents' insurance (as representing general insurance policies), attempted to ascertain the extent to which the self-regulatory measures were complied with in practice in the United Kingdom.

[193]*ICOB* 4.3.2.

[194]*ICOB* 4.3.3.

[195]*ICOB* 7.3.6.

[196]*ICOB* 7.3.6 (d) (ii).

[197]*ICOB* 7.5.18.

[198]This is by virtue of s150 of the *Financial Services and Markets Act 2000* (UK).

[199]Section 66 of the *Financial Services and Markets Act 2000* (UK).

[200]English and Scottish Law Commission Joint Consultation Paper Summary (2007, p. 6).

3.2.9 The Effect of Intermediaries on Non-disclosure and Misrepresentation

It is important to note that often issues pertaining to non-disclosure and misrepresentation involve acts or omissions by intermediaries such as agents and brokers. This raises the question as to who is bound by such acts or omissions, the insurer or the insured, which may in turn have serious implications to the parties. In general, insurance brokers have been deemed to be the insured's agent[201] whereas insurance agents were deemed to be the insurer's agent, although not always the case, as it depended on the nature of the dealing.[202] With respect to brokers however, there have been cases where the broker has been held to be the insurer's agent instead,[203] but this was due to the fact that there was a close relationship between the insurer and broker in question, with the broker even being authorised to conclude the insurance cover at times.

The biasness of the 'prudent insurer' test against the insured as it was applied in the United Kingdom prior to the recent reforms, has been compounded by the fact that in reality, insurance agents often dictate the questions in the proposal form to the proposer and fill in the answers, with the proposer merely signing the form thereafter. In such cases, there should be no room for non-disclosure or misrepresentation to be raised later by the insurer to avoid the policy, as the insured would have no way of knowing of this residual duty.

However, English law not just permitted this practice but lent support to it by holding that an insurance agent in such circumstances became the insured's agent, thereby absolving any adverse knowledge from being imputed onto the insurer, as seen in the often cited case of *Newsholme Bros v Road Transport and General Insurance*.[204] This was the case in the United Kingdom for a long time, despite the Law Reform Committee in 1957[205] having recommended that the position be reversed, whereby an insurance agent negotiating a policy should be deemed to be the insurer's agent instead for the purposes of formation of the insurance contract, so that the agent's knowledge could be imputed to the insurer.

It is important to note that the recent amendments in the United Kingdom, namely ss12 (5), 9 and Paragraphs 2, 3 and 4 of *Schedule 2* to the *Consumer Insurance (Disclosure and Representations) Act 2012* (UK) with respect to consumer insurance; and ss4 (6), 4 (7), 4 (8) (b) and 5 of the *Insurance Act 2015* (UK) with respect to non-consumers, have limited the application of the common law by focussing on the intermediary's capacity at the time of the action in question

---

[201] *Roberts v Plaisted* [1989] 2 Lloyd's Rep. 341; *Winter v Irish Life Assurance Plc* [1995] 2 Lloyd's Rep. 274.

[202] *Newsholme Bros v Road Transport and General Insurance* [1929] 2 KB 356.

[203] *Stockton v Mason* [1978] 2 Lloyd's Rep. 430; *Woolcott v Excess Insurance Co Ltd* [1979] 1 Lloyd's Rep. 231. See: Birds, above n 3, 210–211.

[204] [1929] 2 KB 356.

[205] *Conditions and Exceptions in Insurance Policies* (1957).

instead, in determining on whose behalf they were acting. This is a more balanced approach which takes into account the practical realities involved and is a welcome change.[206]

3.2.10 *The Effect of 'Basis of Contract' Clauses on Warranties*

Since an insurance contract comprises not only the policy documentation itself, but also the completed proposal form and renewal notices, a meaningful assessment of the law on misrepresentation invariably requires an examination of the 'basis of contract' clause commonly found at the foot of proposal forms and its effect on the terms of the insurance contract. There are in essence three types of terms in insurance contracts, namely, warranties, conditions and clauses descriptive of the risk.

The terms warranty and condition have 'acquired a meaning peculiar only to insurance law'[207] and have an opposite effect from its conventional usage in the general law of contract.[208] The least important to our present analysis are terms descriptive of or delimiting the risk. These terms define the scope of the purpose(s) for which the insured subject matter may be used, in order for the insurer to be liable for any loss suffered. If the insured subject matter is used for a purpose outside the said scope, the risk is not covered by the policy, although there is no breach of the insurance contract by the insured as such and the policy remains in full force.[209]

A condition in insurance contracts in turn, entitles the insurer to a claim of damages only, in the event of breach by the insured.[210] This is because it is usually of a collateral nature to the insurance policy that pertains for example, to the claims procedure or the insurer's subrogation rights, etc. An exception to this however, would be breaches of clearly stipulated conditions precedent because the insurer's liability under the insurance policy in such cases is made conditional only upon the insured strictly satisfying the condition precedent.[211]

Warranties on the other hand, are the most important type of term in insurance contracts. There are three types of warranties, namely, warranties of existing fact,

---

[206]It is in line with the approach adopted by Australia via s71 of the *Insurance Contracts Act 1984* (Cth).

[207]Poh (2005, p. 385).

[208]*New Zealand Insurance Co Ltd v Ong Choon Lin* [1992] 1 CLJ 44, 53 (Vohrah J).

[209]*De Maurier (Jewels) Ltd v Bastion Insurance Co* [1967] 2 Lloyd's Rep. 550; *L'Union des Assurance de Paris IARD v HBZ International Exchange Co (Singapore) Pte Ltd* [1993] 3 SLR 161.

[210]*Stoneham v Ocean Railway and General Accident Insurance Co* (1887) 19 QBD 237.

[211]*Chong Kok Hwa v Taisho Marine & Fire Insurance Co Ltd* [1977] 1 MLJ 244.

promissory warranties and warranties of opinion. Failure by an insured to strictly adhere to a warranty, whether a warranty of existing fact or a promissory warranty,[212] would discharge the insurer from all liability under the policy as from the date of the breach.[213] The insurer however, remained liable for all insured losses which may have occurred prior to the breach of warranty. This was apparent from the words of s33 (3) of the *Marine Insurance Act 1906* (UK) which defined a warranty as:

> [A]condition which must be exactly complied with, whether it is material to the risk or not. If it be not so complied with, then, subject to any express provision in the policy, the insurer is discharged from liability, as from the date of the breach but without prejudice to any liability incurred by him before that date.

Section 33 (3) and the House of Lord's decision in *The Good Luck*[214] pertaining to the effect of a breach of warranty have been accepted and applied to non-marine insurance contracts in the United Kingdom in *Hussain v Brown*[215] and *Kumar v AGF*.[216] The same principle has also been applied in non-marine insurance in Malaysia as far back as 1966 in *Suhaimi bin Ibrahim v United Malaya Insurance Co Ltd*.[217]

The third type of warranty is the warranty of opinion which is the least severe in nature, and merely warrants that certain facts are to the best of the insured's knowledge and belief, true. All that is required of the insured is to exercise care when making such a warranty, for only a dishonest or reckless warranty of opinion would amount to a breach.[218]

Warranties of past or present facts, promissory warranties and warranties of opinion may either be created in the body of the policy itself or by way of a provision or declaration contained at the foot of the proposal form containing a list of questions which the insured is required to sign, termed the 'basis of contract' clause. A typical 'basis of contract' clause would read: 'I declare that the particulars and statements made by me above are true, and I agree that they shall be the basis of the contract between me and the company'.[219]

---

[212] A promissory warranty requires performance by the insured of a warranty in the future during the duration of the policy, for example, maintaining the sprinkler systems in a commercial fire insurance policy; whereas a warranty of existing fact is often made in the proposal form, for example, that the insured of a life insurance policy is a non-smoker.

[213] *Bank of Nova Scotia v Hellenic Mutual War Risks Association (Bermuda) Ltd (The Good Luck)* [1991] 2 Lloyd's Rep 191.

[214] *Bank of Nova Scotia v Hellenic Mutual War Risks Association (Bermuda) Ltd (The Good Luck)* [1991] 2 Lloyd's Rep 191.

[215] [1996] 1 Lloyd's Rep 627.

[216] [1999] Lloyd's Rep IR 147.

[217] [1966] 1 MLJ 140.

[218] *Huddleston v RAC Insurance Pty Ltd* [1975] VR 683.

[219] Hasson (1971, p. 29).

Such clauses have had the effect of incorporating the insured's answers into the insurance policy and converting them into warranties of past or present facts. Hence, an incorrect answer by the insured to any of the questions posed in the proposal form preceding the 'basis of contract' clause would amount to a breach of warranty. As the warranty is breached at the inception of the policy itself, it would have the effect of discharging the insurer from liability ab initio, which would be a harsh consequence to the insured. The severity of the blow has in the past been compounded by the fact that the 'materiality' of the insured's misrepresentation or inaccurate answer having been irrelevant,[220] and so is the fact that the insured may have had answered the questions posed in good faith and to the best of his or her knowledge and belief.[221]

Such potential for mischief created by 'basis of contract' clauses has often left the lay insured helpless. This fact, was highlighted back in the 19th Century by Lord St Leonards in *Anderson v Fitzgerald*[222] where his Lordship said 'no prudent man [would] effect a policy of insurance with any company without having an attorney at his elbow to tell him what the true construction of the document is' (clarification added).[223] What is surprising is that this clause which was developed in the 19th Century[224] has continued to wreak havoc in the United Kingdom and Malaysia up until the recent amendments in 2012–2015, despite lacking a juridical basis for its continued existence.

In view of this, it is useful to take stock of the 'basis of contract' clause's development from the 18th to the 20th Century as analysed by R A Hasson in his article.[225] His analysis is that the 18th Century English cases have been unnecessarily and unfortunately accredited with the development of the doctrine that a breach of warranty, however immaterial, would relieve the insured from liability. This is despite the fact that none of the decided cases from that period involved a clearly immaterial fact.[226]

In fact, in *Ross v Bradshaw*[227] which was a non-marine insurance case decided at the time, a warranty pertaining to the insured being of good health was interpreted rather liberally, so as not to have been breached by palsy giving rise to incontinence, as it was merely an inconvenience and not dangerous to the insured's life. Furthermore, Lord Mansfield in at least two cases decided at the time,

[220]*McKay v London General Insurance Co.* (1935) 51 Ll L R 201.

[221]Birds, above n 3, 173–174.

[222](1853) 4 HLC 483.

[223]Ibid. 514.

[224]The first reported decision was *Duckett v Williams* (1834) 2 C & M 348.

[225]See: Hasson, above n 188.

[226]See: *Bean v Stupart* (1778) 1 Doug 11; *De Hahn v Hartley* (1786) 1 TR 343, both concerning the number of seaman on board the insured vessel. *McDowell v Fraser* (1779) 1 Doug 266, in turn, concerned the sighting of a ship which was in fact lost at the time.

[227](1761) 1 Wm Bl 313.

expressly limited the creation of warranties through means such as memorandums and attachments folded or incorporated into the policy.[228]

The problem however, was created by subsequent 19th Century decisions which contained some unnecessary statements of principle explicitly removing the requirement of materiality from having to be established for breaches of warranty, which in turn produced unfortunate results in later cases.[229] This led to the 'basis of contract' clause formally rearing its ugly head in a reported case, in *Duckett v Williams*.[230]

This was a case concerning reinsurance where the trustees of the Provident Life Assurance Company had represented to the Hope Insurance Company that the life insured was in good health. The life insured was in fact found to be uninsurable and on those facts, the court rejected Provident's argument that the obligation to answer 'truly' as per the 'basis of contract' clause only required that it was made to the best of their knowledge. This resulted in the reinsurers forfeiting the premiums paid and being discharged of any liability. Although the decision was justifiable as it was a reinsurance matter as opposed to an original application for insurance, this distinction was unfortunately not highlighted, thus, leaving it as an authority for all cases concerning 'basis of contract' clauses.

More damage was done in *Anderson v Fitzgerald*[231] where the House of Lords held that the 'basis of contract' clause had the effect of removing any question of materiality from consideration by the jury. The most important case on point in this area was *Thompson v Weems*[232] which concerned a life insurance policy containing a 'basis of contract' clause. Although the decision against the insured was in principle correct, it should have been on the ground that the insured had acted in bad faith. It was unfortunate however, that Lord Blackburn instead chose to state that 'insurers have a right if they please to take a warranty against [the applicant's] ...disease, whether latent or not, and it has very long been the course of business to insert a warranty to that effect' (clarification added).[233] His Lordship went on to acknowledge that was so despite it being a hard bargain for insureds who innocently warranted inaccurate information without any moral guilt.

This unfortunate trend involving 'basis of contract' clauses continued in the 20th Century, with the requirement of materiality of the misrepresentation being completely done away with.[234] The most important case on 'basis of contract' clauses is *Dawsons v Bonnin*,[235] which is also reflective of the grave injustice it is capable of

[228]*Parson v Barnevelt* (1779) 1 Doug 12; *Bize v Fletcher* (1779) 1 Doug 284.

[229]See: Lord Eldon in *Newcastle Fire Insurance Co v Macmorran* (1815) 3 Dow 255, 265.

[230](1834) 2 C & M 348.

[231](1853) 4 HLC 483.

[232](1884) 9 App Cas 671.

[233]Ibid. 682.

[234]*Yorkshire Insurance Co v Campbell* [1917] AC 218 (PC).

[235][1922] 2 AC 413.

doing. The case concerned an insurance policy taken out on a lorry which was subsequently destroyed by a fire at the garage in which it was parked. The House of Lords held that the insured was not entitled to recover owing to a misstatement made in the proposal form which contained a 'basis of contract' clause as to where the lorry was garaged.

This was despite the fact that the misstatement was inadvertent and immaterial, as the premium charged would have been exactly the same even if the true address was stated. Furthermore, the lorry was parked in a garage outside Glasgow, which is less dangerous than had it been parked in a garage in central Glasgow as insured. All this however, mattered to nought, as the House of Lords held that a 'basis of contract' clause incorporated into a policy would have the effect of making statements made therein 'contractually material'.[236]

This unfortunate state of affairs was highlighted by Swift J in *Mackay v London General Insurance Co*[237] where his Lordship, although being bound by precedent to deny the insured recovery, was convinced that the misrepresentation was immaterial and had not misled the insurers in the least.

In view of the historical account of the law above on warranties and 'basis of contract' clauses, it is not surprising that there has been a long standing call for reform in this area. There has been no valid justification for removing the materiality requirement from an actionable breach of warranty. Questions in proposal forms (pertaining to the insured's health and value of the insured subject matter) should not be treated as warranties of fact, as they should logically be treated as the insured's statement of his honest opinion instead. The original purpose of the 'basis of contract' clause as an 'educative' tool to draw proposers' attention to the importance of the information required is no longer there, as it has been easily replaced by the statutory warning in proposal forms.[238] These factors together with the present gross inequality in bargaining positions between insurers and insureds which was absent in the 18th Century, have formed the basis of numerous calls for reform seeking materiality to be proved for an actionable breach of warranty; a causal connection to exist between the breach and loss; and the abolition of the 'basis of contract' clause altogether.[239]

These calls have been answered, as 'basis of contract' clauses have been abolished in the United Kingdom for both consumer and non-consumer insurance contracts via s 6 (2) of the *Consumer Insurance (Disclosure and Representations) Act 2012* (UK) and ss9 (2) and 10 (1) of the *Insurance Act 2015* (UK), respectively. Furthermore, the second line of s33 (3) and the whole of s34 of the *Marine Insurance Act 1906* (UK) have been deleted by ss10 (7) (a) and 10 (7) (b) of the

---

[236]Ibid. 435 (Lord Dunedin).

[237](1935) 51 Ll L R 201, 202. See also: *West v National Union and Accident Insurance Co* [1954] 2 Lloyd's Rep 461.

[238]Hasson, above n 188, 32 and 38.

[239]See: Law Commission (1980). Australia has long abolished the same via s24 of the *Insurance Contracts Act 1984* (Cth) (Australia).

Insurance Act 2015 (UK), respectively, thereby removing the insurer's right to be discharged from liability from the date of the breach of warranty.

3.3 Development and Application of the Pre-contractual Duties in Malaysia

3.3.1 The Prudent Insurer Test in Malaysia

The position in Malaysia prior to the enactment of the *Financial Services Act 2013* (Malaysia) and the *Insurance Act 1996* (Malaysia) for that matter, was such that the courts had consistently applied the 'prudent insurer' test with respect to materiality,[240] even before the Court of Appeal's decision in *Lambert v Co-operative Insurance Society Ltd.*[241] That is, except for the Federal Court decision in *Abu Bakar v Oriental Fire and General Insurance Co Ltd*[242] that involved a proposal for a fire insurance policy.

The appellant in the case had answered the questions as to what purposes the premises in question were being occupied, by stating that there was a sundry shop downstairs and a dwelling on the first floor. The insurers denied liability when a claim was made, on the basis that the appellant had failed to disclose the existence of four electrically operated grinding mills located at the back of the shop. The Federal Court by a majority reversed the decisions of both the lower courts and held in favour of the insured, saying that there was no actionable non-disclosure, as the insured had answered the questions posed in the proposal form correctly and that any non-disclosure was not material.

It is interesting to note that in so holding, Azmi LP endorsed the prudent insurer test but introduced two qualifications to it by saying:

> I would further add that if a fact even though material [by virtue of the prudent insurer test] is one which the proposer did not and could not have been expected to know or if its materiality could not have been apparent to the reasonable man, his failure to disclose should not in my view be regarded as breach of his duty. (clarification added)[243]

The first qualification of being duty bound to disclose only information that the insured knows or ought to know, is trite law, as can be seen in the words of s18 (1) of the *Marine Insurance Act 1906* (UK) itself. It is the second qualification that seems to adopt a two-fold approach to fuse both the prudent insurer and reasonable insured tests in providing greater protection for the insured.

---

[240] *Teh Say Cheng v North British and Mercantile Insurance Co Ltd* (1921) 2 FMSLR 248; *Wong Lang Hung v National Employees' Mutual General Insurance* [1972] 2 MLJ 191.

[241] [1975] 2 Lloyd's Rep 485.

[242] [1974] 1 MLJ 149.

[243] Ibid. 151.

As Mahmood described, this introduction of the 'appreciation of materiality' qualification by Azmi LP was 'an innovative step' serving 'as a useful temporary measure' to help 'strike a balance between the interest of the insurer and that of the insured' until the legislature deemed it 'fit to change the test of materiality from one that is based on the prudent insurer to that based on the reasonable insured'.[244]

Such a bold restatement of the law by the Federal Court not only reflects an appreciation of the otherwise harsh consequence to the insured but was also the foundation for the change introduced by the Malaysian legislature in 1996 and subsequently in 2013. Further attempt to do justice to the insured was made by the Malaysian Supreme Court in the case of *United Oriental Assurance Sdn Bhd Kuantan v WM Mazzarol (The Melanie)*[245] by holding that the insured's failure to disclose an earlier accident to its vessel in the proposal form was not its fault but that of the insurer in framing ambiguous questions.

Despite the bold attempt at balancing the law on non-disclosure by the Federal Court in *Abu Bakar v Oriental Fire and General Insurance Co Ltd*,[246] subsequent Malaysian cases have nevertheless continued to adopt the 'prudent insurer' test on materiality. In *Tang Tung Thian v United Oriental Assurance Sdn Bhd*[247] the insurer was held to be entitled to avoid a motor insurance contract on the basis that the insured had misrepresented and failed to disclose a fact material to a prudent insurer that the insured vehicle was in fact involved in an accident before. Another case decided in a like manner was *Aetna Universal Insurance Sdn Bhd v Fanny Foo May Wan*.[248] Here, the insurer was held to be entitled to avoid a life insurance policy on grounds that the insured (deceased) had misrepresented and made material non-disclosure of certain medical tests that were run on him in the past, as this was material to a prudent insurer in determining whether to undertake the risk and the premium to charge.

The most recent of such cases decided based on the old *Insurance Act 1963* (Malaysia) (prior to the enactment of the *Insurance Act 1996* (Malaysia)) which bears proof of the perils and pitfalls of the common law on pre-contractual duty of disclosure and misrepresentation, especially with respect to disclosure at renewals is *Leong Kum Whay v QBE Insurance (M) Sdn Bhd*[249] that has been discussed in Chap. 2.

---

[244]Mahmood, above n 47, 55.

[245][1984] 1 MLJ 260.

[246][1974] 1 MLJ 149.

[247][2000] 5 MLJ 696.

[248][2001] 1 MLJ 227. It should be noted that although this case was decided after the *Insurance Act 1996* (Malaysia) came into effect, the provisions of the Act were not considered, as the events giving rise to the claim occurred prior to the enforcement of the said Act, hence based on the earlier repealed *Insurance Act 1963* (Malaysia).

[249][2006] 1 CLJ 1.

3.3.2 Pre-contractual Disclosure Under the Insurance Act 1996

In 1996, the Malaysian legislature passed the *Insurance Act 1996* (Malaysia) with respect to non-marine insurance, repealing the *Insurance Act 1963* (Malaysia). The *Insurance Act 1996* (Malaysia) came into effect on 1st January 1997 and was in force in Malaysia until its repeal by the *Financial Services Act 2013* (Malaysia) on 30th June 2013. Although the *Insurance Act 1996* (Malaysia) was primarily a regulatory piece of legislation, it nevertheless introduced some important substantive provisions, one of which being s150 (1) which for the first time in Malaysia codified the provision on pre-contractual disclosure by the insured. Section 150 (1) provided:

Before a contract of insurance is entered into, a proposer shall disclose to the licensed insurer a matter that—

(a) he knows to be relevant to the decision of the licensed insurer on whether to accept the risk or not and the rates and terms to be applied; or
(b) *a reasonable person in the circumstances* could be expected to know to be relevant. (Emphasis added)

It was indeed an improvement to the insured's predicament under the 'prudent insurer' test of materiality contained in s18 (2) of the *Marine Insurance Act 1906* (UK), as the relevance of a matter warranting disclosure was to be judged from the insured's perspective instead. Section 150 (1) replaced the common law requirement of materiality with that of relevance, with subsection (a) being purely subjective, in that the insured need only disclose matters 'he knows' to be relevant to 'the insurer' in question. Subsection (b) was in turn both an objective and subjective test, requiring the insured to disclose matters which 'a reasonable person in the circumstances' could be expected to know to be relevant to the said insurer.

It was applied in *Ngu Siew Kong v ING Insurance Bhd*[250] where the insurer was held to be entitled to avoid a life insurance policy on grounds that the insured who made a claim for prostate cancer had misrepresented and made material non-disclosure. He had done so by answering 'no' to two questions on the proposal form as to whether he had received treatment for his prostate and had any blood or urine tests done in the past 5 years, which he had, as this was clearly material to the risk undertaken and the premium charged. The converse applied in *Tan Jing Jeong v Allianz Life Insurance Malaysia Bhd & Anor*[251] where the insured was entitled to avoid an investment linked life insurance policy, for non-disclosure and misrepresentation of a material fact by the insurer relating to the amount and nature of subsequent premium payments that involved substantial sums.

250[2011] MLJU 719.

251[2012] 7 MLJ 179.

Section 150 (1) was in fact modelled after the Australian s21 (1) of the *Insurance Contracts Act 1984* (Cth), and as such, Australian cases have provided valuable insight into the application of this section, in the absence of many Malaysian cases on point.

For example, the fact not disclosed to the insurer must first be known to the insured or his agent or employee (whose knowledge could be imputed to the insured).[252] In addition, the insured must also know that the said matter was relevant to the insurer or that a reasonable person in the circumstances could be expected to know of its relevance to the insurer.

As for what was meant by requiring disclosure of a matter that the insured knows to be relevant to the decision of 'the licensed insurer' in s21 (1) (a) of the *Insurance Contracts Act 1984* (Cth) (Australia),[253] in that whether it concerned a prudent insurer or the actual insurer, it was after some debate resolved to mean the actual insurer in question.[254]

Another element of the provision, namely the test in s21 (1) (b)[255] as to 'a reasonable person in the circumstances', was also subject to some debate over the years as to whether the subjective element of the test envisaged by the words 'in the circumstances' covered both the insured's intrinsic (individual idiosyncrasies) as well as extrinsic factors,[256] or extrinsic factors only. This was resolved in favour of it encompassing only the latter extrinsic factors, as endorsed by the High Court of Australia in *CGU Insurance Ltd v Porthouse*[257] which applied the decision in *Twenty-first Maylux Pty Ltd v Mercantile Mutual Insurance (Aust) Ltd.*[258]

As there was no explanatory note that came with the Malaysian s150 (1) to help decipher the true purpose behind its enactment, the observations of the Australian Law Reform Commission provided a useful guide:

> Fairness to the insured can only be achieved by taking account of differences between individual insureds … [l]iteracy, knowledge, experience and cultural background are vitally important factors affecting the behaviour which can reasonably be expected of insureds, by insurers and by the legal system which regulates the insurance relationships … [t]he existing requirement of disclosure imposes obligations on those individuals which many of them acting in the utmost good faith, are unable to discharge.[259]

Although a step in the right direction, s150 (1) however left many issues unaddressed. The most important of which was the remedies available in the event of breach of s150 (1) by the insured. The Act was silent on this, therefore, leaving

---

[252] *Hammer Waste Pty Ltd v QBE Mutual Ltd* [2002] NSWSC 1006.

[253] This is analogous to s150 (1) (a) of the *Insurance Act 1996* (Malaysia).

[254] *Permanent Trustee Australia Co Ltd v FAI General Insurance Co Ltd* [2001] 50 NSWLR 679.

[255] This is analogous to s 150 (1) (b) of the *Insurance Act 1996* (Malaysia).

[256] Examples of this would be the level of informality attendant upon negotiations, whether cover was arranged over the telephone, the type of policy in issue, exposure to advertising, etc.

[257] [2008] HCA 30.

[258] [1990] VR 919.

[259] Australian Law Reform Commission (1982) [183].

the solitary common law remedy of avoidance of contract and a refund of premiums paid, intact.

It is worth noting however, that Australia on the other hand had introduced a package of remedies available in the event of innocent and fraudulent non-disclosure or misrepresentation by the insured, in the form of ss28 and 29 of the *Insurance Contracts Act 1984* (Cth) (Australia).

Section 28[260] read together with s33 makes the following the only remedies available for non-disclosure by the insured. Section 28 (1) requires the insurer to be induced to enter into the contract as a result of the non-disclosure as a pre-requisite to remedy. Once that is satisfied, the insurer is only entitled to avoid the contract where the non-disclosure was fraudulent although some leeway is provided to the insured under s31 in instances of a little bit of fraud.[261] Failing which, s28 (3) provides that the insurer can only reduce the claim to an amount that is representative of the non-disclosure not having occurred.[262]

The Australian position therefore, is that 'the insurer's remedy for non-fraudulent non-disclosure is made proportionate to the prejudice suffered by the insurer, as a result of the insured's breach of duty', whereas by contrast in the United Kingdom and Malaysia prior to the recent reforms, 'the insurer may avoid the policy from inception for breach of the duty of disclosure irrespective of whether it [was] flagrantly fraudulent, completely inadvertent or anything in between.'[263] (Clarification added)

It is unclear as to why this was not adopted by the Malaysian legislature, when s150 (1) of the *Insurance Act 1996* (Malaysia) was modelled after s21 (1) of the *Insurance Contracts Act 1984* (Cth) (Australia) to begin with.

Section 150 (1) therefore, besides having laid down a 'reasonable insured' test for pre-contractual disclosure, left other aspects of the duty of utmost good faith

---

[260]Section 29 is the equivalent provision applying to life insurance. Both sections apply to non-disclosure and misrepresentations as well. This section draws on research appearing in: Thanasegaran (2004, p. 154).

[261]*Insurance Manufacturers of Australia Pty Ltd v Heron* [2005] VSC 482. Under s31 the court has a discretion to disregard the insurer's avoidance if it 'would be harsh and unfair not to do so' thereby allowing the insured recovery of the whole or part of the claim as it thinks 'just and equitable,' provided the insurer has not been prejudiced by the fraudulent non-disclosure or misrepresentation in question.

[262]See: *Prime Form Cutting Pty Limited v Balitca General Insurance Co Ltd* [1991] 6 ANZ Ins Cas ¶61-028; *Fruehauf Finance Corporation Pty Ltd v Zurich Australia Insurance Limited* [1990] 20 NSWLR 359; and more recently, *Prepaid Services v Atradius (no 2)* [2014] NSWSC 21 which have established that the remedy under s28(3) can include reducing the insurer's liability under the policy to nil (if the insurer can prove that it would not have entered into the contract at all but for the non-disclosure or misrepresentation) and reducing its liability for a claim to nil (if it can prove that it would have excluded the relevant claim from cover by way of an excess or exclusion under an alternative policy which it would have issued had there been a proper disclosure or if the additional premium which it would have charged would have exceeded the amount of the claim): Mann and Lewis (2014, p. 197).

[263]Hawke (2006, p. 13). This section draws on research appearing in: Thanasegaran (2008, p. 158).

unaddressed,[264] for example, the application of the general principle of utmost good faith itself, the duty of disclosure independently of any proposal form,[265] the common law relating to material misrepresentations, and the harsh remedy of avoidance in the event of breach. This is unlike the more comprehensive Australian position where the law relating to utmost good faith is addressed in ss12–14; non-disclosure and statutory warnings in ss21–22; misrepresentation in ss23–27 and remedies in ss28, 29, 54 and 56 of the *Insurance Contracts Act 1984* (Cth) (Australia). It is not surprising therefore, that this package of provisions has withstood the test of time. There has only been a minor revision of its provisions made via the *Insurance Contracts (Amendment) Act 2013* (Cth) (Australia) in order to keep it up to date.

Another observation made against s150 (1) of the *Insurance Act 1996* (Malaysia) was that the element of inducement may not have been addressed in s150 (1), thereby raising the question of whether an insurer could have avoided a contract of insurance on grounds of non-disclosure despite not having been induced by the said non-disclosure.[266] This was unlikely, as the words of s150 (1) in itself indicated that the matter undisclosed must have been relevant to the decision of 'the licensed insurer', thereby requiring the particular insurer to have been induced. In fact, the Victorian Supreme Court in *Burns v MMI—CMI Insurance Ltd*[267] accepted that 'the insurer' referred to in s21 (1) of the *Insurance Contracts Act 1984* (Cth) (Australia) was the actual insurer and not a hypothetical prudent insurer. That, which remained unclear, however, was whether the actual insurer had to be induced in the 'mere influence' or 'decisive influence' sense.

Lastly, s150 (3) of *the Insurance Act 1996*(Malaysia),went on to provide that where a person failed to provide or gave an incomplete or irrelevant answer to a question included in a proposal form, the insurer would be deemed to have waived compliance with the duty of disclosure in relation to the matter. This was another feather on the insured's cap modelled after s21 (3) of the *Insurance Contracts Act 1984* (Cth) (Australia), with the difference being that the Australian provision requires the insured's failure to provide or provision of answer to amount to an 'obviously' incomplete or irrelevant one, connoting a heavier burden to be satisfied by the insured.[268]

It may be worthwhile noting that s21A of the *Insurance Contracts Act 1984* (Cth) (Australia) for which there was no equivalent provision in the *Insurance Act 1996* (Malaysia), provides additional protection to consumers. Particularly so in domestic and personal lines insurance (known as 'eligible contracts') because such insureds frequently lack the knowledge and awareness to fully understand those issues which may be of significance to an insurer with its wealth of experience and

[264]Gan (1997, p. 191).

[265]*Tan Mooi Sim & Anor v United Overseas Bank (M) Bhd & Anor* [2011] 8 MLJ 556.

[266]Abdul Mubarak (2002, p. 8).

[267](1995) 8 ANZ Ins Cas ¶61-287.

[268]*Orb Holdings Pty Ltd v Lombard Insurance Co (Aust) Ltd* [1995] 2 Qd R 51.

knowledge in underwriting. Section 21A is meant to redress this imbalance and improve the insured's capacity to comply with the duty of disclosure by requiring insurers to ask specific questions in proposal forms, failing which the insurer is deemed to have waived the duty of disclosure with respect to the same. This notion has however, been modelled in the recent Malaysian reforms relating to consumer insurance contracts, which will be examined shortly.

In practice, the issuance of an insurance policy raises a presumption that things are in order, thus, putting the onus of proving that there was a non-disclosure of a relevant fact on the insurer who alleges it.[269] Once this burden has been discharged on a balance of probabilities, the onus then shifts to the insured to rebut it by showing that adequate disclosure was made or that the fact allegedly undisclosed was in fact not relevant or that it was a fact which did not require disclosure to begin with, by virtue of s150 (2) of the *Insurance Act 1996* (Malaysia).

Section 150 (2) which covered matters not requiring disclosure by the insured was in fact a mirror image of s21 (2) of the *Insurance Contracts Act 1984* (Cth) (Australia) and was broadly modelled after s18 (3) of the *Marine Insurance Act 1906* (UK),[270] set out earlier in this chapter.

Section 150 (2) of the *Insurance Act 1996* (Malaysia) provided that:

The duty of disclosure does not require the disclosure of a matter that—

(a) diminishes the risk to the licensed insurer;
(b) is of common knowledge;
(c) the licensed insurer knows or in the ordinary course of his business ought to know; or
(d) in respect of which the licensed insurer had waived any requirement for disclosure.

Subsections (a), (b) and (c) above are self-explanatory and do not warrant much discussion. In relation to waiver of disclosure by the insurer on the other hand, there are two relevant provisions in the *Insurance Act 1996* (Malaysia) namely s150 (2) (d) and s150 (3).[271]

Section 150 (2) (d) made disclosure of a matter that the insurer has waived, as being unnecessary, whereas s150 (3) provided that:

> Where a proposer fails to answer or gives an incomplete or irrelevant answer to a question contained in the proposal form or asked by the licensed insurer and the matter was not

[269] *Butcher v Dowlen* [1981] 1 Lloyd's Rep 310.

[270] Section 150 (2) departs from s18 (3) of the *Marine Insurance Act 1906* (UK) in some important respects, namely, the proviso 'in the absence of inquiry' appearing in s18 (3) has been dropped, along with s18 (3) (d) which deals with circumstances which are superfluous to disclose by reason of any express or implied warranty.

[271] Section 150 (3) is in fact a reproduction of the Australian s21 (3) of the *Insurance Contracts Act 1984* (Cth).

pursued further by the licensed insurer, compliance with the duty of disclosure in respect of the matter shall be deemed to have been waived by the licensed insurer.

The question of waiver however, only arose where the insurer has acted with full knowledge of the facts concerning non-disclosure and the insured has in turn specifically pleaded and proved an allegation of waiver. If there was evidence that insurers in general do not inquire about a particular matter, it was an indication that the matter was not material. Also, if the insurer asked a question of limited scope, such restraint by implication would have excluded and therefore waived related matters falling outside the scope of the question.[272] The scope of the inquiry therefore, determining the scope of the duty of disclosure.

Failure by the insurer to ask all relevant questions in full on the other hand, could only amount to a waiver if the insured has been placed in genuine doubt as a result. In *Orakpo v Barclays Insurance*[273] for instance, the insured's defence to a claim of misrepresentation was rejected on the basis that despite the proposal form requiring the insured to tick in 'yes' and 'no' boxes, the insured ought not have ticked in the box indicating that his house was sound, when in fact it was badly affected by dry rot.

Having said that, the introduction of s150 (3) of the *Insurance Act 1996* (Malaysia) by the Malaysian legislature was indeed a positive step for insureds, as it placed the burden on the insurer to pursue an incomplete or irrelevant answer to a question posed to the insured, before being entitled to claim non-disclosure.

Although it was largely based on s21 (3) of the *Insurance Contracts Act 1984* (Cth) (Australia),[274] it appeared to be more insured friendly in two respects. First, it covered answers given to questions asked by the insurer outside the proposal form and secondly, the Malaysian provision did not require the insured's answers to be 'obviously' incomplete or irrelevant in order for s150 (3) to apply.[275] The requirement of an 'obviously incomplete' answer for the purposes of s21 (3) however, must be looked at in light of other information coming to the insurer's knowledge.[276]

---

[272] *Mazzarol v United Oriental Assurance* [1983] 1 MLJ 328.

[273] [1995] LRLR 443.

[274] Section 21(3) in turn provides that:

Where a person failed to answer or gave an *obviously* incomplete or irrelevant answer to a question included in a proposal form about a matter, the insurer shall be deemed to have waived compliance with the duty of disclosure in relation to the matter (emphasis added).

[275] *Rocco Pezzano Pty Ltd v Unity Insurance Brokers Pty Ltd* [1995] 8 ANZ Ins Cas ¶61-288; The fact that only one claim was disclosed for a business which was in existence for more than 20 years was held not to be unusual enough a circumstance so as to put the insurer on notice that the information given was 'obviously' incomplete.

[276] *Dew v Suncorp Life and Superannuation Ltd* [2001] QCA 459.

Upon a closer look at the package, however, it would appear that s21 (3) has a wider effect of being able to cover misrepresentation as well, when read together with s27 of the *Insurance Contracts Act 1984* (Cth) (Australia). The effect of this is to prevent clauses being inserted by insurers stating that a lack of or unclear answers would be construed in the negative. There was however, no equivalent provision to s27 in Malaysia.

Apart from this, compliance by the insurer with respect to the requirement in s22 of the *Insurance Contracts Act 1984* (Cth) (Australia) to provide a statutory warning in proposal forms warning prospective insureds of the duty of disclosure and the duty to refrain from making misrepresentations, is a pre-requisite to reliance by the insurer on s21 of the *Insurance Contracts Act 1984* (Cth) (Australia) with respect to any claim of non-disclosure against the insured.[277] Again, this was not adopted with respect to the consequences of failure by insurers to provide a statutory warning in Malaysia under s149 (4) of the *Insurance Act 1996* (Malaysia), as explained in Chap. 2 of this book.

Although the *Insurance Act 1996* (Malaysia) was an improvement from the pre-existing common law position in some respects, it should be borne in mind that the residual pre-contractual duty of disclosure per se and the common law on pre-contractual misrepresentation along with avoidance of the contract being the only remedy available in the event of breach, still remained.

3.3.3 The Effect of Intermediaries on Non-disclosure and Misrepresentation

As far as Malaysia is concerned, the *Insurance Act 1963* (Malaysia) and its successor in 1996 have introduced some positive change from the common law position with respect to pre-contractual negotiations and the 'transferred agency' rule. Section 44A of the *Insurance Act 1963* (Malaysia) which was modelled after the English Law Reform Committee Report of 1957[278] was introduced through the *Insurance Amendment Act 1979* (Malaysia). It provided that:

1. A person who has at any time been authorised as its agent by an insurer and who solicits and negotiates a contract of insurance in such a capacity shall in every such instance be deemed for the purpose of the formation of the contract to be the agent of the insurer and the knowledge of such person relating to any matter

---

[277] *Delphine v Lumley General Insurance* [1990] 6 ANZ Ins Cas ¶60-986.

[278] Law Reform Committee (1957) [14].

relevant to the acceptance of the risk by the insurer shall be deemed to be the knowledge of the insurer.

2. Any statement made or any act done by such person in his representative capacity shall be deemed, for the purposes of the formation of the contract, to be a statement made or act done by the insurer notwithstanding any contravention of section 16A[279] or any other provision of this Act by any such person.[280]

This was a welcome improvement over the common law, as it reversed the 'transferred agency' rule in *Newsholme Brothers v Road Transport and General Insurance Co Ltd*[281] and made insurance agents the agent of the insurer even at the pre-contractual stage. Section 44A was applied in a string of cases, namely, *Lim Gaek Ling v East West-UMI Insurance Bhd*,[282] *Titiria Sdn Bhd v Zurich Insurance (M) Sdn Bhd*,[283] *Syarikat Uniweld Trading v The Asia Insurance Co Ltd*[284] and by the Court of Appeal in *Leong Kum Whay v QBE Insurance (M) Sdn Bhd*.[285] In all these cases, s44A was used to impute the agent's acts, omission and knowledge of material facts unto the insurer, so as to prevent the insurer from relying on pre-contractual non-disclosure and misrepresentation in trying to avoid the insurance contract.

The now repealed *Insurance Act 1996* (Malaysia) then introduced a similar s151 in place of s44A. The difference in wording was in its reference to 'a person who is authorised by a licensed insurer to be *its insurance agent*' in s151(1) and 'a statement made or an act done by the *insurance agent*' in s151(2), whereas, s44A(1) had a

---

[279]Under s16A, it was an offence for any person to make misleading statements, promises or forecasts in order to induce another person to enter into any contract of insurance.

[280]Section 44A(3) however, prevented the application of subsections (1) and (2) where there was collusion between the insured and agent or the insurer has taken reasonable steps to notify all concerned of the cessation of the agency. It is worth noting that s44A was enacted to replace s18E introduced in 1975, as the latter only applied to home-service policies and even then, contained an opening phrase providing that 'where an agent or servant of an insurer fills in a proposal form,' hence not addressing the 'transferred agency' problem because an agent helping the insured to fill in proposal forms was not deemed to be the insurer's agent.

[281][1929] 2 KB 356.

[282][1994] 2 CLJ 405.

[283][1996] 1 CLJ 105.

[284][1996] 2 MLJ 160.

[285][2006] 1 CLJ 1. Mahmood, above n 47, 114, is however, of the view that although s44A reversed the 'transferred agency' rule, it did not address the fact that the proposer was responsible for what he signs and the effect of the parol evidence rule in ss91and 92 of the *Evidence Act 1950* (Malaysia). Nevertheless, in practice, a specific provision like s44A governing the area should take precedence over the general evidentiary rules in ss91 and 92.

broader reference to 'a person who *has at any time* been authorised *as its agent* by an insurer' and s44A(2) to 'any statement made or any act done *by such person* in his representative capacity'.[286]

Section 151 was applied in *Chan Yoke Lain v Pacific & Orient Insurance Co Sdn Bhd*[287] wherein the knowledge of the insurer's agent's clerk who filled in the proposal for a personal accident policy and signed it on behalf of the insured, was imputed to the insurer in preventing them from avoiding the policy.

It appears that both s151 of the *Insurance Act 1996* (Malaysia) and its predecessor, s44A of the *Insurance Act 1963*(Malaysia) were a marked improvement from the common law with respect to imputing liability unto the insurer for the acts, omissions and knowledge of the insurance agent. What remained uncertain however, was its applicability to insurance brokers, financial advisers and alike. A literal interpretation of ss151 (1) and (2) indicated that it would not, as s151 referred to a person authorised by an insurer to be 'its insurance agent' whereas s44A had previously made a broader reference to a person who has 'at any time been authorised as its agent by an insurer,' which could be interpreted to cover brokers authorised by or acting on behalf of the insurer.[288] In this sense, it would appear that s44A was a better drafted provision than s151.

Furthermore, all these provisions only seemed to address the acts or omissions and knowledge of intermediaries at the point of formation of the insurance contract, thereby not applying to notices of loss or claims made to them, which would still be governed by the common law. These deeming provisions would have had a wider scope had they been amended to extend to 'any matter relating to insurance'.[289]

As for Australia on the other hand, the position of intermediaries was previously governed by the *Insurance (Agents & Brokers) Act 1984* (Cth) (Australia), until its repeal in 2001 by the *Financial Services Reform Act* (Cth) (Australia) which

---

[286]Section 151 (1) provided that:

> A person who is authorised by a licensed insurer to be *its insurance agent* and who solicits or negotiates a contract of insurance in that capacity shall be deemed, for the purpose of the formation of the contract of insurance, to be the agent of the licensed insurer and the knowledge of that *insurance agent* shall be deemed to be the knowledge of the licensed insurer.

Section 151 (2) provided that:

> A statement made, or an act done, by *the insurance agent* shall be deemed, for the purposes of the formation of the contract of insurance, to be a statement made, or act done, by the licensed insurer notwithstanding *the insurance agent's* contravention of subsection 150 (4) or any other provision of this Act.

Section 151 (3) provided that:

> Subsection (1) shall not apply—(a) where there is collusion or connivance between the *insurance agent* and the proposer in the formation of the contract of insurance; or (b) where a person has ceased to be an *insurance agent* of a licensed insurer and it has taken all reasonable steps to inform, or bring to the knowledge of potential policy owners and the public in general of the fact of such cessation.

[287][1999] 1 CLJ 179.

[288]This was in fact the view taken by Mahmood, above n 47, 121.

[289]This would be similar to s12 of the repealed *Insurance (Agents & Brokers) Act 1984* (Cth) (Australia), instead of just referring to the formative part of the insurance contract.

extensively reformed and consolidated the larger financial services industry, with intermediaries as a part of it.[290] There is however, no distinction made between agents and brokers in Australia, and the common law 'transferred agency' rule has long been abolished via s12 of the *Insurance (Agents & Brokers) Act 1984* (Cth) (Australia).

3.3.4 Statutory Warnings in Proposal Forms

In addition to ss150 and 151, s149 (4) of the *Insurance Act 1996* (Malaysia) required insurers to display a warning of the duty to disclose in proposal forms and request for particulars. It provided that:

> A proposal form and, where no formal proposal form is used, a request for particulars by the licensed insurer shall prominently display a warning that if a proposer does not fully and faithfully give the facts as he knows them or ought to know them, the policy may be invalidated.

Unfortunately however, the provision did not expressly stipulate a penalty for non-compliance, which should perhaps be the inability to avoid the insurance policy on grounds of non-disclosure, as is the case in Australia by virtue of s22 of the *Insurance Contracts Act 1984* (Cth) (Australia). It is also worth noting Mahmood's criticism of s16 (4) of the *Insurance Act 1963* (Malaysia) (which was the precursor to s149 (4) of the *Insurance Act 1996*(Malaysia)) as being a 'feeble legislative attempt' to caution potential policy holders of the harshness of the law relating to the duty of disclosure.[291]

Feeble, perhaps because the warning had to be displayed only where a proposal form or a request for particulars was used by the insurer, as opposed to whenever an insurance contract was concluded, for instance, so as to cover renewals as well. The said warning did not require insurers to 'clearly inform' insureds in writing of the nature and effect of the duty of disclosure, thereby resulting in its effectiveness being dependent entirely on consumers' ability to understand and appreciate its significance. Furthermore, it not only lacked a consequence for non-compliance by insurers but retained the harsh remedy of ab initio avoidance of the contract for non-disclosure, all of which have been discussed in Chap. 2.

---

[290]The Act came into effect on 11 March 2002 (subject to a two year transition period for some measures) and was the result of the Corporate Law Economic Reform Program (1997) (CLERP 6).

[291]Mahmood, above n 47, 48.

3.3.5 *Misrepresentation and 'Basis of Contract' Clauses*

As far as Malaysia is concerned, since there was no provision in the *Insurance Act 1996* (Malaysia) pertaining to misrepresentation (save for provisions on misstatement of age),[292] ss20 and 33 (3) of the *Marine Insurance Act 1906* (UK) along with the common law on the matter were accepted and applied in Malaysian cases.[293] The consequences of a breach of warranty and the effect of 'basis of contract' clauses at common law, were therefore, also applicable to insurance contracts in Malaysia.

The scope and application of misrepresentation in life insurance was however, restricted by the Malaysian legislature by virtue of the now repealed s147 of the *Insurance Act 1996* (Malaysia).[294]

Section 147 (1) provided that:

> A licensed life insurer shall not dispute liability under a life policy by reason only of a misstatement of the age of the life insured.

Sections 147 (2) and (3) went on to provide the method by which proportionate adjustments could be made by the insurer either to the sum insured or to the premium payable or to both on discovery of the correct age.[295]

A drawback of s147 (1) however, was that it made no exception for fraudulent misstatement of age and could as a result be unfair to insurers if they were

---

[292]This is by virtue of s147 of the *Insurance Act 1996* (Malaysia).

[293]This is facilitated by s5 of the *Civil Law Act 1956* (Malaysia).

[294]Section 147 is similar to the Australian s30 of the *Insurance Contracts Act 1984* (Cth).

[295]Section 147 (2) provided that:

Where the true age as shown by the proof is greater than that on which the life policy is based, the licensed life insurer may vary the sum insured by, and the bonuses allotted to, the life policy so that, as varied, they bear the same proportion to the sum insured by, and the bonuses allotted to, the life policy before variation as the amount of the premiums that have been paid under the life policy as issued bears to the amount of the premiums that would have become payable if the life policy had been based on the true age.

Section 147(3) provided that:

Where the true age as shown by the proof is less than that on which the life policy was based, the licensed life insurer—

(a) may vary the sum insured by, and the bonuses allotted to, the life policy so that, as varied, it bears the same proportion to the sum insured by, and the bonuses allotted to, the life policy, before variation as the amount of the premiums that have been paid under the life policy as issued bears to the amount of the premiums that would have become payable if the life policy had been based on the true age; or

(b) may reduce the premium as from the date of issue of the life policy, to the amount that would have been payable if the life policy had been based on the true age and repay the policy owner the amount of over-payments of premium less any amount that has been paid as the cash value of bonuses in excess of the cash value that would have been paid if the life policy had been based on the true age.

prevented by this provision from raising an allegation of fraudulent misstatement of age in appropriate cases.

Another provision of significance was s147 (4) which read:

> A licensed life insurer shall not dispute the validity of a policy after the expiry of two years from the date on which it was effected on the ground that a statement made or omitted to be made in the proposal for insurance or in a report of a doctor, referee, or any other person, or in a document leading to the issue of the life policy, was inaccurate or false or misleading unless the licensed life insurer shows that the statement was on a material matter or suppressed a material fact and that it was fraudulently made or omitted to be made by the policy owner.

This provision generally restricted the application of the common law principles relating to misrepresentation and non-disclosure in life policies. In doing so, it significantly restricted the avenues open to insurers in avoiding a life policy that has been in force for two years or more. Neither the existence of a 'basis of contract' clause nor the mere fact of the materiality of misrepresented or non-disclosed information was a sufficient ground for avoiding such policies. The insurer could only avoid liability if it could be shown that the misrepresentation or non-disclosure was material and that it was fraudulently made.[296]

Section 147 (5) went on to describe a 'material matter' or 'material fact' in s147 (4) as meaning:

> … a matter of fact which, if known by the licensed life insurer, would have led to its refusal to issue a life policy to the policy owner or would have led it to impose terms less favourable to the policy owner than those imposed in the life policy.

This was a useful provision with respect to potential claims of misrepresentation or non-disclosure against the insured of a life insurance policy after the expiry of two years from the insurance contract coming into existence. It however, did nothing for an insured alleged to have committed misrepresentation or non-disclosure of a relevant matter within the two year period, even if the misrepresentation or non-disclosure had no bearing on the loss suffered.

There was also no provision preventing the use of 'basis of contract' clauses in Malaysia like that of s24 of the *Insurance Contracts Act 1984* (Cth) with respect to Australia. This was exacerbated by the fact that, almost every type of insurance proposal form used in Malaysia contained a 'basis of contract' clause. These clauses had the effect of doing away with the element of materiality to be proven in a claim of misrepresentation, thereby having the potential to cause significant harm to unwary insureds.

One such case was *Suhaimi bin Ibrahim v United Malaya Insurance Co Ltd*,[297] which concerned a workmen's compensation policy containing a 'basis of contract' clause in the proposal form. The fact that the insured stated that six persons would be employed by him on a timber extraction project, when in fact there were 23

---

[296] *Azizah bt Abdullah v Arab Malaysian Eagles Sdn Bhd* [1996] 5 MLJ 569.

[297] [1966] 1 MLJ 140. The decision in *Dawsons v Bonnin* [1922] AC 413 was applied here.

employees at the time of loss which was the death of one of the tree fellers by a falling tree, was held to be a breach of warranty due to the 'basis of contract' clause. This therefore entitled the insurer to avoid liability for the loss despite the immateriality of the misrepresentation. A similar decision was also arrived at in *Leong Chee Yeong v China Insurance Co Ltd*[298] which was a case involving a breach of a promissory warranty created by a 'basis of contract' clause in the proposal form of a personal accident policy. The Court of Appeal in *American International Assurance Co Ltd v Nadarajan a/l Subramaniam*[299] in fact, went so far as to hold that it was not the court's function to inquire into the materiality of the answers where there was a 'basis of contract' clause in the proposal form.

The continuation of this unfortunate state of affairs is apparent from the Court of Appeal's decision in *Leong Kum Whay v QBE Insurance (M) Sdn Bhd.*[300] Apart from the damage done by the said decision to the law on non-disclosure, the fact that the 'basis of contract' clause contained in the proposal form of the original personal accident policy taken out by the insured was held to be operative in the renewed policy merely by way of reference in the renewal certificate, shows the extent to which such clauses could reach and hence, cause injustice to unwary insureds.

Australia on the other hand, has by virtue of ss23–29 of its *Insurance Contracts Act 1984* (Cth) (Australia) provided for a comprehensive method of dealing with pre-contractual misrepresentation, whereby causal connection to the loss is required to be shown in order for it to be actionable. It also provides for the availability of damages in the event of breach, as is the case for non-disclosure as well, to be assessed proportionately for misrepresentation pertaining to life insurance[301] and according to common law damages when it concerns general insurance.[302]

Section 23 of the *Insurance Contracts Act 1984* (Cth) (Australia) in turn, addresses the issue of ambiguous questions whereby such questions would be interpreted in the manner in which a reasonable person in the circumstances would have understood them to be. Failure to answer a question in the proposal form or giving an obviously incomplete or irrelevant answer to such a question would also not in itself amount to misrepresentation.[303]

Also, pre-contractual statements made by the insured unless made knowingly or a reasonable person in the circumstances could be expected to have known that it would be relevant to the insurer's decision on whether to accept the risk and on

---

[298] [1952] MLJ 246.

[299] [2013] 5 MLJ 195.

[300] [2006] 1 CLJ 1. This has been discussed in detail in Chap. 2. This section draws on research appearing in: Thanasegaran (2007, p. clv).

[301] Section 29 of the *Insurance Contracts Act 1984* (Cth) (Australia).

[302] Section 28 of the *Insurance Contracts Act 1984* (Cth) (Australia). Limited recourse to avoidance is only available (subject to s31) in the event of fraudulent misrepresentation by the insured.

[303] Section 27 of the *Insurance Contracts Act 1984* (Cth) (Australia).

what terms, would not amount to a misrepresentation.[304] Furthermore, if untrue statements were made by the insured at the pre-contractual stage based on the insured's belief, being a belief that a reasonable person in the circumstances would have held, it would also not amount to a misrepresentation.[305]

3.3.6 *Central Bank Guidelines*

Prior to the recent reforms in 2013, the law in Malaysia on matters such as non-disclosure and minimum disclosure requirements was governed by the *Insurance Act 1996* (Malaysia) and certain Guidelines and Codes of Practice issued by the Central Bank to insurers, as and when the need arose.

Clause 5 of the *Guidelines on Minimum Disclosure Requirements in the Sale of Insurance Products* (Malaysia) which came into effect on 2 January 2006 for instance, requires insurers to use clear and simple language in their communication with proposers of insurance. It also requires insurers to avoid using technical terms and be accurate and complete in substance.[306] Pursuant to Clause 6, insurers are required to give priority to conveying the importance of completing the proposal form accurately, along with the consequences of failing to do so, with the aim of reducing inadvertent misrepresentation or non-disclosure by proposers of insurance.

Clause 3.4 of the *Guidelines on Claims Settlement Practices* (Malaysia) ('*Claims Settlement Guidelines*') in turn, provides that insurers should not repudiate a claim for technical breaches of warranty or policy conditions which are not material or unconnected to the loss unless it has prejudiced the insurer's interest or exceeded the time bar under law; or on grounds of non-disclosure or misrepresentation unless it is a deliberate or negligent non-disclosure or misrepresentation of material facts.[307] Furthermore, any repudiation is required to contain a prominent statement about recourse to the Insurance Mediation Bureau or its successor the Financial Mediation Bureau which was set up in 2005, so as to both educate insureds of this and deter attempts by insurers to avoid policies based on innocent or non-fraudulent non-disclosure.

However, the *Claims Settlement Guidelines* lack effectiveness since they do not provide for any sanctions against insurers in the event of non-compliance. They

---

[304]Section 26 (2) of the *Insurance Contracts Act 1984* (Cth) (Australia).

[305]Section 26 (1) of the *Insurance Contracts Act 1984* (Cth) (Australia).

[306]Central Bank of Malaysia (2006). Similarly, Clause 8 of the Central Bank of Malaysia (1997) which came into effect on 1 January 1998, requires proposal forms to be written in clear and simple language and questions posed therein to be specific in nature.

[307]Central Bank of Malaysia (2003). This is presumably the most important of the Guidelines issued by the Central Bank, with the revised version coming into effect on 16 September 2003. The purpose of which is to further enhance the minimum standards to be observed by insurers in claims processing and settlement including fraud control and risk management measures: Clause 2.

have also not been given effect to by the Malaysian courts in the cases that have come before them on claims settlement, as they lack the force of law.[308]

That which is promising nevertheless, is the fact that the Mediators of both the Insurance Mediation Bureau (from 1995 to 2004) and the Financial Mediation Bureau (from 2005)[309] have regularly invoked the *Claims Settlement Guidelines* in determining the reasonableness of the conduct of both insurers and insureds, in insurance matters.[310] This has in turn contributed positively to somewhat balance the scales between insurers and insureds in claims settlement, as the Bureau hears most of the complaints or cases on alleged breaches of utmost good faith by insurers in the area as opposed to the civil courts.[311]

3.3.7 Pre-contractual Disclosure and Misrepresentation Under the Financial Services Act 2013

The *Financial Services Act 2013* (Malaysia) which came into effect on 30th June 2013, repeals the *Insurance Act 1996* (Malaysia)[312] and is influenced in part by the provisions of the *Insurance Contracts Act 1984* (Cth) (Australia), as well as the

---

[308]See: *Leong Kum Whay v QBE Insurance (M) Sdn Bhd* [2006] 1 CLJ 1. This section draws on research appearing in: Thanasegaran (2011, pp. 197–198).

[309]This is acknowledged and reported in the Financial Mediation Bureau (2008, p. 14). It is in line with and pursuant to the Financial Mediation Bureau's Terms of Reference as embodied in its Memorandum and Articles of Association:
Mediators are required (i) to have regard to and act in conformity (a) with the terms of any contract; (b) any applicable rule of law, judicial authority or statutory provision; and (c) the general principles of good insurance, investment or market practice, the Central Bank's *Guidelines on Claims Settlement Practices* for insurance and *takaful* matters but with (c) prevailing over (b) in favour of the complainant; (ii) to have regard to (without being bound by) any previous decision of any Mediator; (iii) in light of (i) and (ii), to assess what solution would be fair and reasonable in all the circumstances.

[310]Acknowledgment of this fact is reflected in the Financial Mediation Bureau (2009, p. 20), where the Mediator stressed that the *Claims Settlement Guidelines* have been adopted by the Bureau and its predecessor since 1995 as being reflective of good insurance practice rather than industry practice per se.

[311]This is apparent from the fact that the Financial Mediation Bureau is very popular amongst complainants, with an average of more than 1000 new cases being referred annually from 2000 to 2014 and a large proportion of them comprising allegations by insurers of breach of utmost good faith by insureds in one form or another: See: Table of Cases Referred to the Financial Mediation Bureau from 2000 to 2014 in the Appendix. This can be compared to there being less than 100 reported decisions on insurance from the courts for the same period. In fact, the Mediator's Report in the Financial Mediation Bureau (2006, p. 19), acknowledged this trend of a scarce number of insurance cases being filed in the courts in recent years, stating that insurance intermediaries have now resorted to the Case Review published in the Bureau's Annual Reports for their guidance and reference.

[312]Section 271 of the *Financial Services Act 2013* (Malaysia) repeals the *Insurance Act 1996* (Malaysia) but s272 retains the application of the *Insurance Regulations 1996* as amended in 2013.

English and Scottish reforms introduced via the *Consumer Insurance (Disclosure and Representations) Act 2012* (UK).

As set out above, the *Insurance Act 1996* (Malaysia) had a provision setting out the insured's pre-contractual duty of disclosure in s150 which applied the 'reasonable insured' test but was silent on the duty to refrain from making misrepresentations. As a result, pre-contractual misrepresentations were governed by the common law and s20 of the *Marine Insurance Act 1906* (UK) which required the insured to refrain from making misrepresentations that the *insurer* would deem *material,* thereby imposing the onerous 'prudent insurer' and 'mere influence' tests of materiality of information disclosed, on the insured and its corresponding problems to insurance contracts in Malaysia. The application of 'basis of contract' clauses has continued to create problems for unwary insureds by incorporating their answers in proposal forms into the insurance policy and converting them into warranties of past or present facts, thereby enabling insurers to avoid liability ab initio for incorrect representations, without having to prove materiality of the representations.

The *Insurance Act 1996* (Malaysia) also failed to address the remedies available in the event of breach of these obligations, thus, leaving the all or nothing common law remedy of avoidance of contract and a refund of premium paid, as the only recourse available, instead of a more balanced remedy that corresponds with the loss suffered.

The *Financial Services Act 2013* (Malaysia) addresses these problems in the following manner. Section 129 provides that 'Schedule 9 sets out the pre-contractual duty of disclosure and representations for contracts of insurance in Part 2, and the remedies for misrepresentations relating to contracts of insurance in Part 3.' Paragraph 4 of *Schedule 9* to the Act which relates to *non-consumer insurance contracts* essentially adopts the voluntary disclosure mechanism applicable in Australia[313] that requires the insured before the contract is entered into to disclose matters he or she knows to be relevant to the insurer in accepting the risk or the rates and terms to be applied or that which 'a reasonable person in the circumstances' could be expected to know to be relevant. Paragraph 5 of *Schedule 9* in turn, which relates to *consumer insurance contracts* adopts the inquiry based disclosure mechanism applicable in the United Kingdom and in Australian-eligible contracts[314] that requires the insured before the contract is entered into to take reasonable care not to misrepresent to the insurer when answering specific questions posed by the insurer or when confirming or amending any matters previously disclosed as provided by the insurer in writing. The standard of care required in doing so is 'what a reasonable consumer in the circumstances would have known.'[315]

[313]See: Section 21 of the *Insurance Contracts Act 1984* (Cth) (Australia).

[314]See: Section 2 (2) of the *Consumer Insurance (Disclosure and Representations) Act 2012* (UK) and s21A of the *Insurance Contracts Act 1984* (Cth) (Australia).

[315]See: Paragraph 6 (2) of *Schedule 9* to the *Financial Services Act 2013* (Malaysia) which is based on s3 of the *Consumer Insurance (Disclosure and Representations) Act 2012* (UK) and s21A of the *Insurance Contracts Act 1984* (Cth) (Australia).

According to Paragraphs 4 (3), 5 (5) and 5 (6) of *Schedule 9*, the insurer is deemed to have waived any non-disclosure or incomplete disclosure by proposers, should it fail to pursue the said non-compliance any further.

The *Financial Services Act 2013* (Malaysia)'s provisions relating to pre-contractual non-disclosure are fairly comprehensive in tackling the obligations clearly and also address both consumer and non-consumer insurance contracts. However, the remedies for breach of the duty have not been clearly set out. It may have been intended to be covered by the remedies appearing in Part 3 of *Schedule 9* which relate to misrepresentations. Nevertheless, Part 3 only contains headings and provisions that make specific reference to remedies for misrepresentation. Although many alleged non-disclosures would in essence amount to misrepresentations, especially with respect to consumer insurance contracts requiring inquiry based disclosure, it would nevertheless be good to provide for a residual remedy for a breach of the duty of disclosure per se.

Paragraph 7 (3) of *Schedule 9* classifies pre-contractual misrepresentation by consumers as being deliberate or reckless, careless and innocent. Paragraph 7 (4) provides that a deliberate or reckless misrepresentation is where the consumer knew that the misrepresentation was untrue or misleading or did not care if it was *and* knew that the misrepresentation was relevant to the insurer or did not care if it was. It is for the insurer to prove on a balance of probability that a misrepresentation is deliberate or reckless, with a dishonest representation being regarded as being made deliberately or recklessly.[316] Paragraph 7 (6) on the other hand, provides that a misrepresentation is careless or innocent if it is not deliberate or reckless.

Under Paragraph 13 (2) of *Schedule 9*, misrepresentations made in consumer or non-consumer life insurance contracts in effect for more than 2 years cannot entitle the insurer to avoid the contract unless the 'insurer shows that the statement was on a material matter or suppressed a material fact *and* that it was *fraudulently* made or omitted.' On the question of materiality, it is dependent on whether if it was known by the insurer it would have led to its refusal to issue an insurance certificate or the imposition of terms less favourable to the insured; and should the insurer be permitted to avoid the contract, it must refund payments received there under.[317]

With respect to misrepresentations made in a *consumer* life insurance contract in effect for 2 years or less or in a *consumer* general insurance contract, the insurer is under Paragraph 15 entitled to avoid the contract, refund payments received pursuant thereto and refuse all claims, should the misrepresentation be deliberate or reckless. If the misrepresentation was careless or innocent on the other hand, Paragraph 16 provides that if the insurer would not have entered into or renewed the contract on any terms, it may avoid the contract, refund payments received and

---

[316]See: Paragraphs 7 (7) and 7 (5) respectively of *Schedule 9* to the *Financial Services Act 2013* (Malaysia). It should be noted that Paragraph 7 (8) contains a balanced provision that unless the contrary is shown, it is presumed that the consumer knew that a matter about which the insurer asked a clear and specific question was relevant to the insurer.

[317]See: Paragraphs 13 (4) and 13 (3) respectively of *Schedule 9* to the *Financial Services Act 2013* (Malaysia).

refuse all claims. However, if it would have entered into or renewed the contract on different terms other than the contribution amount, the contract is treated as being on those terms. Lastly, if it would have entered into or renewed the contract by charging a higher premium, then it may proportionately reduce the amount payable under the claim.

The express duty not to make pre-contractual misrepresentation coupled with detailed remedies in the event of breach is a major improvement in the law. The said provisions would have however, been more comprehensive had they applied to **all** insurance contracts. Instead, as it stands, non-consumer general insurance contracts and non-consumer life insurance contracts in effect for 2 years or less have been left out. As a result, there are no residual remedies applicable in the event of misrepresentations in these contracts. To compound matters, it is unclear whether s20 of the *Marine Insurance Act 1906* (UK) would apply to those insurance contracts, in which case insureds would again be bound by the sole remedy of avoidance of the contract with only a refund of premium paid, in the event of breach, which would be unsatisfactory.

Arising from the duty of disclosure is the requirement for insurers to provide a clear warning in insurance proposal forms to proposers of insurance, of the consequences of pre-contractual non-disclosure on the insurance contract. Section 149 (4) of the *Insurance Act 1996* (Malaysia) had provided for this, albeit without reference to the remedy applicable in the event of failure to do so by the insurer. Paragraphs 5 (7) and 4 (4) of *Schedule 9* to the *Financial Services Act 2013* (Malaysia) provide an improvement to this with respect to consumer and non-consumer insurance contracts respectively, by requiring insurers before an insurance contract is entered into, varied or renewed, to *clearly inform* a proposer *in writing* of the pre-contractual duty of disclosure and that it shall *continue until* the contract is entered into, varied or renewed.[318]

A related issue is the question of the relationship between insurers and insurance agents and the effect of information and knowledge received by the insurance agent during negotiations, for the purposes of formation or variation of the insurance contract. Paragraph 12 (1) reinforces the previous position in s151 of the *Insurance Act 1996* (Malaysia) that the insurance agent is deemed to be the insurer's agent in this regard with respect to the formation of the insurance contract and has expanded its scope to cover any variation of the contract as well. As a result, the agent's knowledge is deemed to be that of the insurer.

A major problem in insurance contracts so far has been the inclusion of 'basis of contract' clauses in insurance proposal forms that have the effect of turning answers and information provided by insureds into warranties. This has severely reduced the requirement for insurers to have been 'induced' by any misrepresentation in order for it to be actionable. Almost all insurance proposal forms in Malaysia have in the

[318]This provision takes into account the improvement made to s22 of the *Insurance Contracts Act 1984* (Cth) (Australia) by the *Insurance Contracts Amendment Act 2013* (Cth) (Australia).

past contained 'basis of contract' clauses which have had a detrimental effect on unassuming insureds, despite there being no juridical basis for its use.

This problem has been addressed by Paragraph 10 of *Schedule 9* that abolishes the use of 'basis of contract' clauses in *consumer* insurance contracts. This provision appears to have been based on s6 (2) of the *Consumer Insurance (Disclosure and Representations) Act 2012* (UK) which as its name and scope suggests, applies to consumer insurance contracts alone. The *Financial Services Act 2013* (Malaysia) on the other hand, replaces the *Insurance Act 1996* (Malaysia) which is an Act that is applicable to **all** types of insurance contracts in Malaysia and hence, should cover both consumer and *non-consumer* insurance contracts alike. In this sense, s24 of the *Insurance Contracts Act 1984 (Cth)* (Australia) would have been a better provision to emulate as it abolishes 'basis of contract' clauses in **all** insurance contracts.

3.4 Conclusion

Paragraphs 5 and 4 of *Schedule 9* to the *Financial Services Act 2013* (Malaysia) are fairly comprehensive in setting out the pre-contractual duty of disclosure with respect to both consumer and non-consumer insurance contracts, respectively. The drawback however, is that the remedies for breach of the duty have not been addressed, unlike the clear reference made in Part 3 of *Schedule 9* with respect to pre-contractual misrepresentations.

As for misrepresentation, on the other hand, the provisions would have been more comprehensive had they applied to **all** insurance contracts instead of leaving out non-consumer general insurance contracts and non-consumer life insurance contracts in effect for 2 years or less. As a result, there are no residual remedies applicable in the event of misrepresentations in these contracts, which begs the question as to whether s20 of the *Marine Insurance Act 1906* (UK) and the remedy of avoidance of contract would be applicable to the same.

Lastly, the abolition of 'basis of contract' clauses in *consumer* insurance contracts by virtue of Paragraph 10 of *Schedule 9* would have been more effective in dealing with the long-standing mischief caused by such clauses, had it applied to **all** types of insurance contracts in Malaysia, instead of omitting *non-consumer* insurance contracts.

Malaysia needs to address this in a uniform manner and not discriminate between consumer and non-consumer insurance contracts with respect to utmost good faith in general, the application of basis of contract clauses and aspects of pre-contractual non-disclosure and misrepresentation as highlighted above. Non-consumer insurance contracts cannot be left to rely merely on the Central Bank's *Claims Settlement Guidelines* which direct insurers to conduct themselves in a fair and reasonable manner in settling claims as they lack enforceable sanctions[319]; and the flexible and proactive way in which the Mediators of the Financial Mediation Bureau of Malaysia have resolved the disputes appearing before them.[320]

References

Abdul Mubarak A (2002) Test of Materiality under the Insurance Act 1996. Current Law Journal xlix 2:8

Association of British Insurers (1986a) Statement of general insurance practice, London (Rev 1986)

Association of British Insurers (1986b) Statement of long term insurance practice, London (Rev 1986)

Australian Law Reform Commission (1982) Report No 20, Insurance contracts

Birds J (1982) The Reform of Insurance Law. J Bus Law 449

Birds J (2013) Birds' modern insurance law, 9th edn. Sweet & Maxwell, London

Birds J, Hird N (1996) Misrepresentation and non-disclosure in insurance law—identical twins or separate issues? Mod Law Rev 59:285

Brooke H (1985) Materiality in insurance contracts'. Lloyd's Maritime Commercial Law Quarterly, 43

Central Bank of Malaysia (1997) Code of good practice for life insurance business, Kuala Lumpur

Central Bank of Malaysia (2003) Guidelines on claims settlement practices, Kuala Lumpur (Rev 2003)

Central Bank of Malaysia (2006) Guidelines on minimum disclosure requirements in the sale of insurance products, Kuala Lumpur

Clarke M (1988) Failure to disclose and failure to legislate: is it material?—II. J Bus Law, 298

Clarke M (2003) Refusing rescission: contracts of utmost bad faith. Camb Law J, 556

Eggers P (2003) Remedies for the failure to observe the utmost good faith. Lloyd's maritime commercial law quarterly, 249

English and Scottish Law Commission Joint Consultation Paper Summary on Insurance Contract Law: Misrepresentation, Non-Disclosure and Breach of Warranty by the Insured, 17 July 2007

Evans RC (1984) The role of expert evidence as to materiality in insurance contracts. Aust Bus Law Rev 12(4)

Financial Mediation Bureau (2006–2014) Annual reports 2005–2013, Kuala Lumpur

Financial Ombudsman Service (1990–1991) Insurance Ombudsman Annual Report 1989–1990, London

Financial Services Authority (2005a) Insurance Conduct of Business, London

Financial Services Authority (2005b) Conduct of Business, London

Forte ADM (1986) The revised statements of insurance practice. Mod Law Rev 49:754

Gan CC (1997) Non disclosure. J Malays Comp Law 24:185

Hamilton J (1995) The duty of disclosure in insurance law—the effectiveness of self-regulation. Aust Bus Law Re 23:359

Hasson RA (1971) The "Basis of the Contract Clause" in insurance law. Mod Law Rev 34:29

[319]See: Clause 3.4 of the *Claims Settlement Guidelines*. A major drawback is that the Guidelines have no clear sanctions set out as being applicable in the event of non-compliance.

[320]See: Financial Mediation Bureau (2009, p. 20). This section draws on research appearing in: Thanasegaran and Shaiban (2014, p. 343).

Hasson RA (1984) The special nature of insurance contracts: a comparison of the American and English law of insurance. Mod Law Rev 47:505
Hawke F (2006) The innocents abroad. Insur Law J 17:2
Hertzell D, Burgoyne L (2013) The law commissions and insurance contract law reform: an update. J Int Marit Law 19:105
Hird N (1995a) Rationality in the house of lords? J Bus Law, 194
Hird N (1995b) Pan Atlantic—yet more to disclose? J Bus Law, 608
Law Commission (1980) Insurance law: non-disclosure and breach of warranty, Report No 104, Cmnd 8064
Law Commission and Scottish Law Commission (1975) Exemption clauses, Law Com No 69 and Scot Law Com No 39
Law Reform Committee (1957) Conditions and Exceptions in Insurance Policies, Report No 5, Cmnd 62
Legh-Jones N, Birds J, Owen D (eds) (2003) MacGillivray on Insurance Law, 10th edn. Sweet & Maxwell, London
Mahmood NR (1992) Insurance law in Malaysia. Butterworths, Malaysia
Mann P, Lewis C (2014) Mann's Annotated Insurance Contracts Act, 6th edn. Lawbook Co
Merkin R (1976) Uberrimae Fidei Strikes Again. Mod Law Rev 39:478
Merkin R (ed) (2000) Kluwer's Insurance Contract Law, Revised ed. vol 1. Croner CCH Group Ltd, London
Poh CC (2005) Principles of insurance law, 6th edn. Butterworths, Singapore
Thanasegaran H (2004) Insurers' good faith in Malaysia: does a search for a fairer balance in non-marine insurance contracts lead to Australia? Insur Law J 15:143
Thanasegaran H (2007) To renew or not to renew—what are the questions? An evaluation of the statutory warning in insurance contracts. Malayan Law J 2:cxlvii
Thanasegaran H (2008) Growth of Islamic Insurance (Takaful) in Malaysia: a model for the region? Singapore J Leg Stud, 143
Thanasegaran H (2011) Settlement of claims by Malaysian Insurance and *Takaful* Companies: a genuine prospect or merely suspect? Int Company Commer Law Rev 22(6):191
Thanasegaran H, Shaiban M (2014) Harmonization of Takaful (Islamic Insurance) regulation—a realistic goal or improbable ideal? Singapore J Leg Stud, 328
Ying YH (1990) Common law materiality—an Australian alternative. J Bus Law, 97

Chapter 4
Post-contractual Good Faith and Claims Settlement

Abstract This chapter evaluates the post-contractual duty of utmost good faith which primarily arises in relation to claims management and settlement practices. It looks at the implications of strict construction of contract terms by insurers, the prevalence of wide exclusions often contained in insurance contracts, as well as undesirable claims settlement practices that often cause undue delay, rejection and reduction of settlement sums by insurers. In this context, the making of improper and fraudulent claims by insureds is also examined and a comparative analysis of the English, Malaysian and Australian reforms pertaining to post-contractual good faith will be made.

4.1 Introduction

This chapter examines the post-contractual aspect of the duty of utmost good faith which arises in claims management and settlement practices. It looks at the implications of strict construction of contract terms and the reliance on wide exclusions in insurance contracts by insurers, as well as undesirable claims settlement practices that lead to undue delay, rejection and reduced settlements by insurers. The chapter also examines improper and fraudulent claims made by insureds.[1]

The justification and juridical basis for the continuing post-contractual duty of good faith has been set out in Chap. 2 of this book. In essence, although such a duty exists, it is not as extensive as once thought[2]; and owing to its different juridical

[1]Fraudulent claims by insureds is only briefly considered here, as it has been discussed in Chap. 2 of this book.

[2]This was following Hirst J's wide formulation of the duty in *Black King Shipping Corp v Massie (The Litsion Pride)* [1985] 1 Lloyd's Rep 437.

H. Thanasegaran, *Good Faith in Insurance and Takaful Contracts in Malaysia*,
DOI 10.1007/978-981-10-0383-7_4

basis from that of the pre-contractual duty of good faith,[3] the remedies available in the event of breach would also differ.

This justification for the post-contractual duty is the prevalence of a lack of control in insurance contracts over the years, which has resulted in insurers freely dictating their own terms.[4] The juridical basis for this can in turn be divided into two. With respect to the application of post-contractual terms and claims handling, it has been convincingly argued to be based on an implied term of the contract to that effect. This would give rise to the more proportionate remedy of prospective avoidance of the claim in question and/or damages rather than come within the purview of s17 of the *Marine Insurance Act 1906* (UK)'s remedy of avoidance ab initio.[5] The juristic basis for fraudulent claims on the other hand, has been held to be founded on the public policy reasoning that one should not benefit from one's own wrongdoing, and hence, technically falls out of the ambit of the continuing duty of good faith.[6]

Based on this reasoning, there has been increasing support for invoking the post-contractual duty of utmost good faith to claims handling and management, where insurers deliberately delay paying genuine claims and act unfairly in rejecting or reducing valid claims, thereby causing unnecessary loss to insureds.[7] A clear example of such an instance is *Sprung v Royal Insurance Co (UK) Ltd*,[8] where Evans LJ in delivering the judgment of the Court of Appeal recognised the existence of an implied term of contract which required insurers to act fairly.[9] It is in this vein that this chapter is written.

Upon the occurrence of the event insured under the policy, an insured is in principle entitled to make a claim against the insurer either for the sum insured or to the extent of the loss occasioned.[10] It is imperative however, for the insured to strictly comply with the terms of the policy when making such a claim. To begin with, the insured must notify the insurer of the loss and then, go on to prove the truth of the claim, that the insured has in fact suffered a loss proximately caused by

---

[3]The pre-contractual duty of utmost good faith has been based on the common law pronouncement in s17 of the *Marine Insurance Act 1906* (UK).

[4]Hasson (1984, pp. 517–518).

[5]See: Naidoo and Oughton (2005, p. 371), Soyer (2003, p. 79); *The Star Sea* [2001] 1 Lloyd's Rep 389 (Lord Hobhouse).

[6]See: *The Star Sea* [2001] 1 Lloyd's Rep 389 (Lord Hobhouse), *The Mercandian Continent* [2001] EWCA Civ 1275 (Longmore LJ), *Agapitos v Agnew (The Aegeon)* [2002] 2 Lloyd's Rep 42 (Mance LJ).

[7]See: Bennett (1999, 197); Soyer, above n 5, 70; *Manifest Shipping & Co Ltd v Uni-Polaris Insurance Co Ltd* [1997] 1 Lloyd's Rep 360, 370 (Leggatt LJ).

[8][1999] Lloyd's Rep I R 111.

[9]The insured in this case was however, unsuccessful on the grounds of losses consequent on failure to pay a valid insurance claim being irrecoverable in English law.

[10]An indemnity insurance pays based on the actual value of the loss occasioned from the peril insured whereas a contingency insurance pays based on an amount stipulated in the insurance contract when a specified event occurs, both of which are addressed in this chapter.

an insured peril.[11] This is often a challenging task, as insureds generally tend not to read their policies until a loss arises or a claim is made and even then, many insureds end up not understanding the full extent of the terms. The insured is placed at a serious disadvantage as neither of these are a defence in law.

The insurer on the other hand, upon a claim being made, will ensure that the policy in question is examined thoroughly, in order to establish the existence of an insurable interest in the policy on the part of the insured; and strict compliance by the insured of the pre-contractual duty of disclosure as well as all the terms of the policy. There will also be a thorough investigation of the loss by the insurer to ensure that it falls within the scope of the risk insured, in order to eventually determine the actual amount of loss suffered.

The nature of claims handling in insurance, when viewed in totality, makes it clear how an otherwise genuine insured loss may end up being rejected or not indemnified in full. It is imperative to appreciate that this process is inherently fraught with conflict and therefore, requires utmost good faith to be observed by both parties. This is crucial in order to achieve the true objective of indemnifying a genuine insured (who has kept up with premium payments) for an insured loss suffered.[12]

Since the law concerning the post-contractual duty of utmost good faith in Malaysia has been largely based on English common law, the position in the United Kingdom right up to the recent amendments in the *Insurance Act 2015* (UK) will first be set out before analysing the position in Malaysia and Australia.

4.2 Application of the Law in the United Kingdom

It is important to understand that an insurance contract is not a stand-alone contract but is instead made up of various documents. It comprises the insurance policy itself, the cover note, the proposal form which precedes the policy and any other document incorporated by reference in the proposal form. The most common of which are medical forms completed by the examining doctor in life insurance policies. The cover note is usually issued prior to the policy and lapses when the actual policy documentation is issued. In this context, insurance policies have also been described as being 'often notoriously complex documents riddled with jargon, their layout is often muddled to the untrained eye, and the print, or some of it, may be very small'.[13]

Hence, it can be an insurmountable challenge for an insured to make a successful claim on the policy. First, the insured would have to give notice of the loss to the insurer in the exact manner and form required by the policy. The insured would then have to prove the actual claim being made. This would require the insured to

[11]Clarke (2005, p. 182).

[12]This section draws on research appearing in: Thanasegaran (2011, pp. 191–192).

[13]Birds (2013, p. 232).

show that the loss arose within the terms of the policy providing cover; was not caught out by any exclusion clauses in the policy; and was proximately caused by the peril insured against. It becomes clear when viewed from this perspective that the entire process relies substantially on the construction and interpretation of the words used in the insurance contract.[14]

4.2.1 Construction of Policies

The rules of construction applicable to the terms of an insurance contract are in essence the same as those applying to any other type of contract.[15] The crucial difference however, stems from consumer insurance contracts being widely acknowledged as 'contracts of adhesion.' The significance of this is that the insured, who is normally the party not responsible for drafting the standard form contract, has in essence, no clout or opportunity for that matter, to influence the insurer in producing the insurance contract or incorporating any terms within.[16]

The basic rule of construction is that the terms of a written contract must be construed in the context of the contract as a whole. This is apparent from the English Court of Appeal's decision in *Hamlyn v Crown Accidental Insurance Co Ltd*[17] where an insured who dislocated his knee whilst trying to pick up a marble dropped by a child was held to come within the cover of 'bodily injury caused by violent, accidental, external and visible means'. This was on the basis that the term 'external' covered causes not arising from internal disease or weakness and therefore, fell outside the scope of the exclusion clause in the policy which prevented injury from 'natural disease or weakness'. A more recent application of this principle can be seen in *Rohan Investments Ltd v Cunningham*.[18]

Written words in a contract must be given their plain and ordinary meaning where they are reasonably clear, unless they have acquired a more special meaning as a result of trade usage.[19] Where there is a conflict between printed and written words, the written word must take precedence as being representative of the specific intention of the parties.[20] When the terms of a policy are reasonably clear, the courts are required to give effect to them even though the requirement itself or the result they bring about is unreasonable. On the other hand, when there is ambiguity in the

---

[14]This section draws on research appearing in: Thanasegaran, above n 12, 193–194.

[15]*Cementation Piling and Foundations Ltd v Aegon Insurance Co Ltd* [1995] 1 Lloyd's Rep 97, 101 (Sir Ralph Gibson).

[16]See: Kessler (1943). It should be noted however, that not all insurance policies are contracts of adhesion, for example commercial policies.

[17][1893] 1 QB 750.

[18][1999] Lloyd's Rep I R 190.

[19]*Aswan Engineering Establishment Co Ltd v Iron Trades Mutual Insurance Co Ltd* [1989] 1 Lloyd's Rep 289; *Hammersley v National Transport Insurance* [2015] TASFC 5.

[20]*Robertson v French* (1803) 4 East 130.

words of a policy which is capable of giving rise to more than one meaning, the courts would apply the *contra proferentum* rule and construe the term against the party seeking to rely on it.[21] The rule however, cannot be used to create or magnify an ambiguity where the terms of contract are clear.[22]

In *Harris v Poland*[23] for example, an insured who took out a householder's comprehensive policy which covered 'loss or damage caused by fire' was held to be entitled to claim for the loss of her pearl necklace. She had wrapped and hidden the necklace in her fireplace when she left home and accidentally destroyed it later that day upon her return, when she absent-mindedly lit a fire therein. The court decided that the coverage was for unintentional loss by fire, irrespective of whether the 'fire comes to the insured property or the insured property comes to the fire'.[24] However, it is not always clear whether a term is indeed ambiguous and judicial disagreement on the matter is not uncommon.[25]

As explained, the *contra proforentum* rule is of no assistance where there is no ambiguity on the face of the contract even if it results in an unreasonable outcome. In such instances, the courts in the United States have been more willing to construe policy terms so as to fulfil the 'reasonable expectations of the insured'.[26] The Supreme Court of New Jersey in *Gerhardt v Continental Insurance Companies*[27] for instance, held the insurer of a householder's comprehensive insurance policy providing indemnity against third party liability, not to be entitled to rely on an otherwise clear exclusion. This was on the basis that an exclusion of third party liability in the form of bodily injury to the insured's domestic employee is not that which an average insured would expect of third party liability coverage.

It is interesting to note that the Canadian courts have adopted a more restrictive version of the 'reasonable expectation of the insured' approach to construction. For instance, in *Wigle v Allstate Insurance Co of Canada*,[28] the Ontario Court of Appeal noted that there were three versions of the reasonable expectations doctrine in the United States, with only the first being applied in Canada. One was used to resolve ambiguity in some cases; the other a means to impose coverage reasonably expected to be provided except in the face of clear exclusion; and lastly, to give effect to the reasonable expectation of an insured addressed objectively, irrespective of any policy terms to the contrary.[29]

---

[21] *Zurich General Accident and Liability Insurance Co Ltd v Morrison* [1942] 2 KB 53.

[22] See: *Cornish v Accident Insurance Co Ltd* (1889) 23 QBD 453, 456 (Lindley LJ).

[23] [1914] 1 KB 462.

[24] Ibid. 468.

[25] See: the Court of Appeal's decision in *Alder v Moore* [1961] 2 QB 57.

[26] *Krisa v Equitable Life Assurance Society*, 113 F Supp 2d 694, 701 (MD Pa 2000); *Barrer v Metropolitan Life Ins Co*, 151 F Supp 2d 617 (ED Pa 2001).

[27] 48 NJ 291, 299, 225 A2d 328, 333 (1966); This case was also reported in the United Kingdom as [1967] 1 Lloyd's Rep 380.

[28] (1984) 49 OR (2d) 101 (CA).

[29] Brown in Webb and Rowe (2004, p. 42).

Most rules of construction are generally uncontroversial and subscribe to legal formalism in retaining traditional respect for the sanctity of contract. The doctrine of reasonable expectations however, subscribes to legal functionalism in order to provide relief to parties based on what they would have reasonably expected.[30] Although there have been glimpses of the application of this doctrine in a few cases in the United Kingdom, it has not gained much momentum.[31]

Its more subtle influence perhaps, may be observed in modern English cases where the aim of construction of documents has leaned somewhat towards finding the meaning which the document would convey to a reasonable person based on the information available at the time of the contract. This is apparent from cases like *Investors Compensation Scheme v West Bromwich Building Society*[32] and *Rohan Investments Ltd v Cunningham.*[33]

In order to illustrate the complexities of policy construction, it may be useful at this juncture, to consider the construction of some commonly used terms in insurance contracts. The term 'accident' for example, indicates an event which happens unexpectedly or fortuitously and causes injury or damage to the insured or insured property.[34] Hence, the English Court of Appeal in *Re Deep Vein Thrombosis Litigation*[35] held that deep vein thrombosis suffered by passengers of the insured air carrier arising from cramped seating arrangements and insufficient oxygen and fresh air supply in the cabin, was not recoverable because it was not caused by an 'accident'.

The term 'loss' can in turn, be of many kinds and happen under diverse circumstances.[36] The voluntary parting with the insured property under a sale which turns out to be fraudulently perpetrated by the purchaser with a worthless cheque has not been held to be a 'loss'[37] whereas the voluntary handing of possession of the insured property to an agent for sale, who turned out to fraudulently misappropriate the proceeds, has.[38]

Likewise, in life and personal accident policies, the success of a claim can hinge entirely on the construction of terms such as 'loss,' when it comes to injuries sustained. In the Malaysian case of *Chiew Swee Chai v British American Insurance Co Sdn Bhd,*[39] the insured made a claim against the insurers upon completely losing

[30]Tarr (2001, p. 15).

[31]*First Energy (UK) Ltd v Hungarian International Bank Ltd* [1993] 2 Lloyd's Rep 194; *Cook v Financial Insurance Co* [1998] 1 WLR 1765.

[32][1998] 1 All ER 98.

[33][1999] Lloyd's Rep I R 190.

[34]*Mills v Smith* [1964] 1 QB 30.

[35][2004] QB 235; Lord Phillip MR in the case referred to the Oxford English Dictionary definition of 'accident' in coming to the decision: at 247.

[36]*Moore v Evans* [1917] 1 KB 458, 471 (Banks LJ).

[37]*Eisinger v General Accident, Fire and Life Assurance Co* [1955] 2 All ER 897.

[38]*Webster v General Accident, Fire and Life Assurance Co* [1953] 1 QB 521.

[39][1987] 1 MLJ 53.

the use of his arm after a road accident. His life policy had included coverage for loss of limb by accidental means, with the term 'loss' being defined in the policy as 'dismemberment by severance at or above the wrist or ankle joint'. As a result, the insured was denied coverage because he had refused to have the non-functioning arm amputated. Nevertheless, the court felt bound to apply the clear policy meaning accorded to the term 'loss', although the insurer's good faith in refusing coverage was in itself questionable.

In this context, the lack of clearly and comprehensively drafted policy documentation has resulted in many insureds being 'bemused by their policies and find it difficult if not impossible without expert advice, to work out what cover they are afforded and what their obligations are'.[40] Hence, it is crucial that plain language policies are developed. These policies should be required to comply with a prescribed layout covering essential terms and be made subject to the approval of a statutory body.[41]

4.2.2 *Exclusions and Proximate Cause*

Insurance policies commonly contain exclusion clauses that are inserted by insurers in order to limit the coverage provided by such policies. In principle, where a loss suffered by the insured falls within the words of the policy as well as comes within an exclusion provision in the policy, the exclusion is deemed to have priority. As a result, the insurer's liability is negated by the exclusion.[42]

The burden of proof is however, on the insurer to establish that the loss was within the exclusion clause sought to be relied on.[43] To satisfy this, the insurer need not in principle, show the existence of a causal link between the excluded peril and the loss in question.[44] However, the matter ought to be viewed from a construction as well as a causation angle to ascertain if the policy in fact covers an insured loss. This is based on the common law principle codified in s55 (1) of the *Marine Insurance Act 1906* (UK) that the insurer is only liable for losses proximately caused by the insured peril.[45]

---

[40]Birds (1982, pp. 455–456).

[41]This section draws on research appearing in: Thanasegaran, above n 12, 194.

[42]*Browning v Phoenix Assurance Co Ltd* [1960] 2 Lloyd's Rep 360; *Seddon v Binions* [1978] 1 Lloyd's Rep 381; *Kuwait Airways Corporation v Kuwait Insurance Co SAK* [1999] 1 Lloyd's Rep 804, 815 (Lord Hobhouse).

[43]*People's Insurance Co of Malaya v Ho Ah Kum* [1967] 2 MLJ 134; *American Home Assurance Co v Nalin Industries Sdn Bhd* [1993] 2 MLJ 409.

[44]*Louden v British Merchants' Insurance Co Ltd* [1961] 1 Lloyd's Rep 154.

[45]Section 55 (1) of the *Marine Insurance Act 1906* (UK) provides:

Subject to the provisions of this Act, and unless the policy otherwise provides, the insurer is liable for any loss proximately caused by a peril insured against, but subject as aforesaid, he is not liable for any loss which is not proximately caused by a peril insured against.

In a practical sense however, this only poses a problem where there is more than one cause which contributes to the loss in question. Where two or more dominant causes operate towards causing a loss, the insurer is not liable for the loss if one of them is an excluded peril.[46] On the other hand, if one of the dominant causes is an insured peril whereas the other is not an excluded peril, the insurer would be liable for the loss. It is a question of fact as to whether any cause of the loss amounts to a dominant cause or otherwise.[47] Be that as it may however, the proximate cause rule may be expressly displaced by the terms of the policy where insurers go so far as to exclude liability even for losses indirectly caused by an excluded peril.[48]

4.2.3 Claims Settlement Practice

Utmost good faith is central to the claims settlement practices of both insurers and insureds, in addition to its role in the construction of policy terms and exclusion clauses in claims handling.

On the insured's part, utmost good faith has to be observed in the procedural sense of strictly complying with the requirements of the policy terms; as well as substantively, in having to act honestly and refrain from making fraudulent claims. Failure to do so would entitle the insurer to avoid the claim.[49]

Instances where an insured would be deemed to have put forward a fraudulent claim is where the insured has not suffered a loss or has deliberately caused the insured event or in the case of indemnity policies, has exaggerated the quantum of loss suffered.[50] Where the insured puts forward a claim with the intention to defraud the insurer, the insurer is entitled to avoid the claim, provided it can discharge its burden of proving fraud.[51] This is because it satisfies the definition of fraud which is making a representation either knowingly without belief in its truth or recklessly without caring whether it is true or false.[52]

---

[46]*Wayne Tank and Pump Co Ltd v Employers' Liability Assurance Corporation Ltd* [1973] 3 WLR 483; *Singatronics Ltd. v Insurance Co of North America* [1994] 1 SLR 500.

[47]*Killick v Rendall* [2000] 2 All ER (Comm) 57 (Court of Appeal) (Evans LJ) at 64–67.

[48]*Oei v Foster* [1982] 2 Lloyd's Rep 170.

[49]*Britton v Royal Insurance Company* (1866) 4F & F 905; *Tuong Aik (Sarawak) Sdn Bhd v Arab-Malaysian Eagle Assurance Bhd* [1996] 1 AMR 871; See: Chap. 2 for a discussion on fraudulent claims.

[50]Mahmood (1992, p. 136).

[51]*Galloway v Guardian Royal Exchange (UK) Ltd* [1999] Lloyd's Rep IR 209. The standard for this at common law is somewhere between the balance of probability and beyond reasonable doubt: *Hornal v Neuberger Products Ltd* [1957] 1 QB 347.

[52]*Derry v Peek* (1889) 14 App Cas 337.

However, an inflated claim per se is not in itself conclusive proof of fraud. Often it is merely used as a means to facilitate bargaining,[53] in order to counter insurers' general reluctance to settle claims submitted without contesting, rejecting or reducing the claim where possible. This essentially comes down to a question of proving fraudulent intent. Should a claim be found to be fraudulent, it would fall outside the ambit of the continuing duty of utmost good faith and be disallowed on the basis of public policy instead.[54]

In order to make a successful insurance claim therefore, the insured would in addition to having a strong substantive case, also have to satisfy the procedural requirement of strict compliance with the terms of the insurance policy or face avoidance of the claim by the insurer. This would be the case even if the insured has suffered a genuine loss. The insured's first obligation when an insured loss occurs is to give written notice to the insurer of the loss within the time frame expressly stipulated in the policy. In the absence of such an expressed provision, it is implied that the insured must notify the insurer within a reasonable time.[55]

Express terms requiring the insured to give notice of loss may take various forms. The insured has more flexibility where notice is required to be given as soon as possible after the insured event occurs, as it would require the courts to consider the surrounding circumstances in determining the time-frame to do so.[56] Where however, notice is required to be given within a specified time-frame, for instance within 14 days from the occurrence of the insured event, it must be strictly complied with even if the loss only manifested itself later.[57] It is worth noting that Malaysia has in fact taken a more positive construction of such notice requirements, and shall be discussed later in this chapter.

On the part of the insurer in turn, to be able to disclaim or avoid liability for non-compliance by the insured, the term requiring notice must have been a condition precedent to liability.[58] Failing which it would only amount to a mere condition entitling the insurer to damages alone, provided there has been a loss or prejudice suffered.[59] It should be noted that the lack of a clear description as a

---

[53]Judicial acknowledgement of this commercial phenomenon can be seen in *Ewer v National Employers' Mutual General Insurance Association Ltd.* [1937] 2 All ER 193, 203 (Mac Kinnon J); *Wong Cheong Kong Sdn Bhd v Prudential Assurance Sdn Bhd* [1998] 3 MLJ 724, 737–38 (Vincent Ng J).

[54]This section draws on research appearing in: Thanasegaran, above n 12, 195. Also see. *Hayward v Zurich Insurance Company plc* [2015] EWCA Civ 327.

[55]*Hadenfayre Ltd v British National Insurance Society Ltd* [1984] 2 Lloyd's Rep 393.

[56]*Verelst's Administratrix v Motor Union Insurance Co.* [1925] 2 KB 137.

[57]*Cassel v Lancashire and Yorkshire Accident Insurance Company* (1885) 1 TLR 495; See also: *Adamson & Sons v Liverpool and London and Globe Insurance Co Ltd* [1953] 2 Lloyd's Rep 355. This section draws on research appearing in: Thanasegaran, above n 12, 195.

[58]*Pioneer Concrete (UK) Ltd v National Employer's Mutual General Insurance Association Ltd* [1985] 1 Lloyd's Rep 274.

[59]*McAlpine v BAI* [1998] 2 Lloyd's Rep 694.

condition precedent would also result in a *contra proferentum* construction of it being made, as a mere condition warranting damages in the event of loss.[60]

In addition to this, insurance contracts may also require the insured to give a written notice of loss directly to the insurer. Failure to strictly comply with this requirement can entitle the insurer to avoid liability, where for example notice is given orally and/or to the agent who sold the policy to the insured.[61] However, where notice of loss is given to a duly appointed officer of the insurer like its district manager, as in *Ayrey v British Legal and United Provident Assurance Company Ltd*,[62] it may be imputed to the insurer and suffice.

Furthermore, some policies may require the insured to provide additional information when giving notice of loss as a condition precedent to liability, so as to enable the insurer to assess the loss in question. The insurer would have another ground to avoid liability, should this requirement not be complied with,[63] unless of course the insurer had nevertheless obtained the said information from a third party, as no prejudice would have then been suffered as a result.[64] Where an insurer however, delays in rejecting a claim despite knowing of the insured's breach of policy terms, it only operates as a bar to rejection if the delay was such as to unduly prejudice the insured.[65]

Insureds usually have a limitation period of up to six years from the insurer's rejection of a claim to bring an action for breach of contract.[66] However, insurers have often found ways to reduce this six year limitation period to commence an action in contract by contractually reducing or limiting it to about 12 months for the claim to be referred to arbitration. This poses yet another obstacle to insureds.

It should be noted that as far as the insurer's duty of utmost good faith is concerned, it would cover having to act fairly and reasonably when assessing the insured's compliance with the requirements of the policy; processing and settling claims without delay; refraining from reducing and rejecting claims without good reason; and in essence, not acting in bad faith.[67]

It is important to note that, where the insured is required to prove the loss to the insurer as a 'condition precedent' to recovery, it involves the insurer's exercise of discretion. Since the insurer is an interested party in the matter, it would invariably be acting as a judge in its own cause. This would in turn give rise to doubts as to procedural and substantive propriety in its decision making. English courts have

---

[60] *Stoneham v Ocean Railway and General Accident Insurance Co* (1887) 19 QBD 237.

[61] *Herbert v Railway Passenger Assurance Co Ltd* (1938) 158 LT 417.

[62] [1918] 1 KB 136.

[63] *Welch v Royal Exchange Assurance* [1939] 1 KB 294.

[64] *Barrett Bros (Taxis) Ltd. v Davies, Lickiss and Milestone Motor Policies at Lloyd's (Third Parties)* [1966] 1 WLR 1334.

[65] *Allen v Robles* [1969] 2 Lloyd's Rep 61; This section draws on research appearing in: Thanasegaran, above n 12, 196.

[66] *Walker v Pennine Insurance Co Ltd* [1979] 2 Lloyd's Rep 139.

[67] This section draws on research appearing in: Thanasegaran, above n 12, 196.

generally accepted that insurers must when exercising their discretion, act honestly, in good faith, for a proper purpose and not arbitrarily.[68] That which is not universally accepted however, is whether the insurer is required to act reasonably as well.

The apprehension in introducing the additional possibly objective requirement of reasonableness is apparent in the English Court of Appeal's decisions in *Nash v Paragon Finance plc*[69] and *Gan Insurance Co Ltd v Tai Ping Insurance Co Ltd (No 2)*.[70] They did not wish to extend 'the concept of reasonableness beyond whether the insurer's decision was reasonable [in comparison to a range of reasonable decisions open to insurers], to a consideration of what the reasonable person on the 'Clapham omnibus' would decide' (clarification added).[71]

The processing and settlement of claims on time is yet another important obligation on the insurer's part. Non-compliance with this would amount to a breach of the insurer's post-contractual duty of utmost good faith and also cause unnecessary additional anxiety and hardship to an already affected insured.[72]

A further issue arising from this is the question of availability of indemnity, damages and interest in the event of late payment or improper non-payment or reduced payment of claims by the insurer. English law has long recognised the availability of an action in breach of contract, against the insurer to recover damages in the sum of the indemnity and interest calculated from the date of the loss. The Court of Appeal in *Sprung v Royal Insurance (UK) Ltd*[73] however, made it clear that additional damages for further loss caused by any delay in the insurer's claims settlement would not be available, on the basis that damages is not available as a result of failure to pay damages.[74] The decision was despite a three and a half year delay by the insurer to indemnify, on questionable grounds which resulted in the insured being put out of business and suffering a further loss of £75,000.[75] This has been the unfortunate state of affairs in the United Kingdom prior to the recent reforms where an insurer delays unjustifiably, and is not the case in Malaysia and Australia.[76]

---

68 *Gan Insurance Co Ltd v Tai Ping Insurance Co Ltd (No 2)* [2001] Lloyd's Rep IR 291; *Abu Dhabi National Tanker Co v Product Star Shipping Ltd. (The Product Star)* [1993] 1 Lloyd's Rep 397.

69 [2002] 1 WLR 685.

70 [2001] Lloyd's Rep IR 291.

71 Hobbs in Webb and Rowe (2004, pp. 124–25).

72 This section draws on research appearing in: Thanasegaran, above n 12, 196.

73 [1990] Lloyd's Rep IR 111.

74 *President of India v Lips Maritime Corporation* [1988] AC 395.

75 It is worth noting that the Scottish Court of Session in *Davidson v Guardian Royal Exchange Assurance* [1979] 1 Lloyd's Rep 406 decided otherwise and awarded additional damages to the insured for the loss of use of the insured car for 40 weeks instead of a reasonably estimated eight weeks which is what it should have taken the insurer to repair the car.

76 See: *Pacific & Orient Insurance Co Sdn Bhd v Woon Shee Min* [1980] 1 MLJ 291 (Malaysia); and ss 57 (1) and (2) of the *Insurance Contracts Act 1984* (Cth) (Australia).

This is because the continuing duty of utmost good faith in insurance contracts exists until the settlement or rejection of a claim.[77] As such, just as the insured is required to lay all the cards on the table and not knowingly conceal material facts; the insurer is in turn required to be 'frank and forthcoming' in the claims settlement process.[78] Lord Bingham in *Director General of Fair Trading v First National Bank*[79] duly articulated that good faith:

> ... is one of fair and open dealing [which necessitates that insurers]...should not whether deliberately or unconsciously, take advantage of the consumer's necessity, indigence, lack of experience, unfamiliarity with the subject matter of the contract, weak bargaining position or any other factor listed (clarification added).

Malcolm Clarke also pointed out that the Financial Times on 28 March 1994 carried an article which reflected the United Kingdom as having one of the worst records in Europe for delay in claims settlement, which had not changed much.[80] It is worth noting that in the United States on the other hand, delay in claims settlement by insurers without proper justification would give rise to bad faith, that made insurers liable for punitive damages 'even where the policy does not, in fact, cover the claim'.[81]

A more balanced approach would be to apply the duty of utmost good faith in the handling and settlement of claims, where there is undue delay without justification and indiscriminate reduction and rejection of claims. This is in tandem with the justification for the imposition of the duty on insureds at the pre-contractual stage of insurance contracts, owing to the information imbalance existing in favour of insureds at that stage of the contract. A corresponding duty should therefore, be imposed on insurers with respect to claims handling, as insureds' are vulnerable to insurers' claims handling techniques. More so since insurance contracts are contracts of adhesion which justifies the imposition of a duty to act in utmost good faith, on insurers. This would therefore, facilitate claims being processed and settled fairly and in a timely manner, with recourse to damages being available in the event of breach.[82]

4.2.4 English Proposals for Law Reform

The unsatisfactory state of the law on post-contractual good faith and claims settlements in particular, in the United Kingdom was subject to a major review by the

---

[77]*The Star Sea*[2001] 1 Lloyd's Rep 389.

[78]Clarke, above n 11, 235.

[79][2002] 1 AC 481, 497. Although this was a banking case, the dicta was directed at suppliers of financial services like banks, financial institutions and insurance companies.

[80]Clarke, above n 11, 244–245. For criticism of the English position, see: Campbell (2000).

[81]Brown (2002, pp. 458–459).

[82]This section draws on research appearing in: Thanasegaran, above n 12, 197. Also see: Campbell in Webb and Rowe (2004, p. 213).

English and Scottish Law Commissions which commenced in 2006. This has since resulted in the reforms introduced in the *Insurance Act 2015* (UK) for both consumer and non-consumer insurance contracts.

It is interesting to note that the *Insurance Contracts Bill 2014* (UK) ("the Bill") which was eventually passed as the *Insurance Act 2015* (UK) in February 2015 had originally contained a provision on "Implied Term about Payment" in s14. This provision was dropped from the Bill by the Treasury before it was presented to Parliament as there was criticism of this proposal which made its inclusion unsuitable for the special procedure for uncontroversial Law Commission Bills that was used to pass the Act. Nevertheless, the government had during the Bill's passage through Parliament, indicated its inclusion in future forthcoming insurance provisions. This will remain to be seen in light of the Law Commission's proposed third and final report in 2015 on insurance issues yet to be addressed in the reforms thus far.

Section 14 (1) of the Bill had proposed an 'implied term' into 'every contract of insurance that if the insured makes a claim under the contract, the insurer must pay any sums due in respect of the claim within a reasonable time.' Sections 14 (2) and (3) went on to provide that reasonable time included the time taken to investigate and assess the claim; with what is reasonable depending on all relevant circumstances, particularly the type of insurance, the size and complexity of the claim and compliance with relevant rules and factors outside the insurer's control. Insurers however, would not breach the implied term by merely failing to pay the claim or part of it if *they can show* that there were reasonable grounds for disputing the claim, although their conduct in handling the claim may be a relevant factor in deciding this.[83]

Section 14 (5) went on to explicitly provide for remedies like damages to be available for breach of this implied term which would be in addition to and distinct from the right to enforce payment of the sum due and any right to interest on those sums. This would have been a marked improvement in the law which addressed situations similar to that of *Sprung v Royal Insurance Co (UK) Ltd*[84] and has appeared to have received the support of insurers and insureds alike. The proposal was also 'targeted at specific instances of bad claims handling rather than forcing insurers generally to make decisions more quickly or to pay out more claims'[85] and was to be supplemented by an increased regulatory focus on claims handling via the Financial Conduct Authority's 'thematic review' of claims handling in the insurance industry.[86] It is left to be seen as to whether and how soon these measures would be implemented.

---

[83]Section 14 (4) of the *Insurance Contracts Bill 2014* (UK).

[84][1999] Lloyd's Rep I R 111.

[85]Hertzell and Burgoyne (2013, p. 119).

[86]Ibid. 118. See: Wheatley (2013) http://www.fca.org.uk/news/speeches/meeting-the-growth-challenge. Accessed 30 June 2015.

With respect to fraudulent claims on the other hand, the common law position has been described as being 'convoluted and confused.'[87] This is because not only does the fraudulent insured forfeit the fraudulent claim; the duty of utmost good faith in s17 of the *Marine Insurance Act 1906* (UK) also theoretically gives the insurer a right to avoid the contract and recover any sums previously paid out to the insured, even on genuine claims. It is therefore, crucial that this uncertainty is addressed in a clear manner with insurers being granted remedies that are 'principled and proportionate' in order to deter fraud as well as ensure that insureds are treated fairly with respect to prior untainted claims.[88]

Section 12 (1) of the *Insurance Act 2015* (UK) provides that where such a claim is made by an insured, the insurer is not liable to pay the claim; may recover from the insured any sums paid by it there under; and may by notice to the insured treat the contract as having been terminated with effect from the time of the fraudulent act. Section 12 (2) goes on to provide that in the event that the insurer treats the contract as having been terminated, it may refuse all liability to the insured under the contract in respect of a *relevant event* which occurs *after* the fraudulent act, without having to refund any premiums paid there under.

The insurer's rights are prospective in nature and do not affect the rights and obligations of the parties which have arisen with respect to relevant events occurring before the fraudulent act,[89] with what amounts to a 'relevant event' being events which give rise to the insurer's liability under the contract, for example the occurrence of a loss and the making or notification of a claim or potential claim.[90] Section 13 completes this provision by prescribing a fair treatment of fraudulent claims made in group insurance policies that essentially entitles the insurer to only exercise its remedies against the insured concerned without affecting the cover provided to anyone else in the group.

Sections 15 (1) and 16 (1) go on to provide that parties cannot contract out of any term of a consumer or non-consumer insurance contract if it would put the insured in a worse position. Such contracting out in non-consumer insurance contracts, however, would be possible if the 'disadvantageous term' was clear and unambiguous,[91] and the insurer had taken sufficient steps to draw the said term to the insured's attention before the contract was entered into or varied.[92]

This provision which is mandatory for consumer insurance contracts and provides a default regime for non-consumer insurance with the possibility of contracting out where parties are clearly informed, represents a fair balance between the

[87]Hertzell and Burgoyne, above n 85, 119.

[88]Ibid.

[89]Section 12 (3) of the *Insurance Act 2015* (UK).

[90]Section 12 (4) of the *Insurance Act 2015* (UK).

[91]Section 17 (3) of the *Insurance Act 2015* (UK); See: Carnwath LJ in *Tektrol v International Insurance Co of Hanover* [2005] 2 CLC 339 at 347.

[92]Section 17 (2) of the *Insurance Act 2015* (UK).

interests of insurers and insureds but had dropped its original reference which included the insurer's duty to pay claims within a reasonable time.[93]

Before moving on to examine the application of the post-contractual duty of good faith and claims settlement in Malaysia, the English proposals for reform in the area which were the forerunners to the recent reforms, will be briefly alluded to, so as to provide an insight into the development of the law in Malaysia.

It started with the *Fifth Report of the Law Reform Committee* in 1957[94] which reported that the state of insurance law in the United Kingdom coupled with the widespread use of certain terms and exclusions in policies by insurers could lead to abuse even against an honest and reasonably careful insured. This is because it gave rise to various circumstances enabling insurers to avoid liability in respect of claims made, which had in fact sometimes occurred, as insurers were often placed as judges in their own cause in determining insureds' claims. However, the Committee felt that in this respect, the prejudice to the insured arose largely from express contractual provisions rather than principles of insurance law per se. Since altering that would interfere with the parties' freedom of contract, which required the consideration of matters concerning social policy, the Committee felt that it was outside its scope of reference.[95]

In 1977, the *Unfair Contract Terms Act* (UK) was passed based on the Law Commission and Scottish Law Commission's Report on *Exemption Clauses*,[96] which had an element of 'reasonableness' added in order for any exclusion of liability to be effective. Although the Law Commissions in fact recommended that their proposal be applied to *all types* of contracts, insurance contracts were however excluded from its ambit, due to successful lobbying by the industry.[97]

As a trade-off, the insurance industry adopted self-regulation in 1976 through the *Statement of General Insurance Practice* ('*SOGIP*') covering general insurance[98] and the *Statement of Long Term Insurance Practice* ('*SOLTIP*') covering life and investment insurance[99] (together referred to as 'the Statements'), which were revised in 1986 and remained in use until statutory regulation by the Financial Services Authority was introduced in January 2005 in the form of the *Insurance Conduct of Business* ('*ICOB*')[100] and *Conduct of Business* ('*COB*')[101] respectively.

In 1980 however, The English Law Commission[102] whilst not set up to consider claims and exclusions per se, nevertheless made a very strange recommendation.

---

[93]Hertzell and Burgoyne, above n 85, 120.

[94]*Conditions and Exceptions in Insurance Policies*, Report No 5, Cmnd 62, 1957 [11]–[12].

[95]Ibid. [12].

[96]Law Commission and Scottish Law Commission (1975) [240]–[47].

[97]Birds, above n 13, 233.

[98]Association of British Insurers, *Statement of General Insurance Practice* (1986a).

[99]Association of British Insurers, *Statement of Long Term Insurance Practice* (1986b).

[100]Financial Services Authority, *Insurance Conduct of Business* (2005b).

[101]Financial Services Authority, *Conduct of Business* (2005a).

[102]English Law Commission (1980).

The Commission correctly observed that insurers frequently limited their liability by inserting into insurance contracts terms like conditions precedent or exclusions (not amounting to warranties), which were outside the Commission's scope of address. They however, went on to state that:

> We do not intend to interfere with the manner in which insurers describe or limit the risk which they are prepared to cover: this can be left to competition and market forces… we do not think that any attempt should be made to control the use of such terms even though they may be used to achieve indirectly the functions which can be performed by a warranty.[103]

RA Hasson criticized this as being 'a very strange statement', as the United Kingdom has had a:

> … remarkable lack of control over the terms of insurance contracts [and] if market forces can be trusted to get rid of unfair policy terms, they can also be trusted to get rid of the "basis of contract" clause and to abolish (or attenuate) the duty of disclosure.[104]

In view of the above, it is not surprising therefore, that up until the major reforms in 2012–2015, the United Kingdom was only subject to the self-regulating rules of the *SOGIP* and *SOLTIP* and thereafter, statutory regulation by the Financial Services Authority under the *COB* and *ICOB* from 2005.

Both the Statements were revised in 1986 and applied only to policies taken out by individuals resident in the United Kingdom in their private capacity. With respect to notification of claims or loss by the insured, Clause 2 (a) of *SOGIP* provided that 'the policyholder shall not be asked to do more than report a claim and subsequent developments as soon as reasonably possible'.[105] The effect of this was to do away with tight timelines like notification within 14 days of occurrence of the insured event, especially where the loss only manifested itself much later.

Clause 2 (b) went on to provide that insurers should exercise good claims settlement practice by not repudiating liability on the basis of technical claims like non-disclosure, misrepresentation and breach of warranty or condition by the insured.[106] As far as the legality and content of policy documents were concerned,

---

[103]Ibid. [8.17]. This was expressed despite Professor Gower's observations in 1957 that 'there can be few countries …where the insurance companies are allowed the same freedom to dictate their own terms': Ginsberg (1959, p. 163).

[104]Hasson, above n 4, 517–518. He went on to say that law reform was necessary as English law's main weapon in dealing with unfair contract terms in insurance policies, namely the *contra proferentum* rule, was inadequate as it was not clear if and when it would apply, depending much on the varying views of the judges hearing the cases. He cited as examples, the interpretation of the terms 'riot' and 'flood' in *Bolands Ltd. v London and Lancashire Fire Insurance* [1924] AC 836; and *Young v Sun Alliance and London Insurance* [1977] 1 WLR 104.

[105]This is so except in the case of legal processes and claims which a third party requires the policyholder to notify within a fixed time where immediate advice may be given. Clause 3 (c) of *SOLTIP* was the comparable provision for life insurance and did not contain the proviso above.

[106]Clause 2 (b) provided that:

> An insurer will not repudiate liability to indemnify a policyholder (i) on grounds of non-disclosure of a material fact which a policyholder could not reasonably be expected to have disclosed; (ii) on grounds of misrepresentation unless it is a deliberate or negligent

Clause 5 required insurers to 'continue to develop clearer and more explicit proposal forms and policy documents whilst bearing in mind the legal nature of insurance contracts'.[107]

On the issue of prompt settlement of claims, Clause 2 (c) provided that 'liability under the policy having been established and the amount payable by the insurer agreed, payment will be made without avoidable delay'. The effectiveness of this provision was however, questionable. This is because the obligation to settle without avoidable delay (although having an imperative ring to it) only arose once the insurer's liability was established and the amount payable had been agreed, thereby leaving much scope for delay.[108]

Finally, Clause 6 of *SOGIP* provided that the provisions 'shall be taken into account in arbitration and any referral procedures which may apply in the event of disputes between policyholders and insurers relating to matters dealt with in the Statements'.[109] Again, its effectiveness was questionable as the words 'taken into account' fell short of the provisions having a binding effect on the parties which was enforceable. The only mitigating factor in this respect was the pro-active stance taken by the Insurance Ombudsman who had been known to insist on compliance by insurers with the Statements, in the cases that appeared before him.[110]

In 2000, the general insurance industry established a self-regulatory body called the General Insurance Standards Council ('GISC'), which had a voluntary membership open to insurers and intermediaries engaged in general insurance business.[111] The GISC issued a *General Insurance Code for Private Consumers* ('*GISC Private Code*')[112] and a *Commercial Code* ('*GISC Commercial Code*')[113] (together known as the 'GISC Codes') to regulate the sales, advice and service standards of insurers and intermediaries, so as to ensure the fair treatment of its customers.

(Footnote 106 continued)

misrepresentation of a material fact; (iii) on grounds of breach of warranty or condition where the circumstances of the loss are unconnected with the breach unless fraud is involved.

It did not however, apply to marine and aviation policies. Similar provisions appeared in Clause 3 (a) and (b) of *SOLTIP* covering life insurance.

[107] An identical version appeared in Clause 2(a) of *SOLTIP* for life insurance.

[108] By contrast, the corresponding provision in Clause 3 (d) of *SOLTIP* although identical, was helped to an extent by Clause 3 (e) which required the insurer to pay interest on the sum due if the delay in payment was more than two months, albeit the initial criticism of the payment obligation only arising once liability is established and the amount agreed, still applied.

[109] An identical version appeared in Clause 4 of *SOLTIP*.

[110] See: Financial Ombudsman Service (1990–1991) [2].

[111] This was as a result of the *Financial Services Act 1986* (UK) which introduced a two-tier system of regulation for investment business not covering the ambit of general insurance.

[112] General Insurance Standards Council, *General Insurance Code for Private Customers* (2000a).

[113] General Insurance Standards Council, *General Insurance Commercial Code* (2000b).

Amongst the items covered by the *GISC Private Code* were the obligations to deal with customers fairly and reasonably[114]; handle claims fairly and promptly[115]; explain to customers any significant or unusual exclusions, conditions and obligations which must be met[116]; and provide details of how a claim and complaint against them may be made.[117] Its drawback however, was that since the *GISC Private Code* was a contract between GISC and its members, it was not enforceable by the individual insureds concerned.[118] The said GISC Codes co-existed with the Statements until they were replaced by statutory regulation in 2005.

Apart from this, the 1993 European Community's Directive on *Unfair Terms in Consumer Contracts*[119] was implemented in the United Kingdom through the *Unfair Terms in Consumer Contract Regulations 1999* ('the Regulations') to provide some reprieve in this area. It however, only applied to consumers who did not individually negotiate the insurance contract with the insurer.[120] The Regulations in the main provided that all insurance terms must be 'plain and intelligible',[121] and considered terms which created a 'significant imbalance' between parties to be contrary to the requirement of good faith and therefore 'not binding on the consumer'.[122] However, enforcement of the Regulations was only possible by the Director General of Fair Trading (to whom individual complaints were made) and certain organs of government listed as 'qualifying bodies' in *Schedule 1*, Part 1 of the Regulations,[123] which left affected individuals and organisations unable to initiate proceedings on their own.

This was followed by the *Financial Services and Markets Act 2000* (UK) which came into force in December 2001, replacing the two-tier system of regulating investment business and general insurance set up by the *Financial Services Act 1986* (UK) and the various complaints handling mechanisms then in place.[124] In January 2005, the Financial Services Authority officially took over the regulation of the general and life insurance industriesand issued new statutory regulation in the form of the *ICOB* and *COB* replacing all previous self-regulating codes.[125]

---

[114]Clause 1.1 of the *GISC Private Code*.

[115]Ibid. Clauses 6 and 9.

[116]Ibid. Clause 3.3.

[117]Ibid. Clauses 3.6 and 6.1.

[118]Ibid. Clause 10.2.

[119]*Directive on Unfair Terms in Consumer Contracts 1993* (European Community).

[120]Regulation 5 (4) of the *Unfair Terms in Consumer Contract Regulations 1999*.

[121]Ibid. Regulations 6 (2) and 7.

[122]Ibid. Regulations 5 and 8.

[123]Ibid. Regulations 10 (1) and 12 (1).

[124]The Insurance Ombudsman Bureau and Personal Investment Authority Ombudsman were amongst the said mechanisms in place.

[125]The regulations drew a distinction between 'retail customers' who were individuals acting outside their trade or profession and 'commercial customers' who were anyone other than retail customers (on the basis of the former requiring more protection than the latter) with some

Most of the provisions of the *ICOB* essentially mirrored those of the *SOGIP* but were set out in greater detail. For example, information to be provided to customers included a summary of the policy[126]; list of significant and unusual exclusions and limitations[127]; the policy documents[128]; and information pertaining to the claims handling process.[129] Information on other rights of the insured, like cancellation rights,[130] extent and level of cover[131] and reference to the Financial Ombudsman Service[132] were also required to be provided.

Simple and plain English was required, with technical terms where necessary being explained to customers.[133] Where customers indicated that they wished to make a claim under the policy, reasonable guidance was to be provided to them.[134] Insurers were also required to not unreasonably reject a claim made by a customer; and save where there was evidence of fraud, not refuse to meet claims by retail customers on grounds of non-disclosure or non-negligent misrepresentation of material facts or breach of warranty or condition unless it was connected to the loss.[135] Lastly, insurers were required to settle claims by retail customers promptly,[136] within five business days after both parties had reached a settlement.[137]

The distinctive feature of the *ICOB* and *COB* was that unlike their self-regulatory predecessors, damages was available for the aggrieved party[138] and the Financial Services Authority could impose a penalty or publish a statement of the said misconduct against the party in breach.[139]

In addition to this, the Financial Services Authority had also separately published the *Principles for Business*[140] which expressed the broad spirit running

(Footnote 125 continued)

concession being made for small businesses, mainly with respect to additional protection as to product disclosure and advice provided.

[126] *ICOB* 5.5.1R.

[127] *ICOB* 5.3.20G.

[128] *ICOB* 5.5.27R.

[129] *ICOB* 5.3.9R and 5.3.4R.

[130] *ICOB* 5.3.12R.

[131] *ICOB* 5.5.1R (2) (b).

[132] *ICOB* 4.2.2R.

[133] *ICOB* 4.4.6G.

[134] *ICOB* 7.3.5.

[135] *ICOB* 7.3.6.

[136] *ICOB* 7.5.17.

[137] *ICOB* 7.5.18.

[138] Section 150 of the *Financial Services and Markets Act 2000* (UK).

[139] Section 66 of the *Financial Services and Markets Act 2000* (UK).

[140] Financial Services Authority, *Principles for Business* (2005c).

through the detailed rules of the *ICOB* and *COB*, for breach of which the Financial Services Authority could impose fines on firms.[141]

These developments have finally culminated in the progressive reforms introduced under the *Insurance Act 2015* (UK) for both consumer and non-consumer insurance contracts, via s12's handling of fraudulent claims and ss15 and 16's restriction on contracting out of these provisions, which have been set out above.

It is left to be seen however, if the originally proposed s14 of the *Insurance Contracts Bill 2014* (UK)'s 'implied term' into 'every contract of insurance that if the insured makes a claim under the contract, the insurer must pay any sums due in respect of the claim within a reasonable time' with damages being available as a remedy, would also be legislated upon in due course.

4.3 Development and Application of the Law in Malaysia

4.3.1 Post Contractual Good Faith and Claims Settlement Under the Insurance Act 1996

The law in Malaysia prior to the enactment of *Financial Services Act 2013* (Malaysia) in this area, both before and after the enactment of the *Insurance Act 1996* (Malaysia) has been governed by the broad pronouncement in s17 of the *Marine Insurance Act 1906* (UK).[142] This is evident from the Malaysian courts' continued reference to the 'duty of utmost good faith' as being the cornerstone of insurance contracts in Malaysia.[143] Section 17 in essence provided that insurance contracts are based on utmost good faith and failure by either party to observe the same would entitle the other party to avoid the contract.

Gopal Sri Ram JCA at the Court of Appeal in *Leong Kum Whay v QBE Insurance (M) Sdn Bhd,*[144] referred to the judgments of Montgomery J in *Maschke Estate v Gleeson*[145] and Taliano J in *Katotikidis v Mr Submarine Ltd*[146] in stressing upon the importance of insurers acting in utmost good faith towards insureds. These

[141]The *Principles for Business* required insurers to conduct their business with integrity; observe proper standards of market conduct; treat customers fairly; manage conflicts of interest fairly; take reasonable care to ensure the suitability of advice and that discretion is exercised; and address the information needs of their clients by communicating information to them clearly and fairly without misrepresentation.

[142]This is by virtue of ss5 (1) and (2) of the *Civil Law Act 1956* (Malaysia), owing to the lack of a corresponding provision in Malaysian statutes.

[143]See: *Leong Kum Whay v QBE Insurance (M) Sdn Bhd* [2006] 1 CLJ 1; *Jong Set Fah v Asia Life Assurance Society Ltd.* [1966] 2 CLJ 667; *Leong Brothers Industries Sdn Bhd v Jerneh Insurance Corporation Sdn Bhd* [1991] 1 MLJ 102.

[144][2006] 1 CLJ 1, 6.

[145][1986] 54 OR (2d) 753 and 756.

[146][2002] ACWSJ 10135.

judgments essentially require the insurer to act promptly and in good faith once a claim is received from its insured or face being in breach of its duty. This is because the insurer's position of power over the insured upon the occurrence of an insured loss, inevitably places the latter in a vulnerable position and dependent on the former.[147]

Despite this however, the Malaysian legislature failed to legislate upon this fundamental duty up until the *Financial Services Act 2013* (Malaysia). As a result, Malaysian insurance law and practice has until the recent reforms in 2013 been subject to the same criticisms and uncertainty as English law with respect to the juristic basis and nature of the duty of utmost good faith at claims handling.[148]

In light of this, the Malaysian position prior to the enactment of the *Financial Services Act 2013* (Malaysia) with respect to the application of the rules pertaining to construction of policies, exclusions and claims settlement practice will first be examined.

The rules of construction applying to insurance contracts in Malaysia have been largely based on English common law. In this respect, since insurance contracts are commercial in nature, the rules of construction applying to contracts in general have also applied to insurance.[149] Hence, written or type-written words in a policy take precedence over printed words[150]; the words in a policy are to be construed in the context in which they are used[151]; and terms in a policy will be given effect to by the courts so long as they are reasonably clear,[152] to name a few. This was in fact the case in *Chiew Swee Chai v British American Insurance Co (M) Sdn Bhd*[153] despite the fact that the strict application of the term 'loss' as expressly defined in the policy to be 'dismemberment by severance at or above the wrist or ankle joint' resulted in the insured of a life policy not being able to claim for his limp and non-functional arm (caused by an accident) unless he had it amputated.

It follows therefore, that the construction of some commonly used terms in policies is also similar. For example, the Malaysian Supreme Court in *American Home Assurance Co v Nalin Industries Sdn Bhd*[154] found the term 'accident' to cover an unexpected or unintended or fortuitous event. In *Pacific & Orient Insurance Co Sdn Bhd v Kathirvelu,*[155] the Supreme Court approved the application of the decision in *Pocock v Century Insurance Co Ltd*[156] with respect to 'permanent

---

[147]This section draws on research appearing in: Thanasegaran, above n 12, 192–193.

[148]See: Naidoo and Oughton, above n 5; Bennett, above n 7; Hasson (1969); Soyer, above n 5.

[149]*Malaysia National Insurance Sdn Bhd v Abdul Aziz bin Mohamed Daud* [1979] 2 MLJ 29.

[150]*Tay Hean Seng v China Insurance Co Ltd* [1953] MLJ 38.

[151]*Provincial Insurance Co Ltd v Yeo Chee Swee* [1984] 2 MLJ 60; *Sawarn Singh a/l Mehar Singh v RHB Insurance Bhd* [2014] 7 MLJ 416.

[152]*Chiew Swee Chai v British American Insurance Co (M) Sdn Bhd* [1987] 1 MLJ 53.

[153][1987] 1 MLJ 53.

[154][1993] 2 MLJ 409.

[155][1992] 2 MLJ 249.

[156][1960] 2 Lloyd's Rep 150.

total disablement' as denoting a situation where an insured was unable to engage in his or her then or any substituted type of occupation.

Apart from this, the *contra proferentum* rule has also been consistently applied by the Malaysian courts to resolve ambiguities in policies against the party responsible for or seeking to rely on it. This can be seen in cases like *Malaysia British Assurance Bhd v Syarikat Pembenaan Karun Sdn Bhd,*[157] *Borhanuddin Bin Haji Jantara v American International Assurance Co Ltd,*[158] *Union Insurance (M) Sdn Bhd v Chan You Young*[159] and *Central Lorry Service Co Sdn Bhd v American Insurance Co*[160] Where, the terms of the policy as a whole are clear and unambiguous however, the *contra proferentum* rule would not apply.[161]

The rules pertaining to the effect of exclusion clauses inserted in insurance policies by insurers and the doctrine of proximate cause contained in s55 (1) of the *Marine Insurance Act 1906* (UK)[162] have been equally applicable to Malaysia. The Federal Court in *Wong Kon Poh v New India Assurance Co Ltd*[163] for instance, stated that:

> An exception must clearly and expressly be made known to the party insured—not by implication to be inferred from omission. To require that the ordinary man taking out a policy should read into it not only what was expressed but also to construe omissions as exceptions is an absurd proposition which this court cannot countenance.[164]

The Malaysian Supreme Court in *American Home Assurance Co v Nalin Industries Sdn Bhd*[165] also went on to reiterate that an insurer could only rely on an exclusion provision to deny liability if it could show that the insured's loss came within the exclusion and that it was not for the insured to disprove the same.

On the requirement of utmost good faith in claims settlement practices by the insured and insurer, the Malaysian position has also generally mirrored that of English common law. For instance, the insured must refrain from putting forward fraudulent claims[166] but the mere submission of an exaggerated claim is not conclusive proof of fraud, in view of judicial recognition of 'price haggling' between parties.[167]

---

[157][2008] 6 MLJ 533.

[158][1987] 1 MLJ 22.

[159][1999] 1 MLJ 593.

[160][1981] 2 MLJ 40.

[161]*Norani bin Maniran v Maybank General Assurance Bhd* [2012] 9 MLJ 610.

[162]This is by virtue of ss5 (1) and (2) of the *Civil Law Act 1956* (Malaysia) and applied in *Commercial Union Assurance (M) Sdn Bhd v Pilihan Megah Sdn Bhd* [1998] 7 MLJ 33.

[163][1970] 2 MLJ 287.

[164]Ibid. 289 (Ong CJ).

[165][1993] 2 MLJ 409. See also: *People's Insurance Co of Malaya v Ho Ah Kum* [1967] 2 MLJ 134.

[166]Failure to abide by this would entitle the insurer to avoid the claim and retain the premiums paid: *Tuong Aik (Sarawak) Sdn Bhd v Arab-Malaysian Eagle Assurance* [1996] 1 AMR 871.

[167]*Globe Trawlers Pte Ltd v National Employers' Mutual General Insurance Association Ltd* [1980] 1 MLJ 463; *Wong Cheong Kong Sdn Bhd v Prudential Assurance Sdn Bhd* [1998] 3 MLJ 724, 735 and 737 (Vincent Ng J).

The insured has also been required to meet all procedural requirements contained in the policy strictly, failing which the insurer may avoid the policy, provided the requirement breached was a condition precedent.[168] In this regard, the insured is required to give notice (often written)[169] of the insured loss to the insurer within the time period prescribed in the policy along with any expressly prescribed additional information.[170] The Malaysian courts have however, adopted a more positive construction in *Pacific & Orient Insurance Co Sdn Bhd v Kathirvelu*[171] by holding that a duty to notify the insurer of an accident only arose if the accident was sufficiently serious to give rise to a claim and not trivial in nature. Furthermore, an insurer who despite the insured's failure to provide adequate notification, had obtained all the information from another source, was also not entitled to avoid the contract, as no prejudice was suffered.[172]

With respect to the possible reduction of the six year limitation period within which an insured can institute a claim against the insurer, by the contractual requirement of reference to arbitration within a prescribed shorter time, Malaysia has been in a better position than the United Kingdom. This is because s29 of the *Contracts Act 1950* (Malaysia) provides that a term seeking to limit the time within which an action might be instituted against an insurer, would be void, with the courts regularly applying the same to invalidate such time limits.[173]

The insurer's obligation of utmost good faith in claims settlement has in turn been to act fairly and reasonably; process and settle claims without delay; and refrain from reducing[174] and rejecting claims, without proper grounds. The Malaysian courts have in this regard taken a more progressive stance than the English in granting additional damages to the insured beyond the insured sum, where further damage or loss is suffered directly as a result of the insurer's delay or unreasonable refusal to settle a genuine claim. This is apparent from the Federal Court's decision in *Pacific & Orient Insurance Co Sdn Bhd v Woon Shee Min*[175] where additional damages were awarded for the loss to the insured vehicle as a

---

[168] *Public Insurance Co Ltd v Muthu* [1965] 2 MLJ 201.

[169] *Chong Kok Hwa v Taisho Marine and Fire Insurance Co Ltd* [1977] 1 MLJ 244 where it was held that an insurance agent usually has no authority to waive such a requirement for written notice.

[170] *Cheong Heng Loong Goldsmiths (KL) Sdn Bhd v Chan Kim Swi* [1997] 5 MLJ 191; *AXA Affin Assurance Bhd v MTD Construction Sdn Bhd* [2013] 6 MLJ 323.

[171] [1992] 2 MLJ 249.

[172] *China Insurance Co Ltd v Ngau Ah Kau* [1972] 1 MLJ 52. This was applied again in *Talasco Insurance Bhd v Goh Thiam Hock* [1999] 1 MLJ 179.

[173] See: *Asean Security Paper Mills Sdn Bhd v Commercial Union Assurance (M) Sdn Bhd* [2003] 6 CLJ 505; *New Zealand Insurance Co Ltd v Ong Choon Lin* [1992] 1 CLJ 44. This section draws on research appearing in: Thanasegaran, above n 12, 196.

[174] *Arasis Sdn Bhd v Pacific & Orient Insurance Co Bhd* [2013] 1 MLJ 784 where the High Court held the insurer's payment of a reduced sum to be in breach of the insurance contract and awarded the insured a full settlement of the claim.

[175] [1980] 1 MLJ 291.

result of being left out in the open for six months without being repaired due to the insurer's delay and rejection of even its own repairer's estimate.

In *Wong Cheong Kong Sdn Bhd v Prudential Assurance Sdn Bhd*,[176] Vincent Ng J in awarding interest to the insured from the date of loss, for the unreasonable delay and conduct of the insurer, went so far as to justify his decision on the ground that:

> ... the plaintiffs had, in their properly insured and securely assured claim on the policy, been made to travel through an exceedingly difficult path laid out with sharp stones... [and] travel through an inferno no less searing than the heat that gutted the risk premises.[177]

In *Cheong Heng Loong Goldsmiths (KL) Sdn Bhd v Capital Insurance Bhd*[178] the Court of Appeal yet again applied the duty of utmost good faith to claims settlement where it held the insurer's handling of the insured's claim to 'smack of bad faith'. The insurers here avoided liability and the contract altogether by alleging that the insured had faked the robbery of its items. This was despite their adjuster's report to the contrary, which prompted the Court of Appeal to say that 'bad faith onthe part of the insurer would also restrict them from raising or complaining of lack of good faith by the insured'.[179]

Despite this however, it is worth taking note of Australia's progressive *Insurance Contracts Act 1984* (Cth) which has long provided for a comprehensive manner of dealing with utmost good faith in general, and claims settlement practice in particular, via its ss12–14 and ss54–57. The Act was based on the Australian Law Reform Commission's recommendations made in 1982 that 'legislation should make it clear that the duty of utmost good faith applied to all aspects of the relationship between insurer and insured, including the settlement of claims'.[180]

For a start, s12 entrenches Part II of the Act which is based on the duty of utmost good faith, from being limited or restricted in any way by subsequent provisions as well as any other law.[181] Section 13 goes on to set out the duty as follows:

> A contract of insurance is a contract based on the duty of utmost good faith and there is *implied in such a contract* a provision requiring each party to it to act towards the other party, *in respect of any matter arising under or in relation to it*, with the utmost good faith (emphasis added).

---

[176][1998] 3 MLJ 724.

[177]Ibid. 751. The court's discretion to grant interest is generally available under s11 of the *Civil Law Act 1956* (Malaysia).

[178][2004] 1 CLJ 357.

[179]Ibid. 364–365.This section draws on research appearing in: Thanasegaran, above n 12, 196.

[180]Australian Law Reform Commission (1982) [328]. Further endorsement of this can be found in the Explanatory Memorandum, Insurance Contracts Bill 1984 (Cth) [35].

[181]In fact, the Notes to the draft Insurance Contracts Bill 1982 (Cth) described the duty of utmost good faith as being 'paramount' and should not be displaced by further or other duties imposed by the Act. This view was shared in *Entwells Pty Ltd. v National and General Insurance Co. Ltd.* (1991) 6 WAR 68 (Ipp J) which was a case concerning the effect of s54 on remedies for post-contractual breach and s13.

The implications of this provision vis-à-vis the common law duty of utmost good faith is three-fold. Section 13 makes the duty an *implied term* of the insurance contract and removes the common law restriction on the remedy of avoidance of contract and a refund of premium paid, as the sole consequence of breach. This has resulted in damages being available as a substantive remedy. Furthermore, the words 'in respect of any matter arising under or in relation to it' in s13 give the duty of utmost good faith a wide and overarching reach over all aspects of an insurance contract, from the pre-contractual stage right up to claims settlement.[182]

In relation to construction of policies, exclusions and claims settlement, this translates into the insurer's potential exposure to breach of utmost good faith on a range of matters. This would encompass the unclear drafting of proposal forms and policies; making unsubstantiated allegations of breach of utmost good faith against the insured; making unfounded denials of claims[183]; proposing low claims settlement; as well as causing unreasonable delay in the admission of liability and eventual settlement of claims.[184]

In this regard, the Supreme Court of Western Australia in *Beverley v Tyndall Life Insurance Co Ltd*[185] held that s13 provides for the insurer of a life policy to be duty bound to act fairly, reasonably and in good faith when determining whether the insured was totally and permanently disabled within the purview of the policy, more so because it was acting as a judge in its own cause.

A further effect of s13 directed towards insurers[186] is apparent when read together with ss14 and 37 of the Act. Section 14 (1) provides:

> If reliance by a party to a contract of insurance on a provision of the contract would be to fail to act with utmost good faith, the party may not rely on the provision.

The Australian Law Reform Commission in fact noted that such a provision 'should provide sufficient inducement to insurers and their advisers to be careful in drafting their policies and to act fairly in relying on their strict terms'.[187]

Section 14 (3) goes on to clarify that:

> In deciding whether reliance by an insurer on a provision of the contract of insurance would be to fail to act with the utmost good faith, the court shall have regard to any notification of the provision that was given to the insured, whether a notification of a kind mentioned in Section 37 or otherwise.

---

[182]This section draws on research appearing in: Thanasegaran (2004, pp. 152–153).

[183]Such denials could be based on the unduly strict construction of policy terms or ambiguous exclusions: *Hammer Waste Pty Ltd v QBE Mercantile Mutual Ltd.* [2002] NSWSC 1006.

[184]*Moss v Sun Alliance Aust Ltd.* (1990) 6 ANZ Ins Cas ¶60-967 where the insurer initially denied liability and later, upon admission, delayed in settling the insurance claim.

[185](1999) 10 ANZ Ins Cas ¶61-453. The same reasoning was applied in *McArthur v Mercantile Mutual Life Insurance Company Ltd* [2002] 2 Qd R 197.

[186]Although s14 is theoretically applicable to both insurers and insureds, it would most likely be deployed against insurers, as they are normally the party seeking to rely on provisions of the policy to avoid liability. This section draws on research appearing in: Thanasegaran, above n 182, 153.

[187]Australian Law Reform Commission (1982) [51].

Section 37 in turn covers the position with respect to the notification of unusual policy terms.[188] The combined effect of ss13, 14 and 37 would therefore, neutralize any attempt by insurers to rely on unusual terms, unduly strict construction of policy terms or wide exclusion clauses in policies, so as to defeat an otherwise genuine claim put forward. In this regard, Cox J in *Australian Associated Motor Insurers Ltd v Ellis*[189] held that the combination of ss13 and 14 (3) placed the obligation of utmost good faith on the insurer to notify the insured of any post-contractual conditions which had the effect of permitting it to refuse to indemnify the insured, and could not be discharged by merely including such a condition in the proposal form or policy. This would therefore, compel insurers to exercise care in drafting their policy documentation so as to avoid unfair practices.

With respect to utmost good faith in claims settlement, ss54 (1)–(4) of the *Insurance Contracts Act 1984* (Cth) (Australia) provide that:

1. Subject to this section, where *the effect of a contract of insurance* would, but for this section, be that the insurer may refuse to pay a claim, either in whole or in part, by reason of some act of the insured or of some other person, being an act that occurred after the contract was entered into but not being an act in respect of which subsection (2) applies, the insurer may not refuse to pay the claim by reason only of that act but the insurer's liability in respect of the claim is reduced by the amount that fairly represents the extent to which the insurer's interests were prejudiced as a result of that act (emphasis added).
2. Subject to succeeding provisions of this section, where the act could reasonably be regarded as being capable of causing or contributing to a loss in respect of which insurance cover is provided by the contract, the insurer may refuse to pay the claim.
3. Where the insured proves that no part of the loss that gave rise to the claim was caused by the act, the insurer may not refuse to pay the claim by reason only of the act.[190]
4. Where the insured proves that some part of the loss that gave rise to the claim was not caused by the act, the insurer may not refuse to pay the claim so far as it concerns that part of the loss, by reason only of the act.

---

[188]Section 37 provides that:

An insurer may not rely on a provision included in a contract of insurance (not being a prescribed contract) of a kind that is not usually included in contracts of insurance that provide similar insurance cover unless, before the contract was entered into, the insurer clearly informed the insured in writing of the effect of the provision (whether by providing the insured with a document containing the provision or the relevant provisions of the proposed contract or otherwise).

[189](1990) 6 ANZ Ins Cas ¶60-957.

[190]Sections 54 (5) and (6) complete the provision by preventing the insurer from avoiding liability where the act was necessary to protect persons or property or where the act was not reasonably avoidable; with any reference to 'act' including omissions as well.

A connection between the duty of utmost good faith set out in s13 and the remedies in s54 in the event of post-contractual breach thereof, was held to exist by the Supreme Court of Western Australia in *Entwells Pty Ltd v National and General Insurance Co Ltd*[191] and was in fact, intended to be so by the Australian Law Reform Commission[192] which introduced the provision. Other cases in which this has been successfully applied are *Moss v Sun Alliance Aust Ltd,*[193] *Beverly v Tyndall Life Insurance Co Ltd*[194] and *McArthur v Mercantile Mutual Life Insurance Company Ltd.*[195]

This dual limb approach in ss54 (1) and (2) entitles the insurer to refuse to pay the sum insured for post-contractual breach (whether by act or omission) only if the breach was reasonably capable of causing or contributing to the insured loss, with the burden of proving the lack of a causal link placed on the insured.[196] Otherwise, the insurer is only entitled to claim damages for any prejudice suffered by way of a proportional reduction of the policy monies, to the extent of the prejudice. This was in fact proposed by the Australian Law Reform Commission as a means necessary to strike a fair balance between insurers and insureds.[197] This dichotomy between s54 (1) on the one hand and ss54 (2)–(4) on the other was examined by the High Court in *Ferrcom Pty Ltd v Commercial Union Assurance Co. of Australia Ltd.*[198] Section 54 (1) was held to apply in this case, as the insured's failure to notify the insurer of its registration of a mobile crane for road use was not capable of causing or contributing to the insured loss.

The Australian courts have gone on to give effect to the spirit and intent of the Australian Law Reform Commission's proposal that s54 should not be affected by form. Section 54 would be applicable where 'the effect of the contract of insurance' may lead to the insurer refusing to pay the claim, be it for allegations of the insured's breach of condition, warranty, clause descriptive of the risk,[199] non-fulfilment of notice requirements[200] or exclusions.[201]

---

[191](1991) 6 WAR 68.

[192]The Australian Law Reform Commission's Notes to the draft Insurance Contracts Bill 1982 (Cth) also contains an example of s 54's application as an illustration of this.

[193](1990) 6 ANZ Ins Cas ¶60-967.

[194](1990) 10 ANZ Ins Cas ¶61-453.

[195][2002] 2Qd R 197.

[196]*Antico v Heath Fielding Australia Pty Ltd* (1997) 188 CLR 652.

[197]Australian Law Reform Commission (1982) [228]. In order to achieve this, the Law Commission envisaged that the application of s 54 should not be affected by matters of form and would also cover matters such as breaches of conditions subsequent and exclusions.

[198](1993) 176 CLR 332.

[199]*East End Real Estate Pty Ltd (t/a City Living) v C E Heath Casualty and General Insurance Ltd* (1992) 25 NSWLR 400.

[200]*FAI General Insurance Co Ltd v Australian Hospital Care Pty Ltd* (2001) 204 CLR 641.

[201]It is worth noting that s55 provides that the remedies in s54 apply exclusively to such post-contractual breaches (as opposed to previous common law remedies which depended on the form of breach rather than its effect): *Antico v Heath Fielding Australia Pty Ltd* (1997) 188 CLR

As for fraudulent claims made by the insured, s56 (1) provides that the insurer may refuse payment of the claim but not avoid the contract. However, if only a minimal or insignificant part of the claim is made fraudulently and non-payment of the remainder of the claim would be harsh and unfair, the court may under s56 (2) order the insurer to pay an amount of the claim which is just and equitable in the circumstances. In doing so however, the court shall have regard to the need to deter insurance fraud and other relevant matters.[202]

Based on Fullagar J's decision in *Gugliotti v Commercial Union Assurance Co of Australia*[203] which was approved by the Victorian Court of Appeal in *Thiep Thi To v Australian Associated Motor Insurers Ltd*,[204] s54 would not apply to cases involving fraudulent claims under s56, as the grounds for and manner of assessing the remedies therein are inconsistent with each other.[205]

The Australian Law Reform Commission's primary purpose in drafting s56 (1) was to ensure that fraud with respect to one claim did not affect other claims under the policy that might entitle the insurer to avoid the contract as a whole, as was the case at common law.[206] This was further qualified by s56 (2) to allow a just and equitable payment of the claim to be made even in cases involving 'a little bit of fraud' on the basis that it would be harsh and unfair not to allow an otherwise legitimate claim for an insured loss, on grounds of 'minimal and insignificant' fraudulent conduct.[207]

Although the reasoning behind this appears logical, it may pose a problem in some cases where the extent of fraud may not be readily quantifiable.[208] Apart from this, some authors[209] have pointed out that in view of the protection already granted to insureds under ss12–14 and s54, this added accommodation of fraudulent insureds under s56 (2) may have swung the pendulum, too far in favour of the

(Footnote 201 continued)

652. Section 55A in turn, empowers the Australian Securities and Investments Commission ('ASIC') to bring representative actions on behalf of insureds that have or are likely to suffer damage as a result of the terms of the contract or conduct of the insurer in breach of the Act.

[202]See: s56 (3).

[203](1992) 7 ANZ Ins Cas ¶61-104 where the insured's claim was rejected for the deliberate provision of a false answer in a claims form as to a blood alcohol test result, as it amounted to a fraudulent claim.

[204](2001) 3 VR 279 which involved the submission of a false claim by the insured that the damage to the insured vehicle occurred after it was stolen, when in actual fact it was damaged whilst being driven by her 15 year-old son without her consent. Although the insured would have otherwise been entitled to claim, her false claim based on a mistaken belief that she would not have been so covered, amounted to fraudulent conduct which barred her claim.

[205]This is especially so with respect to ss54 (1) and 56 (2).

[206]Australian Law Reform Commission (1982) [243].

[207]Ibid. [187].This section draws on research appearing in: Thanasegaran, above n 182, 154–155.

[208]*Ricciardi v Suncorp Metaway Insurance Ltd* (2001) 11 ANZ Ins Cas ¶61-493.

[209]Tarr (1989), Hancy (1994).

insured. It could even bring into question the requirement of both parties having to act in utmost good faith.[210]

Lastly, ss57 (1) and (2) provide that where payment by an insurer is due under an insurance contract, the insurer is also liable to pay interest on it, from the day when it was unreasonable for the insurer to withhold payment until payment is actually made.[211]

4.3.2 Central Bank Guidelines

It is worth noting that prior to the recent reforms in 2013, the law in Malaysia on post contractual good faith and claims settlement was governed by the *Insurance Act 1996* (Malaysia) and certain Guidelines and Codes of Practices issued by the Central Bank ('the *Guidelines*') to insurers, as and when the need arose.

Clause 5 of the *Guidelines on Minimum Disclosure Requirements in the Sale of Insurance Products* effective from 2 January 2006 requires insurers to use clear and simple language; avoid technical terms; and be accurate and complete in substance, in their communication with proposers of insurance.[212]

Clause 3.4 of the *Guidelines on Claims Settlement Practices* (*'Claims Settlement Guidelines'*)[213] which is the most important of the guidelines issued, provides that insurers should not repudiate a claim for a technical breach of warranty or policy conditions, save where it is material and unconnected to the loss, unless it has prejudiced the insurer's interest or exceeded the time bar under law. It also requires any repudiation to contain a prominent statement about recourse to the Financial Mediation Bureau. The purpose being to act as a deterrent to attempts by insurers to avoid policies on technical grounds where notice requirements and time-lines are not strictly complied with by insureds.

In this regard, the Mediator of the Financial Mediation Bureau observed that insurers should give sympathetic consideration to appropriate claims, especially where rejection is based on late notification and technical non-compliance. In doing

---

[210]Tarr, above n 209, 89. This section draws on research appearing in: Thanasegaran, above n 182, 154–155.

[211]The question of when it became unreasonable for an insurer to withhold payment is in turn to be determined objectively: *Settlement Wine Co Pty Ltd v National and General Insurance Co Ltd* (1994) 62 SASR 40.

[212]Central Bank of Malaysia (2006). Similarly, Clause 8 of the Central Bank of Malaysia (1997) which came into effect on 1 January 1998 requires proposal forms to be written in clear and simple language and questions posed therein to be specific in nature.

[213]Central Bank of Malaysia (2003). This revised version came into effect on 16 September 2003 replacing the *Claims Settlement Guidelines* of 25 February 1995.

so, they should make 'ex gratia payments' which are not 'arbitrary figures' but have 'substantive basis', as this would considerably enhance the industry's reputation.[214]

Most of the other provisions in the *Claims Settlement Guidelines* relate to time limits applicable to the insurer at various stages of claims processing. Clause 3.1 provides that insurers must initiate claims processing within seven days from receipt of a claim notification.[215] Within 14 days of receipt of the claim form, the insurer is required to acknowledge receipt in writing and provide the insured with certain requisite information.[216] Clause 3.3 goes on to provide that adjusters must be appointed within seven working days of receipt of the claim form and relevant supporting documents; adjuster's final report must reach the insurer within 14 working days of appointment; and the claimant must be notified of the status of the claim within 60 working days of first notification and every 30 working days thereafter.

Pursuant to Clause 3.4, an offer of settlement must be sent to the claimant within seven working days of receipt of the adjuster's final report, with the adjuster's recommendations being accepted unless there is a dispute as to liability. If the claim is rejected, the claimant must within seven working days of the final report be notified in writing, with reasons for repudiation being stated in a clear and simple manner. Insurers are required not to delay in making payment of claims or reduce the quantum in exchange for early payment pursuant to Clause 3.5. In this regard, full payment of claims is required to be made within 14 working days of acceptance of the settlement offer for sums up to RM1,000,000 and within 21 working days for sums above RM1,000,000.

Despite the detailed provisions above, the *Guidelines* have not proved to be very effective, in that they do not provide for any sanctions to be applicable against insurers should they fail to comply. As a result, the Malaysian courts have not given effect to them in the cases appearing before them on claims settlement.[217]

The *Claims Settlement Guidelines* have however, been applied regularly by the Mediators of the Insurance Mediation Bureau **and** its successor, the Financial Mediation Bureau which took over in 2005, when determining the reasonableness of the parties' conduct, in the cases heard before them.[218]

---

[214]Financial Mediation Bureau (2008, p. 15). This section draws on research appearing in: Thanasegaran, above n 12, 197.

[215]Claims notification through agents must reach insurers within three working days, with the agent not being involved in claims handling on the insurer's behalf, save in assisting the claimant to complete the claim form.

[216]Amongst the information to be provided are the insurer's contact person, expected time frames to process claims, insured's rights, request for additional information and supporting documents, so as to avoid piecemeal repetitive requests for information and is required to send a reminder after 14 days if the requisite information is not provided: Clause 3.2.

[217]This section draws on research appearing in: Thanasegaran, above n 12, 197.

[218]This has been acknowledged and reported in the Financial Mediation Bureau (2009, p. 20). See also: The said *Annual Report 2008*, 8–10, for the Financial Mediation Bureau's Terms of Reference as embodied in its Memorandum and Articles of Association which facilitates this:

Nevertheless, the Mediator's Report in the *Annual Report 2007*,[219] noted several continued indiscretions committed by insurers. Delay in claims settlement was the major complaint, with one case even recording a delay of almost a year after the acceptance of the settlement offer. Insurers have in some cases also delayed in responding to the Mediator's request for particulars. Tactics deployed were to request for extensions of time to appoint adjusters and conduct further investigation when in actual fact, all investigations should have been concluded in full before a claim was even rejected or repudiated. Another instance witnessed insurers putting forward new grounds for repudiating a claim after the Mediator had found the earlier ground for repudiation to be baseless. Although an insurer in its repudiation letter may 'reserve any and all defences which it may have with respect to the claims', such conduct by insurers 'to change their tune' depending on the turn of events is unfair to insureds, unprofessional and lacks good faith.[220]

This has in a practical sense, contributed towards mitigating the lopsided bargaining position between insurers and insureds in claims settlement in Malaysia. In fact, an average of 26.5 % of insurers' decisions in cases brought before the Financial Mediation Bureau annually from 2000 to 2014 has been revised by the Mediator in favour of the insureds.[221] This is because most complaints or cases on alleged breaches of utmost good faith by insurers in Malaysia are lodged with the Bureau rather than the civil courts. This is apparent from an average of about 1,000 new insurance cases being referred to it annually from 2000 to 2014. Of these, an average of 53 % of the cases referred annually involved complaints by insureds on poor claims handling by insurers.[222]

(Footnote 218 continued)

Mediators are required (i) to have regard to and act in conformity (a) with the terms of any contract; (b) any applicable rule of law, judicial authority or statutory provision; and (c) the general principles of good insurance, investment or market practice, the Central Bank's *Guidelines on Claims Settlement Practices* for insurance and *takaful* matters but with (c) prevailing over (b) in favour of the complainant; (ii) to have regard to (without being bound by) any previous decision of any Mediator; (iii) in light of (i) and (ii), to assess what solution would be fair and reasonable in all the circumstances.

[219]Financial Mediation Bureau (2008, pp. 13–16).

[220]This section draws on research appearing in: Thanasegaran, above n 12, 197–198.

[221]See: Table of Cases Referred to the Financial Mediation Bureau from 2000–2014 in the Appendix.

[222]See: Table of Cases Referred to the Financial Mediation Bureau from 2000–2014 in the Appendix. Albeit the fact that the breakdown in terms of types of complaints is no longer available from 2012. This can be compared to there being less than 60 reported insurance cases being decided by the courts for the same period. This section draws on research appearing in: Thanasegaran, above n 12, 198 but the statistics herein have been updated from 2009 up until 2014.

4.3.3 Post-contractual Good Faith and Claims Settlement Under the Financial Services Act 2013

The *Financial Services Act 2013* (Malaysia) which came into effect on 30th June 2013, repeals the *Insurance Act 1996* (Malaysia)[223] and with respect to post contractual good faith and claims settlement, appears to have been influenced primarily by the English and Scottish reforms introduced via the *Consumer Insurance (Disclosure and Representations) Act 2012* (UK). It is unfortunate however, that it did not take into account ss13, 14 and 54 of the *Insurance Contracts Act 1984* (Cth) (Australia) which apply to *both consumer and non-consumer* insurance contracts in Australia. Neither did it consider the proposals for reform pertaining to *non-consumer* insurance contracts in the United Kingdom contained in s14 of the *Insurance Contracts Bill 2014* (UK).

As explained above there was no provision in the *Insurance Act 1996* (Malaysia) that set out the duty of utmost good faith or its application to claims settlement and the ensuing remedies. Hence, s17 of the *Marine Insurance Act 1906* (UK) and the common law applied to claims settlement in Malaysia prior to 2013.

The *Financial Services Act 2013* (Malaysia) however, addresses the problems pertaining to good faith in claims settlement through the enactment of Paragraph 5 (9) of *Schedule 9* to the Act. This is an improvement with respect to *consumer* insurance contracts in that it requires the duty of utmost good faith to be exercised by a *consumer and licensed insurer* in their dealings with each other 'including the making and paying of a claim' after a contract of insurance has been entered into, varied or renewed. Although it is an improvement with respect to consumer insurance contracts, as it expressly requires utmost good faith to be exercised by both parties in claims settlement, the uncertainty remaining is however, with respect to the status of non-consumer insurance contracts and the remedy available in the event of breach in **either** case.

Paragraph 5 (9) of *Schedule 9* to the Act would have been more complete had it been applicable to **all** insurance contracts, with the proportionate remedy of damages being expressly provided to apply in cases of breach of utmost good faith in claims settlement. As a result, it remains unclear if there is still scope for s17 of the *Marine Insurance Act 1906* (UK) and its remedy of avoidance to apply to *non-consumer insurance* contracts in Malaysia. Such a result would indeed be an unfortunate state of affairs.

Instead, it would have been better if the *Financial Services Act 2013* (Malaysia) had modelled its provision on utmost good faith and claims settlement along the lines of ss13 and 14 of the *Insurance Contracts Act 1984* (Cth) (Australia) which introduce an 'implied term' into *every contract* of insurance that utmost good faith must be observed by both parties and failure to act in good faith would prevent the said party from alleging breach of good faith by the other. Furthermore, the

---

[223]Section 271 of the *Financial Services Act 2013* (Malaysia) repeals the *Insurance Act 1996* (Malaysia) but s272 retains the application of the *Insurance Regulations 1996* as amended in 2013.

implications of the duty being an implied term of contract, is that damages would be an available remedy in the event of breach, rather than avoidance alone.

4.4 Conclusion

As explained earlier, although Paragraph 5 (9) of *Schedule 9* to the *Financial Services Act 2013* (Malaysia) provides a marked improvement with respect to claims handling in *consumer* insurance contracts, it would have been more effective had it applied to **all** insurance contracts instead and also provided for a proportionate remedy in the event of its breach by either party. As a result, insureds making a claim under *non-consumer* insurance contracts would appear to be at a disadvantage.

The Malaysian legislature needs to address this in a comprehensive manner and not discriminate between consumer and non-consumer insurance contracts with respect to utmost good faith in general and claims settlement in particular. The insurers' right to avoid liability for breach should also be within defined limits; and fraudulent claims need to be addressed along the lines of s12 of the *Insurance Act 2015* (UK) and s54 of the *Insurance Contracts Act 1984* (Cth) (Australia).

The Central Bank's *Claims Settlement Guidelines* directing insurers to conduct themselves in a fair and reasonable manner in settling claims[224]; and the Financial Mediation Bureau of Malaysia's flexible and proactive resolution of disputes brought before them,[225] cannot be the only recourse for *non-consumer* insurance contracts. There is much to be said therefore, in the *Financial Services Act 2013* (Malaysia) being improved to address these shortcomings, so as to be able to 'strike a balance between the competing interests at play while being legally robust.'[226]

References

Association of British Insurers (1986a) Statement of general insurance practice, London, Rev

Association of British Insurers (1986b) Statement of long term insurance practice, London, Rev

Australian Law Reform Commission (1982) Report No 20, insurance contracts

Bennett H (1999) Mapping the doctrine of utmost good faith in insurance contract law. Lloyd's Marit Commer Law Quart 165

Birds J (1982) The reform of insurance law. J Bus Law 449

Birds J (2013) Birds' modern insurance law, vol 9. Sweet & Maxwell, London

[224]See: Clause 3.4 of the *Claims Settlement Guidelines 1995 @ 2003*. A major drawback is that the Guidelines have no clear sanctions set out as being applicable in the event of non-compliance.

[225]See: The Financial Mediation Bureau (2009, p. 20). This section draws on research appearing in: Thanasegaran and Shaiban (2014, p. 343).

[226]Hertzell and Burgoyne, above n 85, 123.

Brown C (2002) Damages for bad faith denial of insurance claims in Canada: continuing a tradition of judicial restraint. N Z Law Rev 453
Brown C (2004) Determining cover: interpretation of policies, causation and fortuity. In: Duncan W, David R (eds) Insurance law: practice, policy and principles. The Centre for Commercial & Corporate Law, New Zealand
Campbell N (2000) The nature of an insurer's obligation. Lloyd's Marit Commer Law Quart 42
Campbell N (2004) A sceptical view of good faith in insurance law. In: Duncan W, David R (eds) Insurance law: practice, policy and principles. The Centre for Commercial and Corporate Law, New Zealand
Central Bank of Malaysia (1997) Code of good practice for life insurance business, Kuala Lumpur
Central Bank of Malaysia (2003) Guidelines on claims settlement practices, Kuala Lumpur, Rev
Central Bank of Malaysia (2006) Guidelines on minimum disclosure requirements in the sale of insurance products, Kuala Lumpur
Clarke M (2005) Policies and perceptions of insurance law in the twenty-first century. Oxford University Press, New York
Explanatory Memorandum, Insurance Contracts Bill 1984 (Cth)
Financial Mediation Bureau (2008) Annual report 2007, Kuala Lumpur
Financial Mediation Bureau (2009) Annual report 2008, Kuala Lumpur
Financial Ombudsman Service (1990–1991) Insurance Ombudsman Annual Report 1989–1990, London
Financial Services Authority (2005a) Conduct of Business, London
Financial Services Authority (2005b) Insurance Conduct of Business, London
Financial Services Authority (2005c) Principles for Business, London
General Insurance Standards Council (2000) General Insurance Code for Private Customers, London
General Insurance Standards Council (2000) General Insurance Commercial Code, London
Gower (1959) Business. In: Ginsberg M (ed) Law and opinion in England in the 20th Century. Stevens, London
Hancy G (1994) Recent trends in insurance law. Paper presented at the Western Australian Law Society Continuing Legal Education Forum, Perth
Hasson RA (1969) The doctrine of uberrima fides in insurance law—a critical evaluation. Modern Law Review 32:615
Hasson RA (1984) The special nature of insurance contracts: a comparison of the American and English law of insurance. Mod Law Rev 47:505
Hertzell D, Burgoyne L (2013) The law commissions and insurance contract law reform: an update. J Int Marit Law 19:105
Hobbs J (2004) The exercise of a contractual discretion: the insurer as judge in its own cause. In: Duncan W, David R (eds) Insurance law: practice, policy and principles. The Centre for Commercial and Corporate Law, New Zealand
Kessler F (1943) Contracts of adhesion—some thoughts about freedom of contract. Columbia Law Rev 43:629
Law Commission (1980) Insurance law: non-disclosure and breach of warranty, Report No 104, Cmnd 8064
Law Commission and Scottish Law Commission (1975) Exemption clauses. Law Com No 69 and Scot Law Com No 39
Law Reform Committee (1957) Conditions and exceptions in insurance policies, Report No 5, Cmnd 62
Mahmood NR (1992) Insurance law in Malaysia. Butterworths, Malaysia
Naidoo A, Oughton D (2005) The confused post-formation duty of good faith in insurance law: from refinement to fragmentation to elimination? J Bus Law 346
Soyer B (2003) Continuing duty of utmost good faith in insurance contracts: still alive? Lloyd's Marit Commer Law Quart 39
Tarr A (1989) Insurance law and the consumer. Bond Law Rev 1:79
Tarr J-A (2001) The insured's reasonable expectations. Insur Law J 12:9

Thanasegaran H (2004) Insurers' good faith in Malaysia: does a search for a fairer balance in non-marine insurance contracts lead to Australia? Insur Law J 15:143

Thanasegaran H (2011) Settlement of claims by Malaysian insurance and takaful companies: a genuine prospect or merely suspect? Int Co Commer Law Rev 22(6):191

Thanasegaran H, Shaiban M (2014) Harmonization of takaful (Islamic insurance) regulation—a realistic goal or improbable ideal? Singap J Leg Stud 328

Wheatley M (2013) Meeting the growth challenge. British Insurance Brokers' Association conference (May 2013). http://www.fca.org.uk/news/speeches/meeting-the-growth-challenge. Accessed 30 June 2015

Chapter 5
Utmost Good Faith and *Takaful* in Malaysia

Abstract This chapter sets out the concept of *takaful* or Islamic insurance as well as its juridical basis and application in Malaysia with respect to both the pre and post-contractual duty of utmost good faith. It analyses the shortcomings of the duty, pre and post-contract with respect to *takaful*, and evaluates the recent reforms introduced via the *Islamic Financial Services Act 2013* (Malaysia) vis-a-vis its predecessor the *Takaful Act 1984* (Malaysia), the common law and the reforms pertaining to conventional insurance introduced in Australia and the United Kingdom. The chapter also briefly addresses the extent to which the duty of utmost good faith in *takaful* contracts has been regulated, in other Muslim-majority jurisdictions where *takaful* is offered in a large scale, so as to place the Malaysian *takaful* reforms in context.

5.1 Introduction

This chapter sets out the concept of *takaful* or Islamic insurance as well as its juridical basis and application in Malaysia with respect to both the pre and post-contractual duty of utmost good faith. It will in this context, analyse the shortcomings of the duty, pre and post-contract with respect to *takaful*, and evaluate the recent reforms introduced via the *Islamic Financial Services Act 2013* (Malaysia) vis-a-vis its predecessor the *Takaful Act 1984* (Malaysia), the common law and the reforms pertaining to conventional insurance introduced in Australia and the United Kingdom. This chapter will also briefly address the extent to which the duty of utmost good faith in *takaful* contracts has been regulated, in other Muslim-majority jurisdictions where *takaful* is offered in a large scale, so as to place the Malaysian *takaful* reforms in context.

5.2 The Juridical Basis of *Takaful*

Takaful originally arose on religious grounds so as to complement the Islamic banking institution. Its growth over the past 25 years has however, cemented its position as an innovative financial alternative to conventional insurance. It is

H. Thanasegaran, *Good Faith in Insurance and Takaful Contracts in Malaysia*,
DOI 10.1007/978-981-10-0383-7_5

important to note that it is not the concept of insurance where insureds are indemnified for included losses, which contradicts the teachings of Islam but the way in which it is practiced. On this point, Muslim scholars tend to differ in their views with respect to the permissibility (*halal*) or prohibition (*haram*) of insurance. Some scholars have accepted insurance in its traditional form as being necessary for the evolution of modern Islamic concepts. On the other hand, the more conservative scholars continue to argue for its prohibition on the basis that it contains certain elements that are prohibited in Islam, for example, the payment of interest (*riba*), the uncertainty of the outcome (*gharar*) and the element of gambling arising from this uncertainty (*maisir*).[1]

This prohibition was in fact what formed the basis for the initiation of interest-free or Islamic banking years ago. At a more fundamental level, it is linked to a revival of Islam and a desire for Muslims to live all aspects of their lives in accordance with the teachings of Islam.[2] It is interesting to note that socio-cultural research findings in the Malaysian context support this phenomenon. Ethnic Malays, who form the Muslim majority population making up more than 65 %, tend to place a great deal of importance on the fulfilment of their religious obligations and tend not to separate the teachings of Islam from every aspect of their lives.[3]

The application of *Sharia* or Islamic law to financial and commercial matters forms the basis of Islamic finance, and *takaful* or Islamic mutual or cooperative insurance is in turn, a crucial component of it. The *Quran* which is the holy book of Islam; the *Sunnah* which comprises the actions and sayings of Prophet Muhammad; and *Ijmaa* which forms the scholarly consensus in interpreting the *Quran* and *Sunnah*, together form the primary sources of *Sharia*. With *Sharia* as its foundation, Islamic finance has developed over the years into a modern vehicle of economic protection and investment for Muslims that is alternative to conventional finance.[4]

Takaful, has likewise benefitted from this development and emerged as an innovative financial instrument to complement Islamic banking. At its core, *takaful* is essentially an agreement between participants (insureds) to jointly guarantee themselves against any defined loss or damage. Each participant makes a contribution (premium) to the *takaful* fund that corresponds with the risk involved and in the event of a loss arising, the said participant will be paid a sum of money from the fund.[5] In this context, family *takaful* is akin to life insurance whereas general *takaful* refers to general insurance.

It is interesting to note that unlike conventional insurance, where the risk is borne solely by the insurers, *takaful* is a scheme where the participants are in effect

[1]Maysami and Williams (2006) pp. 229–230. This section draws on research appearing in: Thanasegaran (2008, pp. 144–145).

[2]Khorshid (2004, p. 113).

[3]Lim and Abdullah (2001, p. 7). See: The last official population and housing census conducted in 2010 for Malaysia: Department of Statistics Malaysia (2010).

[4]Masud (2011, p. 1133).

[5]This section draws on research appearing in: Thanasegaran and Shaiban (2014, p. 331).

the insureds as well as the insurers and therefore, share in the profit and loss of the operator. Another central feature of *takaful* is the separation of the participants' and shareholders' funds. *Takaful* operators are paid explicit contractual fees from the return on investments for managing the participants' fund on their behalf and after these fees are deducted, any remaining surplus is shared by the participants. This includes underwriting profits which are generally not available to conventional insurance policyholders, except in the case of mutual insurance.[6]

Takaful is however, similar to conventional insurance to the extent that both provide financial protection against unforeseen risks. They are also based on similar actuarial approaches to mortality rates, morbidity rates, loss ratios, claims experience and discounted cash flows for calculating the price of risk and the evaluation of liabilities.[7]

Furthermore, although there is no Islamic contract law as such which recognizes the freedom of contract or an express requirement of good faith or disclosure, there is an inherent element of good faith in Islam that all agreements must fulfil in line with the *Quran*. Verse 16:91 of the *Quran* provides that one should '*fulfil the covenant of God when you have entered into it, and break not your oaths after you have confirmed them*'.[8] It is this element of good faith or *uberrimae fidei* which is also a fundamental principle of conventional insurance.[9] In light of this therefore, the concept of insurance where common resources are pooled so as to help the unfortunate is not in conflict with the teachings of Islam, as the latter in any event propagates solidarity, mutual help and cooperation within its community.[10]

Having acknowledged this, the difference between conventional insurance and *takaful* however, is that insurance is based on a contract of buying and selling, where one party sells protection and the other buys it at a certain cost. In the case of *takaful* on the other hand, the contributions paid by participants are treated as *tabarru* (donation) and *mudarabah* (savings) so as to remove the element of *gharar* (uncertainty). The relationship that exists in insurance is therefore, bilateral in nature, where the aim is to eliminate risk for the individual, whereas *takaful* is a collective endeavour that seeks to eliminate the risk within a given social group.[11]

Apart from this, at a more fundamental level, conventional insurance contracts contain the elements of *gharar* (uncertainties in the operation of the insurance contract), *maisir* (gambling as a consequence of the presence of uncertainty), and *riba* (interest which is strictly prohibited by the *Quran*). Verse 2:275 of the *Quran* in fact explicitly provides that *'Allah has permitted trade and has forbidden*

---

[6]This section draws on research appearing in: Thanasegaran (2013, p. 107); Also see: Swartz and Coetzer (2010, pp. 336 and 338).

[7]Bhatty http://www.newhorizon-islamicbanking.com/index.cfm/section=features&action=view. Accessed 30 May 2012.

[8]See: Masud, above n 4, 1139.

[9]See: Section 17 of the *Marine Insurance Act 1906* (UK) as amended by s14 of the *Insurance Act 2015* (UK); and s13 of the *Insurance Contracts Act 1984* (Cth) (Australia).

[10]This section draws on research appearing in: Thanasegaran, above n 6, 107.

[11]Baker and Simon (2002, pp. 37–38).

interest'.[12] These are all elements which contravene the rules of *Sharia* and are therefore, prohibited in *takaful*. In addition, conventional insurance is also unable to ensure Islamic policyholders that the returns received in claims settlement in actual fact come from investments in companies that produce or deal in *halal* (or permissible) goods or services, rather than that which is *haram* (or prohibited) like alcohol, gambling, weapons sale, pork, etc.[13]

Family *takaful* has also been criticized by some Islamic scholars on the basis that it is unlawful to insure against death under *Sharia*, as life and death are in the hands of God. The appointment of a nominee as beneficiary under family *takaful* policies has likewise been criticized as being contrary to *Sharia* inheritance laws on the distribution of a deceased's estate. The latter criticism has however, been addressed by the nominee in *takaful* being authorised to act only as a trustee, with respect to the distribution of policy monies to the beneficiaries which would be according to *Sharia*.[14]

Lastly, all *takaful* operators are required to have a *Sharia* Supervisory Board within their organization to advice on matters pertaining to the *Sharia* compliance of their *takaful* products and practices. This is not required in conventional insurance companies, as they are run like any other corporate entity.

5.3 *Takaful* Models in Existence

There are at present four types of *takaful* models in operation globally, namely the *Mudharabah*, *Wakalah*, Hybrid and *Wakalah Waaf* models. The *Mudharabah* model is a form of Islamic commercial profit-sharing contract between the participants and the *takaful* operators who actually manage the investment and underwriting functions.[15] Net surplus accruing in the *takaful* pool is shared between the participants and *takaful* operator on an agreed ratio. This model is used extensively in Brunei, the United Arab Emirates and Indonesia and was up until 2012 also used in Saudi Arabia.[16]

The *Wakalah* model on the other hand, is fee driven. The participants own the *takaful* fund on a collective basis whereas the *takaful* operator manages its

[12]See: Masud, above n 4, 1139.

[13]See: Au Pui Khuan and Maysami (1998); Central Bank of Malaysia (1999, p. 256). This section draws on research appearing in: Thanasegaran, above n 1, 145.

[14]See: Masud, above n 4, 1144; This section draws on research appearing in: Thanasegaran, above n 6, 109.

[15]Central Bank of Malaysia, above n 13, 257.

[16]Saudi Arabia has however, since moved to the cooperative insurance model following a directive from the Saudi Arabian Monetary Authority (SAMA).

investment and underwriting functions for a fixed fee. The operator does not have any share in the surplus of funds which reverts to the participants.[17] This model is widely used in Sudan, the United Arab Emirates and the United Kingdom.

The Hybrid or Combined model is in turn, a combination of the *Mudharabah* and *Wakalah models* where the *Wakalah* contract is used for underwriting activities while the *Mudharabah* contract is applied for investment management activities. The participant under this model is entitled to enjoy a return on the premium paid whereas the *takaful* operator is paid a fee for its services.[18] This model has been successfully used in Malaysia and Bahrain which apart from Saudi Arabia are viewed as the forerunners in terms of *takaful* growth and penetration. There is also a growing consensus amongst international standard setting bodies like the Accounting and Auditing Organization for Islamic Financial Institutions (AAOIFI) and the Islamic Financial Services Board (IFSB) that it should be the leading practice. This is because it leverages on the strengths of both the *Mudharabah* and *Wakalah* models.[19]

The fourth is the *Wakalah Waqf* model which is widely used in Pakistan and requires the setting up of a legal entity through an initial donation from the shareholders for the benefit of the participants, with only the investment and returns from the fund being used to pay claims. All other characteristics are however, similar to the *Wakalah* model.[20]

Apart from this, there is the Cooperative Insurance model which in a strict sense differs from *takaful* per se in that there is no need for a separation of policyholder and shareholder funds; investments are not required to be held in accordance with the principles of *Sharia* (although they tend to be); and a *Sharia* Board is not required.[21] As of January 2012, this is the only model permitted to apply in Saudi Arabia, following a directive from the Saudi Arabian Monetary Authority (SAMA). According to this cooperative model, policyholders are entitled to 10 % of the net surplus (with no *Wakalah* fee) and losses will not be transferred to them should the company incur any.[22]

---

[17]Ernst and Young (2012, p. 54).

[18]Ibid 55.

[19]Swiss Re Economic Research and Consulting (2011, p. 6). This section draws on research appearing in: Thanasegaran and Shaiban, above n 5, 334.

[20]Ernst and Young, above n 17, 56.

[21]Ibid 57.

[22]This section draws on research appearing in: Thanasegaran and Shaiban, above n 5, 334.

5.4 The Development and Regulation of *Takaful* in Malaysia

It started with the Malaysian National Fatwa Committee in June 1972 declaring the concept of conventional insurance as contravening the rules of *Sharia*. This led to the Task Force to Study the Establishment of an Islamic Insurance Company in Malaysia being formed in 1982. It was to look into the possibility of launching Islamic insurance as a complement to Islamic banking. Following the recommendations of the Task Force, the *takaful* scheme was born in Malaysia via the enactment of the *Takaful Act 1984* (Malaysia).

The operation of *takaful* in Malaysia has from then until 2013 been regulated by the *Takaful Act 1984* with s54 entrusting the Central Bank of Malaysia ('Central Bank') with the responsibility of administering the Act, and the Governor of the Central Bank also acting as the Director General of *Takaful*.[23] The Malaysian Takaful Association was formed in 2002 as an association for *takaful* operators in order to improve industry self-regulation through uniformity in market practice and the promotion of greater co-operation amongst the operators in developing the *takaful* industry.

All *takaful* operators are however, required to satisfy the following measures. They are required to establish a *Sharia* Advisory Council within their organization to ensure *Sharia* compliance and are bound by the National *Sharia* Advisory Council of the Central Bank (NASC)'s rulings on *Sharia* issues pertaining to Islamic finance. Malaysian *takaful* operators are also subject to the *Sharia Governance Framework 2011* and *Takaful Operating Framework 2012* established by the Central Bank; and are required to separate their life and general business with a minimum capital of RM100 million, pursuant to s16 of the *Islamic Financial Services Act 2013* (Malaysia).[24] As at 30 June 2015 there were 11 *takaful* operators vis-a-vis 33 insurance companies in Malaysia.[25]

It is important to note that *takaful* in Malaysia exists side by side with conventional insurance, with its role clearly defined by the *Federal Constitution*. *Takaful* is considered to be a part of mainstream mercantile law and hence, a part of civil law and subject to the civil court structure of Malaysia. As such, the Federal Parliament has jurisdiction to legislate over it, as it has done via the *Takaful Act 1984* (Malaysia) and now the *Islamic Financial Services Act 2013* (Malaysia) which repeals and replaces the former. *Takaful* in Malaysia is therefore, not subject to *Sharia* law per se and the *Sharia* courts. This is apparent from the combined effect of Articles 73, 74, 75, 121(1), 121(1A) and the *Ninth Schedule* of the *Federal*

[23]The Central Bank is therefore, responsible for administering the regulations (including licensing and fund management requirements) governing both conventional insurance and *takaful* in Malaysia. This has remained unchanged under the *Islamic Financial Services Act 2013* (Malaysia).

[24]This section draws on research appearing in: Thanasegaran and Shaiban, above n 5, 335.

[25]Central Bank of Malaysia www.bnm.gov.my/index.php?ch=li&cat=insurance&lang=en Accessed 30 June 2015.

Constitution of Malaysia[26], which is in line with Malaysia being a moderate Islamic country, with *Sharia* being confined to personal and inheritance matters only.

In fact, *takaful* is treated as being part of mainstream mercantile law by most of the nations that offer it on a fairly large scale. This would include Bahrain, Pakistan, Egypt, Indonesia, Brunei, Iran and the United Arab Emirates which in turn, would be largely based on their respective common law and civil law traditions. *Takaful* is in effect only treated as being a part of *Sharia* per se, in Saudi Arabia and Sudan.[27]

The principal governing statute for *takaful* in Malaysia has been the *Takaful Act 1984* (Malaysia) up until its repeal by s282 of the *Islamic Financial Services Act* (Malaysia) in 2013. It should be noted however, that the *Takaful Act 1984* (Malaysia) was largely regulatory in nature, with very few substantive provisions to boost, let alone those dealing with the application of *Sharia* principles. As a result, the gaps in its provisions have in the past been filled by the common law through the operation of s5 of the *Civil Law Act 1956* (Malaysia).[28] More so, since s67 (2) of the *Takaful Act 1984* (Malaysia) seemed to imply that the *Insurance Act 1996* (Malaysia) and *Takaful Act 1984* (Malaysia) were mutually exclusive in their application, with the former only applying to insurance contracts in Malaysia and not *takaful* matters. This would also appear to be the present position with respect to the *Financial Service Act 2013* (Malaysia) and *Islamic Financial Services Act 2013* (Malaysia), although there is no explicit provision in either statute to the effect, as the provisions in both statutes generally form a mirror image of each other, with some *Sharia* based requirements incorporated into the latter.

It should be noted that although s282 of the *Islamic Financial Services Act 2013* (Malaysia) repeals the *Takaful Act 1984* (and the *Islamic Banking Act 1983*) (Malaysia), the former through s285 nevertheless, retains much of the licensing and *takaful* fund establishment requirements originally set out in the repealed *Takaful Act 1984* (Malaysia).

For instance, *takaful* is defined in s2 of the *Islamic Financial Services Act 2013* (Malaysia) as an arrangement based on mutual assistance under which *takaful* participants agree to contribute to a common fund providing for mutual financial benefits payable to the *takaful* participants or their beneficiaries on the occurrence of pre-agreed events. A *takaful* agent is in turn defined as one who solicits or obtains a proposal for a *takaful* certificate or negotiates it or acts in relation to the issuance or renewal or continuance of a *takaful* certificate on behalf of a *takaful* operator. Section 136 goes on to provide that a 'financial service provider' (defined in s133 as an authorised person and includes *takaful* operators) shall not engage in prohibited business conduct set out in *Schedule 7* to the Act that contains a list of

---

[26]See: Mohamed (2005). This section draws on research appearing in: Thanasegaran, above n 1, 147.

[27]This section draws on research appearing in: Thanasegaran, above n 1, 147.

[28]Mahmood (1992, p. 247). The use of s5 of the *Civil Law Act 1956* (Malaysia) to permit the application of English insurance and mercantile law in force at the time, to Malaysia has been set out in Chap. 2 of this book.

misleading and/or deceptive conduct and inducement to enter into and/or pay for financial services.

It is important to note that since *takaful* is part of the mainstream mercantile law of Malaysia, the application and treatment of the duty of utmost good faith in *takaful* contracts would be similar to its conventional insurance counterpart, save for any additional *Sharia* based requirements. This would also be justified from a juridical stand point, as the concept of utmost good faith is also fundamental to *Sharia*, as explained earlier. The statute governing *takaful* in Malaysia would however, be different, as it would be the *Islamic Financial Services Act 2013* (Malaysia) instead of the *Financial Services Act 2013* (Malaysia) (which applies to insurance contracts) that would apply. Having examined the duty of utmost good faith both at the pre and post contractual stages in the Malaysian insurance context, however, it is interesting to note that most of the provisions of the *Financial Services Act 2013* (Malaysia) and the *Islamic Financial Services Act 2013* (Malaysia) appear to be a mirror image of each other. This is to an extent not surprising, as both pieces of legislation were drafted and enacted around the same time.

5.4.1 Relevance of Utmost Good Faith to Takaful Contracts

Takaful is similar to a cooperative or mutual form of insurance, save for additional *Sharia* compliance requirements.[29] Therefore, core insurance principles such as utmost good faith, disclosure, non-misrepresentation, insurable interest, reciprocity in claims handling and the ensuing remedies, apply equally to both *takaful* and conventional insurance. Industry experts have in fact stressed on the importance of *takaful* following 'the best regulatory and compliance practices currently deployed in the insurance sector'[30] for its continued growth. This can be seen from the Islamic Financial Services Board (IFSB) and the International Association of Insurance Supervisors (IAIS)'s collaboration towards harmonizing *takaful* regulatory standards by adapting IAIS core principles on corporate governance to *takaful*.[31]

Furthermore, as *takaful* and insurance are essentially part of mainstream mercantile law in Malaysia, with English common law forming the basis for both, a comparison can be drawn between conventional insurance principles and *takaful*. One author in fact correctly points out that 'regulations adopted in this respect will obviously vary from one system to another but not so fundamentally as to justify the characterization of a system as 'Islamic' or 'non Islamic,' for the basic

[29]Masud, above n 4, 1141; Hoyle (2012, p. 525).

[30]Tsang and Hodgins (2012, p. 1) http://www.mondaq.com/x/188132/islamic+finance/Asia+Insurance+Review+Takaful+Conference+910+May+2012. Accessed 30 June 2015.

[31]This section draws on research appearing in: Thanasegaran and Shaiban, above n 5, 330.

mechanisms of insurance are universal, as is the concern about limiting unfair advantages of the insurer.'[32]

Malaysia, along with the likes of Pakistan, Bahrain, the United Arab Emirates and Saudi Arabia is amongst the *takaful* elite in so far as *takaful* regulation, the number of operators and market growth is concerned. The *takaful* industry in Malaysia has enjoyed a healthy growth over the years with its *takaful* operators accounting for about 25 % of global gross *takaful* contributions, second only to Saudi Arabia's 50 % strong hold. Its total net family *takaful* contributions have also reached RM4.5 billion in 2014.[33]

In view of this positive outlook, matters such as suitable and sustainable product development and marketing (which are beyond the purview of this book)[34] and substantive legal issues concerning *takaful* regulation need to be addressed, if Malaysia is to remain competitive at the fore-front of *takaful* development. It is therefore, especially crucial that issues of utmost good faith be addressed, as seen from the statistics provided in the Appendix with respect to the number and nature of complaints referred to the Financial Mediation Bureau of Malaysia between 2000–2014 involving *takaful*.[35] These statistics show that a large proportion of public complaints involving *takaful* (and insurance for that matter) consistently stem from alleged breaches of this fundamental duty.

For example, from 2000 to 2014, an average of 93.6 % of the total *takaful* cases referred to the Financial Mediation Bureau concerned allegations of breaches of utmost good faith in one form or another, with an average of 60.5 % out of it involving poor claims handling.[36] These statistics provide a useful measure of the current state of affairs in Malaysia, as most cases on *takaful* (and insurance) are filed with the Bureau as opposed to the courts.

In response to this, however, up until the recent reforms introduced via the *Islamic Financial Services Act 2013* (Malaysia), there was no substantive legislative change made after the enactment of the *Takaful Act* in 1984. During this period, the Malaysian government undertook measures to improve the infrastructure supporting the industry, by way of improving the grievance redress mechanisms and

---

[32]Khorshid, above n 2,160.

[33]Ernst and Young (2014, pp. 7–8).

[34]See: Maysami and Williams, above n 1, 232 which is an interesting article that examined these issues, albeit more particularly with respect to neighbouring Singapore. It provides an indication that Muslims who are supposedly the target recipient of *takaful* products remain largely unaware of the existence of these services and more so, that Muslims with conservative values seem to be less aware of *takaful* compared to the more liberal Muslims.

[35]See: Table of Cases Referred to the Financial Mediation Bureau from 2000 to 2014 in the Appendix.

[36]Ibid. However, it should be noted that the breakdown in terms of the types of *takaful* complaints is no longer available from 2012. This section draws on research appearing in: Thanasegaran (2011, p. 199) but the statistics have been updated up to 2014 from 2009 previously.

introducing the Consumer Education Programme.[37] These measures namely, the amalgamation of the Insurance Mediation Bureau and Banking Mediation Bureau into the Financial Mediation Bureau, although necessary, were however, long-term in nature and needed the supported of more immediate legislative amendment to the *takaful* regulation in place, which eventually came in 2013.

5.4.2 Utmost Good Faith Under the Takaful Act 1984

Before examining the recent reforms introduced by the *Islamic Financial Services Act 2013* (Malaysia), it is useful to take stock of the law applicable prior thereto under the *Takaful Act 1984* (Malaysia), so as to provide an insight into the reforms.

The *Takaful Act 1984* which was the principal regulation governing *takaful* operations in Malaysia has been described by Nik Ramlah Mahmood as being only regulatory in nature.[38] It was not a comprehensive source of the substantive law regulating *takaful,* as it contained very few provisions on how the *takaful* scheme should be implemented. It dealt primarily with the setting up and operations of a *takaful* business, rather than the application of Islamic principles to *takaful*. The application of the substantive principles of *Sharia* to *takaful*, therefore, remained unclear because it was only implied in a few provisions of the *Takaful Act 1984* (Malaysia). To make matters worse, by virtue of s 67 (2) of the *Takaful Act 1984*, the now repealed *Insurance Act 1996* (Malaysia) could also not apply to *takaful* at the time, as both statutes were to be mutually exclusive.[39]

The *Takaful Act 1984* for example, provided for the definition of *takaful*.[40] It also set out the requirement for establishing the *Sharia* Advisory Council within the Central Bank of Malaysia and *Sharia* Committees within each *takaful* operator's organisation. This was to ensure *Sharia* compliance as well as the types of *takaful* business that a licensed operator may undertake.[41] Section 53A was inserted following a review of the *Takaful Act 1984* in 2003, which elevated the *Sharia* Advisory Council as the sole authority on *Sharia* matters pertaining to Islamic banking and finance, with its role enlarged so as to ensure better *Sharia* governance.

---

[37]This was a 10-year programme launched in 2003 to educate consumers (of *takaful* and insurance) of their contractual rights and responsibilities. This was to enable them to make well-informed decisions, both in product selection as well as meeting their legal and contractual obligations.

[38]Mahmood, above n 28, 247.

[39]This is unlike the situation in Pakistan for instance, where its *Takaful Rules 2005* clearly provide that any gap therein shall be filled by reference to the *Insurance Ordinance 2000*.

[40]Section 2 of the *Takaful Act 1984* (Malaysia).

[41]The function of the *Sharia* Committees is supervisory, in that it is to advise the company on matters relating to *Sharia*. The *Takaful Act 1984* (Malaysia) did not however, mention matters such as the status of the committees' advice, for example, as to whether it was binding on the company.

The *Sharia* Advisory Council was also to act as the reference point for the courts and mediators when resolving disputes involving *Sharia* issues on Islamic banking and finance. In this vein, the *Guidelines on the Governance of Sharia Committees* for Islamic financial institutions were issued in 2004 to streamline the functions and duties of the *Sharia* Committees of *takaful* operators and to strengthen their independence.[42]

It should be noted that as far as substantive provisions went, the *Takaful Act 1984* (Malaysia) did not provide any express requirement for the duty of utmost good faith to be observed. There was also no provision governing the pre-contractual duty of disclosure and misrepresentation, nor the post-contractual duty involving exclusions and claims settlement. Nik Ramlah Mahmood in fact hypothesised two possible explanations for this omission.[43] The first is that since *takaful* was a form of insurance, the *takaful* contract would in essence be an insurance contract. And as insurance contracts are contracts *uberrimae fidei* or contracts of utmost good faith, the duty of utmost good faith would apply to *takaful* as well. The other possibility was to treat a *takaful* contract like any other ordinary contract. If this were the case, then it could only be avoided if there has been a positive act of fraud or misrepresentation operating. The more current available literature however, suggests that this is no longer in doubt, as utmost good faith is viewed as a principle that is central to *takaful*,[44] much like its conventional insurance counterpart and would therefore, be governed by s17 of the *Marine Insurance Act 1906* (UK).

This being the case therefore, parties to a *takaful* contract would have to act with utmost good faith towards each other or the contract would be void ab initio at the option of the innocent party. The problems with this have been addressed in earlier chapters pertaining to conventional insurance and are equally applicable to *takaful*. Should one party to the contract breach or fail to carry out the duty, the other party would be entitled to avoid the contract with a refund of premiums paid, subject to fraud being involved, in which case, the premiums would be forfeited. The *Takaful Act 1984* (Malaysia) like the *Insurance Act 1996* (Malaysia) did not provide for damages as a remedy, and this has been a problem in instances where the participant had suffered substantial losses.

Another disadvantage of this solution is due to the application of this duty itself, where parties are required to disclose all material facts. This may result in a party being punished for innocent non-disclosure, as there was no requirement for a causal connection to be shown to exist between the non-disclosure and loss in question, in the Malaysian context.[45] This would presumably go against basic

---

[42]This section draws on research appearing in: Thanasegaran, above n 1, 154.

[43]Mahmood, above n 28, 250.

[44]See: *Seah Cheoh Wah v Malayan Banking Bhd & Anor* [2009] 7 CLJ 485 and the Table of Cases Referred to the Financial Mediation Bureau from 2000 to 2014 involving *takaful* in the Appendix.

[45]On the contrary, this is a necessary requirement for avoidance of conventional insurance policies in Australia under ss28 and 29 of the *Insurance Contracts Act 1984* (Cth).

Islamic principles where fairness and justice are paramount. Instead however, the *Takaful Act 1984* (Malaysia) left even more to be desired than its conventional counterpart.[46]

There was in fact no express provision for the duty of utmost good faith or the availability of damages as a remedy for a breach thereof. The *Takaful Act 1984* (Malaysia) even lacked some of the basic utmost good faith provisions which could be found in the *Insurance Act 1996*(Malaysia). Examples of these are the pre-contractual duty of disclosure required of the insured in s150 (1) of the *Insurance Act 1996* (Malaysia); the insurer's deemed waiver of incomplete or irrelevant answers provided by insureds in proposal forms in s150 (3); and the statutory warning required to be given by insurers in proposal forms on the effects of non-disclosure by insureds, in s149 (4).

Since the *Insurance Act 1996* (Malaysia) did not apply to *takaful* matters,[47] ss149 (4), 150 (1) and 150 (3) could not be imported to fill the gap in *takaful* regulation, which resulted in the less favourable common law provisions and even s18 of the *Marine Insurance Act 1906* (UK) with respect to the 'prudent insurers' test for disclosure as opposed to the 'reasonable insured' test in s150 (1) of the *Insurance Act 1996* (Malaysia), being applicable to *takaful*. Also, like conventional insurance, there was no provision for pre-contractual misrepresentation and therefore, s20 of the *Marine Insurance Act 1906* (UK) and its heavily criticized 'prudent insurer' test resulted in applying to *takaful* as well.[48]

In addition to this, an anomaly existed in a number of *takaful* proposal forms in Malaysia. They displayed a statutory warning to proposers to disclose material facts or face avoidance of the policy but referred to s28 of the *Takaful Act 1984* (Malaysia) instead, as the basis for doing so.

Section 28(1) provided:

> Any person who, by any statement, promises or forecasts which he knows to be misleading, false, or deceptive, or by any fraudulent concealment of a material fact, or by the reckless making (fraudulently or otherwise) of any statement, promise or forecast which is misleading, false or deceptive, induces or attempts to induce another person to enter into or offer to enter into any contract of *takaful with an operator* shall be *guilty of an offence* and shall, on conviction, be liable to a fine not exceeding twenty thousand ringgit or to imprisonment for a term not exceeding one year or to both (emphasis added).

An examination of this provision clearly shows that it was intended to deter unconscionable conduct on the part of *takaful* agents and brokers. This is compounded by the fact that it made it an 'offence' to make misleading statements, promises or forecasts which induce persons to enter into *takaful* contracts with '*takaful* operators'. The fact that there was no provision made for the consequence of avoidance of the *takaful* contract as a remedy, is further proof that s28 was not

[46]This section draws on research appearing in: Thanasegaran, above n 1, 155.

[47]This is pursuant to s67 (2) of the *Takaful Act 1984* (Malaysia).

[48]This section draws on research appearing in: Thanasegaran, above n 1, 155–156.

meant to be a statutory warning but was nevertheless used as such in a blatant way.[49]

On the other hand, it should be noted that the *Takaful Act 1984* (Malaysia) did contain some important substantive provisions and as such, ought not to be labelled as a purely regulatory piece of legislation either. Section 66 for instance, provided that the knowledge of and statement by an authorised agent is deemed to be that of the *takaful* operator, which is in tandem with s151 of the *Insurance Act 1996* (Malaysia) and was an important protection for the participant. Sections 27 and 28 went on to impose controls on proposal forms, certificates and brochures as well as any statements made by insurers or their agents which may have been misleading or deceptive. Furthermore, s26 much like its conventional insurance counterpart in s147 of the *Insurance Act 1996* (Malaysia), provided that a misstatement of the age of the participant or insured in a family *takaful* policy did not warrant avoidance of the contract by the *takaful* operator. Unfortunately however, it did not go on to provide for any proportionate adjustment of the sum insured and bonuses to address the matter.[50]

This therefore, substantiates the view that the *Takaful Act 1984* (Malaysia) was indeed meant to govern the regulatory as well as substantive aspects of *takaful* in Malaysia but poor drafting and major oversights have hampered its effectiveness over the years.

5.4.3 Utmost Good Faith Under the Islamic Financial Services Act 2013

As a result of the legal framework of Malaysia (a former colony) being based on English common law, the *Marine Insurance Act 1906* (UK) and the common law have applied to *takaful* contracts in Malaysia, in so far as it is not inconsistent with the *Takaful Act 1984* (Malaysia).[51] To this end, the *Islamic Financial Services Act 2013* (Malaysia) forms the first substantive review of *takaful* regulation in Malaysia since 1984. It has also led to the repeal of the *Takaful Act 1984* (Malaysia) with its numerous shortcomings highlighted above.[52]

Most of the key provisions pertaining to utmost good faith in *takaful* contracts are found in *Schedule 9* to the *Islamic Financial Services Act 2013* (Malaysia) with a clear distinction being made between the treatment of consumer and non-consumer *takaful* contracts. Paragraph 5 (9) of *Schedule 9* to the *Islamic*

---

[49]This section draws on research appearing in: Thanasegaran, above n 1, 158–159.

[50]Ibid.

[51]See: Section 5 of the *Civil Law Act 1956* (Malaysia); Mahmood, above n 28, 43. Judicial acknowledgement of the application of s17 of the *Marine Insurance Act 1906* (UK) to *takaful* contracts in Malaysia is apparent in *Seah Cheoh Wah v Malayan Banking Bhd* [2009] 7 CLJ 485.

[52]This is by virtue of s282 of the *Islamic Financial Services Act 2013* (Malaysia).

Financial Services Act 2013 (Malaysia) explicitly sets out the duty of utmost good faith with respect to consumer *takaful* contracts by requiring 'the *duty of utmost good faith* to be exercised *by a consumer and licensed takaful operator* in their *dealings* with each other, *including the making and paying of a claim*, after a contract of *takaful* has been entered into, varied or renewed.' Paragraph 2 of *Schedule 9* in turn defines a 'consumer *takaful* contract' as a contract of *takaful* entered into, varied or renewed by an individual wholly for purposes unrelated to the individual's trade, business or profession.

This provision for a general duty of utmost good faith that includes claims handling, is a substantial step in the right direction. It would however, have been more effective had it applied to **all** *takaful* contracts and not just *consumer* contracts and also addressed the remedy available in the event of its breach by either party. This is because utmost good faith is a fundamental principle to *takaful* as a whole.[53]

As a result of this omission, the law on utmost good faith in *takaful* contracts in Malaysia remains uncertain in the following respect. It is unclear whether the remedy for a breach of Paragraph 5 (9) of *Schedule 9* to the Act with respect to *consumer takaful* contracts is avoidance of the contract or damages proportionate to the loss suffered. It is also unresolved if s17 of the *Marine Insurance Act 1906* (UK) still forms the basis for the application of the duty of utmost good faith in *non-consumer takaful* contracts. If this is still the case, participants in a *takaful* contract would be bound by the harsh remedy of avoidance of the contract with only a refund of premium paid, in the event of breach, which would remain a grossly inadequate remedy.[54]

As highlighted above, the *Takaful Act 1984* (Malaysia) also lacked provisions outlining the participant's pre-contractual duty of disclosure and duty to refrain from making misrepresentations, as well as the remedies available in the event of breach. This resulted in the said duties in the *takaful* context being governed by the common law and ss18 and 20 of the *Marine Insurance Act 1906* (UK) along with the onerous 'prudent insurer' and 'mere influence' tests of materiality of information to be disclosed, as well as the remedy of avoidance in the event of breach.[55]

These issues are addressed by the *Islamic Financial Services Act 2013* (Malaysia) as follows. Section 141 starts the ball rolling by providing that 'Schedule 9 sets out the pre-contractual duty of disclosure and representations for *contracts of takaful* in Part 2, and the remedies for misrepresentations relating to *contracts of takaful* in Part 3.' Paragraph 4 of *Schedule 9* adopts the Australian[56] voluntary disclosure mechanism for *non-consumer takaful contracts* which requires the participant before the contract is entered into, to disclose matters he or she knows to be relevant to the *takaful* operator in accepting the risk or the rates and

[53]This section draws on research appearing in: Thanasegaran and Shaiban, above n 5, 338.

[54]Ibid.

[55]Ibid 338–339.

[56]See: Section 21 of the *Insurance Contracts Act 1984* (Cth) (Australia).

terms to be applied or that which 'a reasonable person in the circumstances' could be expected to know to be relevant.[57]

Paragraph 5 of *Schedule 9* in turn, incorporates the English and Australian-eligible contract's[58] inquiry based disclosure mechanism for *consumer takaful contracts* which requires the participant before the contract is entered into, to take reasonable care not to misrepresent to the *takaful* operator when answering specific questions posed by the operator or when confirming or amending any matters previously disclosed as provided by the *takaful* operator in writing. The standard of care required here is 'what a reasonable consumer in the circumstances would have known.'[59] In this context, pursuant to Paragraphs 4 (3), 5 (5) and 5 (6) of *Schedule 9*, the *takaful* operator is deemed to have waived any non-disclosure or incomplete disclosure by proposers if the non-compliance was not pursued further by them.[60]

Although the recent provisions pertaining to pre-contractual non-disclosure are a welcome improvement to the previous position, they unfortunately fail to clearly set out the remedies for breach of the duty. It may be that they were intended to be covered by the remedies appearing in Part 3 of *Schedule 9* that apply to misrepresentations. However, the headings and the provisions in Part 3 make no reference to non-disclosure, referring instead, only to remedies available for misrepresentation. Although it could be the case that many alleged non-disclosures are essentially misrepresentations, especially with respect to consumer *takaful* contracts, as they require inquiry based disclosure, it would have been more comprehensive to provide for a residual remedy for a breach of the duty of disclosure separately, owing to its wider scope, especially with respect to non-consumer *takaful* contracts.[61]

Paragraph 7 (3) of *Schedule 9* classifies pre-contractual misrepresentation by consumers as deliberate or reckless, careless and innocent. Paragraph 7(4) defines a deliberate or reckless misrepresentation as one where the consumer knew that the misrepresentation was untrue or misleading or did not care if it was *and* knew that the misrepresentation was relevant to the *takaful* operator or did not care if it was. The *takaful* operator bears the burden of proving on a balance of probability that a misrepresentation is in fact deliberate or reckless, with a dishonest representation being regarded as being made deliberately or recklessly.[62] A misrepresentation is careless or innocent on the other hand, under Paragraph 7 (6) if it is not deliberate or

---

[57]This section draws on research appearing in: Thanasegaran and Shaiban, above n 5, 339.

[58]See: Section 2 (2) of the *Consumer Insurance (Disclosure and Representations) Act 2012* (UK) and s21A of the *Insurance Contracts Act 1984* (Cth) (Australia).

[59]Paragraph 6 (2) of *Schedule 9* to the *Islamic Financial Services Act 2013* (Malaysia) which is based on s3 of the *Consumer Insurance (Disclosure and Representations) Act 2012* (UK) and s21A of the *Insurance Contracts Act 1984* (Cth) (Australia).

[60]This section draws on research appearing in: Thanasegaran and Shaiban, above n 5, 339.

[61]Ibid.

[62]Paragraphs 7 (7) and 7 (5) respectively of *Schedule 9* to the *Islamic Financial Services Act 2013* (Malaysia).

reckless.[63] It is interesting to note that Paragraph 7 (8) contains a balanced provision that unless the contrary is shown, it is presumed that the consumer knew that a matter about which the *takaful* operator asked a clear and specific question was relevant to the *takaful* operator.

Paragraph 13 (2) goes on to cover misrepresentations made in consumer or non-consumer family *takaful* contracts that are in effect for more than 2 years. In such cases, the *takaful* operator is not entitled to avoid the contract unless it 'shows that the statement was on a material matter or suppressed a material fact *and* that it was *fraudulently* made or omitted.' The materiality of the matter is in turn dependent on whether had it been known by the *takaful* operator, it would have led to its refusal to issue a *takaful* certificate or the imposition of terms less favourable to the participant. In the event that the *takaful* operator is permitted to avoid the contract, it must refund payments received there under.[64]

Paragraph 15 which covers misrepresentations made in *consumer* family *takaful* contracts in effect for 2 years or less or in *consumer* general *takaful* contracts, provides that in cases of deliberate or reckless misrepresentation, the *takaful* operator is entitled to avoid the contract and refund payments received there under as well as refuse all claims. In the event of a careless or innocent misrepresentation, Paragraph 16 provides that should the *takaful* operator not have entered into or renewed the contract on any terms, it may avoid the contract, make a refund of payments received there under and refuse all claims. However, if it would have entered into or renewed the contract on different terms (other than that pertaining to the contribution amount), the contract is treated as being on those terms. Lastly, if it would have entered into or renewed the contract by charging a higher *takaful* contribution instead, then the amount payable under the claim may be proportionately reduced.[65]

The *Islamic Financial Services Act 2013* (Malaysia) has indeed markedly improved the previous position with respect to pre-contractual misrepresentations, by clearly addressing the issue and setting out the remedies available in the event of breach. The said provisions however, would have been more comprehensive had they applied to **all** *takaful* contracts instead of failing to address *non-consumer* general *takaful* contracts and *non-consumer* family *takaful* contracts in effect for 2 years or less. As a result, there are no residual remedies within the Act that would be applicable in the event of misrepresentations in such contracts. This would in turn beg the question as to whether s20 of the *Marine Insurance Act 1906* (UK) might still apply to those *takaful* contracts. Should this be the case, then the participants of such *takaful* contracts would remain shackled by the inadequate remedy of avoidance of the contract with only a refund of premium paid, in the event of breach. [66]

---

[63]This section draws on research appearing in: Thanasegaran and Shaiban, above n 5, 339–340.

[64]Paragraphs 13 (4) and 13 (3) respectively of *Schedule 9* to the *Islamic Financial Services Act 2013* (Malaysia); Ibid 340.

[65]Ibid 340.

[66]Ibid.

An extension of the duty of disclosure is the requirement for *takaful* operators to provide a clear warning of the consequences of pre-contractual non-disclosure on the *takaful* contract, to prospective participants, in *takaful* proposal forms. As alluded to earlier, the *Takaful Act 1984* (Malaysia) did not address this issue. Paragraphs 5 (7) and 4 (4) of *Schedule 9* to the *Islamic Financial Services Act 2013* (Malaysia) however, adequately provide for this with respect to consumer and non-consumer *takaful* contracts respectively. The said provisions require *takaful* operators before a *takaful* contract is entered into, varied or renewed, to *clearly inform* a proposer *in writing* of the pre-contractual duty of disclosure and that it shall *continue until* the contract is entered into, varied or renewed.[67]

A question related to this is the relationship between *takaful* operators and agents and the status of information and knowledge received by *takaful* agents during their negotiations with the proposer, in the formation or variation of the *takaful* contract. Paragraph 12 (1) retains the previous position in s66 of the *Takaful Act 1984* (Malaysia) that the *takaful* agent is deemed to be the *takaful* operator's agent in this regard. As a result, the agent's knowledge is rightfully deemed to be that of the *takaful* operator.[68]

It should be noted that a major drawback in *takaful* contracts thus far, has been the use of 'basis of contract' clauses in *takaful* proposal forms. *Takaful* operators have used it to convert answers and information provided by participants into warranties. This has severely impaired the requirement for *takaful* operators to have been 'induced' by any misrepresentation in order for it to be actionable. An examination of *takaful* proposal forms in Malaysia shows their rampant use of such clauses. Although this has proved detrimental to unwary *takaful* participants over the years, it has nevertheless remained as a testament to the imbalance in favour of *takaful* operators in Malaysia, despite there being no juridical basis for its use.[69]

This has been addressed by Paragraph 10 of *Schedule 9* which abolishes the use of 'basis of contract' clauses in *consumer takaful* contracts which appears to have been based on s6 (2) of the *Consumer Insurance (Disclosure and Representations) Act 2012* (UK). The drawback however, is that 'basis of contract' clauses have now only been abolished with respect to consumer *takaful* contracts in Malaysia. Section 6 (2) of the *Consumer Insurance (Disclosure and Representations) Act 2012* (UK) as its name and scope suggests, correctly applies to consumer insurance contracts alone. The *Islamic Financial Services Act 2013* (Malaysia) on the other hand, in replacing the *Takaful Act 1984* (Malaysia) is an Act which should be applicable to all types of *takaful* contracts in Malaysia and should therefore, apply to **both** consumer and *non-consumer takaful* contracts alike. Such an oversight needs to be addressed promptly, in order to accord participants in non-consumer

[67]This provision takes into account the improvement made to s22 of the *Insurance Contracts Act 1984* (Cth) (Australia) by the *Insurance Contracts Amendment Act 2013* (Cth) (Australia). Ibid 341.

[68]Ibid.

[69]Ibid.

takaful contracts the same protection. This is in effect what s24 of the *Insurance Contracts Act 1984 (Cth)* (Australia) does, as it abolishes 'basis of contract' clauses in *all* contracts of insurance.[70]

The absence of an express pronouncement of utmost good faith in *takaful* contracts in the *Takaful Act 1984* (Malaysia) has also contributed to the wide spread use of exclusion clauses and strict construction of policy terms by *takaful* operators. These measures along with other undesirable claims settlement practices such as undue delay, rejection and frequent reduction of claims, have been deployed in defeating participants' otherwise legitimate claims.[71]

Such was in fact the case in *Seah Cheoh Wah v Malayan Banking Bhd & Anor.*[72] The *takaful* operator in this case issued a Mortgage Redemption Term Assurance (MRTA) policy under a housing loan taken by the participant and refused to settle the outstanding loan upon the participant's death six months later. The *takaful* operator's argument was based on the fact that despite an official receipt being issued to the participant for payment of the premium, a *takaful* policy was not yet issued at the time of participant's death. This thereby prevented a valid *takaful* contract from coming into existence. This argument was rejected by the High Court of Malaya. It was held that the payment of the premium, followed by its acceptance and issuance of an official receipt by the *takaful* operator was sufficient to give rise to a valid *takaful* contract. The High Court however, went on to say that this was the case as there was no declaration in the MRTA form that the policy would only take effect subject to a policy being issued.[73]

It should be noted that this decision in favour of the participant is only a partial vindication for *takaful* participants. The High Court's unfortunate qualification pertaining to the absence of a declaration in the policy at hand, has raised the possibility of *takaful* operators in the future being able to avoid liability by inserting such a declaration in *takaful* proposal forms that *takaful* contracts would only be effective once a policy was issued. This, although the participant may have performed all his or her obligations in good faith and would have no control over the duration of time it may take the *takaful* operator to issue a policy after accepting the risk and premium. For a *takaful* operator to be entitled to do this however, would surely amount to a lack of good faith on its part.[74]

In this regard, Paragraph 5 (9) of *Schedule 9* to the *Islamic Financial Services Act 2013*(Malaysia) is indeed a substantial improvement with respect to *consumer takaful* contracts, as it clearly requires 'the *duty of utmost good faith* to be exercised *by a consumer and licensed takaful operator* in their *dealings* with each other, *including the making and paying of a claim*, after a contract of *takaful* has been entered into, varied or renewed.' Such an express pronouncement of a general duty

---

[70]Ibid.

[71]This section draws on research appearing in: Thanasegaran, above n 6, 115–116.

[72][2009] 7 CLJ 485.

[73]This section draws on research appearing in: Thanasegaran, above n 6, 116.

[74]This section draws on research appearing in: Thanasegaran and Shaiban, above n 5, 342.

of utmost good faith that covers claims handling as well is a progressive step forward. However, it would have been more effective in eliminating any mischief had it applied to **all** *takaful* contracts and not just consumer contracts, and provided for a proportionate remedy in the event of its breach by either party. In failing to do this, the *Islamic Financial Services Act 2013* (Malaysia) has placed participants making a claim under *non-consumer takaful* contracts at an unnecessary disadvantage.[75]

5.5 Conclusion

It is important to note that Malaysia, which has positioned itself as a global leader in *takaful* regulation and market practice, has indeed come a long way in terms of substantive *takaful* regulation since its inception in 1984. A look at the *takaful* regulations in other Muslim-majority jurisdictions where *takaful* is offered in a large scale like Bahrain, Pakistan, Brunei, Indonesia, the United Arab Emirates, Egypt, Saudi Arabia, Sudan and Iran, further reinforces this. This is because the said jurisdictions have focussed primarily on regulating licensing, product development and market conduct instead of substantive principles like utmost good faith.

The *takaful* regulations of Bahrain, Pakistan, Brunei, Egypt, Sudan and Indonesia for instance, make no provision for any aspect of utmost good faith. This is startling, as *takaful* is offered in a large scale in most of these jurisdictions. The United Arab Emirates via Articles 3 (2) and 6 (3) of its *Board Resolution No. 3 of 2010* on *Professional Practice and Code of Conduct for Insurance Companies* which regulates both insurance and *takaful* contracts, makes some provision for utmost good faith and statutory warnings in proposal forms. Iran on the other hand, via Articles 12 and 13 of the *Iran Insurance Act 1937* which also regulates insurance and *takaful* contracts, has provided for pre-contractual disclosure, misrepresentation and its ensuing remedies. Saudi Arabia has in turn, via Articles 32, 42, 52 and 53 of the *Insurance Market Code of Conduct Regulation 2008* and Articles 44 and 55 of the *Implementing Rules for the Cooperative Insurance Companies Control Law 2003* made some provision to regulate disclosure, misrepresentation, statutory warnings and claims handling in cooperative insurance schemes.[76]

Malaysia has therefore, come a long way in terms of its *takaful* regulation via the enactment of its *Islamic Financial Services Act 2013* (Malaysia). All that is left, therefore, is for the gaps in *takaful* regulation to be addressed in a comprehensive manner so as not to discriminate between consumer and non-consumer *takaful* contracts, with respect to utmost good faith in general and claims handling in particular. Non-consumer *takaful* contracts cannot be left to rely merely on the

[75]Ibid.

[76]Ibid 354.

Central Bank's *Claims Settlement Guidelines*, namely Clause 3.4 which directs *takaful* operators to conduct themselves in a fair and reasonable manner in settling claims. This is particularly so as the said Guidelines do not provide for clear sanctions to apply in the event of non-compliance. Nor can the aggrieved party rely primarily on the flexible and pro-active way in which the Mediators of the Financial Mediation Bureau of Malaysia have resolved the disputes appearing before them.[77]

To this end, the progressive reforms in Australia's *Insurance Contracts Act 1984* (Cth) as amended in 2013 and the United Kingdom's *Insurance Act 2015* set out in previous chapters, could be looked to as a guide. This is particularly so since *takaful* would have to operate alongside conventional insurance in Malaysia, and as such would be viewed by the insuring public as a more viable alternative if it was comparable to rather than completely different from the existing laws on conventional insurance, subject of course to the requirements of *Sharia*.

Further justification for the reforms suggested above along with additional structural reform will be provided in the following chapters, this time from a socio-economic perspective, so that a comprehensive reform of the law and practice governing insurance and *takaful* contracts in Malaysia may be achieved.

References

Au Pui Khuan A, Maysami RC (1998) Islamic Insurance in Malaysia: a successful model in operation. Int Ins Law Rev 6(3):79

Baker T, Simon J (eds) (2002) Embracing risk: the changing culture of insurance and responsibility. University of Chicago Press, US

Bhatty A (2012) *Takaful* in North America: a global view for a local perspective, Takaful Focus, 1. http://www.newhorizon-islamicbanking.com/index.cfm/section=features&action=view. Accessed 30 May 2012

Central Bank of Malaysia (2015) List of licensed insurance companies and Takaful operators in Malaysia. www.bnm.gov.my/index.php?ch=li&cat=insurance&lang=en. Accessed 30 June 2015

Central Bank of Malaysia (1999) The Central Bank and the financial system in Malaysia—a decade of change 1989–1999, Kuala Lumpur, 1999

Department of Statistics Malaysia (2010) Population Distribution and Basic Demographic Characteristics Report, Putrajaya 2010

Ernst and Young (2012) The World Takaful Report 2012—Industry Growth and Preparing for Regulatory Change, 2012

Ernst and Young (2014) Global Takaful insights 2014—market updates: growth momentum continues, 2014

Hoyle M (2012) Research handbook on international insurance law and regulation. Edward Elgar Publishing, Cheltenham

Khorshid A (2004) Islamic insurance: a modern approach to islamic banking. Routledge Curzon, London

Lim Lrong, Abdullah Asma (2001) Cultural dimensions of Anglos, Australians and Malaysians. Malays Manag Rev 36(2):1

[77]See: Financial Mediation Bureau (2009, p. 20).

Mahmood NR (1992) Insurance Law in Malaysia. Butterworths, Malaysia
Masud H (2011) Takaful: an innovative approach to insurance and Islamic Finance. Univ PA J Int Law 32(4):1133
Maysami RC, Williams JJ (2006) Evidence on the relationship between Takaful insurance and fundamental perception of islamic principles. Appl. Financ Econ Lett 2(4):229–230
Mohamed S (2005) The legislative jurisdiction of the federal parliament in matters involving Islamic Law. Malayan Law J 3:cv
Swartz N, Coetzer P (2010) Takaful: an islamic insurance instrument. J Dev Agric Eco 2(10):333
Swiss Re Economic Research and Consulting (2011) Islamic Insurance Revisited, Sept 2011
Thanasegaran H (2008) Growth of islamic insurance (Takaful) in Malaysia: a model for the region? Singap J Leg Stud 143:144–145
Thanasegaran H (2011) Settlement of claims by Malaysian insurance and Takaful companies: a genuine prospect or merely suspect? Int Company & Commercial Law Rev 22(6):191
Thanasegaran H (2013) Making an entrance—can Australia contribute to takaful (Islamic insurance) law reform? Insur Law J 24:104
Thanasegaran H, Shaiban M (2014) Harmonization of Takaful (Islamic insurance) regulation—a realistic goal or improbable ideal? Singap J Legal Stud 328
Tsang W, Hodgins P (2012) Asia Insurance Review *Takaful* Conference 9–10 May 2012, Hong Kong, 24 July 2012, 1. http://www.mondaq.com/x/188132/islamic+finance/Asia+Insurance+Review+Takaful+Conference+910+May+2012. Accessed 30 June 2015

Chapter 6
Law Reform from a Social Science Perspective

Abstract The previous chapters of this book undertook a detailed doctrinal analysis of the need for and type of legal reform of the law and practice governing insurance and *takaful* contracts in Malaysia. This penultimate chapter proposes additional justification for such reform, from a socio-cultural perspective. This is due to an appreciation of law reform as being part of the broader social sciences namely sociology, economics and political science and that an examination of this is necessary for any suitable law reform proposal. This chapter in focusing on the social aspects of law reform will pay particular attention to the law and society movement which is an amalgam of law, sociology, political science, anthropology and history, with lesser bits of economics and psychology. In doing so it will set out the relevant empirical studies in the field, with principal reference to Malaysia, to justify reform being undertaken in a holistic sense.

6.1 Introduction

The previous chapters of this book have thus far been dedicated to a detailed doctrinal analysis of the need for and type of legal reform of the law and practice governing insurance and *takaful* contracts in Malaysia. This penultimate chapter aims to propose additional justification for such reform, from a socio-cultural perspective.

The starting point for this is the appreciation that law reform is a part of the broader social sciences namely sociology, economics and political science and that an examination of this is necessary for any suitable law reform proposal. This chapter will however be focusing on the social aspects of law reform and hence, will pay particular attention to the law and society movement which is an amalgam of law, sociology, political science, anthropology and history, with lesser bits of economics and psychology.

Lastly, it is important to note that the insurance and *takaful* industry also forms a key component of the financial services industry. This is because it provides an

H. Thanasegaran, *Good Faith in Insurance and Takaful Contracts in Malaysia*,
DOI 10.1007/978-981-10-0383-7_6

important social service to individual consumers and underlines most forms of economic activity. Therefore, the next and final chapter of this book will examine the role of law and economics in evaluating the law reform package undertaken by the Malaysian government via the *Financial Services Act 2013* (Malaysia) and *Islamic Financial Services Act 2013* (Malaysia) in regulating the duty of utmost good faith in insurance and *takaful* contracts, in order to determine if it strikes a fair and workable balance between the competing interests of insurers and insureds.[1]

The layout of this chapter is as follows. First, the role and place of law within the broader social sciences will be established. This will be followed by an examination of Lawrence Friedman's proposition that for any legal system (and by analogy law) to be effective, there must be structure and substance, and the prevailing legal culture must support it.[2] The structure and substance regulating utmost good faith in insurance and *takaful* contracts in Malaysia will then be briefly revisited. Finally, a detailed examination will be made of Malaysian legal culture, which is largely based on its national culture, to ascertain if it supports this existing structure and substance following the recent reforms introduced via the *Financial Services Act 2013* (Malaysia) and *Islamic Financial Services Act 2013* (Malaysia).

6.2 Legal Culture

It has been accepted since the 1920s and 1930s, that the law and the legal system was an integral part of the broader social sciences as opposed to an autonomous science of its own.[3] Lawrence Friedman has in turn, since the late 1960s developed and fine-tuned this view by postulating that a legal system comprises three basic components: the structure and substance of a legal system, as well as legal culture.[4] Legal structure refers to the institutions and processes within a legal system, for example the court system, alternative dispute resolution mechanisms and the legislature. Substance in turn, refers to the substantive and procedural laws and regulations in place in a given legal system; and 'legal culture' refers to 'the attitudes, values and opinions held in society with regard to law, the legal system and its various parts.' [5]

---

[1]The reason law and society and law and economics are addressed separately in this chapter and Chap. 7 of this book is because the former is used to provide additional justification for reform (alongside the doctrinal reasons set out in Chaps. 2–5) whereas the latter is used to evaluate the viability or economic efficiency of the reforms undertaken.

[2]Lawrence Friedman is both America's leading legal historian and main proponent of the law and society movement. See: Friedman (1975, p. 2).

[3]Huffman (1984, p. 579).

[4]Friedman's earliest exposition of this concept appears in Friedman (1969); Friedman, above n 2, and continues to form the basis of his more current work found in Friedman (1994, 2006, pp. 185–199).

[5]Friedman, above n 2, 15–16.

Friedman, the acknowledged father of the term 'legal culture' is a firm believer of legal culture being the most important amongst the three components of a legal system, for 'it is the legal culture which determines when, why and where people use the law, legal institutions or legal processes; and when they use other institutions or do nothing.'[6] This view has been echoed by others.[7]

It should be noted that culture has been acknowledged by sociologists and anthropologists alike, to be one of those words which are 'difficult to define and easy to abuse'[8] and has been described as 'one of the two or three most complicated words in the English language'.[9] However, for our present purposes of evaluating the utility of the concept of 'legal culture,' the problem with definition does not become overwhelming if the term 'culture' is divided into cultural practices and cultural values.

As Geert Hofstede explains, cultural practices are 'the rituals, symbols and heroes used within a particular society as part of its identity,' which can change over a short period of time; whereas *cultural values* are the values of people within a society, whereby value systems are the core elements of culture and do not change easily.[10] When anthropologists and sociologists like Geert Hofstede and Harry Triandis talk of culture, it is the latter 'cultural values' that they are referring to. This is in sync with Friedman's definition of legal culture as being the '...ideas, attitudes, opinions, and expectations with regard to the legal system.'[11] That it is very difficult to change the (internalized) values of a society in a short period of time has also been independently substantiated by the World Values Survey, which is an investigation of socio-cultural and political change carried out by an international network of social scientists.[12]

Legal culture is 'the source of law ...a kind of intervening variable' between social forces which make or influence the law, and the law or legal system itself; '...in other words ...[it] translates social change into legal change.' It is also in principle measurable, '...either directly through questioning the public, indirectly by observing what people do and making inferences of their attitudes from that or both, in order to get a more accurate picture.'[13]

In this context, legal culture has been recognized to be an especially important concept for legal transplants with regard to 'developing and transitional countries which often import laws or even entire legal systems from industrialized Western nations in attempting to modernize their domestic legal frameworks.'[14] Others

---

[6]Friedman (1977, p. 76).

[7]See: Yngvesson (1998), Macaulay (1998).

[8]See: Kuper (1999).

[9]Williams (1983, p. 87).

[10]Hofstede and Jan (2005, pp. 2–5).

[11]Friedman, 'The Place of Legal Culture in the Sociology of Law', above n 4, 189.

[12]Inglehart and Baker (2000).

[13]Ibid. 19.

[14]Tabalujan (2002).

like Oscar Chase have highlighted the importance of culture in shaping legal institutions, namely dispute resolution institutions, which are a product of and reflect the culture from which they arise.[15] It is important therefore, to appreciate the importance of legal culture in law reform, as '...law reform is doomed to failure if it does not take legal culture into account...[as] legal systems are products of society—more specifically, of legal culture; hence reform is a subtle and complex task. One has to take into account the limits imposed by culture; one has to re-examine whether the 'failures' of the law are real failures, or whether we are neglecting to cut with instead of against the grain.'[16]

Although this chapter does not propose to examine legal transplants as such,[17] it is based on the premise that the legal culture in Malaysia does not support the existing legal structure in terms of the primary dispute resolution mechanism for the insurance and *takaful* industry being litigation, as well as some of the substantive reforms introduced that are limited to only *consumer* insurance and *takaful* contracts. There is thus, a need to review the effectiveness of the primary dispute resolution mechanisms supporting insurance and *takaful* in Malaysia, as well as some aspects of the recent reforms introduced via the *Financial Services Act 2013* (Malaysia) and *Islamic Financial Services Act 2013* (Malaysia), along the lines set out towards the end of this chapter.

This chapter will in evaluating Malaysian legal culture, also take stock of the sub-debate within legal culture circles on the appropriate unit or units of culture which ought to be evaluated, namely the national or state level; sub-national or ethnic level; individual levels; or even the impact of globalization.[18] More recent commentators like Susan Silbey and David Nelken appear to place emphasis on some level; the former on micro-level social action she calls 'legal consciousness' which is 'specifically the ways in which individuals interpret and mobilize legal meanings and signs'[19] whilst the latter towards a more macro-level construct of culture in the aggregate.[20]

Neither author however, can nor tries to realistically exclude the other and Nelken in fact, goes on to say that '...there is much to be gained by inserting an investigation of legal consciousness into the larger framework of inquiries into legal culture'.[21] Such analysis would perhaps come closest to truly measuring legal

[15]Chase (1997). Still others who have used the concept of legal culture in a similar vein include Lev (1972, p. 247), who in fact acknowledged the work of Friedman on legal culture; Former Indonesian Minister of Justice Kusumaatmadja (1982, p. 6); Lindsey (2000, p. 284), who refers to 'hard law' which can be equated with Friedman's legal structure and substantive law and 'soft law' with Friedman's legal culture; Tabalujan (2001).

[16]Friedman, 'Is there a Modern Legal Culture?' above n 4, 130.

[17]For legal transplants, see: Watson (1993, p. 108).

[18]Nelken (2004, p. 1).

[19]Silbey (2001, p. 8623).

[20]Nelken (2006).

[21]Ibid. 223. Also see: Webber (2004, p. 32).

culture, which is why this chapter will analyze Malaysian legal culture from both a macro national/societal level as well as a more micro intra-national/ethnic sub-cultural level.

6.3 Legal Structure

Building on the premise set out above, that for any legal system and by analogy any law to be effective, there must be structure, substance and the prevailing legal culture must support it; the following paragraphs will briefly examine the legal structure and substance of the Malaysian insurance and *takaful* industry.

With respect to legal structure, the Malaysian insurance and *takaful* industry as set out in Chap. 1 of this book is essentially regulated by the Central Bank and the regulatory requirements of the *Financial Services Act 2013* (Malaysia) and *Islamic Financial Services Act 2013* (Malaysia). Insurance companies and *takaful* operators are licensed and regulated by the same. They are also required to be members of their respective trade associations, namely the Life Insurance Association of Malaysia ('LIAM'), General Insurance Association of Malaysia ('PIAM') or the Malaysian *Takaful* Association ('MTA').[22] Insurance and *takaful* agents employed by them in turn, have to be registered with their respective trade associations and meet certain minimum entry requirements.[23]

As for insureds on the other hand, their rights and responsibilities arising under the insurance contract are regulated by the terms of the contract, the proposal form filled out by them prior to purchasing the policy and the provisions of the *Financial Services Act 2013* (Malaysia) or *Islamic Financial Services Act 2013* (Malaysia) respectively. In the event of a dispute or disagreement arising under the insurance or *takaful* policy, the insured's first recourse is to raise it with the Complaints Unit within the insurance company or *takaful* operator concerned.

The insured is then left with one of three options should it fail to obtain a satisfactory resolution from the Complaints Unit concerned. The most popular of

---

[22]Insurance brokers and loss adjusters on the other hand, are members of the Insurance Brokers' Association of Malaysia ('IBAM') and Association of Malaysian Loss Adjusters ('AMLA') respectively.

[23]They need to pass a Pre-Contract Examination for Insurance Agents set by the Malaysian Insurance Institute ('MII'), the Malaysian Certificate of Examination and satisfy the requisite number of hours of continuous professional development (annually) set by the Central Bank: Central Bank of Malaysia (2006, p. 2). A similar requirement applies to *takaful* agents as well. Insurance brokers and loss adjusters who on the contrary, are viewed as independent contractors (as opposed to employees of the insurer) have to meet the requisite paid-up capital and solvency criteria, instead.

which would be to lodge a complaint with the Financial Mediation Bureau which is an effective alternative to litigation in dispensing justice.[24] The way in which the Financial Mediation Bureau operates is that legal representation is not permitted in the mediation process; the Mediator is not bound solely by legal rules; the Mediator's award is binding on the insurer and *takaful* operator whereas the complainant has a choice on whether to accept or reject the award; and there is no appeal procedure available within the Bureau.

The insured could alternatively, direct the more minor complaints and enquiries to the Customer Services Bureau of the Central Bank which was set up in 1998. The Customer Services Bureau's function is to analyze complaints received and liaise with industry and relevant trade associations to resolve the same. It also has the additional task of identifying insurance and *takaful* practices that may require regulatory action by the Central Bank.

Pursuant to these developments, the Malaysian government launched a 10-year Consumer Education Programme in 2003. Its primary aim was to educate consumers of their rights and responsibilities that arose under insurance and *takaful* contracts. This was to enable them to make well informed decisions in selecting insurance and *takaful* products.[25] There was also talk of plain language policies being used to complement this move in December 2005, but nothing concrete has been proposed thus far.[26]

The final alternative for aggrieved insureds is of course the civil courts, which handle both insurance and *takaful* matters.[27] Although the civil courts have no issue with respect to a limitation on monetary jurisdiction like the Financial Mediation Bureau which has a limit of RM200,000 for motor, fire insurance and *takaful* matters; RM5000 for third party property damage and RM100,000 for other matters, the Financial Mediation Bureau has been the preferred choice of dispute resolution amongst complainants, as reported in the Bureau's *Annual Report 2005*.[28]

---

[24]The Financial Mediation Bureau is an amalgamation of the Insurance Mediation Bureau and the Banking Mediation Bureau and started operations on 20 January 2005. It was set up by the 90 member financial institutions including commercial banks, merchant banks, Islamic banks, insurance companies, *takaful* operators and credit or charge card issuers: Financial Mediation Bureau (2006, p. 8): and is in line with the Central Bank of Malaysia, *Financial Sector Master Plan*, Kuala Lumpur, 2001.

[25]This was done through bilingual booklets called *InsuransInfo* made available at all banks, financial institutions, insurance companies, *takaful* operators, the Financial Mediation Bureau, as well as posting the same on an interactive website.

[26]The Central Bank called for insurance firms to make their policies and cover notes simple and consumer friendly: *The Star* (Kuala Lumpur) (2005, p. 10).

[27]As explained in Chap. 5 of this book, *takaful* in Malaysia is treated as part of general mercantile law as opposed to *Sharia* law, and has therefore, been subject to compliance with the specific *Sharia* based requirements of the now repealed *Takaful Act 1984* and its successor, the *Islamic Financial Services Act 2013*. See: Articles 73, 74, 75, 121 (1), 121 (1A) and the *Ninth Schedule* of the *Federal Constitution of Malaysia*.

[28]See: Financial Mediation Bureau (2006, p. 19).

The popularity of the Financial Mediation Bureau over the courts is apparent from the number of insurance and *takaful* complaints referred to them annually since the year 2000. The Financial Mediation Bureau has had an average of 1000 new cases referred to it each year from 2000 to 2014. Comparatively however, less than 100 reported cases on insurance and *takaful* have been decided by the Malaysian courts for the same period.[29] The insuring public's preference for alternative dispute resolution via the Financial Mediation Bureau has been due to it being free,[30] convenient and efficient, as it has proven to be as independent as the courts. Furthermore, as it will be explored later, the fact that Malaysians are in general not a litigious society, also points to this.

Apart from this it appears that the Financial Mediation Bureau has an added appeal of the Mediators consistently demonstrating (in their mediation awards) their willingness to be flexible and pro-active and not to be strictly bound by legal rules alone, in dispensing justice. In fact, as the Mediator's Case Review contained in the *Annual Reports 2005–2014* bear proof,[31] many of the decisions have been made by giving effect to the spirit of the Central Bank's *Guidelines on Claims Settlement Practices* ('*Claims Settlement Guidelines*')[32] in addition to the former (now repealed) *Insurance Act 1996* (Malaysia) and *Takaful Act 1984* (Malaysia), albeit the *Claims Settlement Guidelines* surprisingly lack formal sanctions for non-compliance. In contrast, the courts have been only strictly guided by the two pieces of legislation and policy terms.

6.4 Legal Substance

Having set out the legal structure of the Malaysian insurance and *takaful* industry, the following paragraphs shall briefly recap the shortcomings of the *Financial Services Act 2013* (Malaysia) and *Islamic Financial Services Act 2013* (Malaysia) that form the legal substance of the industry, pertaining to the requirement of utmost

---

[29] See: Table of Cases Referred to the Financial Mediation Bureau from 2000 to 2014 in the Appendix. This section draws on research appearing in: Thanasegaran (2011, pp. 198–199), but the statistics herein have been updated from 2009 up until 2014.

[30] The operational costs of the Financial Mediation Bureau (and its predecessor, the Insurance Mediation Bureau) are funded through levies on individual insurance companies and *takaful* operators. The Bureau's independence however, is maintained by its structure comprising the Board of Directors and Director of Operations being separate from the Mediators.

[31] See: Financial Mediation Bureau (2006–2014, 2015); This is a continuation of the trend initiated by the Mediator of the Insurance Mediation Bureau before it, from 2000 to 2004 as reflected in the Insurance Mediation Bureau (2001–2005).

[32] It was issued on 25 February 1995 and revised with effect from 16 September 2003, regulating insurance companies and *takaful* operators (and loss adjusters as to general insurance); with the purpose of further enhancing the minimum standards to be observed in claims processing and settlement, including fraud control and risk management measures. This section draws on research appearing in: Thanasegaran, above n 29, 198–199.

good faith.[33] This will then enable an assessment to be made on whether the prevailing legal culture in Malaysia supports the recent reforms or requires further improvement to be effected instead.

The drawbacks of the two pieces of legislation pertaining to the duty of utmost good faith will be reiterated as it affects the various stages of the insurance and *takaful* contract, from the pre-contractual stage right through to claims settlement.

For a start, Paragraph 5 (9) of *Schedule 9* to both the *Financial Services Act 2013* (Malaysia) and the *Islamic Financial Services Act 2013* (Malaysia), provides that both *consumers* and insurers or *takaful* operators shall exercise the duty of utmost good faith in their dealings with each other, including the making and paying of a claim, after a contract has been entered into, varied or renewed. Although the express pronouncement of a general duty of utmost good faith that covers claims handling and renewals is a positive step, the provisions would have been more effective had they been made applicable to **all** insurance and *takaful* contracts instead of just consumer contracts, and should have also addressed the remedy in the event of its breach by either party. This has resulted in unnecessary uncertainty for *non-consumers* and has failed to resolve the question of whether there remains any room for the common law remedy of avoidance to apply under the new regime or has it been abolished altogether.

With respect to the pre-contractual duty of disclosure, Paragraph 4 of *Schedule 9* to both the *Financial Services Act 2013* (Malaysia) and the *Islamic Financial Services Act 2013* (Malaysia) essentially adopts the voluntary disclosure mechanism applicable in Australia for *non-consumer insurance/takaful contracts* that requires the insured/participant before the contract is entered into, to disclose matters he or she knows to be relevant to the insurer or *takaful* operator in accepting the risk or the rates and terms to be applied or that which 'a reasonable person in the circumstances' could be expected to know to be relevant. Paragraph 5 of *Schedule 9* to the Acts in turn, which relates to *consumer insurance/takaful* contracts adopts the inquiry based disclosure mechanism applicable in the United Kingdom and in Australian-eligible contracts that require the insured/participant before the contract is entered into, to take reasonable care not to misrepresent to the insurer/*takaful* operator when answering specific questions posed by the insurer/*takaful* operator or when confirming or amending any matters previously disclosed as provided by the insurer/*takaful* operator in writing. The standard of care required in these cases is 'what a reasonable consumer in the circumstances would have known.'

Although these provisions are fairly comprehensive, the drawback is that the remedies for breach of the duty have not been clearly set out. It may have been intended to be covered by the remedies appearing in Part 3 of *Schedule 9* to the Acts which relate to misrepresentations. However, Part 3 only contains headings and provisions that make specific reference to remedies for misrepresentation and not non-disclosure.

[33]This has been examined in depth in Chaps. 2–5.

With respect to pre-contractual misrepresentation by consumers, Paragraphs 7 (3)—7 (8) of *Schedule 9* to both Acts classify it as being deliberate or reckless, careless and innocent, along with their consequences. Paragraph 13 (2) provides that misrepresentations made in life insurance/*takaful* contracts (whether consumer or non-consumer) in effect for more than 2 years cannot entitle the insurer/*takaful* operator to avoid the contract unless the 'insurer/*takaful* operator shows that the statement was on a material matter or suppressed a material fact *and* that it was *fraudulently* made or omitted.' Paragraphs 15 and 16 of *Schedule 9* to both Acts in turn provide for remedies in the event of misrepresentations made in *consumer* life insurance/family *takaful* contracts in effect for 2 years or less or in *consumer* general insurance/general *takaful* contracts.

The express duty not to make pre-contractual misrepresentation coupled with a detailed set of remedies for its breach is indeed a step in the right direction. The provisions would have however, been more comprehensive had they applied to **all** insurance and *takaful* contracts instead of omitting *non-consumer general* insurance and *takaful* contracts and *non-consumer life* insurance and family *takaful* contracts in effect for 2 years or less. As a result, there are no residual remedies applicable in the event of misrepresentations arising in these contracts and hence, it is unclear whether there is still room for s20 of the *Marine Insurance Act 1906* (UK) and the remedy of avoidance to apply to them, which would be an unsatisfactory state of affairs.

Paragraph 10 of *Schedule 9* to both Acts addresses the major drawback in Malaysian insurance and *takaful* contracts with respect to the indiscriminate inclusion of 'basis of contract' clauses in proposal forms, by abolishing the use of such clauses in *consumer* insurance and *takaful* contracts. This provision should however have been made applicable to *non-consumer* insurance and *takaful* contracts as well, as there is no justifiable reason for non-consumers to have been disadvantaged in this manner.

The final aspect affecting utmost good faith in insurance and *takaful* contracts is the widespread use of exclusion clauses and strict construction of policy terms by insurers and *takaful* operators to defeat valid claims made by insureds and participants, as well as other claims settlement practices such as inordinate delay and reduced settlement of claims. In fact, an average of 57 % of the insurance and *takaful* cases referred to the Financial Mediation Bureau (and Insurance Mediation Bureau before it) annually from 2000 to 2014 related to delay in processing of claims, dissatisfaction with settlement sums, repudiation of liability and delay in responding to enquiries.[34]

Paragraph 5 (9) of *Schedule 9* to both Acts addresses the issues pertaining to good faith in claims settlement in *consumer* insurance and *takaful* contracts by requiring a *consumer and licensed insurer or takaful operator* to exercise the duty

[34]See: Table of Cases Referred to the Financial Mediation Bureau from 2000 to 2014 in the Appendix. The breakdown of the number of insurance and *takaful* cases according to the type of complaints made is however, no longer available in the Financial Mediation Bureau's Annual Reports since 2012.

of utmost good faith in their dealings with each other 'including the making and paying of a claim' after a contract of insurance or *takaful* has been entered into, varied or renewed. Although it is an improvement with respect to consumer insurance and *takaful* contracts, there remains an uncertainty however, with respect to *non-consumer* contracts, as well as the remedy available in the event of breach in either case. Paragraph 5 (9) of *Schedule 9* would have been more complete had it been applicable to **all** insurance and *takaful* contracts instead, with the proportionate remedy of damages being expressly catered for in cases of breach of utmost good faith in claims settlement, so as not to unnecessarily disadvantage non-consumers.

Non-consumer insurance and *takaful* contracts should not be left out of these reforms. It is inadequate for these contracts to be addressed merely by the Central Bank's *Claims Settlement Guidelines* which direct insurers and *takaful* operators to settle claims in a fair and reasonable manner and the Mediators of the Financial Mediation Bureau of Malaysia who have resolved disputes appearing before them in a flexible and pro-active way.[35] This is because the courts which are the primary dispute resolution mechanism in Malaysia are strictly bound by legal rules and as a result, have not given effect to the *Claims Settlement Guidelines* in arriving at their decisions.[36]

Having set out the various shortcomings of the law and practice governing insurance and *takaful* contracts in Malaysia, with respect to its legal structure and substance; this chapter will go on to examine and measure Malaysian legal culture. This is done to ascertain whether the prevailing legal culture supports the current infrastructure and regulation in place or in fact calls for further reform of the same.

6.5 Measuring Legal Culture

In measuring Malaysian legal culture with respect to the appropriate structural and substantive reform to be adopted to adequately facilitate the insurance and *takaful* industry, it is important to note the different empirical studies conducted by academics and researchers like Hofstede, Triandis and the Global Leadership and Organizational Behaviour Effectiveness Research Programme (Project GLOBE) in identifying, explaining and measuring cultural values.

When cross-cultural researchers study or measure national or societal cultural values, what they are observing is in fact the common values apparent across different cultures of all the nations or societies within the study, albeit they are referred to in different terms, for example 'dimensions' of culture by Hofstede and 'cultural constructs' by Project GLOBE.

---

[35]See: Clause 3.4 of the *Claims Settlement Guidelines 1995 @ 2003*. A major drawback is that the *Guidelines* have no clear sanctions set out as being applicable in the event of non-compliance. Also see: The Financial Mediation Bureau (2009, p. 20). This is because their Terms of Reference do not bind them strictly to legal rules alone.

[36]This section draws on research appearing in: Thanasegaran and Shaiban (2014, pp. 338–343).

In this chapter, Malaysian legal culture will be assessed by analyzing data on Malaysian national culture, using Hofstede's dimensions of culture as improved and refined by Project GLOBE, as well as ethnic or intra-national culture, so as to obtain as accurate an account possible of both the macro and micro perspectives. The importance and effect of this will in turn be examined, in relation to the legal structure and substance of the law and practice governing insurance and *takaful* contracts in Malaysia.

This chapter will however, only examine two of the studies, namely Hofstede's first study of 54 nations between 1967 and 1973 and the more recent Project GLOBE study of 62 nations conducted between 1992 and 2002, as both these studies have specific data on Malaysia. Despite some criticism leveled at Hofstede and other cross-cultural icons' clustering of 'national culture' as perhaps being too simplistic, this chapter will be based on the dimensions of culture developed by Project GLOBE and Hofstede because thus far, such research has not been able to do away with reliance on them and more so, research on Malaysia is still heavily reliant on both models. [37]

The reason for this two-fold macro-micro approach of assessing Malaysian culture is mainly due to its heterogeneous population of about 28.3 million, with 67.4 % of the population being ethnic Malays and indigenous peoples,[38] 24.6 % Chinese, 7.3 % Indians and 0.7 % made up of others.[39] In this context, although individual differences will exist in any culture,[40] there is no empirical data involving Malaysia at such a micro (individual) level of analysis. As such, this chapter will analyze intra-cultural differences at an ethnic level, as they would be more pronounced in a multi-ethnic society like Malaysia. It is hoped that this macro-micro assessment of culture would alleviate the common criticism that researchers tend to use nations as a surrogate for culture and in the process overlook differences that exist within a national boundary.[41]

Although Hofstede's ground-breaking study was carried out at the macro-national level, he did acknowledge that cross-cultural issues could be viewed from a national, organizational or even individual level.[42] Some researchers believe that it might make sense to use an 'etic' approach (which measures similarities between cultures) when comparing countries or societies and an 'emic' approach (which measures the differences within cultures) when evaluating individuals[43] or even ethnic sub-cultures. However, both 'etic and 'emic' approaches will be used in this

[37]See: Abdullah (1992, pp. 3–15).

[38]The indigenous peoples are called 'bumiputra' which literally translated, means 'sons of the soil'.

[39]This is according to the last official population and housing census conducted in 2010: Department of Statistics Malaysia (2010).

[40]Maruyama (1985).

[41]Schollhammer (1969).

[42]Hofstede (2001, p. 15).

[43]Fontaine and Richardson (2003, p. 76).

chapter when analyzing national as well as intra-national culture or multiculturalism.[44]

Hofstede was the first to quantify the values held within different cultures by identifying several dimensions of culture in the process; which are used extensively till today. They are the dimensions of *power distance*, *individualism versus collectivism*, *masculinity versus femininity*, *uncertainty avoidance* and long term versus short term orientation. Although subsequent researchers, namely Project GLOBE, have developed more dimensions of culture, like *power distance,* institutional collectivism, *in-group collectivism, assertiveness, uncertainty avoidance*, gender egalitarianism, humane orientation, future orientation and performance orientation, they have their origins in Hofstede's original dimensions.

Project GLOBE is a worldwide, multi-phase, multi-method project comprising an extensive quantitative and qualitative study of 62 societies on the effect of culture on leadership and organizational effectiveness. The researchers were however, first required to conduct an extensive in depth study of the cultures of the 62 participating nations; and it is this data on societal culture, which this chapter is based on. This project uncovered nine dimensions of culture common in all the nations studied; with six of them having their 'origins in the dimensions of culture identified by Hofstede.'[45] This study has to date, resulted in providing one of the best possible empirical data to determine cross-cultural values and practices.

The said nine dimensions of culture studied by Project GLOBE and their definitions are reproduced in Table 6.1.[46]

As not all of the cultural dimensions set out above are relevant to this book, only the relevant constructs of *power distance*, *collectivism, assertiveness* and *uncertainty avoidance* will be discussed.

6.5.1 Power Distance

Project GLOBE's definition of power distance set out above, is based on Hofstede's definition and essentially concerns 'human inequality' which measures the interpersonal power or influence between the powerful and powerless or less powerful, as perceived by the less powerful.[47]

Many relationships in society mirror this inequality in power, including parent-child, teacher-student and boss-subordinate relationships. At a larger state or national level, high power distance countries tend to have relatively stable, authoritarian governments whereas those at the opposite spectrum have relatively

[44]The meaning imputed to the term 'multiculturalism' generally takes into account the notion of a national culture being the sum total of several sub-cultures: See: Magala (2005).

[45]House et al. (eds) (2004, p. 3).

[46]This is adapted from Table 1 in House et al. (2002, p. 6).

[47]See: Hofstede, above n 42, 79; Hofstede and Jan Hofstede, above n 10, 46.

Table 6.1 Nine dimensions of culture studied by Project GLOBE

Cultural construct	Definition
Power distance	The degree to which members of a collective expect power to be distributed equally
Uncertainty avoidance	The extent to which a society or group relies on social norms, rules and procedures to alleviate unpredictability of future events
Humane orientation	The degree to which a collective encourages and rewards individuals for being fair, altruistic, generous, caring and kind to others
Institutional collectivism	The degree to which societal institutional practices encourage and reward collective distribution of resources and collective action
In-group collectivism	The degree to which individuals express pride, loyalty, cohesiveness in the families
Assertiveness	The degree to which individuals are assertive, confrontational and aggressive in their relationships with others
Gender egalitarianism	The degree to which a collective minimizes gender inequality
Future orientation	The extent to which individuals engage in future-oriented behaviours such as delaying gratification, planning and investing in the future
Performance orientation	The degree to which a collective encourages and rewards group members for performance improvement and excellence

stable pluralist systems.[48] The former supports characteristics such as larger status disparity and special privileges associated with power and this appears true for Malaysia which has an authoritarian government.[49]

The Project GLOBE study recorded an average level of power distance for Malaysia with a practices score of 5.17 ranking it 34th amongst 61 nations.

In analyzing power distance, the researchers of Project GLOBE have identified four factors which have influenced power distance in cultures, mainly religion, democratic government, role of the middle class and a high proportion of immigrants in any given society.[50] A powerful influence on power distance has been religion, with different religions having had differing impact on the level of power distance in a culture. Islam and Christianity, for instance, whilst preaching equality in terms of ideology, have in fact resulted in a strict hierarchical system instead, mainly due to the way in which they were organized. The Roman Catholic Church's strict hierarchical system was broken by the Protestant movement led by Martin Luther in the 16th Century, thereby explaining the visibly lower levels of power distance in Western cultures with a Protestant tradition, as compared with a Roman Catholic tradition.[51]

[48]Hofstede, above n 42, 111.

[49]See: Kennedy (2004, p. 20).

[50]House et al. (eds), above n 45, 518.

[51]Ibid. 520.

Islam in turn, whilst having no hierarchy of leaders during the Prophet Muhammad's time, nevertheless gave rise to one upon his death.[52] Hinduism on the other hand, does not promote social inequality but the caste system was manipulated by the Brahmins during the post-Vedic times to maintain the social positions of the wealthy in the name of ensuring order in society.[53] As for Confucianism which is more of a philosophical tradition, it embodies a patriarchal, hierarchical structure stressing on the reciprocal obligations between the five pivotal relationships of ruler-subject, father-son, husband-wife, elder-younger brother and senior-junior friend.[54] Lastly, Buddhism instead endorses low power distance, owing to its central aim of bridging social castes and emphasis on spirituality.[55] In modern times however, the major religions of the world, with the exception of Islam, do not stress on high power distance as such.

It is not clear whether the relatively high power distance practices in predominantly Muslim cultures, is due to religious dogma or its leadership. Amongst these, fundamentalist Muslim cultures tend to reflect higher power distance practices, even though the Project GLOBE study indicates that the general Muslim population in such cultures reflects lower power distance values.[56]

Power distance within a culture is also influenced by prevailing political practices, whereby cultures with a strong democratic tradition (like Western societies) have low power distance values. People in these cultures are less tolerant of social inequality as compared to Asian and African societies where such inequality is more acceptable.[57]

The third factor influencing power distance within a culture is the role of the middle class, predominantly due to the increased level of education and wealth in such societies.[58] Members of the middle class generally believe that they are responsible for their own lives and thus, demand for their rights and to be heard. The fourth factor identified as bearing on power distance is the high proportion of immigrants within a culture, whereby it is believed that the high proportion in societies like the United States, Australia and Canada, is instrumental in breaking down traditional barriers laid down by the powerful.[59] Although true for the United States, Australia and Canada which have a very low rate of power distance, this factor may not be completely substantiated, as the Nordic states of Sweden, Finland and Denmark which do not have a high proportion of immigrants, also have very low power distance practices scores.

---

[52]Ibid. 521.

[53]Ibid. 522.

[54]Ibid. 523.

[55]Ibid.

[56]Ibid. 539–540.

[57]Ibid. 523–525.

[58]Ibid 525; See also: Hofstede, above n 42, 93–96.

[59]House et al. (eds), above n 45, 525–526.

The researchers of Project GLOBE however, believe that the existence of a democratic government is the most important factor influencing power distance in a culture. Endorsement for this can be found by looking at Malaysia for instance, where even though a strong middle class exists, there are relatively high levels of power distance. This is mainly due to the authoritarian form of democracy practiced, as well as the central role of Islam in government.

In this context, the Malaysian population of about 28.3 million with an ethnic mix of about 67.4 % Malays and indigenous peoples, 24.6 % Chinese, 7.3 % Indians and 0.7 % made up of others,[60] has been aptly described as a 'distinctive mix of Asian cultural values' with the historical Malay social structure being 'overlaid by Islamic principles and leavened with British colonial management philosophies and Chinese and Indian religious and cultural values'.[61]

In an interesting article using the findings of the Project GLOBE study on Malaysia, Jeffrey Kennedy has sought to identify the important values of Malays as being generally representative of Malaysian organizational outlook based on it being the overwhelming ethnic majority in the country.[62] According to the said article,[63] although the level of power distance practices in Malaysia is not as extreme as portrayed by Hofstede's original work,[64] Malay culture places a great deal of importance on clear recognition of status differences, emphasizes the correct use of titles and protocol, with honorifics widely used to indicate one's social status and level of authority. Subordinates are also unlikely to argue with their superiors for it would be seen as a loss of face to the latter. There is loyalty to authority and deference and obedience towards elders, with authoritarian government or management being prevalent.[65] Hence, there is tension between egalitarian Islamic values and the traditional Malay hierarchical social structure.[66]

In fact, political scientist Harold Crouch went so far as to coin the phrase 'repressive-responsive regime' to describe Malaysian political leadership, whereby the government is said to exert authoritarian control over the opposition to stay in power, whilst seemingly maintaining democratic structures to respond to societal pressures.[67] This is not surprising if one considers certain facts about Malaysia. For example, that the country has been ruled by the United Malay National Organization as the major partner in a coalition of ethnic parties since independence in 1957. Until October 2003, the country has had Dr. Mahathir Mohammad as its

[60]The figures are derived from the last official population and housing census conducted in 2010: Department of Statistics Malaysia (2010).

[61]Kennedy, above n 49, 15.

[62]Ibid.

[63]Ibid. 17.

[64]Support for this is also available in a study using Hofstede's Value Survey Module by Lim (2001).

[65]Abdullah, 'The Influence of Ethnic Values on Managerial Practices in Malaysia', above n 37, 11–12.

[66]Mansor and Ali (1998).

[67]Crouch (1996, p. 96).

prime minister, for 22 years.[68] The Malaysian government's aggressive social re-engineering policies like the New Economic Policy (NEP) is in essence an affirmative action policy[69] to improve the majority ethnic Malay access to educational and job opportunities, as well as their share of the country's wealth from 4 to 30 % equity ownership in the country. Lastly, the use of emergency orders under its *Internal Security Act 1960* to incarcerate those whom the government calls dangerous militants and the opposition claims, are legitimate opponents.[70]

The link between power distance and legal reform is however, indirect. When the level of power distribution in a society is relatively high, so is the level of authoritarianism in that society, and vice versa. In such societies, the less powerful are not used to enforcing their rights and are more accepting of power making people unequal.[71] They are therefore, *more intimidated by formal court processes* and *tend to rely on clear consumer centric laws* giving distinct rights to the (insuring) public, as they are unlikely to claim the same otherwise.

6.5.2 Individualism Versus Collectivism

Collectivism as defined by Hofstede 'stands for a preference for a tightly knit social framework in which individuals can expect their relatives, clan, or other in-group to look after them, in exchange for unquestioning loyalty'.[72] In contrast, he describes individualism as '…a preference for a loosely knit social framework in a society in which individuals are supposed to take care of themselves and their immediate families only'.[73] The general distinction is the emphasis on self- interest in individualistic cultures and group interests in collectivist cultures.[74] Triandis like

---

[68]This is far longer than any democratically elected leader anywhere in the world. See: *The Economist* (London) (2003, p. 5).

[69]This is despite the fact that human rights and employment legislation in many Western countries makes preferential treatment based on ethnicity illegal and affirmative action programmes address minority rather than majority rights: Kennedy, above n 49, 23.

[70]*The Economist* (London) (2003, p. 5). For example, in November 2007, five leaders of an ethnic Indian civil rights movement, the Hindu Rights Action Force ('HINDRAF') were detained under the said Act without trial, on the ruling government's charge of it having links to Sri Lanka's Liberation Tigers of Tamil Eelam ('LTTE'): *The Economist* (London) (2008, p. 32). In February 2006, the Sarawak Tribune, a 61-year old daily newspaper in the state was indefinitely suspended by the Internal Security Ministry under the *Printing Presses and Publications Act 1984* following the publication of an article by the daily entitled 'Cartoon not much impact here' which was accompanied by a caricature of the Prophet Muhammad which was circulating in the European press at the time: *The Star* (Kuala Lumpur) (2006a, b, c, p. 4). The *Internal Security Act 1960* has since been repealed and replaced by the *Security Offences (Special Measures) Act 2012* (Malaysia).

[71]Hofstede, above n 42, 29.

[72]Hofstede (1985, pp. 347–348).

[73]Ibid.

[74]Erez and Early (1993).

Hofstede believes that individualism and collectivism is probably the most important distinction amongst different cultures, as the behaviour of people in individualistic societies differs substantially from collectivist societies.

Hazel Markus and Shinobu Kitayama[75] point out that at the individual level, people in collectivist societies are more socio centric and have an interdependent view of the self, being more inclined to sacrifice their personal gain for the greater welfare of the group. Individualistic societies on the other hand, are egocentric, autonomous, separate and self-contained and have an independent view of the self. According to Triandis, each person has a concept of the self which could be the private self focusing on the concept of 'I am…' which he calls 'idiocentric'; or public self-focusing on what people think of a person; or collective self which is like the public self but is concerned with what a particular in-group thinks, both of which he calls 'allocentric'.[76]

It is not surprising therefore, that in interdependent collectivist cultures, it is important 'to belong' to an in-group where loyalty to the group is paramount; conflicts are often 'swept under the carpet' as criticism and face to face confrontation is not valued. This is viewed as a 'loss of face' and as such, members are not used to enforcing their individual rights.[77] In independent individualistic cultures on the other hand, people value personal goals and are encouraged to be independent in their thinking and relationships. They have less tolerance for in-group demands and are more likely to take proactive steps in resolving conflicts even if it involves direct confrontation or even legal action.[78]

Generally, Asian, Latin American and African cultures tend to be collectivist, whilst Western cultures are more individualistic.[79] Collectivist societies may therefore prefer *less direct methods of confrontation like mediation and conciliation rather than adversarial dispute resolution processes like the courts* in individualistic societies.

The researchers of Project GLOBE have divided the individualism vs collectivism dimension into 'institutional collectivism' and 'in-group collectivism'. The former measures the degree to which societal institutional practices encourage and reward collective distribution of resources and collective action. The latter on the other hand, which has its roots in research conducted by Triandis and Hofstede measures the degree to which individuals express pride, loyalty and cohesiveness in their groups or families,[80] and is the dimension that is relevant to this chapter.

Malaysia was ranked 13th amongst 61 nations measured for institutional collectivism practices with a score of 4.61, where the average score was 4.25; and

---

[75]Markus and Kitayama (1991).

[76]Triandis (1990).

[77]Triandis (1988).

[78]Bhagat et al. (2002).

[79]Hofstede and Jan Hofstede, above n 10, 78–79.

[80]Gelfand et al. (2004, pp. 463–464).

more importantly, was placed 26th out of 62 countries in terms of in-group collective practices with a score of 5.51 which is well above the average score of 5.13. Interestingly, Malaysia has an even higher values score of 5.85 which places it at 18th position overall and shows that Malaysians in general exude pride and loyalty towards their families and in-group members and would like to invest more in it.[81]

These results go to show in Triandis's terms, that Malaysia is allocentric and collectivist as compared to Australia for example, which is idiocentric and individualist.[82] Hence, Malaysians work well in a team environment as they have a strong sense of belonging, with the 'we' orientation or collective spirit reigning over individuality. They prefer compromise to confrontation and avoid open public criticism and outspokenness for fear of undermining harmonious relationships.[83]

Apart from this, Hofstede, Triandis and the Project GLOBE researchers have all acknowledged a link between collectivism and power distance.[84] This is supported by a cultural insider, Asma Abdullah who notes that Malaysians are in general group oriented, respect elders and hierarchy, emphasize loyalty and consensus and place importance on harmony in relationships.[85] This positive correlation between relatively high power distance and collectivism is supported by the Project GLOBE researchers, specifically with respect to their in-group collectivism dimension.[86]

Another indirect link to this would be the general unwillingness of Malaysians to be assertive and enforce their rights. Using Project GLOBE's data on in-group collectivism and power distance scores, along with observations of the value placed on paternalistic and patronage relationships in Malaysia, Malays who make up more than 65 % of the Malaysian population are generally unwilling to challenge superiors and are less likely to assertively promote their achievements.[87]

Furthermore, there is a correlation between Project GLOBE's in-group collectivism practices and values scores and the World Economic Forum's Competitiveness Rankings ('WEFCR') , the United Nations Human Development Report ('UNHDR') and the World Values Survey ('WVS'),[88] which lend strength to Project GLOBE's results. This reflects a positive correlation between politics and in-group collectivism, whereby high in-group collective practices are linked to passiveness and a lack of voice when dealing with the government.

---

[81]In contrast, although Australia also has a high values score of 5.75, their in-group collectivism practices score is well below average at only 4.17, placing it 52nd overall.

[82]See: Bochner (1994).

[83]Abdullah, above n 37, 12.

[84]See: Hofstede (1991).

[85]See: Abdullah (1996); Abdullah, above n 37. See also: Schermerhorn and Bond (1997, p. 188).

[86]Kennedy, above n 49, 20.

[87]Kennedy, above n 49, 23.

[88]Gelfand et al., above n 80, 481–490.

In high in-group collectivist cultures like Malaysia, paternalistic and patronage relationships are also common, with decisions often being based more on connections than on merit.[89] A typical example of this in Malaysia is where large companies (known as '*Ali Baba*' companies) may have well connected Malays as figure-heads on their boards, with the business actually being run by a Chinese or Indian partner.[90]

Also, the lack of individualism and assertiveness amongst the public translates into a preference for alternative mediation and conciliatory means to enforce their rights, as opposed to more confrontational legal action in court. In the insurance and *takaful* context, this is apparent from an average of more than 1000 new cases being referred to the Financial Mediation Bureau, annually from 2000 to 2014, as compared to less than 100 reported cases being decided in the courts for the same period.[91]

The link between collectivism or lack of individualism and legal reform is also indirect, in that high in-group collectivism is compounded by the existence of a relatively high power distance culture, resulting in a vertical collectivist society. This in turn transcends into lack of assertiveness, hence, *a greater preference for alternative mediation or conciliation methods of dispute resolution* over the strict enforcement of legal rights through the court system.

6.5.3 Assertiveness

The researchers of Project GLOBE made a major contribution to the study of cross-cultural research when they identified and developed assertiveness as a dimension of culture. They define assertiveness as 'the degree to which individuals are assertive, confrontational and aggressive in their relationships with others'.[92]

Until then, assertiveness had only been studied as a personality trait at an individual level, that is a person is either assertive or not. Hofstede in his seminal work on cross-cultural empirical research had identified assertiveness but as just one of the aspects of societies that were masculine, under his masculinity versus femininity index.[93] His research showed that masculine societies valued tough competition, achievement and assertiveness more than feminine societies. The researchers of Project GLOBE however, found Hofstede's masculinity index to be confounded by many items and felt it best to develop two distinct dimensions of

---

[89]Javidan and House (2002).

[90]*The Economist* (London) (2001, p. 38).

[91]See: Table of Cases Referred to the Financial Mediation Bureau from 2000 to 2014 in the Appendix.

[92]House et al., above n 46, 6.

[93]Hofstede, above n 42, 280.

'assertiveness' and 'gender egalitarianism' instead.[94] They believe assertiveness is a dimension of culture, as it reflects a society's shared belief on whether people should be tough and assertive or tender and unassertive instead.[95]

Independent validation for this view can be found in Fons Trompenaars and Charles Hampden-Turner's study of various societies' adaptability to their surroundings.[96] They found that societies in general have two orientations towards nature. They are either 'inner directed' believing that they can control and subjugate their surrounding environment; or 'outer directed' believing in the need to maintain harmony with and even sometimes subjugating themselves to their surrounding environment.

Project GLOBE's score for assertiveness societal practices in Malaysia is 3.87, ranking 46th in a survey of 61 countries, well below the average score of 4.14.[97] Malaysians however, recorded one of the highest scores for assertiveness values at 4.81, where the average was a much lower 3.82.[98] Although in general, most societies surveyed valued lower assertiveness than currently practiced, Malaysia like most of the Asian societies wanted more assertiveness. This is presumably due to the general below average practices scores found amongst them.[99] Western societies on the other hand, in general had high assertiveness practices scores and valued lower assertiveness instead.[100]

The above results broadly support Trompenaars and Hampden-Turner's research which concludes that Western societies are more assertive, aggressive and competitive than Eastern or Asian societies, except for Japan.[101] This is because Eastern or Asian societies, unlike the West, do not focus on the 'self' as much and place importance on compromise and maintaining the peace as the way to lead life. Chan, Gelfand, Triandis and Tzeng have also pointed out that in collectivist Southeast Asia where basic Confucianism is often adhered to individuals believe more in common interests and social harmony than self-interest and enjoyment, therefore, again leaning towards non-assertive behaviour.[102]

---

[94]House and Javidan (2004, p. 13).

[95]Den Hartog (2004).

[96]Trompenaars and Hampden-Turner (1997).

[97]This data was used in an article identifying important values of Malays in relating them to preferred organizational leadership styles, by Kennedy, above n 49, 22.

[98]Den Hartog, above n 95, 410–411.

[99]Hong Kong and Singapore however, were the only exceptions, valuing even higher societal assertiveness despite already having high assertiveness practices scores.

[100]An example of this is Australia, which has an above average 4.28 practices score and a slightly below average 3.81 values score. Switzerland, New Zealand and the Nordic states however, had low practices scores and with the exception of New Zealand and Sweden which reflected slightly higher assertiveness values scores, valued even lower assertiveness in their society. Not surprisingly, they were all described as 'feminine societies' under Hofstede's cultural construct.

[101]Trompenaars and Hampden-Turner, above n 96, 141–156.

[102]Chan et al. (1996).

It is not surprising therefore, that Malaysia's score on assertiveness practices is below average, as the Malays who form its ethnic majority comprising more than 65 % of the population, originally evolved from a history of communal living, where individual displays of assertion and confrontational behavior was discouraged.[103] Their attitude towards life is to accept everything that comes their way, albeit good or bad, even death and illness as the will of Allah. Further proof of the Malay culture being non-assertive is the use of polite and non-aggressive language so as not to upset others and preferring to refer to them-selves in the third person, instead of using the pronoun 'I'.[104] Compromise is preferred to confrontation, with open public criticism and outspokenness being avoided at all costs, for fear of undermining harmonious relationships. Also, overt displays of anger and aggressive behaviour are shunned upon, with 'go-getting' and 'take charge' methods of dealing with people being perceived as brash, rough and insensitive.[105]

Malaysia's ethnic Chinese on the other hand, who make up 24.6 % of the population and are the most successful at commerce, in turn believe that success is attained and maintained by maintaining harmony with nature through the practice of *Feng Shui*.

As indicated above, there is a link between the cultural dimensions of power distance, institutional and in-group collectivism and assertiveness, and the operation of this can be seen with respect to Malaysia. Malaysia has a high institutional and in-group collectivism practices score and an average power distance practices score. Not surprisingly, it has a very low assertiveness practices score. This translates into Malaysian society valuing loyalty to family and other in-groups, whereby the interests of in-groups take priority over individual interests. This lack of individualism, coupled with average power distance practices and an authoritarian government, contribute to Malaysians in general being non-assertive.

Examples of this are a plenty in the Malaysian context. Malaysia's multi-ethnic mix of Malays, Chinese and Indians have on the whole lived together in relative harmony since independence from British colonial rule in 1957, save for a bloody clash between the ethnic Malays and Chinese in 1969. Tough government action through affirmative action policies, provide preferential treatment for the Malay majority in terms of preferential access to tertiary education, loans, financial aid and other benefits.[106] This has for the most part been grudgingly accepted by the Chinese and Indians, without overt displays of challenge, as the price they must pay for stability in the country.[107]

Further incidents bearing proof of the lack of assertiveness amongst Malaysians is the relatively unchallenged suspension of the 61-year old daily newspaper the 'Sarawak Tribune' in February 2006, following the publication of an article

---

[103]Kennedy, above n 49, 16–17.

[104]Ibid.

[105]Abdullah, above n 37, 12–13.

[106]Kennedy, above n 49, 24.

[107]*The Economist* (London) (2004, p. 44).

accompanied by a caricature of the Prophet Muhammad which was circulating in the European press at the time.[108] In January 2006, a memorandum was submitted to the Prime Minister by nine non-Muslim Cabinet members calling for a review of laws affecting the rights of non-Muslims, following a decision by the *Sharia* Court on the conversion to Islam of an ethnic Indian (who was deceased at the time of the ruling). This caused such a stir amongst the rest of the Cabinet, that the memorandum was retracted at the request of the Prime Minister, in order to preserve the peace so to speak.[109] Finally, the detention without trial of five ethnic Indian civil rights leaders of the group Hindu Rights Action Force ('HINDRAF') in November 2007 for questioning the alleged systematic marginalization of the ethnic Indian minority in Malaysia, under the charge of having links to terrorism has also been largely unopposed.[110]

The link between non-assertiveness and legal reform is more direct, although linked to the foregoing dimensions of high in-group collectivism and average power distance coupled with an authoritarian government. The insuring public is as a result, less likely to resort to confrontational legal action in the courts to enforce their rights, preferring instead the less formal mediation or investigative processes like that offered by the Financial Mediation Bureau. Also, being generally non-assertive, the (insuring) public is unlikely to fight for rights which have not been clearly legislated upon. Hence, legislation according clear rights to the insuring public is required, without any unnecessary distinction being made on the duty of utmost good faith, abolition of basis of contract clauses and fair and timely claims settlement, between consumers and non-consumers that places the latter at a disadvantage.

6.5.4 Uncertainty Avoidance

Uncertainty avoidance has long been a part of organizational behaviour literature and was identified as an attribute of organizational behaviour by Richard Cyert and James March in 1963.[111] It was Hofstede however, who subsequently conceptualized it as a dimension of societal culture, defining it as 'the extent to which the members of a culture feel threatened by uncertain or unknown situations'.[112] Uncertainty avoidance essentially measures the tolerance or intolerance for ambiguity in a society.

According to Hofstede, extreme ambiguity leads to intolerable anxiety and as a result, societies have come to develop ways to manage this, namely through the

---

[108]*The Star* (Kuala Lumpur) (2006a, b, c, p. 4).

[109]*The Star* (Kuala Lumpur) (2006a, b, c, p. 3).

[110]*The Economist* (London) (2008, p. 32).

[111]Cyert and March (1963) cited by House et al. (eds), above n 45, 13.

[112]Hofstede, above n 42, 161.

three mechanisms of technology, religion and law.[113] Technology is used to deal with uncertainty caused by nature, whereas laws are relied on to maintain social order and religion in turn, as a means of handling uncertainties beyond one's control. Of the mechanisms identified, only law however, is important to the discussion of legal reform of the structure and substance of the law and practice governing insurance and *takaful* contracts.

The value of uncertainty avoidance as a cultural dimension is clear, finding validation in the independent works of others such as Triandis and Shalom Schwartz. Triandis divides cultures into those which are 'loose and tight', with tight cultures having many rules and norms for people to follow whilst discouraging deviation, compared to loose cultures which have less rules to formally regulate society.[114]

Schwartz on the other hand, describes this dimension as 'autonomy versus embeddedness' whereby autonomous cultures encourage individuals to use their intellect and explore personal creativity while being positive about life. Embedded cultures on the other hand, focus on more orderly lifestyles where individuals are expected to respect tradition and rely on their in-groups.[115] Still others have described it in terms of 'neuroticism versus emotional stability'[116] and 'traditional versus secular-rational authority'[117] covering much the same ground.

The researchers of Project GLOBE have also identified uncertainty avoidance as a dimension of societal culture, endorsing Hofstede's claim. They however, disagree with Hofstede's survey methodology and analysis, questioning his conclusions which were based merely from analyzing the results of three questions which related to job stress, attitude towards rules and long-term career goals as experienced by IBM employees.[118] They in turn, have defined uncertainty avoidance as 'the extent to which a society, organization or group relies on social norms, rules and procedures to alleviate the unpredictability of future events'.[119]

Hofstede in his study had identified Malaysia as being very low on the uncertainty avoidance index, ranking 46th in a scale of 53 countries surveyed, thereby, indicating that Malaysians have a high tolerance for the uncertainties of life.[120] The researchers of Project GLOBE meanwhile, have found Malaysia to have very high uncertainty avoidance practices. In fact, amongst the highest in the list of countries surveyed, with a practices score of 4.78 where the average was only 4.16. Malaysia

[113]Ibid. 145.

[114]Triandis (1989).

[115]Schwartz (1999).

[116]Lynn and Martin (1995), cited in deLuque and Javidan (2004, pp. 611–612).

[117]Inglehart and Baker, above n 12.

[118]deLuque and Javidan, above n 116, 609–610.

[119]House et al., above n 46, 5.

[120]Hofstede, above n 42, 151.

was in fact (apart from China), the only country surveyed that had a high uncertainty avoidance practices score and an even higher values score of 4.88.[121] All the other countries with high uncertainty avoidance practices generally had a lower values score and vice versa. This result shows that Malaysians are very rule oriented and want even more rules and mechanisms to cope with the anxiety of uncertainty and to promote the predictability of behaviour.[122]

Although it is difficult to determine which of the two studies is accurate, the fact that the Project GLOBE surveys were conducted in the late 1990s against Hofstede's survey done more than 40 years ago; and being aware of the concerns regarding Hofstede's methodology, the researchers of Project GLOBE designed their questionnaire so as to test Hofstede's views; it is more likely that the Project GLOBE results are more accurate than Hofstede's.

Apart from that, the researchers of Project GLOBE agree with Hofstede that technology and law are the main methods of dealing with uncertainty avoidance. They felt that although there is a connection between religion as a coping mechanism and high uncertainty avoidance, it is not as clear and simple as Hofstede's postulation. In fact, they found a clearer link between law and uncertainty avoidance, with societies high on the uncertainty avoidance practices scale, like Malaysia, having more laws and rules to deal with the anxiety of uncertainty.[123] This is supported by the finding that in terms of societal uncertainty avoidance practices, Malaysia is the most rule oriented country in the Southern Asian cluster of nations surveyed.[124]

The link between uncertainty avoidance and legal reform is rather direct. The only anomaly is that despite having a high uncertainty avoidance practices score indicating that Malaysians have a strong desire for laws and rules to regulate the predictability of behaviour, they are not known for steadfastly enforcing their legal rights in court. This however, may be mainly due to the fact that Malaysians are on the whole non-assertive, lack individualism, practice high in-group collectivism, reflect average power distance and have long been subjected to an authoritarian form of government.

As such, the lack of enforcement by the public of their strict legal rights does not translate into there being no need for clearer laws regulating utmost good faith in insurance and *takaful* contracts that accord rights to all segments of the insuring public. On the contrary, the culture of high uncertainty avoidance practices and even higher values supports this.

What it does mean is that the legal infrastructure along with the substantive legal provisions with respect to the law and practice governing insurance and *takaful*

---

[121]deLuque and Javidan, above n 116, 622–623. However, the values score for Malaysia was in itself not amongst the highest.

[122]This can be distinguished from Australia for instance, which has an above average uncertainty avoidance practices score of 4.39 but a values score of 3.98 which is well below the average score of 4.62, indicating the society's preference for fewer laws and more flexibility.

[123]deLuque and Javidan, above n 116, 623.

[124]Gupta et al. (2002, p. 21).

contracts needs to be looked at. The fact that the Insurance Mediation Bureau and its successor, the Financial Mediation Bureau have from 2000 to 2014 been the preferred choice amongst complainants, as opposed to the civil courts, bears out this argument.[125]

Therefore, attention should be focused on enhancing the alternative means of dispute resolution in place, by for instance, increasing the monetary jurisdiction, terms of reference and profile of the Financial Mediation Bureau. The Customer Services Bureau should in turn be retained as a parallel, less formal avenue dealing with enquiries and minor grievances, as well as monitoring industry conduct and compliance.

At this point, it is useful to note that the Guidelines issued by the Central Bank on industry regulation, especially the *Claims Settlement Guidelines*, should have clearly defined sanctions in place to regulate compliance, in order for it to have any real effect. This way, the courts and the Customer Services Bureau will be more effective in being able to enforce breaches of *the Guidelines*, as opposed to merely relying on the Financial Mediation Bureau's pro-active enforcement of it in the cases brought before it.[126]

6.6 Intra-National or Ethnic Culture

Having measured Malaysian legal culture at a macro national or societal level, it is necessary to evaluate the more micro sub-national or ethnic culture within Malaysia, so as to get an accurate reflection of Malaysian legal culture, given the constraints of empirical data available. Although such a macro-micro analysis of culture is necessary for any society examined, it is more so in the Malaysian context.[127] This is because 'while Malaysia is fully engaged in the international economy, it retains a distinctive mix of Asian cultural values'.[128]

Although Hofstede's seminal work on national culture which included an analysis of Malaysia, was conducted without segregating the three major ethnic groups comprising Malays, Chinese and Indians, he nevertheless proposed that Malaysia's ethnic groups 'may really be culturally not so different'.[129]

In testing this assumption, this latter part of the chapter shall examine the literature and empirical research available on Malaysian intra-national culture. This will be done by starting with Lrong Lim's review and synthesis of the current

---

125See: Table of Cases Referred to the Financial Mediation Bureau from 2000 to 2014 in the Appendix.

126This section draws on research appearing in: Thanasegaran, above n 29, 199.

127Failure to account for the ethnic factor may be an enormous source of error in cross-cultural studies: Ronen and Shenkar (1985, p. 441).

128Kennedy, above n 49, 15.

129Hofstede, above n 84, 7.

literature on the cultural attributes of Malays and Malaysian Chinese;[130] followed by an evaluation of two separate empirical studies conducted on the Malay, Chinese and Indian sub-cultures in Malaysia by Lim and Abdullah[131] and a group of academics from Malaysian universities.[132]

Lim reviewed and synthesized the literature on the cultural attributes of the Malays and Malaysian Chinese by examining the empirical works available. He used Hofstede's framework with respect to the definition of culture and cultural dimensions, on the basis of it having the strongest research thrust. Lim argues that although the Malays and Malaysian Chinese share some similar cultural attributes, there exist fundamental differences between them which should not be ignored in cross-cultural research or implicitly overlooked in favour of cultural homogeneity.

On the question of power distance, he refers to a survey conducted on 83 Malay and 89 Malaysian Chinese university students which found the Malay students surveyed to possess stronger societal-oriented values and a greater deference to hierarchy than the Malaysian Chinese students surveyed.[133] Based on this, Lim argues that although conceptually the two ethnic groups reflect fairly high power distance, 'the direction and strength' of it appears to be different.[134]

With respect to collectivism, he refers to the works of Hamzah Sendut, John Madsen and Gregory Thong in arguing that although the overall culture is collectivist, the two groups differ in content and orientation.[135] A strong community spirit and deep sense of responsibility to help their in-group in the name of *gotong-royong* or mutual co-operation is prevalent amongst the Malays and stems from their history of communal living. The Malaysian Chinese on the other hand, have traditionally formed alliances to provide mutual help and security for their in-group by engaging the business community.[136]

Since Lim's review was based on Hofstede's framework, he refers to the masculinity versus femininity dimension, which is broadly representative of the assertiveness aspect of culture.[137] Here, he refers to a survey conducted on 180 Malay, 137 Malaysian Chinese and 133 Malaysian Indian school children which found the Malaysian Chinese school children to possess a higher achievement

---

[130] Lim (1998).

[131] Lim and Asma (2001).

[132] Ahmad Saufi et al. (2002).

[133] Ng et al. (1982).

[134] Lim, above n 130, 83.

[135] Sendut et al. (1990).

[136] Ibid. 128.

[137] This is based on the fact that Hoftede's cross-cultural empirical research had identified assertiveness as one of the aspects of societies that were masculine.

motivation than the Malays.[138] He uses this to submit that Malays are comparatively more feminine or less assertive and relationship oriented than the Malaysian Chinese, who are in turn more masculine or assertive and career-success oriented.

On the aspect of uncertainty avoidance, Lim suggests that Malaysian Chinese are less uncertainty avoiding than Malays, based on their respective views on religion.[139] The Malaysian Chinese who are more comfortable with the acceptance of multiple religions and teachings, as reflected in the concurrent practice of Confucianism, Buddhism and Taoism, exhibit more flexibility towards uncertainty than the Malays, who are required to practice the Islamic faith which on the other hand searches for the one 'truth'.

In an empirical study investigating the cultural similarities and differences amongst Anglos, Australians and Malaysians in general, data was collected from 168 managers representative of the groups studied who attended executive cross-cultural training courses conducted by the lead author.[140] The questionnaire was developed based on eight concepts commonly used in cross-cultural management literature, namely relationships, harmony, shame, group orientation, belief in God, respect for elders, polychronic time orientation and high context form of communication.[141]

The results of the study reveal that the Anglos and Australians differed substantially from the Malaysians in six dimensions with the most significant pertaining to relationships, collectivism and religiosity. What is more interesting, however, is that among the Malaysian ethnic sub-cultures, there was only one significant difference, being the religiosity dimension, where the Malays differed substantially from both the Malaysian Chinese and Indians.[142] This is probably due to the fact that Malays place a great deal of importance on the fulfillment of religious obligations and do not separate the teachings of their religion from all aspects of life, including their work.[143] On all other score, there was no significant difference amongst the three ethnic sub-cultures in the management dimensions

---

[138]Rahman (1988). This is supported by the views of two other works, namely Sendut et al., above n 135, 132; Ismail (1988) p. 104, who describe the Malaysian Chinese as exhibiting a strong security motivation which translates into the acquisition of wealth and ambitiousness to achieve high recognition and status, respectively.

[139]He refers broadly to Hofstede and Bond (1988).

[140]See: Lim and Abdullah, above n 131.

[141]Ibid. 3.

[142]This result supports previous research conducted by Hussin (1997), Yusof and Amin (1999).

[143]Lim and Abdullah, above n 131, 7. In fact, in October 2008, a defamation suit was lodged by one Teresa Kok (an ethnic Chinese Member of Parliament for the Opposition 'People's Justice Party') against a local Malay daily (Utusan Melayu Sdn Bhd) and its columnist for publishing that she had instructed a mosque in Kuala Lumpur to reduce the volume of its loud-speakers during prayer (a fact which she has denied and has also been denied by the mosque in question). This suit was in turn, construed by a division of the ruling coalition limb of the United Malay National Organization as 'challenging the honour of Malays by suing Utusan Melayu as it is a newspaper owned by Malays': *The Star* (Kuala Lumpur) (2008, p. 8). All ethnic Malays in Malaysia are Muslims by religion.

forming the equivalent of the societal cultural constructs of power distance, collectivism and assertiveness. Collectively as a nation however, Malaysians in general differed substantially from the Anglos and Australians.[144]

Another study on Malaysian ethnic sub-cultures which is of interest is a survey conducted on 142 Malaysian managers, representative of all three sub-cultures from both the government and private sector companies.[145] This was in part, to measure how the Malays, Chinese and Indians fared on Hofstede's cultural dimensions of power distance, collectivism, masculinity versus femininity[146] and uncertainty avoidance. In short, all four of Hofstede's cultural dimensions which are central to this chapter were used to measure how the ethnic Malay, Chinese and Indian sub-cultures within Malaysia rank.

In general, the results of this study show that there is no significant difference in the masculinity versus femininity dimension, in that all three races were generally found to be non-assertive.[147] The Malays and Indians however, were found to exhibit higher levels of power distance and uncertainty avoidance and were less individualistic than the Chinese.[148] This result supports Abdullah's contention that Malays and Indians in general place more value on cooperation and teamwork, whereas the Chinese value entrepreneurship, perseverance and hard work instead.[149] Therefore, despite having distinct cultural and religious backgrounds, recent research points toward the work related values of the three major races in Malaysia, namely the Malays, Chinese and Indians, as being similar in many respects, except for the religiosity dimension.[150]

That such intra-national or ethnic sub-cultural differences exist but are relative (except for the religiosity dimension) between the three races is supported by the

---

[144]This broadly supports the results of Abdullah's earlier research on the values of the three ethnic groups based on a series of workshops and dialogues with more than 200 Malaysian and foreign managers working in Malaysian organizations, where the common values of the three ethnic groups were recorded to be in the 'we' orientation, with emphasis on face, modesty and harmony, whereas the values correlating with the 'I' orientation, emphasizing self-esteem, assertiveness and achievement were labeled as being Western: Abdullah, above n 37, 7. There was however, no equivalent of the uncertainty avoidance dimension in the study.

[145]Ahmad Saufi et al., above n 132. It should be noted however, that only part of this study was dedicated to measuring Malaysian intra-national culture using Hofstede's dimensions. The other part which is not relevant to this chapter was to measure the preference of leadership styles of Malaysian managers.

[146]This dimension is again used as being broadly representative of the assertiveness construct.

[147]Most Malaysians however, generally view the ethnic Chinese to be more masculine, assertive and materialistic than the Malays and Indians.

[148]Ahmad Saufi et al., above n 132, 7–8.

[149]Abdullah, above n 85.

[150]Kennedy, above n 49, 16, in referring to the works of Lim and Abdullah, above n 131; Lim (2001).

independent quantitative research of Lim and Abdullah[151] and Mohd Yusoff Zainun Hamzah and associates.[152] In general, the consensus seems to be that except for the issue of religiosity, the Malays and Indians exhibit a 'relatively' higher level of power distance, uncertainty avoidance and collectivism whereas the Chinese are 'relatively' more individualistic, assertive and materialistic.

That this might be the more accurate reflection of the sub-cultural state of affairs in Malaysia is further endorsed by the independent quantitative study on the three races conducted by Rodrigue Fontaine and Stanley Richardson,[153] using Schwartz's SVS Model of 57 cultural values representing 10 dimensions at the individual level and seven dimensions at the cultural level.[154] The researchers based their findings on 324 completed usable questionnaires from individuals of different levels of education and responsibility (mainly managers and non-managers) and from different industries in various locations within the country.

The outcome of the survey showed that 91 % of the values in Schwartz's SVS Model at the individual level and 82 % of the values at the cultural level were shared by all three ethnic groups without significant differences.[155] The researchers found the key difference between the three groups to be the rating of the 'devout' value which is a component of Schwartz's 'embeddedness' dimension. This therefore, broadly confirms the findings of Abdullah and Lim who found the only significant difference between the three races to be in the 'religiosity' dimension, thereby cross validating both instruments.[156]

Based on the qualitative and quantitative evidence available, it appears that despite their distinct cultural heritage, 'Malaysians of various races have more converging cultural values than diverging cultural values'.[157] As suggested by some, this may perhaps be as a result of the three ethnic races having 'streamlined their values under a shared wider socio-cultural environment'.[158]

---

[151]Lim and Abdullah, above n 131.

[152]Ahmad Saufi, Wafa and Zainun Hamzah, above n 132.

[153]Fontaine and Richardson (2005).

[154]The 10 dimensions at the individual level being: power, achievement, hedonism, stimulating, self-direction, universalism, benevolence, tradition, conformity and security; and the seven dimensions at the cultural level being: embeddedness, hierarchy, mastery, affective autonomy, intellectual autonomy, egalitarianism and harmony: Schwartz (1994).

[155]Fontaine and Richardson, above n 153, 69–70.

[156]Lim and Abdullah, above n 131.

[157]Fontaine and Richardson, above n 153, 64.

[158]Lim and Abdullah, above n 131, 6.

6.7 Effect of Legal Culture on Structure and Substance

The main aim of this chapter has been to ascertain Malaysian legal culture in the firm belief that 'every law reform proposal to change some substantive law or legal institution should include an analysis of what aspects of the local legal culture would support or inhibit such change'[159] and not merely be based on doctrinal justification for reform.

From the foregoing analysis, it can be summarized that both from a macro-national or societal level as well as a more micro-ethnic sub-cultural level, Malaysians are essentially non-assertive; collectivist (exhibiting high institutional as well as in-group collectivism); have an average power distance orientation which is compounded by years of authoritarian government; and reflect a very high level of uncertainty avoidance.

Also, 'religiosity' is the only dimension on which the three Malaysian ethnic sub-cultures differ substantially, with the Malaysian Chinese and Indians showing a much lower propensity for it than the Malays. However, this dimension is not relevant to the question of legal reform of the law and practice governing insurance and *takaful* contracts which is essentially a commercial-consumer related matter. Therefore, it can be assumed that the above said converging societal and ethnic culture is reflective of Malaysian legal culture. Nevertheless, the greater propensity for 'religiosity' on the part of the Malays would point towards *takaful* (Islamic insurance) being more appealing to them than conventional insurance as the preferred mode of protection and investment.[160]

That being the case, it can be concluded that the prevailing Malaysian legal culture in fact, supports this book's proposal for further improvement to be made to the recent substantive reforms introduced via the *Financial Services Act 2013* (Malaysia) and *Islamic Financial Services Act 2013* (Malaysia), as well as structural improvement of the law and practice governing insurance and *takaful* contracts by providing greater emphasis to and increasing the jurisdiction of the Financial Mediation Bureau along the lines set out in the next chapter.

[159]Tabalujan, above n 15, 42.

[160]Having said that however, as at June 2013 the ratio of the market penetration of family *takaful* in Malaysia (which has a population of more than 60 % (Muslim) Malays) to conventional life insurance was only 13–55 %: Abdullah (2013, p. 1). This is presumably because of the relative infancy of *takaful* and more importantly, because *takaful* in Malaysia is offered as part of mainstream mercantile law alongside conventional insurance in a dual system: (Kadir and Razif 2007, pp. 3–4).

6.8 Conclusion

The importance and effect of Malaysian legal culture on the proposed legal reform of the substance and structure of the law and practice governing insurance and *takaful* contracts can be summarized as follows. The average to relatively high level of power distance in a society coupled with years of subjugation to an authoritarian style of government would result in the less powerful members of society, namely the general (and in this case, the insuring) public not being used to enforcing their rights. They instead expect the government to take the initiative when matters of public concern arise. This coupled with low individualism and especially, a high level of in-group collectivism would result in vertical collectivism. This in turn translates into a lack of assertiveness amongst the (insuring) public, which is in fact empirically substantiated.

As a result, the (insuring) public is less likely to resort to confrontational legal action in the courts to enforce their legal rights, preferring instead to resort to less formal mediation and investigative processes like that offered by the Financial Mediation Bureau which is hugely popular amongst individual complainants.[161]

A very high level of uncertainty avoidance practices coupled with an even higher value placed on it, is reflective of Malaysians in general having a strong desire for laws and rules to regulate most aspects of their lives, which would include insurance and *takaful* matters. As such, clearer and more balanced legislative provisions regulating utmost good faith that do not unnecessarily discriminate against non-consumers would be welcome, in improving the recent provisions of the *Financial Services Act 2013* (Malaysia) and *Islamic Financial Services Act 2013* (Malaysia).

As explained earlier in this chapter, the fact that Malaysians are not known for steadfastly enforcing their strict legal rights despite having a propensity for laws is not surprising nor is it a reason against a case for improvement of the industry's recent legislative provisions. The former has not much to do with the importance placed on laws but everything to do with the fact that Malaysians, being generally non-assertive, would rather not seek to enforce their strict legal rights in a confrontational court setting. This yet again lends support to the need for enhancing and improving the role of the Financial Mediation Bureau.

The next and final chapter will conclude this book by setting out the details of the proposed reform and addressing the viability of the said reform from a law and economics perspective, so as to ensure that legal reform of the duty of utmost good faith in insurance and *takaful* contracts in Malaysia is undertaken in a balanced and comprehensive fashion.

---

[161]It is not doubted that other reasons for this could be the fact that recourse to the Financial Mediation Bureau is free and the Mediators are more pro-active than the courts in resolving disputes brought before them. See: The Table of Cases Referred to the Financial Mediation Bureau from 2000 to 2014 in the Appendix.

References

Abdullah A (1992) The Influence of Ethnic Values on Managerial Practices in Malaysia. Malays Manage Rev 27(1):3

Abdullah A (1996) Going glocal: cultural dimensions in malaysian management. Malaysian Institute of Management, Kuala Lumpur

Abdullah MIS (2013) (Treasury Secretary General of the Ministry of Finance, Malaysia), keynote address. In: 4th annual world *Takaful* conference: family *Takaful* Summit, Kuala Lumpur, Malaysia, 19 June 2013

Bhagat RS, Harveston PD, Triandis H (2002) Cultural variations in the cross-border transfer of organizational knowledge: an integrative framework. Acad Manag Rev 27(2):204

Bochner S (1994) Cross-cultural differences in the self concept: a test of Hofstede's individualism/collectivism distinction. J Cross Cult Psychol 25(2):273

Central Bank of Malaysia (2006) Insurance Annual Report 2005. Kuala Lumpur

Chan DKS et al (1996) Tightness—looseness revisited: some preliminary analyses in Japan and the United States. Int J Psychol 31:1

Chase O (1997) Legal processes and national culture. Cardozo J Int Comp Law 5:1

Crouch H (1996) Government and society in Malaysia. Allen & Unwin, New South Wales

Cyert R, March J (1963) A behavioral theory of the firm. Prentice Hill, Englewood Cliffs, New Jersey

Den Hartog D (2004) Assertiveness. In: House R et al (eds) Culture, leadership and organizations: the GLOBE study of 62 societies. Sage Publications, California

de Luque S, Mansour J (2004) Uncertainty avoidance. In: House R et al (eds) Culture, leadership and organizations: the GLOBE study of 62 societies. Sage Publications, California

Department of Statistics Malaysia (2010) Population distribution and basic demographic characteristics report, Putrajaya

Erez M, Early C (1993) Culture, self-identity and work. Oxford University Press, New York

Financial Mediation Bureau (2006) Annual report 2005, Kuala Lumpur

Financial Mediation Bureau (2009) Annual report 2008, Kuala Lumpur

Financial Mediation Bureau (2006–2014) Annual Reports 2005–2013, Kuala Lumpur

Financial Mediation Bureau (2015) Statistical Report (January–December 2014), Kuala Lumpur, 7 Jan 2015

Fontaine R, Richardson S (2003) Cross-cultural research in Malaysia. Cross Cult Manag 10(2):75

Fontaine R, Richardson S (2005) Cultural values in Malaysia: Chinese, Malays and Indians compared. J Cross Cult Manag 12(4):63

Friedman L (1969) Legal culture and societal development. Law Soc Rev 4:29

Friedman L (1975) The legal system: a social science perspective. Russel Sage Foundation, New York

Friedman L (1977) Law and society: an introduction, Englewood Cliffs, New Jersey

Friedman L (1994) Is there a modern legal culture?'. Ratio Juris 7:117

Friedman L (2006) The place of legal culture in the sociology of law. In: Freeman M (ed) Law and sociology: current legal issues 2005, vol 8. Oxford University Press, Oxford

Gelfand M et al (2004) Individualism and collectivism. In: House R et al (eds) Culture, leadership and organizations: the GLOBE study of 62 societies. Sage Publications, California

Gupta V et al (2002) Southern Asian cluster: where the old meets the new? J World Bus 37:16

Hofstede G (1985) The interaction between national and organizational value systems. J Manag Stud 22:347

Hofstede G (1991) Management in a multicultural society. Malays Manag Rev 26:3

Hofstede G (2001) Cultures consequences: comparing values, behaviours, institutions and organizations across nations, 2nd edn. Sage Publications, California

Hofstede G, Bond M (1988) The confucius connection: from cultural roots to economic growth. Organ Dyn 16(4):5

Hofstede G, Jan HG (2005) Cultures and organizations: software of the mind, 2nd edn. McGraw Hill, New York

House R, Javidan M (2004) Overview of GLOBE. In: House R et al (eds) Culture, Leadership and organizations: the GLOBE study of 62 societies. Sage Publications, California

House R et al (2002) 'Understanding cultures and implicit leadership theories across the globe: an introduction to project GLOBE. J World Bus 37:3

House R et al (eds) (2004) Culture, leadership and organizations: the GLOBE study of 62 societies. Sage Publications, California

Huffman J (1984) From legal history to legal theory: a comment on the work of Lawrence Friedman. Tulsa Law Rev 40:579

Hussin H (1997) Personal values and identity structures of entrepreneurs: a comparative study of Malay and Chinese entrepreneurs in Malaysia. In: Donckels R, Miettinen A (eds) Entrepreneurship and SME research: on its way to the next millenium. Aldershot

Inglehart R, Baker W (2000) Modernization, change and persistence of traditional values. Am Sociol Rev 65:19

Insurance Mediation Bureau (2001–2005) Mediator's Annual Reports and Case Reviews 2000–2004, Kuala Lumpur

Ismail NAR (1988) Value systems of Malay and Chinese managers: a comparative study. In: Nash M (ed) Economic performance in Malaysia. Professor World Peace Academy, New York

Javidan M, House R (2002) Cultural acumen for the global manager: lessons from project GLOBE. Organ Dyn 29(4):289

Kadir A, Razif M (2007) (Deputy Governor of the Central Bank of Malaysia), keynote address. In 23rd Pacific insurance conference, Kuala Lumpur, Malaysia, 29 Oct 2007

Kennedy J (2004) Leadership in Malaysia: traditional values, international outlook. Acad Manag Executive 16(3):15

Kuper A (1999) Culture: the anthropologists' account. Harvard University Press, Cambridge

Kusumaatmadja M (1982) Law and development in the ASEAN region: the Indonesian experience. ASEAN Law J 1(1):1

Lev D (1972) Judicial institutions and legal culture in Indonesia. In: Holt C (ed) Culture politics in Indonesia. Cornell University Press, Ithaca

Lim L (1998) Cultural attributes of Malays and Malaysian Chinese: implications for research and practice. Malays Manag Rev 33(2):81

Lim L (2001) Work-related values of Malays and Chinese Malaysians. Int J Cross Cult Manag 1 (2):229

Lim L, Asma A (2001) Cultural Dimensions of Anglos, Australians and Malaysians. Malays Manag Rev 36(2):1

Lindsey T (2000) Black letter, black market and bad faith: corruption and the failure of law reform. In: Manning C, Van Diermen P (eds) Indonesia in transition: social consequences of reformasi and crisis. Institute of Southeast Asian Studies, Singapore

Lynn R, Martin T (1995) National differences for 39 nations in extraversion, neuroticism, psychoticism and economic, demographic and other correlates. Pers Individ Differ 19:403

Macaulay S (1998) Popular legal culture: an introduction. Yale Law J 1545

Magala S (2005) Cross cultural competence. Routledge, London

Mansor N, Ali MAM (1998) An exploratory study of organizational flexibility in Malaysia: a research note. Int J Hum Resour Manag 9(3):506

Markus H, Kitayama S (1991) Culture and self: implications for cognition, emotion and motivation. Psychol Rev 98:224

Maruyama M (1985) Mindscapes: how to understand specific situations in multicultural management. Asia Pac J Manag 2(3):125

Nelken D (2004) Using the concept of legal culture. Aust J Leg Philos 29:1

Nelken D (2006) Rethinking legal culture. In: Freeman M (ed) Law and sociology: current legal issues 2005, vol 8. Oxford University Press, Oxford

Ng SH et al (1982) Human values in nine countries. In: Rath R et al (eds) Diversity and unity in cross-cultural psychology. Swets & Zeitlinger, Netherlands

Rahman WRA (1988) The role of achievement motivation in economic development in Malaysia. In: Sinha D, Kao HSR (eds) Social values and development: Asian perspectives. Sage Publications, New Delhi

Ronen S, Shenkar O (1985) Clustering countries on attitudinal dimensions: a review and synthesis. Acad Manag Rev 10(3):435

Saufi RA, Wafa S, Hamzah Z, Yusoff M (2002) Leadership style preferences of malaysian managers. Malays Manag Rev 37(1):1

Schermerhorn J, Bond M (1997) Cross-cultural leadership dynamics in collectivism and high power distance settings. Leadersh Organ Dev J 18(4):187

Schollhammer H (1969) The comparative management theory jungle. Acad Manag J 12(1):81

Schwartz S (1994) Are there universal aspects in the structure and content of human values? J Soc Issues 50(4):19

Schwartz S (1999) A theory of cultural values and some implications for work. Appl Psychol Int Rev 48:23

Sendut H, Madsen J, Thong G (1990) Managing in a plural society. Longman, Singapore

Silbey S (2001) Legal culture and legal consciousness. Int Encycl Soc Behav Sci 8623

Tabalujan B (2001) Legal development in developing countries—the role of legal culture. Business Law Working Paper, Nanyang Business School

Tabalujan B (2002) Why Indonesian corporate governance failed—conjectures concerning legal culture. Columbia J Asian Law 15(2):162 (Spring 2002)

Thanasegaran H (2011) Settlement of claims by Malaysian insurance and *Takaful* companies: a genuine prospect or merely suspect? Int Company Commercial Law Rev 22(6):191

Thanasegaran H, Shaiban M (2014) Harmonization of Takaful (Islamic Insurance) regulation—a realistic goal or improbable ideal? Singap J Legal Stud 328

The Economist (2001) Doctor's orders, 31 Mar 2001 (London), 38

The Economist (2003) The changing of the guard, 3 Apr 2003 (London), 5

The Economist (2004) Forging a nation, 21 Oct 2004 (London), 44

The Economist (2008) Indian Mutiny, 24 Jan 2008 (London), 32

The Star (2005) Insurers told to use simple language, 19 Dec 2005 (Kuala Lumpur), 10

The Star (2006a) Government stands by Accuracy of EPU Data, 13 Oct 2006 (Kuala Lumpur), 4

The Star (2006b) Indefinite suspension, 10 Feb 2006 (Kuala Lumpur), 4

The Star (2006c) Five cabinet ministers meet Pak Lah over Memo, 22 Jan 2006 (Kuala Lumpur), 3

The Star (2008) Cheras UMNO starts Fund for Utusan, 13 Oct 2008 (Kuala Lumpur), 8

Triandis H (1988) Individualism and collectivism: cross cultural perspectives of self—in-group relationships. J Pers Soc Psycholo 54(2):323

Triandis H (1989) The self and social behaviour in differing cultural contexts. Psychol Rev 96:506

Triandis H (1990) Cross cultural studies of individualism and collectivism. In: Berman JJ (ed) Nebraska symposium on motivation, vol 37

Trompenaars F, Hampden-Turner C (1997) Riding the waves of culture: understanding cultural diversity in business, 2nd edn. Nicholas Brealey, London

Watson A (1993) Legal transplants: an approach to comparative law, 2nd edn. University of Georgia Press, London

Webber J (2004) Culture, legal culture and legal reasoning: a comment on Nelken. Aust J Legal Philos 29:27

Williams R (1983) Keywords: a vocabulary of culture and society. Fontana, London

Yngvesson B (1998) Inventing law in local settings: rethinking popular legal culture. Yale Law J 1689

Yusof S, Amin R (1999) Admired values: the case of teenagers in Malaysia. Int J Soc Econ 26 (6):802

Chapter 7
Conclusion

Abstract This concluding chapter summarizes the main theme of the book which is to address the question of 'why and what legal reform' is needed with respect to utmost good faith in insurance and *takaful* contracts in Malaysia. In doing so, it starts with a summary of the proposals for reform of the law and practice governing insurance and *takaful* contracts in Malaysia, that have been suggested throughout the book. This is followed by an examination of the proposed legal reforms to ascertain whether they are viable from a law and economics perspective, so as to strike a fair and workable balance between the competing interests of insurers and *takaful* operators on the one hand and insureds and *takaful* participants on the other.

7.1 Introduction

This concluding chapter summarizes the main theme of the book which is to address the question as to 'why and what legal reform' is needed with respect to utmost good faith in insurance and *takaful* contracts in Malaysia. Legal reform is needed for a number of reasons.

First, because of the social and economic importance of insurance and *takaful* to the nation, the inherent tension between insurer-insured and *takaful* operator-participant expectations needs to be balanced. Secondly, there still remain some shortcomings in the existing legal framework regulating utmost good faith in insurance and *takaful* contracts despite recent reforms introduced via the *Financial Services Act 2013* (Malaysia) and the *Islamic Financial Services Act 2013* (Malaysia). Chapters 2–5 of this book set out how these shortcomings have caused an imbalance or inadequate balancing of the expectations of the respective parties. Some substantive and structural legal reform is therefore, necessary to address this. Thirdly, the Malaysian legal culture of low individualism, high in-group collectivism, lack of assertiveness and high uncertainty avoidance, suggests that reform in favour of clearer and more balanced legislative provisions that apply to both consumers and non-consumers, as well as greater recourse to less formal dispute resolution mechanisms like mediation is necessary.

H. Thanasegaran, *Good Faith in Insurance and Takaful Contracts in Malaysia*,
DOI 10.1007/978-981-10-0383-7_7

This chapter starts with a summary of the proposals for reform of the law and practice governing insurance and *takaful* contracts in Malaysia, that have been suggested throughout the book. This is followed by an examination of the proposed legal reforms to ascertain whether they are indeed viable from a law and economics perspective, so as to strike a fair and workable balance between the competing interests of insurers and *takaful* operators on the one hand and insureds and *takaful* participants on the other. Such an analysis is especially useful in the insurance and *takaful* context, as they are necessarily underpinned by economic considerations.

This 'multicultural'[1] approach to addressing the law reform of utmost good faith in insurance and *takaful* contracts in Malaysia, by combining contributions made by socio-cultural as well as economic analysis to law reform,[2] is hoped would have a compelling effect of not just proposing appropriate law reform but also in assessing its viability.

7.2 Proposed Reforms

7.2.1 General Duty of Utmost Good Faith and Its Effect

For a start, both the repealed *Insurance Act 1996* (Malaysia) and *Takaful Act 1984* (Malaysia) lacked an express provision that dealt with this fundamental duty of utmost good faith. As such, Malaysia was bound by the shackles of s17 of the *Marine Insurance Act 1906* (UK) as the source of this duty and with it, its solitary draconian remedy of avoidance of the contract with only a refund of premium paid, in the event of breach.

Recent reforms in the United Kingdom via ss14 (4), (1) and (3) of the *Insurance Act 2015* (UK) have however, abolished the remedy of avoidance of contract for a breach of utmost good faith under s17 of the *Marine Insurance Act 1906* (UK) in *all* types of insurance contracts, by only retaining the first part of s17 which provides that 'a contract of marine insurance is a contract based upon the utmost good faith' and deleting the rest. This provision was originally introduced to apply to only consumer insurance contracts under s2 (5) of the *Consumer Insurance (Disclosure and Representations) Act 2012* (UK). By adopting it to all insurance contracts, the *Insurance Act 2015* (UK) has paved the way for more proportionate remedies like damages to be available to aggrieved parties. There are however, no specific

[1]Hadfield (1999, p. 61).

[2]In fact, there have been increasing calls for economic analysis to be used as a 'filter' in judicial decision-making as well, in cases where the law is unclear or the use of the law alone is inadequate (bearing in mind that not all cases come within this category, as some issues concern non-economic considerations of ethics and justice): Kirby (1999, p. 125). Note: The use of the 'Brandeis' brief by the Supreme Court in the United States for the past century, where information about the economic and social consequences of the potential decisions is placed before the judges: Mason (1991, p. 174).

provisions made for remedies with respect to a breach of utmost good faith as such in the English statutes, as the emphasis is on the insured's duty of fair presentation and the consequences of failure thereof.

As for Malaysia, Paragraph 5 (9) of *Schedule 9* to both the *Financial Services Act 2013* and the *Islamic Financial Services Act 2013* (Malaysia), provides that both 'consumers' and insurers or *takaful* operators shall exercise the duty of utmost good faith in their dealings with each other, including the making and paying of a claim, after a contract has been entered into, varied or renewed. This express pronouncement of a general duty of utmost good faith which covers claims handling and renewals as well is a major development. The drawback however, is that the provisions should have been made applicable to **all** insurance and *takaful* contracts instead of just consumer contracts and should have also addressed the remedy available in the event of breach by either party. This has resulted in some uncertainties in the law. For example, it is unclear as to whether the duty of utmost good faith which explicitly includes the insurers'/*takaful* operators' conduct in claims handling also applies to *non-consumer* insurance and *takaful* contracts; and whether in the event of a breach of the duty of utmost good faith by either party, there is any room for the common law remedy of avoidance to still apply or has it been abolished.

These issues remain to be addressed and the Australian *Insurance Contracts Act 1984* (Cth) as amended in 2013, with its balanced, progressive and time-tested provisions could be looked to as a suitable guide. The relevant package of provisions would in this regard be ss12, 13, 14, 37, 24, 28, 29, 54 and 56 of the *Insurance Contracts Act 1984* (Cth) (Australia), as they would if adopted, essentially place on the insurer/*takaful* operator the onus of ensuring that the duty of good faith is properly observed by the insured/participant, since this is where the greatest potential for breach lies.[3] Furthermore, since many of the provisions of the repealed *Insurance Act 1996* (Malaysia)[4] were already modelled after the *Insurance Contracts Act 1984* (Cth) (Australia) and applied over the years without any difficulty, additional reform along these lines would pose few problems, thereby, being the logical choice all round.[5]

For a start, s13 of the *Insurance Contracts Act 1984* (Cth) (Australia) implies the duty of utmost good faith as a term of insurance contracts and provides:

> A contract of insurance is a contract based on the utmost good faith and there is *implied in such a contract* a provision requiring each party to it to act towards the other party, *in respect of any matter arising under or in relation to it*, with the utmost good faith (emphasis added).

Section 13 has the effect of making the duty an implied term of the insurance contract and more importantly, does not restrict the remedy for a breach of it to just avoidance of the contract and a refund of premium paid. This is essential for purchasers of insurance and *takaful*, as often, the remedy of avoidance upon breach

---

[3]This section draws on research appearing in: Thanasegaran (2004, pp. 158–159).

[4]Some examples of these are ss149 (4), 150 and 151 of the *Insurance Act 1996* (Malaysia).

[5]The law of transplants is however, beyond the scope of this book.

by the insurer/*takaful* operator is of no benefit to an insured/participant who has suffered substantial loss or been exposed to grave risk. Such an implied contractual provision would also facilitate damages being available as a substantive remedy for its breach.

Apart from this, the words ‘in respect of any matter arising under or in relation to’ contained in s13 have a wide implication, in that all provisions in the insurance contract, as well as provisions governing the terms and operation of insurance contracts under the *Insurance Contracts Act 1984* (Cth) (Australia) are bound by the overriding obligation of utmost good faith. With respect to an insurer/*takaful* operator, this translates into potential exposure to breach of utmost good faith on a wide range of a matters, like drafting of proposal forms and policies; failure to give proper explanation of the policy and its terms; unsubstantiated allegations of a breach of utmost good faith against the insured/participant; unreasonable delay in admitting liability and settling claims; unfounded denial of claims and low claims settlement.

In addition to this, the improvements introduced via ss13 (2)–(4) and 14A of the *Insurance Contracts Amendment Act 2013* (Cth) (Australia) could also be incorporated into the Malaysian context. As far as Australia is concerned, this amounts to a breach of utmost good faith resulting in a breach of the Act itself which entitles the Australian Securities and Investments Commission (ASIC) to take action against the insurer. It also extends the obligation to exercise good faith to third party beneficiaries under the contract, from the inception of the contract; and provides the ASIC with the power to take action against the insurer under the *Corporations Act 2001* (Cth) (Australia), for failure to comply with the duty of utmost good faith in handling claims. Such a provision, if made applicable to insurers and *takaful* operators in Malaysia, could pave the way for the Central Bank of Malaysia's involvement in terms of enforcing adherence to this fundamental duty, in addition to giving rise to a breach of contract.

A further effect of s13 is seen, when construed together with ss14 and 37 of the *Insurance Contracts Act 1984* (Cth) (Australia). Section 14(1) provides that:

> If reliance by a party to a contract of insurance on a provision of the contract or the Act would be to fail to act with the utmost good faith, the party may not rely on the provision.

Section 14(3) goes on to provide that:

> In deciding whether reliance by an insurer on a provision of the contract of insurance or the Act would be to fail to act with the utmost good faith, the court shall have regard to any notification of the provision that was given to the insured, whether a notification of a kind mentioned in Section 37 or otherwise.[6]

---

[6]Section 37 which covers the notification of unusual terms, provides that:

An insurer may not rely on a provision included in a contract of insurance (not being a prescribed contract) of a kind that is not usually included in contracts of insurance that provide similar insurance cover unless, before the contract was entered into, the insurer clearly informed the insured in writing of the effect of the provision (whether by providing the insured with a document containing the provision, or the relevant provisions of the proposed contract or otherwise).

The overall effect of these provisions is that the duty of utmost good faith which is a reciprocal and continuing duty would have to be adhered to by both parties to the insurance contract. Otherwise, the party in breach would not be entitled to enforce its rights arising under the contract or the *Insurance Contracts Act 1984* (Cth) (Australia) which would in turn entitle the innocent party to damages for a breach of an implied term of the contract.

Furthermore, s12 of the *Insurance Contracts Act 1984* (Cth) (Australia) specifically provides that the general duty of utmost good faith in s13 does not impose on the insured a duty beyond that of pre-contractual disclosure in s21. This serves to curb potential allegations by insurers of post-contractual non-disclosure as amounting to a breach of utmost good faith.

As can be seen above, ss12–14 would be of tremendous importance especially to insureds and *takaful* participants if adopted in Malaysia, especially in situations where the overriding duty of utmost good faith conflicts with the strict application of a contractual term, in which case, the former would take precedence.

The remedies available in the event of a breach of ss13, 14 and the like, are in turn addressed in the form of pre-contractual remedies in ss28 and 29 and post-contractual remedies in ss54 and 56 of the *Insurance Contracts Act 1984* (Cth) (Australia) which are dealt with later in this chapter.

7.2.2 Pre-contractual Duty of Disclosure and Its Effect

As set out in Chap. 3 of this book, with respect to the pre-contractual duty of disclosure, s150 (1) of the now repealed *Insurance Act 1996* (Malaysia) was an improvement from the common law position, as it introduced the 'reasonable insured test' in assessing the materiality of any non-disclosure, in place of the more onerous 'prudent insurer's' perspective of the same. Although a positive measure, s150 (1) left many issues unaddressed. The most important of which was the remedy available in the event of its breach by the insured. This resulted in the common law remedy of avoidance of contract and a refund of premiums paid being left intact, as opposed to more equitable remedies like damages and/or a proportionate reduction of policy monies paid out, should a causal connection be shown to exist between the non-disclosure and loss suffered by the insurer.

The *Takaful Act 1984* (Malaysia) on the other hand, did not contain any provision that addressed the pre-contractual duty of disclosure. Section 129 of the *Financial Services Act 2013* (Malaysia) and s141 of the *Islamic Financial Services Act 2013* (Malaysia) have however, since gone on to provide with respect to insurance and *takaful* contracts respectively, that *Schedule 9* sets out the pre-contractual duty of disclosure and representation in Part 2, and the remedies for misrepresentation in Part 3. Both statutes in fact contain mirror images of provisions pertaining to utmost good faith in insurance and *takaful* contracts.

Paragraph 4 of *Schedule 9* to both Acts which relates to *non-consumer insurance/takaful contracts* essentially adopts the voluntary disclosure mechanism applicable in Australia[7] that requires the insured/participant before the contract is entered into to disclose matters he or she knows to be relevant to the insurer/*takaful* operator in accepting the risk or the rates and terms to be applied or that which 'a reasonable person in the circumstances' could be expected to know to be relevant. Paragraph 5 of *Schedule 9* in turn, which relates to *consumer insurance/takaful contracts* adopts the inquiry based disclosure mechanism applicable in the United Kingdom and in Australian-eligible contracts[8] that requires the insured/participant before the contract is entered into to take reasonable care not to misrepresent to the insurer/*takaful* operator when answering specific questions posed by the insurer/ *takaful* operator or when confirming or amending any matter previously disclosed as provided by the insurer/*takaful* operator in writing. The standard of care required in doing so is 'what a reasonable consumer in the circumstances would have known.[9]'

According to Paragraphs 4 (3), 5 (5) and 5 (6) of *Schedule 9*, the insurer/*takaful* operator is deemed to have waived any non-disclosure or incomplete disclosure by proposers should it fail to pursue the said non-compliance any further. This retains the improved position introduced via s150 (3) of the now repealed *Insurance Act 1996* (Malaysia), that was in fact modeled after s21 (3) of the *Insurance Contracts Act 1984* (Cth) (Australia). These provisions could perhaps be further improved by providing that 'any such lack of or incomplete or irrelevant answer shall not be taken to be a response by the insured in the negative', so as to address a practice amongst some insurers/*takaful* operators of inserting such provisions in proposal forms.

The *Financial Services Act 2013* (Malaysia) and *Islamic Financial Service Act 2013* (Malaysia)'s provisions relating to pre-contractual non-disclosure are fairly comprehensive in tackling the obligations clearly and also address both *consumer and non-consumer* insurance and *takaful* contracts. However, the remedies for breach of the duty have not been clearly set out. It may have been intended to be covered by the remedies appearing in Part 3 of *Schedule 9* which relate to misrepresentations. However, Part 3 only contains headings and provisions that make specific reference to remedies for misrepresentation. Although many alleged non-disclosures would in essence amount to misrepresentations, especially with respect to *consumer* insurance and *takaful* contracts requiring inquiry based

---

[7]See: Section 21 of the *Insurance Contracts Act 1984* (Cth) (Australia).

[8]See: Section 2 (2) of the *Consumer Insurance (Disclosure and Representations) Act 2012* (UK) and s21A of the *Insurance Contracts Act 1984* (Cth) (Australia).

[9]See: Paragraph 6 (2) of *Schedule 9* to the *Financial Services Act 2013* (Malaysia) and *Islamic Financial Services Act 2013* (Malaysia) which is based on s3 of the *Consumer Insurance (Disclosure and Representations) Act 2012* (UK) and s21A of the *Insurance Contracts Act 1984* (Cth) (Australia). This section draws on research appearing in: Thanasegaran and Shaiban (2014, p. 339), but is used throughout this chapter in the context of both the *Financial Services Act 2013* (Malaysia) and the *Islamic Financial Services Act 2013* (Malaysia), as an examination of both statutes shows that the Malaysian legislature has used the same numeric sections in referring to this area of the law in both statutes.

disclosure, it would nevertheless be advisable to provide for a residual remedy that applied to a breach of the duty of disclosure per se.[10]

In this context, Australia's package of remedies for innocent and fraudulent non-disclosure by the insured, in ss28 and 29 of the *Insurance Contracts Act 1984* (Cth) might prove useful to address situations where insureds/*takaful* participants are found to be in breach of this duty. It is unclear however, as to why this was not adopted by the Malaysian legislature in 1996, when s150 (1) of the now repealed *Insurance Act 1996* (Malaysia) in fact emulated s21 (1) of the *Insurance Contracts Act 1984* (Cth) (Australia).

Section 28 of the *Insurance Contracts Act 1984* (Cth) (Australia) read together with s33 makes the following the only remedies available for pre-contractual non-disclosure and misrepresentation by the insured in relation to general insurance. Section 28 (1) requires the insurer to be induced to enter into the contract as a result of the non-disclosure or misrepresentation, as a pre-requisite to remedy. Avoidance of the contract is only an option where the non-disclosure or misrepresentation was fraudulent, with some allowance being given in instances where there was a little bit of fraud.[11] Otherwise, the insurer is only entitled to reduce its liability in respect of a claim to the amount that would place the insurer in a position as if the non-disclosure or misrepresentation had not occurred.[12]

Section 29 is in turn, the equivalent provision applicable to life insurance contracts, with the only substantial difference being the application of the proportionality principle instead.[13] In short, these two provisions make 'the insurer's

---

[10]This section draws on research appearing in: Thanasegaran and Shaiban, above n 9, 339.

[11]Section 31 in fact gives the court a discretion to disregard the insurer's avoidance if it 'would be harsh and unfair not to do so' thereby allowing the insured recovery of the whole or part of the claim as it thinks 'just and equitable,' in cases where the insurer has not been prejudiced by the fraudulent non-disclosure or misrepresentation in question.

[12]Section 28 (3); The remedy under s28 (3) can include reducing the insurer's liability under the policy to nil (where the insurer can prove that it would not have entered into the contract at all but for the non-disclosure or misrepresentation) and reducing its liability for a claim to nil (where it can prove that it would have excluded the relevant claim from cover by way of an excess or exclusion under an alternative policy which it would have issued had there been a proper disclosure or where the additional premium which it would have charged would have exceeded the amount of the claim): Mann and Lewis (2014, p. 197).

[13]Section 29(4) provides that:

If the insurer has not avoided the contract, whether under subsection (2) or (3) or otherwise, the insurer may, by notice in writing given to the insured before the expiration of 3 years after the contract was entered into, vary the contract by substituting for the sum insured (including any bonuses) a sum that is not less than the sum ascertained in accordance with the formula SP/Q where:

"S" is the number of dollars that is equal to the sum insured (including any bonuses).
"P" is the number of dollars that is equal to the premium that has, or to the sum of the premiums that have become payable under the contract; and
"Q" is the number of dollars that is equal to the premium, or to the sum of the premiums, that the insurer would have been likely to have charged if the duty of disclosure had been complied with or the misrepresentation had not been made.

remedy for non-fraudulent non-disclosure [or misrepresentation by the insured] … proportionate to the prejudice suffered by the insurer' (clarification added)[14] which would serve as a fair remedy to be adopted for insurers and *takaful* operators in Malaysia.

7.2.3 Pre-contractual Misrepresentation and 'Basis of Contract' Clauses

As for pre-contractual misrepresentation on the other hand, it was not addressed by either the *Insurance Act 1996* (Malaysia) or the *Takaful Act 1984* (Malaysia). Hence, it was left to be governed by s20 of the *Marine Insurance Act 1906* (UK) which entitled insurers/*takaful* operators to avoid the contract for material misrepresentation by insureds/participants, as viewed from the more onerous 'prudent insurer's' perspective. Up until 2013 therefore, the law on pre-contractual misrepresentation in Malaysia played second fiddle to that of non-disclosure, at least with respect to insurance contracts that applied the 'reasonable insured' test to assess the materiality of any non-disclosure, via s150 (1) of the *Insurance Act 1996* (Malaysia). The *Takaful Act 1984* (Malaysia) on the other hand, was completely silent on both pre-contractual duties.

Following the recent amendments however, *Schedule 9* to both the *Financial Services Act 2013* (Malaysia) and *Islamic Financial Services Act 2013* (Malaysia) sets out the pre-contractual duty pertaining to representations made for contracts of insurance and *takaful* in Part 2 and the remedies for misrepresentation in Part 3.

Paragraph 7 (3) of *Schedule 9* to both the Acts classifies pre-contractual misrepresentation by consumers as being deliberate or reckless, careless and innocent. Paragraph 7 (4) provides that a deliberate or reckless misrepresentation is where the consumer knew that the misrepresentation was untrue or misleading or did not care if it was *and* knew that the misrepresentation was relevant to the insurer/*takaful* operator or did not care if it was. It is for the insurer/*takaful* operator to prove on a balance of probability that a misrepresentation is deliberate or reckless, with a dishonest representation being regarded as being made deliberately or recklessly. Paragraph 7 (6) on the other hand, provides that a misrepresentation is careless or innocent if it is not deliberate or reckless.[15]

Under Paragraph 13 (2) of *Schedule 9* to both Acts, misrepresentations made in consumer or non-consumer life insurance/family *takaful* contracts in effect for more

[14] Hawke (2006, p. 13).

[15] See: Paragraphs 7 (7) and 7 (5) respectively of *Schedule 9* to the *Financial Services Act 2013* (Malaysia) and *Islamic Financial Services Act 2013* (Malaysia). It should be noted that Paragraph 7 (8) contains a balanced provision that unless the contrary is shown, it is presumed that the consumer knew that a matter about which the insurer/*takaful* operator asked a clear and specific question was relevant to the insurer/*takaful* operator. This section draws on research appearing in: Thanasegaran and Shaiban, above n 9, 340.

than 2 years cannot entitle the insurer/*takaful* operator to avoid the contract unless the 'insurer/*takaful* operator shows that the statement was on a material matter or suppressed a material fact *and* that it was *fraudulently* made or omitted.' On the question of materiality, it is dependent on whether if it was known by the insurer/*takaful* operator it would have led to its refusal to issue an insurance/*takaful* certificate or the imposition of terms less favourable to the insured/participant; and should the insurer/*takaful* operator be permitted to avoid the contract, it must refund payments received there under.[16]

As for misrepresentations made in a *consumer* life insurance/family *takaful* contract in existence for 2 years or less or in a *consumer* general insurance/ general *takaful* contract, the insurer/*takaful* operator is under Paragraph 15 entitled to avoid the contract, refund payments received pursuant thereto and refuse all claims, should the misrepresentation be deliberate or reckless. If the misrepresentation was careless or innocent on the other hand, Paragraph 16 provides that if the insurer/*takaful* operator would not have entered into or renewed the contract on any terms, then it may avoid the contract, refund payments received and refuse all claims. However, if it would have entered into or renewed the contract on different terms other than the contribution amount, the contract is treated as being on those terms. Lastly, if it would have entered into or renewed the contract by charging a higher premium, then it may proportionately reduce the amount payable under the claim.[17]

The express duty not to make pre-contractual misrepresentation coupled with detailed remedies in the event of breach is a major improvement in the law. The said provisions would have however, been more comprehensive had they applied to **all** insurance and *takaful* contracts. Instead as it stands, non-consumer general insurance/*takaful* contracts and non-consumer life insurance/family *takaful* contracts in existence for 2 years or less have been left out. As a result, there are no residual remedies applicable in the event of misrepresentations made in these contracts. To compound matters, it is unclear whether s20 of the *Marine Insurance Act 1906* (UK) would apply to those insurance/*takaful* contracts, in which case insureds/participants would again be bound by the sole remedy of avoidance of the contract with only a refund of premium paid, in the event of breach, which would be an unsatisfactory state of affairs.[18]

Apart from this, the inclusion of 'basis of contract' clauses in proposal forms for almost every type of insurance and *takaful* contract in Malaysia has been a widespread practice. This has had the effect of giving answers and information provided by insureds and *takaful* participants the status of warranties and thereby removing the requirement for the insurer/*takaful* operator to have been 'induced' by the

[16]See: Paragraphs 13 (4) and 13 (3) respectively of *Schedule 9* to the *Financial Services Act 2013* (Malaysia) and *Islamic Financial Services Act 2013* (Malaysia).This section draws on research appearing in: Thanasegaran and Shaiban, above n 9, 340.

[17]Ibid.

[18]Ibid.

misrepresentation or for any causal connection to be established between the misrepresentation and ensuing loss, in order for it to be actionable.

This major problem has however, been addressed with respect to *consumer* insurance and *takaful* contracts in Malaysia via Paragraph 10 of *Schedule 9* to the *Financial Services Act 2013* (Malaysia) and *Islamic Financial Services Act 2013* (Malaysia) which has abolished the same. This provision appears to have been based on s6 (2) of the *Consumer Insurance (Disclosure and Representations) Act 2012* (UK) which as its name and scope suggests, applies to consumer insurance contracts alone. The *Financial Services Act 2013* (Malaysia) and *Islamic Financial Services Act 2013* (Malaysia) on the other hand, replace the *Insurance Act 1996* (Malaysia) and *Takaful Act 1984* (Malaysia) respectively, which are statutes applicable to **all** types of insurance and *takaful* contracts in Malaysia. They should therefore, cover both consumer and *non-consumer* insurance and *takaful* contracts alike. In this sense, s24 of the *Insurance Contracts Act 1984 (Cth)* (Australia) could be looked to as a guide as it abolishes 'basis of contract' clauses in **all** contracts of insurance.[19]

7.2.4 Statutory Warnings and Matters of Form

Related to the issue of utmost good faith and pre-contractual disclosure is the requirement on the part of insurers and *takaful* operators to provide clear warnings in proposal forms to prospective insureds and *takaful* participants, of the consequences of pre-contractual non-disclosure or misrepresentation on insurance and *takaful* contracts.

Section 149 (4) of the *Insurance Act 1996* (Malaysia) had provided for this with respect to insurance contracts, albeit without reference to the remedy applicable in the event of failure to do so by the insurer. There was no provision for this in the *Takaful Act 1984* (Malaysia) pertaining to *takaful* contracts, although s28 of the Act was used for this purpose in an erroneous way, as highlighted in Chap. 5 of this book. Paragraphs 5 (7) and 4 (4) of *Schedule 9* to the *Financial Services Act 2013* (Malaysia) and *Islamic Financial Services Act 2013* (Malaysia) now provide an improvement to this with respect to consumer and non-consumer insurance/*takaful* contracts respectively, by requiring insurers/*takaful* operators before an insurance/*takaful* contract is entered into, varied or renewed, to *clearly inform* a proposer *in writing* of the pre-contractual duty of disclosure and that it shall *continue until* the contract is entered into, varied or renewed. This provision in fact, takes into account the improvement made to s22 of the *Insurance Contracts Act 1984* (Cth) (Australia) by the *Insurance Contracts Amendment Act 2013* (Cth) (Australia).[20]

---

[19]Ibid 341.

[20]Ibid.

However, what remains lacking is the remedy applicable in the event of the insurer/*takaful* operator's non-compliance with this provision. In this context, a provision along the lines of s22 (3) of the *Insurance Contracts Act 1984* (Cth) (Australia) should be introduced to complete the provision. This would have the effect of preventing an insurer/*takaful* operator in breach from exercising a right against the insured/participant for non-disclosure unless it is fraudulent.

Apart from the proposals set out above, the *Financial Services Act 2013* (Malaysia) and *Islamic Financial Services Act 2013* (Malaysia) should perhaps also formalize the need for proposal forms to contain clear and specific questions covering only genuinely material matters as opposed to 'catch all' questions[21]; have legible and comprehensible plain language policies[22]; and incorporate the possible introduction of 'standard form' policies approved by the Central Bank[23] for commonly acquired domestic or consumer policies, such as house owner's or householder's, motor vehicle, personal accident and illness and travel policies.

7.2.5 *Role and Effect of Intermediaries*

Another aspect affecting utmost good faith is the role of intermediaries such as agents, brokers and now financial advisers and bank staff involved in bancassurance/*bancatakaful* in effecting insurance and *takaful* contracts which is substantial, as insurance and *takaful* agents still appear to be a dominant distribution channel for life insurance and family *takaful* products in Malaysia.[24]

On this count, the now repealed s151 of the *Insurance Act 1996* (Malaysia) and s66 of the *Takaful Act 1984* (Malaysia) were positive measures which treated insurance and *takaful* agents as in fact, agents of the insurer and *takaful* operator respectively, in relation to any information acquired by them from the insured or participant during pre-contractual negotiations. This enabled the agent's knowledge of or any statement made or act done by the agent to be imputed unto the insurer or *takaful* operator concerned.

---

[21]Brown (1994, p. 205).

[22]This should entail the use of simple and consumer friendly language in drafting proposal forms, insurance/*takaful* policies and cover notes.

[23]Such approval should be given in consultation with the relevant trade associations, with the standard cover being re-examined from time to time by the Central Bank, to accommodate possible revision so as to permit flexibility in keeping abreast with changes in insurance and *takaful* practices as well as the reasonable expectations of insureds and *takaful* participants: Australian Law Reform Commission (1982a) [81]. The appropriate terms or content of the said standard cover are however, outside the scope of this book.

[24]Insurance agents and brokers had a 49.4 % market share of new insurance premiums in 2005: Central Bank of Malaysia (2006a) p. 31. *Takaful* agents and brokers in turn, had a 33.5 % market share of new *takaful* premiums for the same period: Central Bank of Malaysia (2006b).

Paragraph 12 (1) of *Schedule 9* to the *Financial Services Act 2013* (Malaysia) and *Islamic Financial Services Act 2013* (Malaysia) now reinforces this position with respect to insurance and *takaful* contracts and has expanded its scope to cover any variation of the contract as well, in addition to the formation of contract prescribed for before.

However, some shortcomings and inconsistencies remain. For example, Paragraph 12 (1) of *Schedule 9* to the 2013 Acts, like ss151 (1) and (2) of the *Insurance Act 1996* (Malaysia) seems limited in scope, applying only to insurance and *takaful* agents whereas ss44A (1) and (2) of the previously repealed *Insurance Act 1963* (Malaysia) and ss66 (1) and (2) of the *Takaful Act 1984* (Malaysia) appeared broad enough to cover brokers as well, as they were phrased as 'authorised by the insurer/*takaful* operator as *its agent*' rather than the present 'its insurance/*takaful* agent' which necessarily omits brokers from the equation. All of the above statutes however, do not clarify the position with respect to the status of financial advisers and bank staff involved in the sale of bancassurance/*bancatakaful* in this regard, although presumably, the former would be more akin to brokers and the latter, agents. Perhaps this could be expressly provided for in any amendment to the *Financial Services Act 2013* (Malaysia) and *Islamic Financial Services Act 2013* (Malaysia), as it would help address issues arising from current insurance and *takaful* distribution channels.

Furthermore, Paragraph 12 (1) of *Schedule 9* to the *Financial Services Act 2013* (Malaysia) and *Islamic Financial Services Act 2013* (Malaysia) only seems to address the acts or omissions and knowledge of intermediaries at the point of 'formation or variation of the insurance/*takaful* contract', thereby not applying to notices of loss or claims made to them subsequently, which are still governed by the common law.[25] Paragraph 12 (1) should therefore be amended to cover agents, brokers, financial advisers, staff involved in bancassurance/*bancatakaful*and alike, and extend to 'any matter relating to insurance or *takaful*' instead of merely referring to the formative part of insurance and *takaful* contracts. This was in fact what was provided for in s12 of the now repealed *Insurance (Agents & Brokers) Act 1984* (Cth) (Australia).

7.2.6 Claims Settlement and Post-contractual Implications

The final substantive aspect affecting utmost good faith in insurance and *takaful* contracts is the frequent use of exclusion clauses and strict construction of policy terms by insurers and *takaful* operators in denying insureds' and participants'

[25]This essentially depends on whether the intermediary concerned has the insurer or *takaful* operator's authority to receive the same, which in turn needs further proof.

legitimate claims, along with undue delay and reduced settlement of claims depicting poor claims handling.[26]

For example, from 2000 to 2014, of the average of more than 1000 new insurance and *takaful* cases referred to the Financial Mediation Bureau per year, an average of 57 % involved complaints by insureds and participants on poor claims handling by insurers and *takaful* operators.[27]

Despite this, however, Malaysia did not have any provision in the *Insurance Act 1996* (Malaysia) or the *Takaful Act 1984* (Malaysia) which clearly dealt with the conduct of parties during claims settlement. Claims settlement practices were until 2013, merely regulated by the *Guidelines on Claims Settlement Practices* issued by the Central Bank ('*Claims Settlement Guidelines*'),[28] which via Clause 3.4 directed insurers and *takaful* operators to conduct themselves in a fair and reasonable manner when settling claims. To compound matters, there was also no structured set of sanctions that could apply should insurers and *takaful* operators fail to comply with the *Claims Settlement Guidelines*. The Central Bank could only issue show-cause letters as an indirect means of exerting pressure on errant insurers and *takaful* operators.

In this respect, only the Mediators at the Financial Mediation Bureau[29] have stepped in to resolve complaints and disputes brought before them in a flexible and pro-active manner, by giving effect to the said Guidelines. They have been able to do this because of their widely drafted Terms of Reference that do not strictly bind them to legal rules alone.[30] The courts and the Central Bank on the other hand, have not been able to enforce industry compliance with the *Claims Settlement Guidelines* due to the lack of sanctions available in the event of non-compliance. The injustice that can result from this is apparent from the Court of Appeal's decision in *Leong Kum Whay v QBE Insurance (M) Sdn Bhd*,[31] which has been examined in Chap. 2 of this book.

The *Financial Services Act 2013* (Malaysia) and the *Islamic Financial Services Act 2013* (Malaysia) now address the problems pertaining to good faith in claims

---

[26]See: *Wong Cheong Kong Sdn Bhd v Prudential Assurance Sdn Bhd* [1998] 3 MLJ 722; *Cheong Heng Loong Goldsmiths (KL) Sdn Bhd v Capital Insurance Bhd* [2004] 1 CLJ 357 (insurance); *Seah Cheoh Wah v Malayan Banking Bhd & Anor* [2009] 7 CLJ 485; *TK0216—Total and Permanent Disability* and *TK0218—Death Claim*, Financial Mediation Bureau, Compilation of Cases 2010, Kuala Lumpur, 2011, 21 (*takaful*). This section draws on research appearing in: Thanasegaran (2013, pp. 115–116).

[27]See: Table of Cases Referred to the Financial Mediation Bureau from 2000 to 2014 in the Appendix. The breakdown of the number of cases referred to the Financial Mediation Bureau according to the types of complaint is however, no longer available from 2012.

[28]Central Bank of Malaysia (2003).

[29]See: Financial Mediation Bureau (2009, pp. 8–10).

[30]See: Table of Cases Referred to the Financial Mediation Bureau from 2000 to 2014 in the Appendix for the percentage of cases in which the insurers' and *takaful* operators' decision was revised by the Mediator. This section draws on research appearing in: Thanasegaran (2011, pp. 197–198).

[31][2006] 1 CLJ 1.

settlement through the enactment of Paragraph 5 (9) of *Schedule 9* to both Acts. This is an improvement with respect to *consumer* insurance and *takaful* contracts in that it requires the duty of utmost good faith to be exercised by a *consumer and licensed insurer/takaful operator* in their dealings with each other 'including the making and paying of a claim' after a contract of insurance/*takaful* has been entered into, varied or renewed. Although it is an improvement with respect to consumer insurance and *takaful* contracts, as it expressly requires utmost good faith to be exercised by both parties in claims settlement, the uncertainty remaining is nevertheless, with respect to the status of *non-consumer* insurance and *takaful* contracts and the remedy applicable in the event of breach, in **either** case.

Paragraph 5 (9) of *Schedule 9* to both Acts would have been more complete had it been made applicable to **all** insurance and *takaful* contracts, with the proportionate remedy of damages being expressly provided to apply in cases of breach of utmost good faith in claims settlement. As a result, it remains unclear if there is still scope for s17 of the *Marine Insurance Act 1906* (UK) and its remedy of avoidance to apply to *non-consumer* insurance and *takaful* contracts in Malaysia. This would indeed be an unfortunate state of affairs.[32]

In this respect, the Australian package of provisions ranging from ss12–14 and ss54–57 of the *Insurance Contracts Act 1984 (Cth)*, have provided for a more comprehensive manner of dealing with utmost good faith in general, and claims settlement practice in particular, which could serve as a guide.[33]

For a start, s12 entrenches Part II of the Act which is on the duty of utmost good faith, from being limited or restricted in any way by subsequent provisions as well as any other law.[34] Section 13 as described earlier, goes on to set out the duty as being implied in all insurance contracts in respect of any matter arising under or in relation to it.[35] Together with ss14 and 37 set out earlier, it would neutralize any attempt by insurers to rely on unusual terms, unduly strict construction of policy terms or wide exclusion clauses in policies, so as to defeat an otherwise genuine claim put forward.

In relation to the construction of policies, exclusions and claims settlement, this translates into the insurer's potential exposure to breach of utmost good faith on a

---

[32]This section draws on research appearing in: Thanasegaran and Shaiban, above n 9, 342.

[33]This was done to implement the Australian Law Reform Commission's recommendations made in 1982 that 'legislation should make it clear that the duty of utmost good faith applied to all aspects of the relationship between insurer and insured, including the settlement of claims': Australian Law Reform Commission (1982b) [328]; Further endorsement of this can be found in the Explanatory Memorandum, Insurance Contracts Bill 1984 (Cth) [35]. This section draws on research appearing in: Thanasegaran, above n 3, 158–159.

[34]In fact, the Notes to the draft Insurance Contracts Bill 1982 (Cth) described the duty of utmost good faith as being 'paramount' and should not be displaced by further or other duties imposed by the Act.

[35]As a result, damages is available as a substantive remedy and gives the duty of utmost good faith a wide and overarching reach over all aspects of an insurance contract, from the pre-contractual stage right up to claims settlement.

range of matters. This would include the unclear drafting of proposal forms and policies; unsubstantiated allegations of breach of utmost good faith against the insured; unfounded denials of claims based on strict construction of policy terms or ambiguous exclusions; low claims settlement; as well as unreasonable delay in the admission of liability and eventual settlement of claims.

The remedies for post-contractual breach of utmost good faith which would inevitably encompass poor claims settlement practices, are addressed in ss54 (1)–(4) of the *Insurance Contracts Act 1984 (Cth)* (Australia) which have been set out in Chap. 4.

An examination of s54 shows the existence of a connection between the duty of utmost good faith set out in s13 and the remedies in s54 in the event of post-contractual breach thereof. The dual limb approach in ss54 (1) and (2) entitles the insurer to refuse to pay the sum insured for post-contractual breach (whether by act or omission) only if the breach was reasonably capable of causing or contributing to the insured loss. The burden of proving the lack of a causal link is in this case, placed on the insured. Otherwise, the insurer is only entitled to claim damages for any prejudice suffered by way of a proportional reduction of the policy monies, to the extent of the prejudice. This was proposed by the Australian Law Reform Commission[36] as a means necessary to strike a fair balance between insurers and insureds.[37]

As for fraudulent claims, s56 (1) provides that where such a claim is made by an insured or under the Act, the insurer may refuse payment of the claim but not avoid the contract. However, if only a minimal or insignificant part of the claim is made fraudulently and non-payment of the remainder of the claim would be harsh and unfair, the court may under s56 (2) order the insurer to pay an amount of the claim which is just and equitable in the circumstances.[38] The main aim of the Australian Law Reform Commission in drafting s56 (1) was to ensure that fraud with respect to one claim did not affect other claims under the policy so as to entitle the insurer to avoid the contract ab initio, as per the common law.[39]

Alternatively, as discussed in Chap. 4 of this book, s12 of the *Insurance Contracts Act 2015* (UK) which provides for the prospective termination of the

---

[36]Report No 20 (1982b) [228]. In order to achieve this, the Law Commission envisaged that the application of s54 should not be affected by matters of form and would also cover matters such as breaches of conditions subsequent and exclusions and has been given effect to by the Australian courts.

[37]Section 55 provides that the remedies in s54 apply exclusively to such post-contractual breaches; and s55A in turn, empowers the Australian Securities and Investment Commission (ASIC) to bring representative actions on behalf of insureds who have or are likely to suffer damage as a result of the terms of the contract or conduct of the insurer in breach of the Act.

[38]In doing so however, the court shall have regard to the need to deter insurance fraud and other relevant matters: Section 56(3). Also, s54 would not apply to cases involving fraudulent claims under s56, as the grounds for and manner of assessing the remedies therein are inconsistent with each other.

[39]Australian Law Reform Commission (1982b) [243] and [187].

contract could be looked to as a guide to address the treatment of fraudulent claims, instead. In which case, insurers would be entitled to prospectively terminate the contract from the occurrence of the fraudulent act, without being liable to pay the claim, as well as be entitled to recover any sums already paid under the policy.

Lastly, ss57 (1) and (2) of the *Insurance Contracts Act 1984* (Cth) (Australia) provide that where payment by an insurer is due under an insurance contract, the insurer is also liable to pay interest on the amount, from the day when it was unreasonable for the insurer to have withheld payment until payment is actually made. The question of when it in fact becomes unreasonable for an insurer to withhold payment is to be determined objectively.[40]

Based on the analysis above, it would appear that the *Financial Services Act 2013* (Malaysia) and *Islamic Financial Services Act 2013* (Malaysia) can therefore, be improved along these lines, so as not to discriminate between the treatment of consumers and non-consumers of insurance and *takaful* contracts and also provide for a clear set of remedies proportionate to the breach and loss suffered. The additional protection provided for insureds in the event of 'a little bit of fraud' by s56 (2) of the *Insurance Contracts Act 1984* (Cth) (Australia), could on the other hand be omitted for Malaysia, as it may be difficult to ascertain in cases where the extent of fraud may not be readily quantifiable. Furthermore, this additional latitude being given to the insured or *takaful* participant appears to be in direct conflict with utmost good faith being expected of both parties and would likely result in greater resistance from the Malaysian insurance and *takaful* industry, that could be avoided.

Apart from this, the Central Bank's *Claims Settlement Guidelines* should also be beefed up in terms of sanctions available in the event of non-compliance by insurers and *takaful* operators, so as to be effective. Perhaps something along the lines of the (British) Financial Services Authority's powers under the *Financial Services and Markets Act 2000* (UK) could be viewed as a guide. In this respect, the Central Bank could perhaps be given the power to impose substantial fines and/or require errant insurers and *takaful* operators to publish an apology and/or compensate aggrieved insureds and *takaful* participants.

In addition, Australia's new s14A of the *Insurance Contracts Act 1984* (Cth) introduced by the *Insurance Contracts Amendment Act 2013* (Cth) that empowers the Australian Securities and Investments Commission (ASIC) to execute its powers against insurers for failing to exercise utmost good faith in the 'handling or settlement of a claim or potential claim under the contract' would also serve as a useful guide to address the present gap in enforcing desirable claims settlement practices in Malaysia.[41]

---

[40]*Settlement Wine Co Pty Ltd v National & General Insurance Co Ltd* (1994) 62 SASR 40; See: Australian Law Reform Commission (1982b) [323] and [324].

[41]This section draws on research appearing in: Thanasegaran and Shaiban, above n 9, 352.

7.2.7 Structural and Miscellaneous Reforms

Lastly, in terms of the structure of the Malaysian insurance and *takaful* industry, it is apparent that most insureds and *takaful* participants prefer to refer their grievances to the Financial Mediation Bureau for redress. There could be three reasons for this. First, the Central Bank's *Claims Settlement Guidelines* have over the years been only enforced by the Mediators of the Financial Mediation Bureau against errant insurers and *takaful* operators due to their broader Terms of Reference and willingness to be pro-active. Secondly, recourse to them is free and thirdly, due to the socio-cultural make-up of Malaysians in general. Malaysians tend to exhibit high in-group collectivism, low individualism, low assertiveness and an average power distance in society, which has been compounded by years of submission to an authoritarian style of government.[42] As such, they prefer to seek redress in the less formal mediation and investigative setting of the Financial Mediation Bureau as opposed to confrontational legal action in the courts to enforce their legal rights.[43]

However, there is a limitation on the Financial Mediation Bureau's monetary jurisdiction which affects its potential to do more. It has a limit of RM200,000 for motor, fire insurance and *takaful* matters; RM5000 for third party property damage and RM100,000 for other matters. To compound matters, the Central Bank of Malaysia's inability to enforce the *Claims Settlement Guidelines* against errant insurers and *takaful* operators for want of formal sanctions, makes it ineffective in balancing the scales between insurers/*takaful* operators and insureds/participants.[44]

It should be noted that despite the recent substantive legal amendments introduced through the *Financial Services Act 2013* (Malaysia) and the *Islamic Financial Services Act 2013* (Malaysia), there has been no change to the Financial Mediation Bureau's monetary limit since its introduction in 2005, nor has the lack of sanctions for non-compliance with the *Claims Settlement Guidelines* been addressed.

To be truly effective, there needs to be an immediate and substantial increase to the Financial Mediation Bureau's monetary limit to about RM1,000,000 or more for each insurance and *takaful* claim across the board, including third party property damage. In line with this, the staffing and infrastructural needs of the Financial Mediation Bureau should also be improved or increased, so as to be able to handle any increase in complaints which would likely result from such a measure.[45]

---

[42]This is so, despite showing a propensity for laws, with a very high uncertainty avoidance score, as shown in Chap. 6.

[43]This is apparent in the number of complaints being referred to the Financial Mediation Bureau annually from 2000 to 2014, which is an average of more than 1000 cases per year, as compared to a total of not more than 100 decided cases on insurance and *takaful* in the civil courts for the entire period. See: Table of Cases Referred to the Financial Mediation Bureau from 2000 to 2014 in the Appendix. This section draws on research appearing in: Thanasegaran, above n 30, 198.

[44]Ibid 199.

[45]Ibid.

This proposal to increase the monetary jurisdiction of the already successful Financial Mediation Bureau would cut with the grain of recent reforms, as the Malaysian government had in 2008 improved its justice system through the enactment of the *Mediation Act* which has facilitated the use of mediation as a means to resolve disputes out of court, in order to address the backlog of cases.[46]

These reforms would complement the major step in substantive law reform already undertaken by the Malaysian legislature in 2013, towards addressing the remaining shortcomings surrounding the duty of utmost good faith in insurance and *takaful* contracts, without invoking drastic reform of the entire financial services industry.

7.3 The Role of Economic Efficiency

Having summarized the reforms required in order to address the remaining shortcomings in the law and practice regulating insurance and *takaful* contracts in Malaysia, this part of the chapter will now turn to briefly examine the role of law and economics as playing the invisible hand in law reform. This is important because all legal change or reform that pertains to commercial matters, of which insurance and *takaful* are a part, will bring about costs and benefits to the parties affected, which in this case would be the insurer/*takaful* operator on the one hand and the insured/*takaful* participant on the other. More so, in modern mixed-market economies, as competing interests are regularly re-determined by society. As a result of this, it is only natural that some will gain and some will lose when any legal reform is pursued.

Therefore in answering the question as to 'what direction shall we change the law?' the issues to be addressed in law and economics, are in actual fact, 'who will have rights?' and 'whose losses will be compensated?' It is in this vein that the concluding part of this chapter is written, with the question as to 'what direction shall we change the law?' being phrased instead as 'whether the legal reforms proposed in this book are viable.'[47]

Addressing this involves a 'normative' legal-economic analysis which deals with the question 'what should be?' which is prescriptive and pertinent to the debate and formulation of legal policy. This is as opposed to a 'positive' legal-economic analysis which is descriptive or predictive in nature and deals with the 'what is?' question instead and as such, is not relevant here.[48]

---

[46]*The Star* (Kuala Lumpur) (2008) p. 8. Ibid.

[47]This section draws on research appearing in: Thanasegaran, above n 26, 119.

[48]Ibid. Positive economic analysis is based on the assumption that 'individuals are rational maximizers of their satisfactions in their non-market as well as their market behaviour' responding to 'price incentives' and 'legal rules and legal outcomes can be assessed on the basis of their efficiency properties': Mercuro and Medema (2006, p. 102).

The 'law' part of law and economics is a set of principles for ordering society whereas the 'economics' part is whether such principles are 'efficient' for such ordering of society. The question then is how much weight should be given to efficiency when it conflicts with other ethical or political principles? In principle, it is accepted in law and economics circles that the criteria for assessing outcomes of legal change should be (the often opposing objectives of) 'efficiency' (or resource allocation) and 'equity' (income distribution) . This is done by first redistributing income in the most desirable or equitable manner and then allocating resources in the most efficient manner, in response to competitive forces. All the time bearing in mind that the ultimate goal is what economists call 'social efficiency.'

However, it is no doubt a formidable task to balance the consideration of the twin goals of efficiency and equity; as efficient resource allocation is a major concern on the 'economic side' and desirable income distribution built on concepts of justice and fairness is on the other hand, the main-stay of the 'law side' of law and economics.[49]

There are in this context, two concepts of social welfare that are used widely in normative economic analysis, namely 'Pareto efficiency' and 'Kaldor-Hicks efficiency' which is in effect a derivative of the former. 'Pareto efficiency' is a proposition that reform or change is welfare enhancing if it makes someone better off and nobody worse off.[50] Although it appears to have initial appeal, there are a number of difficulties associated with it.

For example, there is uncertainty as to what amounts to voluntariness vis-à-vis coercion in decision making, a lack of complete information in deciding one way or another and the effect of third parties who perceive themselves to be negatively affected by the change. It is also very much preference-driven in the sense of change making people 'feel' better off and nobody 'feel' worse off, therefore, being unable to disqualify certain 'monstrous, self-destructive, outrageous or immoral preferences.' In addition, by taking the status quo as a given in any scenario, 'Pareto efficiency' has no concern over matters of distributive justice and as such, provides no limits on what can be bought and sold if there is a willing buyer and seller. This, as long as it makes those involved 'feel' better off. As a result, it would be a concern in certain matters involving 'human personhood' which should not be the subject of transactions.[51]

'Pareto efficiency' also requires the 'gainers' to compensate the 'losers' in any exchange. Failure to do so would entitle the 'losers' to veto any change, resulting in every change to necessarily require unanimous consent. Such a measure would be an almost impossible guide to public policy. Furthermore, it would not be

[49]Normative questions such as 'what is good' and 'what is just' is 'the stuff of law': Hadfield, above n 1, 55; whereas the 'rational maximization of satisfaction' using efficient means is the stuff of economics: Mercuro and Medema, above n 49, 102. This is epitomized by the opposing concepts of 'the reasonable man' and 'the rational man' respectively.

[50]This section draws on research appearing in: Thanasegaran, above n 26, 119.

[51]Trebilcock (1999, pp. 18–20).

applicable in the *takaful* (or Islamic economics) context, as a solution is not recognized as 'Pareto' optimum if it requires sacrifice on the part of some in order to increase the welfare of many. Such sacrifice is however, central to Islam where for instance, all Muslims have an obligation to pay religious dues called '*zakat*' annually to aid the poor, in addition to their national taxes. In Malaysia, this religious contribution by Muslim taxpayers is in fact, tax deductible under s6A (2) of the *Income Tax Act 1967* (Malaysia).[52]

On the other hand, 'Kaldor Hicks efficiency' or 'welfare economics' is a cost-benefit test which weighs the benefits of a measure to the 'winners' against its costs to the 'losers'. Although 'Kaldor Hicks efficiency' also has some of the problems identified with respect to'Pareto efficiency', admittedly, the world for the most part functions whereby 'most people much of the time are doing cost-benefit analyses in their heads in an intuitive fashion'.[53]

In this context, it is widely accepted in 'welfare' or 'Kaldor-Hicks' economics that a change or reform would be deemed to constitute an improvement, in the sense of increasing economic welfare as a whole, if the gains to the 'winners' exceed the losses to the 'losers.' As such, it is the most relevant branch of law and economics to this type of analysis, for it involves legal rule formulation.[54]

It is acknowledged that it is indeed a formidable task to evaluate the relevant costs and benefits involved in a reform, especially so with respect to the sale of future intangible rights, which is the case with insurance and *takaful* contracts. This is because the 'losers' generally tend to overstate their losses whilst the 'gainers' tend to underestimate their gains, in order to affect the financial outcome. Despite this however, an attempt to evaluate the same, is crucial in obtaining valuable economic input to any law reform proposal.[55]

The relevance of 'Kaldor Hicks' welfare economic analysis to insurance and *takaful* contracts in particular is clear, as insurance and *takaful* contracts also serve as a 'welfare enhancing vehicle' to address market failures or imperfections. For instance, the pre-contractual duty to disclose material information placed on insureds has been traditionally justified by the existence of an information imbalance 'inhibiting an efficient contract.' On the other hand, it is important for legal policy to be aimed at 'reducing the reverse information gap between insurer and insured' so as to provide insureds with sufficient information 'to compare insurance offers and appraise policy techniques, terms and exclusions'. This is particularly so, in consumer insurance and *takaful* where it has been acknowledged that 'premium

---

[52]This section draws on research appearing in: Thanasegaran, above n 26, 119.

[53]Trebilcock, above n 52, 22; Ibid 120.

[54]The opposite of this is effect evaluation which is in the realm of positive economics and has an organizational perspective of law and economics which focuses on transactional costs instead: Hirsch (1999, pp. 5–6).

[55]Polinsky (1983, pp. 123–124). This section also draws on research appearing in: Thanasegaran, above n 26, 120.

is the only visible object of competition' whilst it 'seems to be more and more the policy objective' for insureds to have access to transparent information.[56]

The aforesaid relevance of 'welfare economics' rings true as much for *takaful* as it does for conventional insurance. This is because the subject matter of both conventional and Islamic economics is at its core, the efficient allocation and distribution of scarce resources amongst their infinite uses. The fundamental difference is however, that Islamic economics is based on a religious world view, as opposed to secularism and value neutrality which are the pillars of post-Enlightenment conventional economics. Nevertheless, unlike most spheres of conventional economics, Islamic economics' emphasis on social welfare as a criterion for business which discourages wealth maximization as the primary aim augurs well with 'Kaldor Hicks' welfare economics emphasis on the evaluation of both the private and social costs and benefits of any change or reform to be undertaken.[57]

7.4 Viability of Proposed Reforms

A similar method of analysis (albeit not explicitly acknowledged as such) may be observed in the reasoning used by the Australian Law Reform Commission in 1982. An argument rooted in economic efficiency is apparent from a detailed analysis of the Commission's justifications for reform of the Australian insurance industry, in their *Report No 20 on Insurance Contracts* and *Report No 16 on Insurance Agents and Brokers* in 1982. These proposals formed the basis of the hugely successful insurance law reform package introduced via the *Insurance Contracts Act 1984 (Cth)*. This was done in the spirit of proposing reform which struck a balance as far as possible between the interests of insurers and insureds. In fact, 20 years on, in a review of the *Insurance Contracts Act 1984 (Cth)* undertaken by the Australian Treasury in February 2007, it was reported that the reforms have been successful, thereby, needing only a slight adjustment to some provisions in order to keep it abreast with changing times and to address some issues pertaining to the interpretation of its provisions by the courts. This has in fact been done through the *Insurance Contracts (Amendment) Act 2013* (Cth) (Australia).

It is in this spirit, that the viability of the reforms proposed herein to the duty of utmost good faith in insurance and *takaful* contracts will be assessed. The said reforms will be weighed against the 'cost-benefit' arguments employed in 'Kaldor Hicks' economics to determine if they will increase economic welfare as

---

[56] van Boom (2008, p. 11). Ibid.

[57] This section also draws on research appearing in: Thanasegaran, above n 26, 120–123. See: Chapra (2000), Azhar (2009).

a whole. This is done in the firm belief that laws and law reform cannot exist in a vacuum.[58]

It has been shown in Chap. 6 how culture impacts upon law reform. Similarly, economic analysis also influences law reform, particularly so in the realm of commercial type contracts such as insurance and *takaful* which involve a trade-off between the competing interests of insurers/*takaful* operators and insureds/participants.[59] Hence, law reform proposals which are substantiated by the prevailing socio-cultural environment as well as weighed against the relative costs and benefits to the parties affected would go a long way in striking a fair and workable balance between the competing interests involved.

The legal reforms proposed in this book essentially address the issues that remain lacking despite the major reform introduced by the Malaysian government through the *Financial Services Act 2013* (Malaysia) and *Islamic Financial Services Act 2013* (Malaysia). This entails the comparable treatment of *non-consumers* of insurance and *takaful* alongside consumers without unnecessary discrimination with respect to the applicability of a general contractual duty of utmost good faith that also applied to claims settlement as well as the abolition of basis of contract clauses; appropriate remedies being set out for pre-contractual non-disclosure separately from that of misrepresentation, so as to eliminate the application of the common law remedy of avoidance per se, as well as for failure to provide clear statutory warnings on proposal forms by insurers and *takaful* operators; the expansion of the role and jurisdiction of the Financial Mediation Bureau as the primary means of dispute resolution for insurance and *takaful* matters so as to enhance its effectiveness; and to set out the sanctions applicable for non-compliance with the *Claims Settlement Guidelines*, in order to enable the Central Bank of Malaysia and the courts to enforce the same.

This improvement to the legislative reforms introduced by the Malaysian government in 2013, pertaining to the duty of utmost good faith is needed to redress the remaining imbalance in the law, so as to achieve as far as possible a fair and workable balance between insurers'/*takaful* operators' rights on the one hand and insureds'/*takaful* participants' rights on the other. This however, might be perceived to be at the cost of the insurers' and *takaful* operators' more favourable position at present and could hence, be viewed as a 'loss' to them and 'gain' to the insureds and *takaful* participants. Applying the cost-benefit analysis employed in 'Kaldor-Hicks' economics, the general arguments against such reform likely to be put forward by insurers and *takaful* operators as causing a 'loss' to them can be grouped into three main points. This is in fact similar to the objections faced by the

---

[58]A similar approach involving a trade-off between competing interests based on efficiency and equity in order to justify the imposition of certain burdens or standards on certain parties to a contract involving equitable principles like unconscionable dealing was adopted by Duggan (1997).

[59]In fact, it has been said to have 'a great deal of impact on law-making' despite its limits in terms of relevance to some spheres of legal issues, such as child abuse, race and gender discrimination: Trebilcock, above n 52, 27.

Australian Law Reform Commission in 1982,[60] when proposing the reforms contained in the *Insurance Contracts Act 1984* (Cth) (Australia).

First, it is arguable that such broad reform would hamper competition and be at the cost of market efficiency and as such, would not be justified and perhaps even be harmful. Instead, the insurance and *takaful* industry itself might be better placed to solve the problems identified at less cost than substantial legal change for example, through industry self-regulation like that which was in place in the United Kingdom until 2005.

Secondly, even if legal reform of certain common domestic or consumer insurance/*takaful* products like house owners' or householders' or motor vehicle policies is seen as necessary, there is no justification for reform of business/non-consumer insurance/*takaful* as well. The cost of such wide legal intervention would be too high and not be justified hence, any such reform should not be made applicable to all types of non-marine insurance and *takaful* contracts but only certain limited categories.

Thirdly, the indirect effect of the legal reform proposed would be the increase in the cost of insurance and *takaful* which would have to be borne by all insureds and *takaful* participants, whereby the honest and cautious would have to bear the cost of the careless and fraudulent, which would clearly be undesirable. It should be noted however, that this increase in the cost of insurance and *takaful* would not be significant because the recent reforms introduced via the *Financial Services Act 2013* (Malaysia) and *Islamic Financial Services Act 2013* (Malaysia) already help balance the scales to a large extent, especially in consumer insurance and *takaful* contracts.

In response to this on the other hand, arguments for such reform in favour of insureds/participants and the general public as giving rise to a 'gain' or 'benefit' to them can be summarized as follows.[61]

First, although any reform package in order to be workable should operate within the existing legal, social and economic framework within which insurance and *takaful* operate (which is in turn largely regulated by market forces), it is essential for it to promote both economic efficiency and general welfare, if it is to go the distance. Hence, limited government intervention in the market may be justified, as unregulated markets do not necessarily work well and may not be sufficiently competitive, as the requisite availability of information needed for competitive forces to operate may be lacking.

In this regard, in line with the Australian Law Reform Commission's observations, reform should be put in place to make clear information on insurance and *takaful* products readily available to the insuring public so as to facilitate the efficient operation of the market. This is because insurance and *takaful* products are

---

[60] Australian Law Reform Commission (1982a) [20]–[29].

[61] These are in fact similar to and are based on the response articulated by the Australian Law Reform Commission in 1982 when assessing the package of reforms contained in the *Insurance Contracts Act 1984* (Cth): Australian Law Reform Commission (1982b) [20]–[30].

essentially a set of intangible promises and it is a known fact that insureds and *takaful* participants have difficulty understanding what is being purchased and making informed comparisons between the different products available. To compound matters, proposal forms and policy documentation are notorious for their illegibility and incomprehensibility. As such, especially in certain common domestic or consumer insurance contracts, unusual and unexpected exclusions and limitations on cover must be highlighted to proposers of insurance and *takaful* before the contract is concluded. This transparency and openness would in turn enhance competition based on essentials rather than be distorted by a monopoly of information by insurers and *takaful* operators.

Apart from this, although efficiency in the insurance and *takaful* market is important, it is not the sole criteria for regulation. Intervention would be justified if other important social or welfare objectives or benefits outweigh the direct and indirect cost of intervention. Having said this, the form of regulation should however, be that which is least likely to have an adverse effect on the market. In this regard, apart from educating insureds/*takaful* participants and the public on their rights and responsibilities arising under insurance and *takaful* contracts,[62] reform of some of the existing laws on the duty of utmost good faith is necessary despite the 2013 reforms, especially with respect to *non-consumer* insurance and *takaful* contracts which appear to have been discriminated against without adequate justification. Some disproportionate burdens remain imposed on insureds and *takaful* participants, especially in *non-consumer* insurance and *takaful* contracts which exceed any loss which may be suffered by insurers and *takaful* operators. As such, addressing the inequity and prejudice in the existing laws especially with respect to pre-contractual disclosure and misrepresentation, the remedies available and the effect of contractual terms, exclusions and claims handling is ample justification for minor intrusion on the freedom of contract and hence, outweighs the 'loss' to insurers and *takaful* operators. This is particularly so, in light of the progressive reforms undertaken to date.

In this regard, the improvements to the duty of utmost good faith, pre-contractual disclosure and misrepresentation, claims handling and the ensuing remedies proposed herein would cut *with the grain* of the 'cost-benefit' argument as opposed to an outright removal of the duty of disclosure for instance or taking the settlement of claims out of the hands of insurers and *takaful* operators altogether, which would be far too costly a burden placed on insurers and *takaful* operators to independently investigate each and every proposal for insurance and *takaful*[63] and would be an outright suggestion that they lacked integrity in claims settlement.[64]

Furthermore, restating the duty of utmost good faith as a contractual duty between both parties in *non-consumer* insurance and *takaful* contracts as well,

[62]This has been done through the 10-year Consumer Education Programme launched by the Central Bank of Malaysia in August 2003.

[63]Australian Law Reform Commission (1982b) [175] and [183].

[64]Ibid [326].

whereby neither party can rely on a contractual provision when doing so would amount to a breach of utmost good faith, should ensure that insurers and *takaful* operators take care when drafting their policies and relying on strict terms and exclusions, as well as act fairly in claims settlement towards all categories of insureds and *takaful* participants.[65] This measure would also address the current injustice that remains with respect to insureds and participants of *non-consumer* insurance and *takaful* contracts, at minimum cost to the insurer and *takaful* operator,[66] than perhaps more drastic alternatives like administrative control over policy terms or standard form contracts for all types of insurance and *takaful*.

Secondly, in response to the argument against legal reform of business or non-consumer insurance/*takaful*, it is important to note that most businessmen or non-consumers are not legal or insurance/*takaful* experts, and small businessmen in fact do not differ substantially from those purchasing consumer or domestic insurance or *takaful*. Furthermore, the cost to businesses and non-consumers in engaging lawyers and brokers to avoid the perils and pitfalls in the existing law might be reduced by introducing simpler and fairer laws applicable to **all types** of non-marine insurance and *takaful* contracts in a uniform fashion. Having two sets of rules for consumers and non-consumers would instead be arbitrary and increase the cost of dealing with the ensuing difference in the demarcation. This remains a salient problem under the recent reforms instituted in Malaysia in 2013 and needs to be addressed in a uniform manner.

In addition to the above, to address some market failings like inadequate information being available to insureds/*takaful* participants and the inability of insureds/*takaful* participants to understand and appreciate individual terms and the significance of insurance and *takaful* contracts as a whole, which are more pronounced to mainly consumer or domestic type insurance, some 'type' specific reform could be introduced. Standard form policies could perhaps be introduced for common consumer policies which are of most concern to individuals, such as house owner's or householder's insurance/*takaful*, motor vehicle, personal accident and illness and travel insurance/*takaful*. This 'would simplify insurance for insureds and would protect them against unusual and unexpected exclusions and obligations. It might also increase the efficiency of insurers and reduce their cost' by competition proceeding 'on the basis of price, reputation and service' instead.[67] This would help

[65]Ibid [51].

[66]See: Duggan, above n 59, 614, which is akin to the socially costless option of refraining from engaging in exploitative and unconscionable conduct envisaged by him.

[67]Australian Law Reform Commission (1982b) [55]. The reference to 'insurance' in the report is construed to include '*takaful*' as well for the purposes of this book. It should be noted that the possible cost of anti-competitiveness in terms of inhibiting insurers' (and *takaful* operators') development of new and improved products as a result of the introduction of standard cover, has been dealt with by Australia by permitting insurers to derogate from standard cover, provided they specifically draw the limit on cover to the insured's attention at the onset: [57]. However, it is doubtful whether such a proposal would be suitable for Malaysia, in view of the socio-cultural climate within which it is to operate.

tip the 'gains' to the insureds and *takaful* participants over the perceived 'loss' to insurers and *takaful* operators.

Thirdly, with respect to the argument that legal reform would result in an increased cost to all, the Australian experience has shown that the increase may in effect not be substantial.[68] For a start, the proposed reforms retain the insurers' and *takaful* operators' right to avoid the policy if fraud can be proved with respect to pre-contractual non-disclosure or misrepresentation. To retain the right to avoid the policy for anything less than fraud cannot be justified as this often occurs after the insured/*takaful* participant has suffered an insured loss and is left high and dry with only a refund of premiums paid. Substituting avoidance with a right to damages would not only be an adequate deterrent to misrepresentation and non-disclosure, it would also adequately compensate insurers and *takaful* operators for loss suffered as a result of insureds'/*takaful* participants' breach of their duty.[69] Furthermore, insurers and *takaful* operators should not be a judge in their own cause and should no longer be entitled to reject claims on purely technical grounds lacking any merit.

It is true that there would probably be some increase in insurance and *takaful* cost as a result of these improvements suggested. However, it would be minimal in light of the fact that it would for the most part only address the situation relating to *non-consumer* insurance and *takaful* contracts, following the 2013 amendments already in place. Insurers and *takaful* operators will always be dependent to some extent upon the insured/*takaful* participant for information, but it becomes highly questionable when insureds and *takaful* participants are 'retrospectively deprived of the benefit of the policy in respect of legitimate claims because of…conduct falling short of fraud'.[70]

However, any additional cost would appear to pale in comparison when weighed against the potential injustice to insureds and *takaful* participants caused by the somewhat lopsided laws still remaining, especially in *non-consumer* insurance and *takaful* contracts. Fairness between insurer/*takaful* operator and insured/*takaful* participant cannot be achieved if the fundamental promises made by the insurer/*takaful* operator and the reasonable expectations of the insured/*takaful* participant cannot be fulfilled. Hence, the 'gains' to the insured/*takaful* participant brought about by reform of the duty of utmost good faith in insurance and *takaful* contracts as suggested herein would outweigh any 'cost' suffered by the insurer or *takaful* operator as a result.

---

[68]This is because there are 'so many insureds (and participants) and because the combination of non-disclosure and subsequent loss is so infrequent, the effect of the proposed change on premiums would be negligible': Ibid [183].

[69]Ibid [187]; A combination of proportionate damages for life insurance (and family *takaful*) and contractual damages for general insurance (and general *takaful*), appropriately addresses the matter: Ibid [226]–[228].

[70]Bennett (1999, pp. 214–215).

7.5 Conclusion

This book has attempted to draw attention to the need for further legal reform of the duty of utmost good faith in non-marine insurance and *takaful* contracts in Malaysia, to supplement the reforms undertaken in 2013. Such reform is imperative to truly achieve a more balanced environment between the competing interests of insurers/*takaful* operators and *all categories* of insureds/*takaful* participants.

In the words of R.A. Hasson[71] 'would-be reformers frequently make the claim that the changes they propose in any given area of the law are conservative rather than radical in nature. That claim can be made with special force' in this book as the reforms suggested herein do no more than serve to bring the law of utmost good faith in insurance and *takaful* contracts in Malaysia in line with contemporary practices in developed nations in improving its own progressive reforms instituted in 2013.

The Australian experience in such reform over the past 20 years has shown to be a success[72] although the decision to reform the law back in 1984 'was greeted with a chorus of disapproval from the industry which feared for its future'.[73] In spite of this, the reform has not only gone down with relative ease but has also witnessed a change in 'the entire culture which surrounds the insurance industry.' Underwriters have over the years become more generous in their approach towards insureds, thus, showing that 'the market adapts very easily to new laws as long as they strike a fair balance between the interests of the parties'.[74] The same trend is expected with the sweeping reforms undertaken in the United Kingdom via the *Consumer Insurance (Disclosure and Representations) Act 2012* (UK) and the *Insurance Contracts Act 2015* (UK).

Based on the comparative, socio-cultural and economic analysis provided throughout this book, there appears no reason why the same cannot be achieved for Malaysia, especially in light of the reforms already undertaken via the *Financial Services Act 2013* (Malaysia) and *Islamic Financial Services Act 2013* (Malaysia).

It is hoped that the comprehensive analysis provided in this book provides adequate justification for the legal reform proposed herein to be adopted. This would complement the reforms undertaken in 2013 with respect to the duty of utmost good faith in insurance and *takaful* contracts in Malaysia in striking a workable balance between insurer/*takaful* operator and insured/*takaful* participant rights in both *consumer* and *non-consumer* contracts without unnecessary discrimination.

---

[71]Hasson (1969, p. 636).

[72]Coonan (2003).

[73]Merkin (2006, p. 6).

[74]Ibid.

References

Australian Law Reform Commission (1982a) Report No 20, *Insurance Contracts*
Australian Law Reform Commission (1982b) Report No 16, *Insurance Agents and Brokers*
Azhar RA (2009) Economics of an Islamic economy. Brill Hotel Publishing, Leiden
Bennett H (1999) Mapping the Doctrine of Utmost Good Faith in Insurance Contract Law. Lloyd's Maritime Commer Law Quart 165
Brown C (1994) Unfinished business: misrepresentation and non-disclosure in insurance proposals. 16 N Z Univ Law Rev 195
Central Bank of Malaysia (2003) Guidelines on claims settlement practices, Kuala Lumpur, Rev 2003
Central Bank of Malaysia (2006a) Insurance Annual Report 2005, Kuala Lumpur
Central Bank of Malaysia (2006b) Takaful Annual Report 2005, Kuala Lumpur
Chapra MU (2000) Is it necessary to have Islamic economics? J Socio-Econ 29
Coonan H (2003) Insurance Contracts Act Reform Package. Press Release, 10 Sept 2003
Duggan A (1997) Is equity efficient? 113 Law Quart Rev 601
Explanatory Memorandum, Insurance Contracts Bill 1984 (Cth)
Financial Mediation Bureau, Annual Reports 2005–2013, Kuala Lumpur, 2006–2014
Financial Mediation Bureau, Statistical Report (January–December 2014), Kuala Lumpur, 7 Jan 2015
Hadfield G (1999) The second wave of law and economics: learning to Surf. In: Richardson M, Hadfield G (eds) The second wave of law and economics. The Federation Press, Sydney
Hasson RA (1969) The doctrine of uberrima fides in insurance law—a critical evaluation. 32 Modern Law Rev 615
Hawke F (2006) The innocents abroad. 17 Insur Law J 2
Hirsch W (1999) Law and economics: an introductory analysis, 3rd edn. Academic Press, New York
Insurance Mediation Bureau, Mediator's Annual Reports and Case Reviews 2000–2004, Kuala Lumpur, 2001–2005
Kirby M (1999) Law and economics in the courts: is there hope? In: Richardson M, Hadfield G (eds) The second wave of law and economics. The Federation Press, Sydney
Mann P, Lewis C (2014) Mann's Annotated Insurance Contracts Act, 6th edn. Lawbook Co
Mason, Anthony, 'Law and Economics' (1991) 17 *Monash University Law Review* 167, 174
Mercuro N, Medema S (2006) Economics and the law: from posner to post-modernism and beyond, 2nd edn. Princeton University Press, Princeton
Merkin R (2006) Reforming insurance law: is there a case for reverse transportation? Report prepared for the English and Scottish Law Commission on the Australian experience of insurance law reform, London, p 6
Polinsky M (1983) An introduction to law and economics. Little Brown & Company, Boston
Thanasegaran H (2004) 'Insurers' good faith in Malaysia: does a search for a fairer balance in non-marine insurance contracts lead to Australia? 15 Insur Law J 143
Thanasegaran H (2011) Settlement of claims by Malaysian insurance and *Takaful* companies: a genuine prospect or merely suspect? 22(6) Int Company Commer Law Rev 191
Thanasegaran H (2013) Making an entrance—Can Australia contribute to *Takaful* (Islamic Insurance) law reform?' 24 Insur Law J 104
Thanasegaran H, Shaiban M (2014) Harmonization of Takaful (Islamic Insurance) regulation—A realistic goal or improbable ideal? Singapore J Legal Stud 328
The Star, Better justice system, 18 June 2008, Kuala Lumpur, 8
Trebilcock M (1999) The value and limits of law and economics. In: Richardson M, Hadfield G (eds) The second wave of law and economics. The Federation Press, Sydney
van Boom W (2008) Insurance law and economics: an empirical perspective. Paper presented at the Rotterdam Institute of Private Law accepted paper series, Rotterdam, 2008, 11

Appendix

Table of cases referred to the financial mediation bureau (FMB) from 2000 to 2014[a]

Year	Total cases filed	Insurance	*Takaful*	Percentage of insurers' decisions revised	Percentage of cases on utmost good faith in general		Percentage of cases on claims handling in particular[b]	
					Insurance	*Takaful*	Insurance	*Takaful*
2000	515	515 Breakdown N/A		16	92 Breakdown N/A		53 Breakdown N/A	
2001	726	703	23	24	88 Breakdown N/A		58 Breakdown N/A	
2002	932	874	58	18	86	91	51	48
2003	1070	1033	37	20	88	97	53	49
2004	1105	1048	57	20	93	91	56	53
2005	1254	1207	47	23	89	87	48	49
2006	1429	1368	61	31	91	95	54	52
2007	1404	1339	65	39	91	98	53	68
2008	1278	1197	81	47	87	91	50	67
2009	1445	1325	120	55	88	97	54	72
2010	1211	1098	113	49	87	98	46	76
2011	1270	1143	127	45	96	98	63	81
2012	1318	1152	166	10	Breakdown N/A[c]	Breakdown N/A[d]	Breakdown N/A[c]	Breakdown N/A[d]
2013	1229	1012	217	3[e]	Breakdown N/A		Breakdown N/A	
2014	1137	848	289	1[f]	Breakdown N/A		Breakdown N/A	

[a]This table was constructed based on information and statistics obtained from the Insurance Mediation Bureau, *Mediator's Annual Reports and Case Reviews 2000–2004*, Kuala Lumpur, 2001–2005; the Financial Mediation Bureau, *Annual Reports 2005–2013*, Kuala Lumpur, 2006–2014; and the Financial Mediation Bureau, *Statistical Report (January–December 2014)*, Kuala Lumpur, 7 January 2015

[b]The percentage of cases involving claims handling forms part of the overall percentage of cases referred to the Financial Mediation Bureau which concern utmost good faith

[c]The breakdown of the number of cases according to the types of complaint is no longer available from 2012. However, it was noted that 'non disclosure by the prospective assured …in the insurance proposal form, which led to the subsequent rejection of claims by the FSP (Financial Services Provider) was a common and systemic issue raised in 2012.' Also 'complaints relating to rejection of Total Permanent Disability (TPD) claims comprised 20 % of cases in 2012' with the common contention by the FSP being that the 'assured's condition did not fulfil the definition of TPD in the policy,' Financial Mediation Bureau, *Annual Report 2012*, Kuala Lumpur, 2013, 29

[d]'The *takaful* family cases are predominantly related to breach of the Certificate's terms and conditions … non-disclosure of pre-existing illness' etc. '…in some *takaful* cases the grounds and reasons for repudiation are often not provided to the complainant' …despite Clause 4.4.2.1 of the Central Bank's *Claims Settlement Guidelines* imposing 'an obligation on the *takaful* operators to explain their grounds of rejection/repudiation to the

H. Thanasegaran, *Good Faith in Insurance and Takaful Contracts in Malaysia*,
DOI 10.1007/978-981-10-0383-7

(continued)

complainant.' However, an encouraging trend was noted that 'more FSPs are complying with the BNM (Central Bank). Guidelines to ensure complainants clearly understand the grounds of repudiation of their claims,' Financial Mediation Bureau, *Annual Report 2012*, Kuala Lumpur, 2013, 30

[e]The significant drop in the percentage of insurers' decisions that were revised by the FMB was 'attributed generally to the quality of FSPs' decisions that has improved over the years,' Financial Mediation Bureau, *Annual Report 2013*, Kuala Lumpur, 2014, 24

[f]It should be noted that at the Mediation stage of the FMB proceedings, the FSPs revised their own decisions in 59 percent of the cases, thus contributing to the significant drop, Financial Mediation Bureau, *Statistical Report (January–December 2014)*, Kuala Lumpur, 7 January 2015, 3

Index

H. Thanasegaran, *Good Faith in Insurance and Takaful Contracts in Malaysia*,
DOI 10.1007/978-981-10-0383-7

Kolibri 360 GmbH
Ferdinand-Jühlke-Straße 7
99095 Erfurt, Deutschland
produktsicherheit@kolibri360.de